MW01015123

Kant's theory of freedom

Kant's theory of freedom

University of California, San Diego

Published by the Press Syndicate of the University of Cambridge
The Pitt Building, Trumpington Street, Cambridge CB2 1RP
40 West 20th Street, New York, NY 10011-4211, USA
10 Stamford Road, Oakleigh, Victoria 3166, Australia

First published 1990
Reprinted 1991, 1993

Printed in the United States of America

Library of Congress Cataloging-in-Publication Data
Allison, Henry E.
Kant's theory of freedom / Henry E. Allison.
p.   cm.
Includes bibliographical references.
ISBN 0-521-38270-x. – ISBN 0-521-38708-6 (pbk.)
1. Kant, Immanuel, 1724–1804 – Contributions in concept of free
will and determinism.   2. Free will and determinism.   I. Title.
B2799.F8A44   1990
123′.5′–dc20   89-77710

British Library Cataloguing in Publication Data
Allison, Henry E.
Kant's theory of freedom.
1. Freedom. Theories of Kant, Immanuel, 1724–1804
I. Title
323.44092

ISBN 0-521-38270-X hardback
ISBN 0-521-38708-6 paperback

TO THE MEMORY OF ERIC

Contents

CONTENTS

Acknowledgments

I am indebted to many individuals and to some institutions for their generous help and support for this project. Beginning with the latter, I would like to thank the National Endowment for the Humanities for providing me with a fellowship for the academic year 1985–6 and the John Simon Guggenheim Memorial Foundation for a fellowship for the year 1986–7. My thanks also go to the Academic Senate of the University of California at San Diego for two summer grants for research and clerical assistance and to my department for permitting me the luxury of two consecutive years of leave.

Among the individuals, my thanks go first to Allen Wood for his extremely helpful criticisms of a preliminary draft of most of the manuscript. Although I am sure that he will still find much to criticize, his incisive comments were of great assistance to me in my endeavor to formulate the issues separating us. I would also like to thank Karl Ameriks, Barbara Herman, Adrian Piper, and Andrews Reath for their helpful comments on portions of the manuscript and my colleagues Patricia Kitcher and Robert Pippin, not only for their many useful suggestions and criticisms, but also for their ready willingness to discuss Kant. I count myself fortunate indeed to be a member of a department in which there is such interest and expertise in the "Sage of Königsberg." In this group I must also include Michelle Gilmore, who once again has proved invaluable to me as a research and editorial assistant. I likewise wish to thank Peter Mangan for the preparation of the index. Finally, but above all, I must express my deep gratitude to my wife, Norma, who continued to encourage me in my work and to create an atmosphere in which I could pursue it during a time of great sadness for both of us. Without her support, this book would never have seen the light of day.

An earlier version of much of Chapter 2 is contained in my paper "Empirical and Intelligible Character in the *Critique of Pure Reason*," which was presented at the Seventh Jerusalem Philosophical Encounter on Kant's practical philosophy at the Hebrew University in December 1985 and is published in the proceedings of that conference: *Kant's Practical Philosophy Reconsidered*. The basic argument of Chapter 3 is foreshadowed in "The Concept of Freedom in Kant's 'Semi-Critical' Ethics," which appeared in the *Archiv für Geschichte der Philosophie*. That of Chapter 11 was initially presented in "Morality and Freedom: Kant's Reciprocity Thesis," which was published in the *Philosophical Review*. Similarly, early drafts of portions of the argument of Chapter 12 are contained in "The Hidden Circle in *Groundwork* III," which was presented at the Sixth International Kant Congress and is published in its proceedings, and "Kant's Preparatory Argument in *Groundwork* III," which was presented in a conference on the *Groundwork* held at Sigriswil, Switzerland, in June 1986 and is published in *Grundlegung zur Metaphysik der Sitten. Ein kooperativer Kommentar*. Finally, I initially dealt with the issues discussed in Chapter 13 in "Justification and Freedom in the *Critique of Practical Reason*," which was delivered at the Stanford Conference on Kant's Deductions in April 1986 and was published in its proceedings: *Kant's Transcendental Deductions: The Three "Critiques" and the "Opus postumum."* All of this material has been substantially revised for the book and in some cases, particularly the last, my views have changed significantly. Nevertheless, I would like to thank the organizers of these conferences, specifically Yirmahu Yovel, Otfried Höffe, and Eckart Förster, for inviting me to participate and, together with the editors of the above-mentioned journals, for their kind permission to reuse some of the material they initially published.

Note on sources and key to abbreviations and translations

Apart from the *Critique of Pure Reason* and the *Lectures on Ethics,* all references to Kant are to *Kants gesammelte Schriften* (KGS), *herausgegeben von der Deutschen* (formerly *Königlichen Preussischen*) *Akademie der Wissenschaften,* 29 volumes [Berlin: Walter de Gruyter (and predecessors), 1902]. References to the *Critique of Pure Reason* are to the standard A and B pagination of the first and second editions. References to the *Lectures on Ethics* are to *Eine Vorlesung uber Ethik,* edited by Paul Menzer, Berlin: Rolf Heise, 1924. Specific works cited in the main body of the text are referred to by means of the abbreviations listed below. Those cited only in the notes are given with the full title. Kant's letters are usually identified by means of recipient and date, and citations from them are based on the translation of Arnulf Zweig, *Kant: Philosophical Correspondence* (Chicago: University of Chicago Press, 1970). The other translations used are listed in what follows and, except in the case of the *Critique of Pure Reason,* are referred to immediately following the reference to the volume and page of the German text. It should be noted, however, that I have frequently modified these translations significantly. Where there is no reference to an English translation, the translation is my own.

A/B	*Kritik der reinen Vernunft* (KGS 3 and 4).
	Critique of Pure Reason, trans. N. Kemp Smith, New York: St. Martin's Press, 1965.
Anthro	*Anthropologie in pragmatischer Hinsicht* (KGS 7).
	Anthropology from a Practical Point of View, trans. Mary J. Gregor, The Hague: Nijhoff, 1974
Diss	*De Mundi Sensibilis Atque Intelligiblis Forma Et Principiis* (KGS 2).
	On the Form and Principles of the Sensible and Intelligible World (The Inaugural Dissertation), trans. G. B. Kerferd and D. E. Walford, New York: Manchester University Press, 1968
Ethik	*Eine Vorlesung uber Ethik.*
	Lectures on Ethics, trans. Louis Infield, Indianapolis: Hackett, 1981.
Gr	*Grundlegung zur Metaphysik der Sitten* (KGS 4).
	Groundwork of the Metaphysics of Morals, trans. H. J. Paton, New York: Harper & Row, 1964.

SOURCES AND ABBREVIATIONS

KprV   *Kritik der praktischen Vernunft* (KGS 5).
        Critique of Practical Reason, trans. L. W. Beck, Indianapolis: Bobbs-Merrill, 1956.

KU   *Kritik der Urtheilskraft* (KGS 5).
        Critique of Judgement, trans. Werner Pluhar, Indianapolis: Hackett, 1987.

MAN   *Metaphysische Anfangsgründe der Naturwissenschaften* (KGS 4).
        Metaphysical Foundations of Natural Science, trans. James Ellington, Indianapolis, New York: Bobbs-Merrill, 1970.

MK₃   *Metaphysik K₃* (KGS 28).

ML₁   *Metaphysik L₁* (KGS 28).

MM   *Metaphysik Mrongovius* (KGS 29).

MrM   *Moral Mrongovius II* (KGS 29).

MS   *Die Metaphysik der Sitten* (KGS 6).
        The Metaphysic of Morals, Introduction and Part II (*The Doctrine of Virtue*), trans. Mary Gregor, Philadelphia: University of Pennsylvania Press, 1964.

MV   *Metaphysik Volkmann* (KGS 28).

Proleg *Prolegomena zu einer jeden Künftigen Metaphysik die als Wissenschaft wird auftreten konnen* (KGS 4).
        Prolegomena to any Future Metaphysics, trans. L. W. Beck, Indianapolis: Bobbs-Merrill, 1950.

R   *Reflexionen* (KGS 17–19).

Rel   *Die Religion innerhalb der Grenzen der blossen Vernunft* (KGS 6).
        Religion within the Limits of Reason Alone, trans. Theodore M. Greene and Hoyt H. Hudson, New York: Harper & Row, 1960.

xii

Introduction

There can be little doubt regarding the centrality of the concept of freedom in Kant's "critical" philosophy. Together with the doctrine of the ideality of space and time, it constitutes a common thread running through all three *Critiques*. Although Kant does not claim to have established the reality of freedom in the *Critique of Pure Reason,* he does claim, on the basis of transcendental idealism, to have established its conceivability, that is, its compatibility with the causal mechanism of nature. Indeed, he even states that "were we to yield to the illusion of transcendental realism, neither nature nor freedom would remain" (A593/B571). And in the *Critique of Practical Reason,* where he does claim to have shown the reality of freedom, albeit from a "practical point of view," he characterizes the concept of freedom as "the keystone of the whole architecture of the system of pure reason and even of speculative reason" (5: 3; 3). Finally, in the *Critique of Judgment,* Kant suggests that the faculty of judgment, by means of its concept of the purposiveness (*Zweckmässigkeit*) of nature, makes possible a transition from the realm of the concept of nature to that of the concept of freedom (5: 175–6, 195; 14–15, 35). Surely, then, it is no exaggeration to claim that, at bottom, Kant's critical philosophy is a philosophy of freedom.

Unfortunately, it is also no exaggeration to state that Kant's theory of freedom is the most difficult aspect of his philosophy to interpret, let alone defend. To begin with, even leaving aside "outer freedom" or freedom of action, which is central to Kant's legal and political philosophy but which will not be considered here, we are confronted with the bewildering number of ways in which Kant characterizes freedom and the variety of distinctions he draws between various kinds or senses of freedom. Thus, Lewis White Beck distinguishes between five different conceptions of freedom, and as we shall see, this list could easily be expanded with a little fine-tuning.[1] Of itself, this gives one pause to wonder whether it is possible to speak of *a* theory of freedom in Kant.[2]

Nevertheless, it is relatively noncontroversial that at the heart of Kant's account of freedom in all three *Critiques* and in his major writings on moral philosophy is the problematic conception of transcendental freedom, which is an explicitly indeterminist or incompatibilist conception (requiring an independence of determination by all antecedent causes in the phenomenal world). In fact, Kant himself emphasizes the point and insists that it is precisely because freedom involves this transcendental (nonempirical) component that it is the "stumbling block [*Stein des Anstosses*] of all empiricists

1

but the key to the most sublime practical principles for critical moralists" (KprV 5: 7; 8).

Not surprisingly, however, this difficult conception has proven to be far more of a stumbling block than a key for generations of interpreters. Objections have been raised regarding the very intelligibility of the conception as well as against the alleged necessity of appealing to it. Indeed, the movement to replace it with a more palatable, compatibilist conception, which, as we shall see, is very much alive in the recent literature, can be traced back to Kant's own contemporaries.[3]

There are many reasons for this, and most of them are well known to any student of the secondary literature. First and foremost are the standard objections to Kant's appeal to the phenomenal–noumenal distinction, in order to reconcile his indeterministic conception of freedom with the causal determinism to which he is committed by the Second Analogy. The consensus among Kant's critics is that the application of this distinction to the problem of freedom leads to a dilemma from which there is no ready escape: Either freedom is located in some timeless noumenal realm, in which case it may be reconciled with the causality of nature, but only at the cost of making the concept both virtually unintelligible and irrelevant to the understanding of human agency, or, alternatively, freedom is thought to make a difference in the world, in which case both the notion of its timeless, noumenal status and the unrestricted scope within nature of the causal principle must be abandoned.[4]

The objections raised against the ethical dimensions of Kant's theory appear to be equally formidable, particularly insofar as they relate to his moral psychology. Thus, critics from Hegel to Bernard Williams have rejected Kant's account of moral freedom or autonomy, which supposedly requires us to conceive of moral agents as capable of setting aside all their interests and desires as "real-life" human beings and of acting solely from respect for an impersonal moral law. Against this, it is argued, first, that such a conception commits Kant to the absurd view that only genuinely autonomous actions are free, from which it follows that we are not responsible for our immoral acts; second, that it is impossible to set aside all one's interests and desires; third, that if one could, there would be no point to moral deliberation and nothing left to motivate one to act dutifully; and finally, that the attribution of moral worth to actions so motivated, and indeed, only to such actions, conflicts with our basic moral intuitions. Moreover, since (so the argument goes) it is only this understanding of the demands of morality that lends any credence to the assumption that morality requires transcendental freedom, once this is rejected, there is no longer any need to appeal to this problematic conception.

Finally, there are serious difficulties with Kant's endeavor to establish the validity of the moral law and with it his peculiar conception of freedom. Kant attempts this in both the *Groundwork* and the *Critique of Practical Reason,* and although the issue is controversial, it does seem that the attempt takes a radically different form in each work. In *Groundwork* III, Kant's apparent strategy is to provide a deduction of the moral law based on the necessity of presupposing the idea of freedom. Presumably convinced of the futility of such an approach, when he returns to the problem of justification in the second *Critique,* he reverses his course. Instead of attempting to derive the reality of the moral law from the idea of freedom, Kant now insists that the moral law can be established as a "fact of reason," which can, in turn, serve as the basis for a deduction of freedom. This move has been widely regarded, however, as a desperate and question-begging measure, an abandonment of the critical requirement to provide a transcendental deduction for a priori concepts or principles and a lapse into a dogmatism of practical reason.[5] And since Kant holds that it is only by way of the moral law that the actuality (as opposed to the mere conceivability) of freedom can be established, this means that his conception of freedom likewise remains ungrounded.

The problems mentioned in the preceding largely determine the agenda for this study of Kant's theory of freedom, which attempts to provide an analysis and defense of this theory in both its theoretical and practical dimensions. Naturally, I do not claim to be able to prove that Kant's theory is defensible in all of its details or that he is completely consistent on the topic. In fact, we shall see that even under the most charitable interpretation, many problems remain. Nevertheless, I do hope to show that given a sympathetic understanding of transcendental idealism, a good case can be made for Kant's incompatibilistic conception of freedom. In addition, I shall argue that the central features of Kant's moral psychology, including his conceptions of autonomy, moral worth, moral motivation, and radical evil, are much more plausible than they are frequently taken to be and that the standard criticisms (as well as some recent and influential defenses) suffer from a failure to consider these conceptions in connection with Kant's theory of rational agency. Finally, I shall argue that although the appeal to the fact of reason in the second *Critique* will hardly persuade the critic who rejects the basic thrust of Kant's moral theory, specifically the conceptions of the categorical imperative and autonomy, it does suffice to remove the specter of moral skepticism for someone who accepts the analysis of morality offered in the first two parts of the *Groundwork;* and that given the fact of reason (as well as transcendental idealism), there is a successful deduction of freedom from a practical point of view.

Although the overall argument is largely self-contained, it does presuppose the view of transcendental idealism I developed in *Kant's Transcendental Idealism.* Moreover, since this plays a significant role in my analysis of Kant's conception of agency, a word is in order regarding it at this point for the benefit of those not familiar with the earlier work. Reduced to bare essentials, this interpretation of Kant's idealism holds that the transcendental distinction is not *primarily* between two kinds of entity, appearances and things in themselves, but rather between two distinct ways in which the objects of human experience may be "considered" in philosophical reflection, namely, as they appear and as they are in themselves.[6] As such, it can be (and has been) characterized as a version of the "two-aspect" interpretation of this idealism, which is to be contrasted with the familiar "two-object" or "two-world" interpretation, according to which appearances and things in themselves constitute two ontologically distinct sets of entities.[7]

Central to this interpretation is the conception of an "epistemic condition," which I use as a heuristic device in order to explicate the force and the significance of the transcendental distinction. By an epistemic condition I understand a necessary condition for the representation of objects. Space and time, the forms of human sensibility, and the pure concepts of the understanding are the specifically Kantian candidates for epistemic conditions. As conditions of the possibility of the representation of objects, epistemic conditions are distinguished from both psychological and ontological conditions. The former includes propensities or mechanisms of the mind that supposedly govern belief or belief acquisition, for example, Hume's custom or habit. The latter includes conditions of the possibility of the being of things, which, as such, condition things quite independently of their relation to the human mind and its cognitive capacities, for example, Newton's absolute space and time. Epistemic conditions share with the former the property of being "subjective" in the sense that they reflect the structure and operations of the mind and therefore condition our representation of things rather than the things themselves. They differ from them with respect to their objectivating function. Correlatively, they share with the latter the property of being objective or objectivating. They differ from them in that they condition the objectivity of our *"representation"* of things rather than the very being of the things themselves.[8]

Implicit in this conception is the necessity of distinguishing between things insofar as they conform to these conditions and are therefore knowable by the human mind and the same things as they are "in themselves," that is, as they are independently of the human mind and its cognitive apparatus. The former corresponds to things as they appear, or simply appearances; the latter to things as they are in themselves, or simply things in themselves. Although things considered in the latter fashion are by definition unknowable by us, we can think of them as possible objects of a divine mind blessed with nonsensible or intellectual intuition. Thus, we can think, although not know, things as they are in themselves.

Not only does this line of interpretation have abundant textual support, it also enables one to dismiss many of the familiar objections that have been directed against Kant's "noumenalism" on the two-object or two-world interpretation. With respect to the main concern of this study, it makes it possible to avoid attributing to Kant the view (suggested by much of his language) that free agency occurs in a distinct "intelligible world" or that distinct noumenal activities somehow intervene in (without interfering with) the causal order of the phenomenal world. It offers instead the more appealing contrast between two "points of view" or descriptions under which a single occurrence (a human action) can be considered.

4

Admittedly, the two-aspect reading does not of itself suffice to answer all the salient objections to the Kantian theory of freedom. On the contrary, we shall find that it raises some problems of its own, which have not gone unnoticed in the literature. In particular, it leaves us with the problem of explaining the attribution of a double character, in Kant's terms, an empirical and an intelligible character, to a single subject (a rational agent). This is a problem because the two characters seem to be incompatible since the former involves subjection to causal determination (the "causality of nature") and the latter an independence of all such determination. Nevertheless, I shall argue that sense can be made of Kant's position on this crucial issue if one recognizes that it is rational agency that supposedly has both an empirical and an intelligible character.

To anticipate, the importance of this is that it permits us to interpret the contrast between empirical and intelligible character as holding between two models or conceptions of rational agency. The first, which relates to the empirical character of rational agency, amounts essentially to the familiar belief–desire model. This is used for the observation, causal explanation, and (to a limited extent) prediction of human actions, and it presupposes that an agent's empirical character, understood as a set of relevant beliefs and desires, functions as the empirical cause of the action. What is particularly interesting about this model is just that it is a model for the conception and interpretation of the intentional actions of human beings. Thus, although a causal model (roughly like Hume's), it does not involve the reduction of intentional actions to mere events or bits of behavior. In short, it is a model of rational agency and, as such, leaves ample "elbow room" for freedom of the familiar compatibilist sort. Moreover, we shall see that Kant's dissatisfaction with this model, at least as the whole story about rational agency, is the key to his rejection of the compatibilist solution to the free will problem of the kind familiar to him from the work of Leibniz and Hume.

The other model, which pertains to an agent's "intelligible character," appeals to the spontaneity of the agent as rational deliberator. This spontaneity, which is the practical analogue of the spontaneity of the understanding, may be characterized provisionally as the capacity to determine oneself to act on the basis of objective (intersubjectively valid) rational norms and, in light of these norms, to take (or reject) inclinations or desires as sufficient reasons for action. According to this model, then, the intentional actions of a rational agent are never "*merely*" the causal consequences of the agent's antecedent psychological state (or any other antecedent conditions for that matter) but require, as necessary condition, an act of spontaneity. The claim that this spontaneity is an ineliminable component in rational agency is what, for reasons that will become obvious, I call Kant's "Incorporation Thesis."

Since it can be thought but not experienced, this act of spontaneity is, in Kant's terms, "merely intelligible." As such, it does not enter into an empirical account or explanation of human action. Moreover, it is for this very reason that the intelligible character model, involving spontaneity, is compatible with the empirical character model, which lacks it. Since the former

5

is empirically vacuous, they are simply not competitors. Given transcendental idealism, however, it does not follow from the fact that it is empirically vacuous, with no explanatory function, that it is altogether idle. On the contrary, I shall argue that it is an essential ingredient in the conception of ourselves and others as rational agents and that, as such, it functions in contexts of imputation and rational justification.

Among the major consequences of the Incorporation Thesis to be explored in the course of this study is the recognition that even heteronomous or nonmorally based actions are free for Kant in an incompatibilist sense since they are conceived (in accordance with the intelligible character model) as products of the practical spontaneity of the agent. Moreover, we shall see that this is not, as is sometimes thought, a late modification of Kant's views on freedom but rather is an essential ingredient already present in the first *Critique* and *Groundwork* (and, indeed, in the "precritical" writings). Finally, we shall see that the Incorporation Thesis provides the key to much of Kant's moral psychology, including the frequently ridiculed requirement that an act be "from duty" if it is to possess moral worth.

The study is divided into three parts. The first deals with Kant's views on freedom and rational agency as expressed in the *Critique of Pure Reason* and some of his earlier writings. It is concerned primarily with the metaphysics of the problem, although attention is also paid to Kant's moral theory at the time of the first *Critique* and before, insofar as it sheds light on his views of freedom. This part consists of four chapters. The first analyzes the thesis and antithesis arguments of the Third Antinomy and Kant's appeal to transcendental idealism in its resolution. The second deals with Kant's distinction between empirical and intelligible character and with the problematic claim that both characters are to be attributed to rational agents. It is here that the major issues regarding Kant's conception of agency and his transcendental idealism are addressed. The third chapter analyzes the important contrast between practical and transcendental freedom, which, among other things, raises questions about the compatibility of Kant's discussions of freedom in the Dialectic and Canon of the first *Critique*. It is here that I discuss some relevant features of Kant's moral philosophy circa 1781. The fourth contrasts the view of freedom here attributed to Kant with the reconstructions of Lewis White Beck and Ralf Meerbote, each of whom bases his analysis, at least in part, on a two-aspect reading of Kant's idealism.

The second part deals with Kant's conception of moral agency and the central features of his moral psychology in his main writings on moral philosophy from the *Groundwork* on. As such, it is concerned with the concept of freedom as it is operative within what I term Kant's "fully critical" moral theory. This part consists of six chapters. The first (Chapter 5) is concerned mainly with the concept of autonomy, which is the essential ingredient in this fully critical moral theory. It explores the respect in which the attribution of the property of autonomy to the will marks a modification of the original first *Critique* conception of rational agency. The second (Chapter 6) analyzes Kant's views on moral worth as articulated in the *Groundwork* and his account of respect as the moral incentive in the *Critique of Practical Reason*. Together, then, these chapters deal with the central features of Kant's moral psychology as they are expressed in the main writings on moral philosophy in the 1780s.

By contrast, Chapters 7–9 focus on features of Kant's position that, for the most part, are implicit in the *Groundwork* and the second *Critique* but become prominent only in the writings of the 1790s, mainly *Religion within the Limits of Reason Alone* and the *Metaphysic of Morals*. Chapter 7 discusses the *Wille–Willkür* contrast and the associated conception of a *Gesinnung*, or underlying disposition. Chapter 8 analyzes the doctrine of radical evil. Chapter 9 explicates Kant's view of virtue and of holiness as a moral ideal. Finally, Chapter 10 considers and attempts to provide a response to the critiques of Kant's views on moral agency and moral psychology mounted by Schiller, Hegel, and in our own time, Bernard Williams.

The third part is concerned with Kant's attempts to justify the moral law and freedom in the *Groundwork* and the *Critique of Practical Reason*. It consists of three chapters. Chapter 11 analyzes and defends a claim that is common to both works and that constitutes a necessary first step in the Kantian justificatory strategy, namely, that morality and freedom (in the strict or transcendental sense) reciprocally imply one another, which I call the "Reciprocity Thesis." Its significance stems from the fact that it shows that (for better or worse) Kant's moral theory rests ultimately on a "thick" conception of freedom and not on a "thin," relatively unproblematic conception of rational agency. Chapter 12 analyzes Kant's manifestly unsuccessful attempt in *Groundwork* III to provide a deduction of the moral law, which is based on the necessity of presupposing the idea of freedom. Chapter 13 then considers Kant's quite different strategy for certifying the moral law and establishing the reality of freedom through the fact of reason in the second *Critique*. As already indicated, it judges this effort to be a qualified success and, at the very least, a considerable improvement over the approach of the *Groundwork*.

I
Freedom and rational agency in the
Critique of Pure Reason

1
The Third Antinomy

The Third Antinomy is not only the locus of the major discussion of the problem of freedom in the *Critique of Pure Reason,* it is also the basis for Kant's subsequent treatments of the topic in his writings on moral philosophy. His central claim is that it is only because the resolution of this antinomy leaves a conceptual space for an incompatibilist conception of freedom that it is possible to give the claims of practical reason a hearing. The antinomy itself, however, is ostensibly concerned with a conflict between cosmological ideas (ideas of totality), which seems to have nothing directly to do with what is generally regarded as the "free will problem." Consequently, it is not surprising that many commentators tend to gloss over the cosmological dimension of Kant's account, either ignoring it completely or dismissing it as one more example of Kant being deflected from his proper philosophical course by architectonic considerations.[1]

Although certainly understandable, this wholesale neglect of the cosmological dimension of Kant's account of freedom is nonetheless misguided. As I shall argue in the present chapter, the cosmological conflict can best be seen as one between two generic models or conceptions of agency that can and, in the history of philosophy, have been applied both to rational agents in the world and to a transcendent creator of the world. Thus, although the conflict cannot be identified with the familiar debate between libertarianism and determinism, it does provide the conceptual framework in terms of which Kant analyzes this debate. The chapter is divided into four parts. The first presents some preliminary remarks regarding the Antinomy of Pure Reason and its role within the first *Critique.* The second analyzes the arguments of the thesis and antithesis positions of the Third Antinomy. The third considers Kant's claim that transcendental idealism is the key to the resolution of the antinomies and its particular relevance to the Third Antinomy. The fourth discusses the connection between the cosmological question and the question of human freedom. It thus serves as a transition from the mainly cosmological focus of the present chapter to the specific concern with rational agency that will occupy us for the remainder of this study.

I. Some preliminaries[2]

In a famous letter to Christian Garve written in 1798, Kant remarks that it was the Antinomy of Pure Reason that "first aroused me from my dogmatic slumber and drove me to the critique of reason itself in order to resolve the

11

ostensible contradiction of reason with itself" (12: 258; 252). This contradiction or conflict of reason with itself is manifested in the fact that it seems to generate two equally compelling but incompatible answers to some fundamental cosmological questions. Kant also suggests that, if unresolved, the situation would lead to nothing less than the "euthanasia of pure reason" (A407/B434), that is, a radical skepticism concerning the claims of reason. Accordingly, a major goal of the *Critique of Pure Reason* is to resolve this conflict.

One of the keys to Kant's resolution is the location of the source of the conflict in reason itself. Specifically, he claims that it is located in reason's demand for an unconditioned totality of conditions (grounds) for any conditioned. This demand draws its apparent legitimacy from the principle that "*if the conditioned is given, the entire sum of conditions, and consequently the absolutely unconditioned* (through which alone the conditioned has been possible) *is also given*" (A409/B436). Both the demand and the principle reflect the need of reason to arrive at "such a completeness in the series of premises as will dispense with the need of presupposing other premises" (A416/B444). This need, in turn, is simply the logical requirement of the complete justification of every conclusion and explanation of every state of affairs.

Construed as a regulative idea, this requirement is certainly in order. Reason is never satisfied until every *explanans* is itself an *explanandum* and every conclusion grounded in self-evident premises. The problem arises when this regulative idea is construed constitutively, that is, when it is dogmatically assumed that the entire series of conditions for every conditioned is "given" or at hand. If the "conditioned" is the conclusion of an argument, then this assumption is certainly warranted; for the conclusion is not established unless all of the premises from which it follows are likewise given and justified. If, on the other hand, the conditioned is a state of affairs for which an explanation (set of conditions) is sought, then the assumption cannot be made. All that we can do is to look for further conditions, with no guarantee that they are attainable (even in principle).

Although the fallacious nature of this dogmatic assumption might seem obvious on the face of it, Kant insists that it is natural, indeed inevitable, given the identification of appearances with things in themselves. Very roughly, the main point is that if, in the manner of transcendental realism, we construe appearances as things in themselves, then in our legitimate search for conditions (explanations) we inevitably abstract from the temporally successive manner in which items are given in experience, or in Kant's terms, "empirical synthesis." After all, if the items in question are assumed to be things in themselves, that is, things whose nature can be defined independently of the conditions of human knowledge, then these latter conditions may be dismissed as "merely subjective," as limitations of the human cognitive situation that do not have any implications for the things themselves.[3] To do this, however, is to assume the legitimacy of an eternalistic, "God's eye" standpoint with respect to these things; and from such a stand-

12

point (which is not ours) it certainly holds that a complete series of conditions for every conditioned must be presupposed as being at hand. The antinomy arises because any such complete set of conditions may be thought with equal cogency either as bounded by a first member, which is itself unconditioned, or as infinite.

The thought of such a complete series or totality of conditions is, in Kant's technical terminology, a "cosmological idea." Kant connects these ideas very closely with the categories, maintaining that they arise from the illegitimate extension to the whole of the modes of categoreal synthesis used to conceptualize items in the realm of possible experience. But not every category is capable of generating a cosmological idea and with it an antinomy. The only ones that are, according to Kant, are those that involve the thought of a synthesis of subordinate elements or conditions, namely, quantity, reality, causality, and necessity. The claim, then, is that each of the ideas generated by an illicit extension of these categories gives rise to an antinomical conflict, which is itself a particular expression of the underlying conflict of reason with itself.

One of the interesting features of Kant's analysis is his claim that each party to the dispute presents an internally consistent philosophical position. The proponent of the finitistic position maintains that the world has a first moment in time and a limit in space; that matter is composed of simple indivisible elements; that there is a spontaneous free cause outside the series of natural causes that grounds the whole series; and that there is a necessary being that serves as the ground of the contingent beings in the world. By contrast, the opposed infinitistic position maintains that there can be no such beginning, limit, simple, free cause, or necessary being. Kant characterizes the former position as "dogmatism" and the latter as "empiricism," and he links them with Plato and Epicurus, respectively. It seems clear, however, that Kant also had a more contemporary conflict in view; namely, the dispute between Newton and Leibniz, as presented in the correspondence between Leibniz and Clark.[4] Moreover, it turns out that it is Leibniz who is the empiricist, although this empiricism is, in its own way, as dogmatic as the position to which it is opposed.

Kant insists that the equal success of each side in refuting the other renders impossible a dogmatic solution to the conflict. This, in turn, suggests a skeptical impasse, which would amount to the already mentioned "euthanasia of pure reason." He thinks that this can be avoided, however, by the adoption of what he calls the "skeptical method," which consists in an examination of the presuppositions underlying the dispute.

The result of this examination is the discovery that both sides share the initially plausible, but ultimately untenable, presupposition that the sensible world, with respect to which the cosmological questions are raised, is a whole existing in itself. Given this presupposition, it follows necessarily that the conflicting claims are genuine contradictories and, therefore, that one of them must be true. But once this presupposition is rejected, the contradiction is replaced by a "dialectical opposition" between contraries, both of which

13

are false. This reflects Kant's treatment of the first two, or "mathematical," antinomies. The second two, or "dynamical," antinomies receive a quite different treatment. There is, of course, still a false presupposition that generates the appearance of a contradiction; but now it is the assumption that claims are contradictory when they really are compatible (given the transcendental distinction between appearances and things as they are in themselves).[5] Accordingly, the competing claims are here treated as subalternates, rather than contraries, although the conflict between them is still regarded as merely dialectical.

II. The arguments

Both parties to the Third Antinomy assume the validity within experience of "causality in accordance with laws of nature," that is, the mode of causality affirmed in the Second Analogy. In dispute is whether it is also necessary, or even permissible, to appeal to another conception of causality, transcendental freedom, defined as "the power [*Vermögen*] of beginning a state spontaneously [*von selbst*]" (A533/B561), in order to account adequately for any given appearance.[6] In other words, the issue is the justifiability of positing a cause or ground of appearance, the causal activity of which is exempt from the conditions of the causal activity of appearances.

The thesis affirms the necessity of appealing to such causality in order to find the required resting place for reason (the idea of the unconditioned), a place where the explanatory buck stops. Appealing to the distinction between a "beginning in time" and a "beginning in causality" (A450/B478), it also affirms the logical possibility of applying this conception to some occurrences in time, for example, human actions. The antithesis denies both claims. It affirms instead that all causality (without exception) must be of the Second Analogy type. In so doing, it also commits itself to the assumption of an infinite causal chain. As in the case of the other antinomies, the demonstrations are apogogic in nature, that is, each side attempts to establish its case by demonstrating the impossibility of the alternative. Thus, the operative assumption shared by both sides is that the opposing claims are contradictories. This is not readily apparent from the formulation in the text (which suggests a clash between two competing conceptions of causality); but the situation can be easily rectified if the thesis and antithesis are taken to claim, respectively, not everything takes place according to mechanistic causality and everything takes place according to such causality.[7]

A. *The thesis*

As already indicated, the thesis makes a claim about the requirements for an adequate explanation: In addition to "causality in accordance with the laws of nature" (*nach Gesetzen der Natur*), it is necessary to assume a "causality of freedom" in order to account for appearances. The argument can be broken down a number of different ways, but it will be convenient to consider it as consisting of the following seven steps:

1. The assumption of the opposing view: "There is no other causality than that in accordance with laws of nature" (A444/B472).

2. This means that "everything which *takes place* presupposes a preceding state upon which it invariably follows according to a rule" (A444/B472).

3. But this entails (by universalization) that the preceding state must itself have come into existence in time. [If this be denied, i.e., assuming that the preceding state has always existed, then its consequence (the succeeding state) would likewise have always existed.[8] But this contradicts the assumption that the latter has come into existence in time, i.e., taken place.]

4. Since the "causality of the cause through which something takes place is itself . . . something that has *taken place*," it "presupposes, in accordance with the law of nature" (*nach dem Gesetz der Natur*) (A444/B472) its own antecedent cause, and so on.

5. Consequently, on the assumption that "everything takes place in accordance with mere laws of nature" [*nach blossen Gesetzen der Natur*], there will always be only a relative [*subalternen*] and never a first beginning, and consequently no completeness of the series on the side of the causes" (A444–6/B472–4).

6. "But the law of nature [*Gesetz der Natur*] is just this, that nothing takes place without a cause sufficiently determined *a priori*" (A446/B479).

7. Thus, when "taken in unlimited universality," the claim that "no causality is possible save in accordance with laws of nature" (*nach Naturgesetzen*) (A446/B474) is self-contradictory. Consequently, it cannot be regarded as the sole kind of causality.

Strictly speaking, this argument establishes at most the negative conclusion that mechanistic or natural causality (causality according to "laws of nature") is not the only kind of causality, and this might seem to be quite distinct from establishing a positive thesis about a distinct, nonnatural kind of causality involving absolute spontaneity or, equivalently, transcendental freedom. As Kant makes clear in his discussion of the solution to the antinomy, however, he is treating the causality of nature and freedom as the only two modes of causality conceivable to us (A533/B561). Moreover, since freedom is here understood in a purely negative sense (as independence of the conditions of nature), there is nothing particularly problematic in the move from the insufficiency of the former to the assertion of the latter.

The same cannot be said, however, about the argument for the thesis. In fact, the secondary literature suggests that it is difficult to find an argument here that has even a prima facie claim to plausibility. The problem is not with the first five steps, which are relatively straightforward and do nothing more than state and spell out the implications of the position to be refuted. The most important of these implications, the one on which the argument is obviously supposed to turn, is that there would be "no completeness of the series on the side of the causes." There can be no question that this does,

15

indeed, follow from the assumption under attack. The question is why this should be unacceptable; certainly it does not seem unacceptable to the defender of the antithesis position.

The answer is obviously supposed to be provided by the crucial step 6, which refers to the "law of nature" that "nothing takes place without a cause sufficiently determined *a priori*." It is this principle that presumably generates the contradiction with the incompleteness of the causal series and that leads, in turn, to the conclusion asserted in step 7. Consequently, this step bears almost the entire weight of the argument. Unfortunately, it is far from clear that it is capable of supporting this burden.

At the heart of the problem is the notion of "a cause sufficiently determined *a priori*," which constitutes part of the *definiens* of the law of nature. Perhaps the most natural move is to construe this as equivalent to a "sufficient cause," that is, one capable of accounting for the complete effect. This is contrasted with a partial cause, which would be merely a contributing causal factor capable of accounting for only part of the effect. Given the argument of the Second Analogy, it certainly follows that every occurrence must have a sufficient cause in this sense; so that on this reading step 6 might seem unproblematic. The problem is that this reading fails to yield the desired contradiction. As Schopenhauer, who did construe the argument in this way, notes, it is one thing to assert that every event requires a sufficient cause in the sense of a set of simultaneous conditions that are conjointly necessary and sufficient to produce the effect and quite another to assert (as the argument supposedly requires) that there must be a completion in the successive series of antecedent causes leading up to the event.[9] Only by conflating these two claims can the argument, on this interpretation, get off the ground. Basically the same objection is also advanced by Kemp Smith, who remarks that the question of whether A itself is sufficiently explained is distinct from the question of whether A (being given) is sufficient to explain B.[10]

There is, however, little textual support for the Schopenhauer–Kemp Smith reading. As Jonathan Bennett points out, the claim is that the cause must be sufficiently "determined," not that it must be "sufficient." Moreover, he adds (following Heimsoeth) that "a priori" here has its usual pre-Kantian meaning of in advance of or prior to rather than the specifically Kantian sense of "independently of experience."[11] Unfortunately, Bennett does not explain what the requirement that a cause must be sufficiently determined prior to its occurrence amounts to or how the argument based on it is supposed to work. Indeed, he confesses defeat at this point and, in lieu of offering an interpretation of his own, provides a brief survey of some of the supposedly inadequate accounts in the literature.[12]

The most promising of these is a suggestion of Ewing to the effect that if there were only causality of nature, then no explanation would be ultimate in the sense of leaving nothing further to be explained or, equivalently, of providing a resting place for thought.[13] The problem with this suggestion, according to Bennett, is that it takes the target of the thesis to be a version of the principle of causality that holds *both* that there is only the causality of nature *and* that every event has an ultimate explanation. This is deemed unacceptable because it makes the opponent into "such an obvious straw man that Kant cannot have taken it seriously or supposed that the thesis-arguer would do so."[14]

Although correct in his account of the target of the thesis argument on Ewing's reading, Bennett is premature in his rejection of this target as a "straw man" and, therefore, in his dismissal of this line of interpretation. In fact, we need only substitute the principle of sufficient reason for what he terms a "principle of causality" in order to arrive at the Leibnizian position as it is articulated in the polemic with Clarke. There and elsewhere, Leibniz maintains that every occurrence has a sufficient reason *both* in the sense that it has an antecedent cause *and* in the sense that it has an ultimate explanation (accessible only to God) based on its role within the total context of the possible world actualized by the divine will. Much to the dismay of Clarke, Leibniz also extends this principle to the divine will itself, maintaining that it is determined (although not necessitated) by what the divine intellect recognizes as the best. Thus, in his insistence on the strict universality of the principle he explicitly rules out the spontaneity affirmed by Clarke to be necessary to the understanding of divine (or human) agency.[15]

Of perhaps even greater relevance to our present concerns, Leibniz also construes this principle in such a way that it applies equally "to any thing's existing . . . to any event's happening . . . to any truth's taking place."[16] In Kantian terms, this means that he construes it both as a logical principle requiring adequate grounds for any conclusion and as a real or causal principle requiring sufficient preconditions for every occurrence. Moreover, if as Leibniz and his followers seem to have done, one regards these requirements as two expressions of a single principle that has both logical and metaphysical status, then it is certainly natural to take it as requiring an ultimate explanation or grounding for occurrences analogous to the logical grounding in first principles required for the justification of conclusions. In short, in virtue of his interpretation of the principle of sufficient reason, Leibniz is committed to the assumption that there must be both an antecedent cause and an adequate explanation (at least in principle, or for God) for every occurrence or state of affairs.

Applying this to the thesis argument, we can equate a "cause sufficiently determined *a priori*" with a sufficient reason in the Leibnizian sense and the law of nature with the principle of sufficient reason, understood as involving the dual requirement that every occurrence have both an antecedent causal condition and an adequate, that is, complete, explanation. Correlatively, the laws of nature, in terms of which everything is supposed to find its sufficient reason, are just the mechanistic causal laws used to explain occurrences.[17]

Given the ambiguity built into the law of nature, so construed, it is highly significant that it appears twice in the argument (steps 4 and 6).[18] In its first appearance, it expresses the requirement that every occurrence, or more precisely, the "causality" of every cause, have its own antecedent cause. Since any exception would amount to a violation of the principle of sufficient

17

reason, this requirement can be seen as an expression of that principle. Moreover, this leads directly to the assertion of the incompleteness of the causal series (step 5). In its second appearance, it expresses the requirement of complete explicability implicit in the Leibnizian notion of a sufficient reason. The contradiction emerges when it is seen that the two requirements built into the single principle pull in opposite directions: the one demanding that every *explanans* be in turn regarded as an *explanandum* (as it must be if it is itself an occurrence in time), the other demanding that there be an ultimate or unconditioned *explanans* in which the explanatory series is grounded. Finally, since the contradiction is between conflicting demands of a single principle, it is, as Kant states in step 7, a self-contradiction.

The main point of the thesis argument, then, is simply that the requirement of ultimate intelligibility (which is built into the principle of sufficient reason) is incompatible with the exclusion of all causality except that which is "in accordance with laws of nature." Otherwise expressed, there is a conflict between what can be termed the "completeness requirement," that is, the requirement that explanation culminate in an ultimate resting place for thought (an unmoved mover), and the "universalizability requirement," which excludes any such ultimate on the grounds that it violates the principle of sufficient reason since no explanation can be given for it.[19] Thus, in insisting on the latter, the advocate of unrestricted causality, in accordance with the laws of nature, is led to deny the former.

To interpret the argument as a *reductio* of the Leibnizian position, however, leads immediately to a different set of objections: that it is circular or question begging and that it turns on an arbitrary, dogmatic appeal to the principle of sufficient reason.[20] So construed, the critic might very well contend, the thesis argument is aimed at a real target (Leibniz) rather than a straw man; but for that very reason its scope is limited to philosophies with similar metaphysical commitments, in particular, a commitment to a strong form of the principle of sufficient reason. Once we abandon this principle, we are free to reject the thesis on the grounds that it conflates the requirement for the causal explanation of an occurrence (produce a "sufficient" cause) with the requirement for the justification of a conclusion (produce a complete set of premises).

This line of objection, which can be easily generalized so as to apply to the thesis argument of each of the antinomies, seems compelling as long as we consider these arguments in abstraction from the general problematic of the antinomical conflict. In the present case, the troublesome step 6, which expresses the completeness requirement, is, indeed, a fresh premise that goes beyond the implications of the causal principle spelled out in steps 1–5. Why, then, should the defender of the principle that all causality is in accordance with the laws of nature accept it?

The answer, in brief, is that this requirement is nothing more than the application to the sphere of causal explanation of the fundamental principle underlying the antinomical conflict as a whole: *"If the conditioned is given, the entire sum of conditions, and consequently the absolutely unconditioned*

18

(through which alone the conditioned has been possible) *is also given."* In the present case, the "conditioned" refers to any occurrence in time, that is, any event, and the "sum of conditions" to the sum total of causal antecedents required for the complete explanation of this occurrence. Since the proponent of the proposition that all causality is in accordance with laws of nature is, *ex hypothesi,* committed to this principle, he must also respect the completeness requirement. But as the thesis argument shows, this requirement cannot be met on the assumption of the proposition in question because it would render impossible a complete explanation of any occurrence in the causal series.

Admittedly, such a response seems only to push the problem back one step further, thereby delaying the day of reckoning; for it can now be asked why we must accept this principle. Moreover, the problem is complicated by the fact that Kant's critical answer is that we need not, at least not in the dogmatic or constitutive form in which it is operative in the Antinomy of Pure Reason. Thus, Kant's own analysis undercuts the very basis of the antinomical conflict. But although the latter is certainly the case (at least it is claimed to be by Kant), it does not affect the point at issue. This point is simply that the principle in question expresses a necessary requirement of reason (for completeness of explanatory grounds), which is inevitably construed in a dogmatic manner, given the identification of appearances with things in themselves. Since both sides in the dispute make this identification (they are transcendental realists), neither side can avoid appealing to this principle in its dogmatic form. Similar considerations apply, *mutatis mutandis,* to the arguments of the other antinomies.[21]

B. The antithesis

As already indicated, the antithesis denies the possibility of a causality of freedom and affirms instead that "everything in the world takes place solely in accordance with laws of nature" (A455/B473). Like the thesis argument, the argument for the antithesis can be broken down into seven steps, supplemented by some reflections on the "illusion of freedom," which parallel the positive remarks on freedom in the thesis. First the argument:

1. The assumption of the view to be refuted, namely, that there is freedom in the transcendental sense.

2. This means that there is (a) "a power of absolutely beginning a state" and (b) a power "of absolutely beginning a series of consequences of that state" (A445/B473).

3. This, in turn, entails that (a) a series of occurrences will have its absolute beginning in a spontaneous cause and that (b) this causality itself will have an absolute beginning. Consequently, "there will be no antecedent through which this act, in taking place, is determined in accordance with fixed laws" (A445/B473).

4. But as we have learned from the analogies, "every beginning of action presupposes a state of the not yet acting cause" (A445/B473).

5. Moreover, if, as is presumably being assumed, it is not only a *"dynamical* beginning" (the beginning of a causal sequence) but also a first beginning, it "presupposes a state which has no *causal* connection with the preceding state of the cause, that is to say, in nowise follows from it" (A445/B473).

6. Consequently, transcendental freedom is opposed to the conditions of the unity of experience (as specified in the "law of causality") and therefore can never be met within any possible experience.

7. The idea of such freedom is, therefore, "an empty thought entity," that is, there can be no transcendental freedom (A447/B475).

The supplementary remarks reflect the standpoint of a dogmatic determinist. The major brunt of these remarks is that freedom, construed as independence from the laws of nature, is illusory because it entails lawlessness. Here Kant seems explicitly to reject what he elsewhere affirms: that freedom has its own laws, which do not conflict with the laws of nature. As he here puts it, "If freedom were determined in accordance with laws, it would not be freedom; it would simply be nature under another name" (A447/B475).

Since this argument is considerably less problematic than that of the thesis, it requires relatively little analysis. The first three steps state and develop the immediate implications of the hypothesis that there is transcendental freedom. Basically, these are that both a causal activity and a causal series will have an "absolute beginning." Steps 4 and 5 (if these can be considered distinct steps) bring out further implications, which, in turn, lead to the rejection of this hypothesis. First, step 4 introduces a supposedly noncontroversial premise from the analogies, that "every beginning of action presupposes a state of the not yet acting cause," and notes that this must also hold for a putative transcendentally free cause. In other words, even such a cause, or more properly, causal agent, must exist and be in a certain state prior to acting. Step 5 then points out that in this case the action, *ex hypothesi,* does not stand in any causal connection with the antecedent state of the agent; thus, it is in effect a "first beginning." It is this result that is then claimed in step 6 to conflict with the conditions of the unity of experience, from which it follows unproblematically that transcendental freedom cannot be an object of possible experience. Finally, step 7 infers from this that transcendental freedom is impossible.

A crucial feature of this argument, to which we shall return, is that unlike the thesis argument it contends that the proposition to be denied contradicts the conditions of possible experience rather than that it is self-contradictory. It is likewise noteworthy that the move from this result to the absolute rejection of transcendental freedom employs an implicit verificationist premise: Whatever conflicts with the conditions of the unity of experience, or more generally whatever is experientially impossible, is also absolutely impossible. As we shall see, these features of the argument open up the possibility of claiming that both the thesis and the antithesis might be true.

This argument has met with two general types of response in the secondary literature. On the one hand, there is the view of Schopenhauer that it reflects Kant's basic critical position and that it is perfectly satisfactory.[22] A modified version of this view is offered by Strawson, who treats it as a "simple denial of freedom," which is consistent with the results of the Second Analogy.[23] On the other hand, there are those critics who, although they likewise regard the argument as essentially of a piece with the Analytic, nevertheless reject it for that very reason as question begging or circular. The main claim here is that it is illegitimate for Kant to appeal to the results of the Analytic at this point (just as it is illegitimate in the thesis argument to appeal to the principle of sufficient reason). This, it is sometimes argued, is particularly true in that these results (as Kant construes them) are inseparable from a commitment to transcendental idealism, and this idealism is precisely what is at issue in the whole discussion of the antinomies. In addition, it is maintained that the radically un-Kantian equation of freedom with lawlessness is needed to make the argument work; and that by appealing to the conditions of the unity of experience, the argument rules out only a spontaneous cause within nature, which leaves untouched the central contention of the thesis that we must assume such a cause outside of nature.[24]

With regard to the first objection, it is easy to show that the antithesis neither begs the question at issue by illicitly assuming the validity of the causal principle nor presupposes the truth of transcendental idealism. It is not guilty of the former because the validity of this principle (and presumably also the premise "every beginning of action presupposes a state of the not yet acting cause") is accepted by both parties and, therefore, is not at issue in the dispute. As already noted, the issue is merely whether, given this principle, it is also possible to find room for freedom; and the antithesis clearly argues for, rather than assumes, its negative conclusion. Similarly, it is not guilty of the latter because, as I have argued elsewhere, Kant acknowledges that even transcendental realism affirms the validity of the analogies within experience (although it cannot account for this validity).[25] The point here is that the issue between transcendental realism and transcendental idealism does not arise at the empirical level but only when, as in the final step of the antithesis argument, these principles are extended beyond the limits of possible experience. Only then, Kant reflects, "does distinction of the mode in which we view the reality of these objects of the senses become of importance, as serving to guard us against a deceptive error which is bound to arise if we misinterpret our empirical concepts" (A496–7/B525).

The claim that the argument works only by equating freedom with lawlessness, an equation that supposedly conflicts with Kant's own views, is likewise beside the point. Admittedly, the antithesis argument reflects a dogmatic empiricism rather than Kant's critical position; nevertheless, it must be kept in mind that the conception of freedom at issue is an explicitly incompatibilist one. As such, it conflicts with the laws of nature, which are the only laws under consideration within the cosmological context of the antinomy. In that sense, then, even Kant maintains that freedom, so conceived, is "lawless."

The objection that the argument moves illicitly from the rejection of transcendental freedom within nature to the rejection of it outside of nature is a legitimate one, and it points to the previously noted verificationist premise implicit in step 7. It also makes it clear that the antithesis argument goes well beyond the results of the Analytic since these suffice only to rule out freedom within nature, considered as the sum total of objects of possible experience. As with the analogous objection regarding the appeal to the principle of sufficient reason in the thesis argument, however, it must be emphasized that the move is a "natural" one, given the transcendentally realistic assumption within which the entire dispute proceeds. In the present case, this assumption leads to empiricism becoming dogmatic by equating the conditions of possible experience with the conditions of things as they are in themselves. Although Kant certainly rejects such an identification, together with the dogmatic empiricism and verificationism it involves, he nevertheless insists that, given this identification, the reasoning in the antithesis argument is perfectly in order.[26]

Finally, it should be noted that, like its counterpart, the antithesis trades on the ambiguity in the principle of sufficient reason. The difference is simply that whereas the thesis insists upon the completeness requirement at the expense of the universality requirement, the antithesis insists upon the latter at the expense of the former. Another way to put the point, which is somewhat closer to Kant's own, is that the thesis, reflecting a dogmatic rationalism, affirms the demand of reason for totality, that is, for an unconditioned unity that satisfies the conditions of thought, whereas the antithesis, reflecting a dogmatic empiricism, affirms the demand of the understanding for consistency and connectibility, that is, for a unity that satisfies the conditions of experience. The antinomy arises because both demands seem to be equally legitimate and each side takes its claim to be incompatible with its opposite.

III. The resolution of the Third Antinomy

Kant insists that transcendental idealism is the key to the resolution of the entire antinomical conflict, but he also maintains that this idealism yields different resolutions to the different antinomies. Thus, whereas he resolves the first two, or mathematical, antinomies by claiming that neither the thesis nor the antithesis is true, he resolves the last two, or dynamical, antinomies by claiming that both may be (not that they are) true or, more precisely, that the competing claims are compatible.

Not surprisingly, however, this distinction has been met with considerable skepticism by Kant's critics. In fact, it has seemed to many like an ad hoc device, designed to allow Kant to have his cake and eat it too.[27] Typical of this line of response is Strawson, who writes:

It seems obvious what the correct "critical" solution of this conflict should be. Since things in space and time are appearances, the series of ever more remote causes should no more be regarded as existing as a whole than the series of ever more remote temporal states of the world or the series of ever more remote spatial regions of the world. Since the series does not exist as a whole, there is no question of its existing either as an infinite whole or, as is asserted in the thesis, as a finite whole with a first, uncaused member. Every member of the series which is actually "met with" in experience, however, may and must, be taken to have an antecedent cause. The thesis, then, is false, the antithesis true.[28]

Although he was anticipated by Schopenhauer, it is nonetheless somewhat curious to find Strawson claiming that the critical solution to the antinomies is to deny the thesis and affirm the antithesis. Not only does this fly in the face of Kant's explicit claim that in the mathematical antinomies neither the thesis nor the antithesis is true, it also fails to distinguish between the regulative demand always to seek further conditions and the antithesis's dogmatic assertion of the presence of an actual infinity of conditions.[29] In short, it fails to note that Kant regards the antithesis as being as dogmatic in its own way as the thesis.

More to the present point, it glosses over the reason that Kant provides for the distinction between two types of antinomy, namely, the distinct ways in which the regress from conditioned to condition is carried out. In the case of the mathematical antinomies, the conditioned and its conditions are homogeneous, that is, they are all, *ex hypothesi,* members of the same spatio-temporal series. Consequently, assuming that these homogeneous elements constitute a complete set or totality, as seems to be required by the underlying premise of the antinomical conflict (*"if the conditioned is given, the entire sum of conditions, and consequently the absolutely unconditioned... is also given"*), it follows that this set must be composed of either a finite or an infinite number of members. The resolution then consists in the rejection of this assumption, which entails the rejection of both the finitistic and infinitistic alternatives.

In the case of the dynamical antinomies, by contrast, where the regress is from grounded to ground, the homogeneity requirement is not in place. Thus, in the Third Antinomy, where the regress is from effect to cause, the possibility remains open that there is a cause or ground of an event that is not itself sensible, that is, not part of the series of appearances. As non-sensible, such a cause or ground would have to be called "intelligible." The thesis, as we have seen, affirms the necessity for such a cause, whereas the antithesis denies its very possibility. As we have also seen, however, the antithesis does not maintain that the conception of such a cause or ground is self-contradictory but rather that it conflicts with the conditions of possible experience. Accordingly, once the slide from this critical result to the distinct and "dogmatic" claim that such a cause or ground is absolutely impossible is properly diagnosed and eliminated, there is no longer any incompatibility with the thesis. In other words, it becomes possible that both sides may be

23

correct: the thesis, with its assertion of an intelligible, transcendentally free first cause outside of experience; the antithesis, with its refusal to admit such a cause within experience.

Although it is not generally recognized, the difference between the two types of regress and, therefore, the two types of resolution is a function of the difference between the conceptions of a totality or whole underlying the two types of antinomy. Kant himself attempts to characterize this difference in terms of the contrast between "world" and "nature" (A418/B440). The former signifies "the mathematical sum-total of all appearances and the totality of their synthesis, alike in the great and the small." The latter signifies the same sum total conceived as a "dynamical whole." This contrast between a mathematical sum total and a dynamical whole is equivalent to the contrast between a whole in the sense of an aggregate or collection and an explanatory whole, that is, as an all-inclusive series of conditions (explanatory grounds or causes) in terms of which the existence of everything conditioned is to be explained.

The salient difference between these two conceptions of a whole or totality is simply that the former is self-contradictory whereas the latter is not. The concept of a complete set or totality of spatiotemporal items, that is, a "world," is self-contradictory because such a totality (whether it be conceived as containing a finite or an infinite number of members) both purports to be an empirical concept and involves a requirement (completeness) that conflicts with the conditions of possible experience.[30] Accordingly, Kant's strategy for resolving the mathematical antinomies consists essentially in pointing out the self-contradictory nature of its underlying concept. Once this is accomplished, the dogmatic finitistic claim of the thesis is rejected completely, whereas the equally dogmatic, infinitistic claim of the antithesis is replaced by the modest and legitimate regulative demand: Always seek further conditions. With respect to the mathematical antinomies, the problem with the Schopenhauer–Strawson interpretation, which claims that Kant's real solution is to affirm the antithesis, is, as already noted, precisely that it neglects the latter move.

The concept of an explanatory whole likewise conflicts with the conditions of the possibility of experience, but it is not self-contradictory because the concept does not involve the requirement that all the items in the explanation be themselves empirical. Presumably, that is why the antithesis argument of the Third Antinomy does not maintain that the notion of an unconditioned cause, which is required for the completion of an explanatory whole, is itself self-contradictory. In any event, since its underlying concept is not self-contradictory, the resolution of the dynamical antinomies requires a different strategy. Instead of rejecting both thesis and antithesis on the grounds that they flow from a self-contradictory concept, the task here is to show how the two *apparently* conflicting explanatory demands that follow from the concept of an explanatory whole (the completeness and the universality requirements) can be made compatible with one another. It is, therefore, this systematic difference rather than, as is usually assumed, Kant's misguided

24

zeal to reconcile science and morality that accounts for the difference in the treatment of the two types of antinomy.

Finally, we can see from this why only the resolution of the mathematical, and not the dynamical, antinomies yields an indirect proof of transcendental idealism, even though in both cases the rejection of the transcendentally realistic assumption on which the conflict is based is logically equivalent to the assertion of the transcendental ideality of appearances. Once again, the key point is simply that since the concept of an explanatory whole is not self-contradictory, it need not be rejected. Consequently, Kant cannot argue, as he does in the case of the mathematical antinomies, from the self-contradictory nature of their underlying concept (the world, as a complete collection or pregiven totality) to the self-contradictory nature of the position or "standpoint" that entails this concept (transcendental realism) and from the negation of the latter to the affirmation of its contradictory (transcendental idealism).[31]

What he does instead is to appeal to transcendental idealism in order to explain how the apparently incompatible requirements built into the concept of an explanatory whole can be reconciled with each other. In the case of the Third Antinomy, this amounts to creating a logical space for the transcendental idea of freedom. For this line of argument to amount to a proof of transcendental idealism, it would be necessary to establish the reality of such freedom. But this is precisely what Kant denies to be possible, at least on theoretical grounds. Thus, although transcendental idealism resolves the antinomy by showing that "causality through freedom is at least *not incompatible* with nature" (A558/B586), this does not suffice to establish the truth of transcendental idealism.

IV. The Third Antinomy and freedom of the will

Since the "causality of freedom" has so far been considered exclusively with reference to a putative intelligible ground of the series of "natural" causes, that is, with reference to a first cause or unmoved mover, it is not yet clear what, if anything, this cosmological issue has to do with the notion of freedom of the will and the question of its reconcilability with the mechanistic (broadly construed) causality of nature. Kant addresses this question in the observation on the thesis, where he discusses the connection between the transcendental idea of freedom and the ordinary conception of free agency. The main point is that the latter conception, or equivalently, the "psychological concept," which will later be termed "practical freedom," is a hybrid notion. Although mainly empirical, it also contains, as an essential ingredient, the transcendental idea, here characterized as the thought of the "absolute spontaneity of an action as the ground of its imputability." It is further insisted that the transcendental aspect is the source of the difficulty with the concept of freedom, since to admit free agency is to admit a type of "unconditioned causality," that is, "a power of spontaneously beginning a series of successive things or states" (A448/B476). What is at stake, then, according

25

to the standpoint of the thesis, is the coherence of the conception of free agency, here construed in an unabashedly incompatibilistic fashion. To deny the legitimacy of the transcendental idea is to deny what is essential to this conception.

Even granting this, however, it is still necessary to explain how the transcendental idea, which was introduced in order to satisfy the demand of reason for an unconditioned ground outside the series of natural causes, can be also appealed to in connection with occurrences within the course of nature. The explanation offered turns on the contrast between a "beginning in time" and a "beginning in causality." The point is that whereas only the act of divine creation is a beginning in both senses, manifestations of free agency within the world are "beginnings" in the latter sense in that, as involving spontaneity, they cannot be regarded as simple causal consequences of the antecedent state of the agent. But, so the argument goes, it is really a beginning in the latter sense that is affirmed in the thesis. Consequently, once this conception is accepted, there should be no further obstacles to the conception of occurrences within the order of nature as having such a beginning, that is, as having temporal but not causal antecedents. It is admitted that we cannot comprehend how such an unconditioned causality is possible, but this is dismissed as irrelevant on the essentially Humean grounds that "we are not in the least able to comprehend how it can be possible that through one existence the existence of another thing is determined" (A450/B478). In other words, the causality of nature is ultimately as inexplicable as the causality of freedom. In both cases, we must rest content with the recognition of the necessity of presupposing a conception of causality without being able to explain its possibility.

This paradoxical-sounding claim regarding the possibility of a causally unconditioned beginning within the temporal series is illustrated by the example of an ordinary intentional action, that of arising from a chair. The contention that this, or any such action, constitutes a "first beginning in causality" amounts to the claim that it initiates a series of causally related occurrences, without itself being the causal consequence of antecedent conditions, including the antecedent state of the agent. The idea here is that it "follows upon . . . without arising out of" these antecedent conditions. What is explicitly designated in the observation as exempt from the causal series is the "resolution and the act" (*Entschliessung und Tat*) (A451/B479).

This cryptic account suggests a picture of agency in which the decision to act plays a causal role (it starts a new series) while itself, as an expression of spontaneity, standing outside the causal series. As a picture it is somewhat crude and reminiscent of Clarke's position in his polemic with Leibniz.[32] Nevertheless, by insisting upon the "moment" of spontaneity, it does suggest how the transcendental idea of freedom might be viewed as performing a modeling or regulative function with respect to the conception of ourselves (or others) as rational agents. Consequently, it foreshadows an essential feature of the Kantian conception of rational agency, which will be analyzed in the subsequent chapters.

26

Naturally, the observation on the antithesis unequivocally denies this conception of agency, and two aspects of this denial are worthy of attention. First, there is the insistence on the inseparability of mathematical and dynamical beginnings. The claim is that the two notions stand or fall together. Given this connection, the arguments marshalled against the former in the First Antinomy are now applied to the latter. Thus, a first beginning, whether in time or causality, is ruled out on the verificationist grounds that it could not be an object of possible experience. This just makes explicit the verificationism that we have already seen to be at work in the antithesis argument. Second, it is claimed that even if one were to admit the possibility of a first beginning for the causal series as a whole, it would not follow that it is permissible to posit "first beginnings" within the course of nature. In the former case, one is dealing with an empty possibility since such a beginning stands outside the conditions of possible experience. In the latter case, however, there is a direct conflict with these conditions. This, as we shall see, poses the deepest problem for Kant's account of free agency, a problem that he attempts to resolve by introducing the contrast between empirical and intelligible character.

For the present, however, it must be noted that in addition to its rejection of the thesis, the antithesis presents an alternative account of agency, one that is, in all essentials, equivalent to the familiar compatibilist account. Rather than appealing to the transcendental idea of freedom (spontaneity) as a model or regulative principle, it appeals to the "causality of nature," which means that the action must be explicable in terms of the antecedent state of the agent, together with other factors, including background conditions, which collectively constitute the sufficient reason of the action. According to this account, then, to deny that an action has such a sufficient reason is to deny the conditions under which it can be intelligibly attributed to an agent.

It is also noteworthy that the antithesis position is recognizably Leibnizian (although not uniquely so). In his polemic with Clarke, Leibniz insists that "every event should have beforehand its proper conditions, requisites and dispositions, the existence whereof makes the sufficient reason for such an event."[33] Moreover, he insists against Clarke that this principle applies to actions (both human and divine). In general, Leibniz's view is that an action must have its sufficient reason in the antecedent state of the agent, that is, in the agent's motives, which collectively constitute a disposition to act in a certain way under particular circumstances. From this standpoint, then, the suggestion that an agent could act contrary to this disposition is equivalent to the suggestion that it could act without a reason.[34] In order to complete the compatibilist picture of agency, one need only add that an act not causally connected with the antecedent state (disposition) of an agent, that is, a transcendentally free act, could not be coherently attributed to that agent.[35] This is, to be sure, good Leibnizian doctrine, but the same point is made by Hume and many other compatibilists.

27

All of this suggests that intertwined with the official cosmological conflict is an antinomy of agency, which concerns the conditions under which an action may be attributed to an agent. Moreover, just as in the cosmological conflict the issue turns on an ambiguity or tension within the principle of sufficient reason, so the agency conflict turns on an analogous ambiguity or tension in the concept of act attribution. Very roughly, act attribution seems to be subject to two conflicting requirements. First, the action must be regarded as something the agent "does" of itself, as opposed to being the result of something "done" to the agent. This can be called the "activity requirement," which is a necessary condition for an act to be imputed to an agent. Second, the action must be explicable in terms of the agent's nature or character. This may be called the "explicability requirement," and it is a necessary condition for attributing any motivation to the agent. As in the case of the cosmological conflict, each side in this dispute latches on to one of these poles while rejecting the other as incompatible with genuine agency. Once again, then, the task is to show how these apparently conflicting requirements are compatible with one another.

It must be emphasized, however, that since Kant insists that the activity requirement can be met only by an incompatibilist conception of freedom (modeled on the transcendental idea), the usual compatibilist solution to this problem is not open to him.[36] Otherwise expressed, the Kantian project requires not merely the reconciliation of free agency with causal determinism (this being the relatively straightforward and noncontroversial project of compatibilism, with which Kant was familiar through the writings of Leibniz and Hume, among others) but rather the reconciliation of such determinism with an incompatibilist conception of freedom. Thus, in the words of Allen Wood, this project may be appropriately described as the attempt to show the "compatibility of compatibilism and incompatibilism."[37] It is to this attempt, carried out in terms of the contrast between empirical and intelligible character, that we now turn.

2
Empirical and intelligible character

> I readily confess that this double character of man, these two
> I's in the single subject, are for me, in spite of all the expla-
> nations which Kant himself and his students have given of it,
> particularly with respect to the resolution of the well known
> antinomy of freedom, the most obscure and incomprehensible
> in the entire critical philosophy.[1]

After almost two hundred years, the perplexity expressed by Kant's astute
critic, Hermann Andreas Pistorius, is still widely shared. How can both an
empirical and an intelligible character be ascribed to a single agent? How
can one and the same action be conceived both as causally determined by
the antecedent state of the agent and extrinsic factors and as a "new beginning," the product of the spontaneity of the agent?

The present chapter attempts to deal with this problem by focusing on
the distinction between the two types of character as it is depicted in the
Critique of Pure Reason. Contrary to many interpreters, I shall argue that
Kant is there concerned to provide a transcendental framework for a unified
theory of rational agency, one that includes but is not limited to moral
agency. Accordingly, although I shall refer to these texts on occasion, the
modifications of his theory resulting from an exclusive focus on the moral
dimension of agency in the *Critique of Pure Reason* and *Religion within the
Limits of Reason Alone* (specifically, the account of *Gesinnung*) will be reserved for the second part of this study.

The chapter is divided into four parts. The first considers the nature of
the distinction between empirical and intelligible character and analyzes
the conception of rational agency in its empirical character. It concludes
that, in spite of some problems, this conception provides the basis for a
rich compatibilist account of such agency. The second analyzes the conception of an intelligible character and Kant's grounds (apart from moral
considerations) for appealing to it in his account of rational agency. It
thus addresses the reasons for Kant's dissatisfaction with a compatibilistic
position, such as the one advocated by his two major philosophical oppo-
nents, Leibniz and Hume, as well as by most contemporary critics. The
third deals with the problems posed by the ascription of both characters
to a single agent or activity and, therefore, with the question of the coherence of Kant's overall position raised by Pistorius and many others since.
The fourth considers some of the perplexing details of the conception
of rational agency that emerges from this analysis, particularly the notion that "reason has causality" and the alleged "timelessness" of such
causality.

I. The distinction in general and empirical
character in particular

Kant first presents the contrast between an empirical and an intelligible character in general terms, which make no reference to specifically human, or even rational, agency. Only later does he apply it to the human will and its peculiar mode of causality, the "causality of reason." This initial formulation suggests that it should be regarded as the agency version of the phenomenal–noumenal distinction.

"Every efficient cause," he tells us, "must have a character, that is, a law of its causality without which it would not be a cause" (A539/B567). Presumably, this means that every cause, or more properly, causal agent, must have such a law of causality, that is, a determinate *modus operandi*. Apart from the ascription of such a character, there would be no grounds for referring to a particular causal agent or type of cause in the production of a given effect, that is to say, no basis for a causal explanation. Insofar as we are dealing with the empirical character of a causal agent, as we always are in science, this *modus operandi* must conform to the conditions of possible experience (particularly the Second Analogy) and be describable in empirical terms.

Kant also suggests that, in the case of at least some agents, we may have grounds for assigning an intelligible as well as an empirical character. Since "intelligible" here is equivalent to "nonsensible" or "nonempirical," it follows that the intelligible character of such agents and their activity would neither conform to the conditions of possible experience nor be describable in empirical terms. Moreover, since time is the universal condition of possible experience (all appearances are in time), it also follows that with respect to its intelligible character, such an agent "would not ... stand under any conditions of time" (A539/B567). Given Kant's argument in the analogies, this means that we could not speak meaningfully of something happening in or to this agent or of its being determined by antecedent conditions. In short, with this conception of an intelligible character we have the formula for the thought of the empirically unconditioned activity of a noumenal subject.

Whether this conception of an intelligible character is either completely vacuous or incoherent, as most of Kant's critics contend, or perhaps has some relevance for the conception of human agency is the topic of the next section. But before turning to that and the deep issues regarding the attribution of both characters to a single agent, we must consider Kant's account of rational agency in its empirical character. Not only is this account an integral aspect of Kant's overall theory of rational agency, but also, as we shall soon see, it is itself not entirely unproblematic.

The essential feature of Kant's account of empirical character is that he attributes such a character to the will and its causality of reason. This attribution is implicit in the entire discussion; but Kant makes it fully explicit when, after offering a brief account of how reason can be thought to determine conduct by generating imperatives, he notes, "Reason though it be, it must nonetheless exhibit an empirical character" (A549/B577). Moreover, a few lines later, in a passage that deserves to be cited in full, he writes:

Thus, the will of every man has an empirical character, which is nothing but a certain causality of his reason, so far as that causality exhibits, in its effects in the [field] of appearance, a rule from which we may gather what, in their kind and degrees, are the actions of reason and the grounds thereof, and so may form an estimate concerning the subjective principles of his will. Since this empirical character must itself be discovered from the appearances which are its effect and from the rule to which experience shows them to conform, it follows that all the actions of men in the [field of] appearance are determined in conformity with the order of nature, by their empirical character and by the other causes which cooperate with that character; and if we could exhaustively investigate all the appearances of men's wills, there would not be found a single human action which we could not predict with certainty, and recognize as proceeding necessarily from its antecedent conditions. So far, then, as regards this empirical character there is no freedom; and yet it is only in the light of this character that man can be studied – if, that is to say, we are simply *observing,* and in the manner of anthropology seeking to institute a physiological investigation into the motive causes of his actions. (A549–550/B577–8)

As the passage makes clear, Kant is advocating not only a strict determinism at the empirical level but also a *psychological* determinism. Human actions, regarded empirically, are caused by the empirical character of the agent, defined as a causality of reason, together with other "cooperating causes." Similarly, the predictability of such actions would require sufficient knowledge of the "appearances of men's wills," together with the relevant background conditions. Thus, in contrast to most contemporary theorists, Kant's determinism at the empirical level does not rest on the assumption of either the reducibility of action explanations to neurophysiological ones or of a token–token identity between physical and psychological states. On the contrary, the relevant causal factors seem to be largely psychological in nature, that is, the beliefs, desires, and intentions of the agent.[2] Moreover, although the point is not spelled out, it seems reasonable to assume that the cooperating causes are supposed to work by influencing the agent's psychological state.

Quite apart from the question of the tenability of such a psychological determinism, Kant's identification of human agency, in its empirical character, with a causality of reason raises at least two major exegetical puzzles, which, if left unresolved, call into question the coherence of his overall position. The first problem is that given Kant's unrelenting insistence on the spontaneous, nonsensible nature of reason and its activity, it is not immediately obvious how he can attribute an empirical character to it at all. Is not reason the paradigmatically noumenal capacity, and how can anything noumenal have an empirical (i.e., phenomenal) character? The second problem concerns the compatibility of Kant's insistence on a psychological determinism at the empirical level with his denial of the possibility of psychological laws. If reason and its causality do, indeed, exhibit an empirical character, then the study of that character must pertain to the province of empirical psychology (or perhaps anthropology). But Kant denies that empirical psychology is a science, insisting that the most it can provide is a "natural description ... but not a science of the soul" (MAN 4: 471; 8).[3] Since anthropology, which Kant does regard as the actual "science" of human behavior, seems to differ from empirical psychology mainly in that it prescinds from the question of whether human beings have souls, it is apparent that this stricture must apply to it as well.[4]

The resolution of the first problem is complicated by the fact that Kant offers two distinct versions of the relationship between empirical and intelligible character, only one of which appears to leave room for the attribution of an empirical character to the causality of reason.[5] Sometimes Kant describes the relationship in straightforwardly causal terms. On this view, the intelligible character is the noumenal cause and the empirical character its phenomenal effect.[6] In addition to raising the specter of ontologically distinct noumenal causes and all of the problems that this involves, since this view attributes such causality solely to the intelligible character, it seems to foreclose the possibility of regarding the empirical character as itself an expression or instantiation rather than merely as a product of a causality of reason. In short, on this view it is not reason but merely the occurrences in the phenomenal world supposedly produced by it that can be said to have an empirical character. Sometimes, however, apparently without noticing the difference, Kant also speaks of the empirical character as the appearance or sensible schema of the intelligible character.[7] Unlike the first version of the relationship, this view does allow for the possibility that the causality of reason, although intelligible, might nonetheless be said to have an empirical character, namely, its phenomenal expression, appearance, or schema. Unfortunately, it suffers from the disadvantage of suggesting that there might be an inference route from the empirical to the intelligible, a consequence that the "critical" Kant could hardly accept.[8]

It is clear from the preceding that what is needed is an account of empirical character that enables us to regard it as in some sense an expression or manifestation (and not simply a result) of an intelligible activity, without requiring us to assume that it yields any insight into the true nature of that activity. Although it is hardly free from ambiguity, some such view does seem to be suggested by the previously cited passage in which Kant describes the empirical character of a human will as

nothing but a certain causality of his reason, so far as that causality exhibits, in its effects in the [field of] appearance, a rule from which we may gather what, in their kind and degree, are the actions of reason and the grounds thereof, and so may form an estimate concerning the subjective principles of his will. (A549/B577)

The main ambiguity in this passage concerns the expressions "the actions of reason" and "the subjective principles of his will." If these are taken to refer to an agent's intelligible character, then we are right back to the problem already noted, namely, we are construing Kant to be allowing for the possibility of inferring something about the nature of an intelligible activity or character from its empirical manifestation. This is avoided, however, if we take the expressions to refer to the empirical character of the will. Moreover, this latter reading is strongly supported by Kant's subsequent claim that it is the empirical (not the intelligible) character that "must itself be discovered from the appearances which are its effects and from the rule to which experience shows them to conform" (A549/B577). If we take this latter claim seriously, then we are led naturally to the view that the empirical character of the will of a rational agent consists in the subjective principles or "maxims" on the basis of which that agent acts or, more properly, in the disposition to act on the basis of these principles. Construed dispositionally, this character can be inferred from "appearances," that is, from behavior. The basic idea here is that a person's behavior exhibits sufficient regularity so as to enable one to reconstruct the rule or principle on which that person tends to act in given situations. This rule or principle can then be used (to some extent at least) to predict future behavior.

Significantly, on this reading, it becomes meaningful to attribute a causality of *reason* to the empirical character of the will of a rational agent. The crucial point here is that, so construed, the empirical character involves not simply a disposition to behave or to respond in certain predictable ways in given situations but a disposition to act on the basis of certain maxims, to pursue certain ends, and to select certain means for the realization of these ends. That is why even the empirical study of human behavior, particularly that which is provided by "pragmatic anthropology," is, in a very real sense, a study of *rational* agency.[9] Presumably, that is also why Kant speaks of a "psychological" concept of freedom, which he admits is "mainly empirical" (A448/B476).

Unfortunately, this resolution of the initial puzzle also seems to exacerbate the second. Given this account of rational agency together with his denial of nomological status to the empirical generalizations of psychology or anthropology, it becomes increasingly difficult to understand how Kant could insist upon a causal determinism for human actions at the phenomenal level. Causal determinism, so it would seem, presupposes strict causal laws. Certainly, the kind of predictability to which Kant refers requires covering laws similar (if not identical) to those contained in Newtonian physics. As we have seen, however, Kant denies that there are any such laws in the psychological domain. Moreover, the puzzle only increases if one includes in the picture the distinction drawn in the *Critique of Judgment* between mechanistic and teleological explanation. Clearly, the causality of reason, even at the empirical level, is inherently purposive. Consequently, explanations of its activity must be teleological rather than mechanistic in nature.

We shall return to the problem of the relationship between causality according to the model of the Second Analogy and teleology in Chapter 4. For the present, it must suffice to note that the Second Analogy attempts to prove only that every event must have some cause, not that similar causes must have similar effects. Accordingly, it does not follow from it alone that nature is "lawful" in the sense that all occurrences must be subsumable under empirical laws.[10] The latter conception of lawfulness (empirical lawfulness) is a regulative principle of scientific enquiry, not a constitutive principle of the possibility of experience. Moreover, Kant treats it as such in both the Appendix to the Dialectic of the first *Critique* and the Introduction to the third.[11] Thus, for all that one can infer from the argument of the Second Analogy (or indeed, the Transcendental Analytic as a whole), it remains possible that nature does not exhibit any empirically accessible lawlike regularities.[12]

Nevertheless, none of this undermines Kant's psychological determinism. Although Kant denied that the chemistry of his day had achieved full scientific status and contained genuine laws, he would hardly have denied that chemical changes fall within the scope of the Second Analogy.[13] The same can be said, *mutatis mutandis,* for organic phenomena and human actions, even though both of them are supposedly amenable to teleological rather than to mechanistic explanation. Kant makes his position somewhat clearer in the *Critique of Practical Reason,* where, after agreeing with Leibniz that human actions have psychological rather than physical causes, he denies that this exempts them from the "mechanism of nature" broadly construed (KprV 5: 97; 100–1). In order to belong to this mechanism, it is sufficient that an occurrence (whether mental or physical) has its determining ground in antecedent time or, as Kant sometimes put it, that it be subject to the "conditions of time." Since psychological phenomena, including the human will in its empirical character, are subject to these conditions, they must fall under the scope of the Second Analogy.

Finally, it should be noted that this conception of empirical character is capable of providing the basis for a rich and potentially attractive form of compatibilism. It would differ from most contemporary forms because of its focus on psychological rather than neurophysiological determination; but in that respect it would be in accord with the views of Leibniz and Hume. As such, it would also leave "elbow room" for freedom in a deterministic (although not Laplacian) universe by allowing for the description and explanation of human action in terms of the beliefs, desires, and intentions of agents, that is, for a "naturalized" version of the causality of reason. Moreover, it is clear from his remarks about a "psychological" or "comparative" concept of freedom in the first two *Critiques* as well as from his more or less naturalistic account of human freedom as a historically conditioned capacity in the third *Critique,* the *Anthropology,* and the essays on the philosophy of history that Kant was well aware of that fact. Nevertheless, instead of resting content with such a view, which would have been in at least rough accord with the main thrust of the Transcendental Analytic, Kant explicitly denies freedom with respect to the empirical character. Thus, the question inevitably arises: Why did Kant reject such a compatibilist solution to the free will problem and insist instead on introducing the problematic notion of an intelligible character together with all of the difficulties this involves?

34

II. Intelligible character

The usual explanation of Kant's rejection of compatibilism and consequent appeal to an inaccessible noumenal domain or intelligible character is his concern to ground morality. Starting with this assumption, which is itself a reasonable one, if one reads the first *Critique* account of freedom in light of that of the second, it is sometimes also maintained that the main reason for Kant's dissatisfaction with a compatibilist account of freedom lies in his manifestly inadequate view of nonmoral motivation. According to this line of criticism, which can be traced back at least to T. H. Green and has been reaffirmed recently by both Terence Irwin and Allen Wood, Kant believed that all nonmorally motivated actions must be motivated and, therefore, "caused" by the desire for pleasure.[14] Given this belief, Kant could account for the possibility of nonhedonistic or nonegoistic action, as required by his moral theory, only by locating such action in a distinct noumenal world and assigning to it a separate intelligible cause. As Wood succinctly puts it, "the free will problem arises for Kant [in the radical form in which it does] because he is a thoroughgoing psychological hedonist about all the natural causes that might act on our will."[15] The clear implication of this, which is drawn by both Irwin and Wood, is that were it not for this unfortunate thesis in empirical psychology, the way would have been open for Kant to have treated the free will problem along standard compatibilist lines.

I shall argue later (Chapter 5) that Kant does not, in fact, hold such a theory of motivation or, more simply, that he is not a psychological hedonist. But even if he were, it could not account for his analysis of freedom in the *Critique of Pure Reason*. What is distinctive about this analysis is Kant's contention that *both* moral *and* pragmatic or prudential imperatives indicate a causality of reason. Given this, it is clearly a mistake to claim that, in the first *Critique* at least, Kant introduces his noumenalism merely to account for the possibility of acting on the basis of the categorical imperative (as contrasted with the capacity to act on the basis of imperatives in general).

Two passages, one from the Dialectic and one from the Canon, should suffice to make this clear. In the first, shortly after stating that reason imposes imperatives in "all practical matters [*in allem Praktischen*]," which presumably includes prudential as well as moral matters, he contends that "the *'ought'* pronounced by reason" is at work "whether what is willed be an object of mere sensibility (the pleasant) or pure reason (the good)." In either case, Kant suggests:

Reason does not . . . follow the order of things as they present themselves in appearance, but forms for itself with perfect spontaneity an order of its own according to Ideas . . . according to which it declares actions to be necessary, even though they have never taken place, and perhaps never will take place. (A548/B576)

In the second, after distinguishing between moral laws (which dictate our duty) and pragmatic laws (which dictate the means necessary to the ends stemming from our sensuous nature), he notes that both count equally as "objective laws of freedom which tell us what *ought to happen,* although perhaps it never does happen" (A802/B830).

These passages make it clear that in the *Critique of Pure Reason,* if not in his later works in moral philosophy, Kant regards the capacity to act on the basis of imperatives in general (not merely the categorical imperative) as the defining characteristic of free agency. They also suggest that the spontaneity presumably required to act on the basis of an ought (whether moral or prudential) is the source of Kant's dissatisfaction with the compatibilist account of agency in terms of empirical character and, therefore, the reason for his introduction of the conception of an intelligible character.

What is not clear at this point is why Kant should think that this introduction is necessary, particularly when one considers its implications. Let us grant, as seems reasonable, that to engage in practical reasoning is to deliberate about what one ought to do (whether in a moral or a prudential sense). Let us further grant that this deliberation requires the "spontaneity" of reason in that it involves the forming of ends or "ought-to-bes" and rules that are not based solely on what one in fact desires at a given moment but rather reflect what one would choose if one were perfectly rational. The problem is that none of this appears to require the abandonment of the compatibilist conception of agency, much less the appeal to any noumenal or "merely intelligible" activities. Thus, we are brought back to our original question: What, apart from specifically moral considerations, is the basis for Kant's dissatisfaction with the compatibilist account of agency available to him on the basis of the "naturalized" construal of the causality of reason?

In order to understand Kant's seemingly gratuitous insistence on a merely intelligible moment of spontaneity in the conception of rational agency, we must look not to his moral theory or motivational psychology but rather to his views on the spontaneity of the understanding and reason in their epistemic functions. Indeed, Kant himself indicates the connection when, in a famous passage, he states that through mere apperception we are conscious of certain faculties, namely, understanding and reason, "the action of which cannot be ascribed to the receptivity of sensibility" (A547/B575). Since the operative contrast with the receptivity of the senses for Kant is always the spontaneity of the understanding (and reason), the clear implication is that apperception provides us with a consciousness of this spontaneity and that this consciousness is an inseparable component of the conception of ourselves as cognitive subjects.

Kant's claim that the understanding is spontaneous (A51/B75) can best be understood in terms of his identification of its fundamental activity with judgment (A73/B94). Largely against the empiricists, he argues that the senses provide the mind with the data for thinking objects, but not with the thought or knowledge thereof. The latter, he maintains, requires the active taking up of the data by the mind, its unification in a concept or synthesis, and its reference to an object. All this is the work of judgment, which is simply the spontaneity of the understanding in action.

A helpful way of explicating what Kant means by the spontaneity of the understanding in its judgmental activity (epistemic spontaneity) is to consider judgment as the activity of "taking as" or, more precisely, of taking something as a such and such.[16] Thus, in the simplest case, an indeterminate something $= x$ is taken as an F; in more complex cases, Fx is qualified by further "determinations" or predicates, for example, Fx is G. In still more complex cases, distinct takings (categorical judgments) are combined in a single higher order "taking" (hypothetical and disjunctive judgments). The key point, however, is that in all cases the activity of "taking as" is constitutive of judgment.

This same picture of judgment also clarifies the connection between the spontaneity of the understanding and apperception, which is a central theme of the Transcendental Deduction, particularly in the second edition. Eschewing all details, the main point is simply that although we can perfectly well perceive or intuit x's that are F's (such a capacity falls within the sphere of sensibility and can be attributed even to animals), we cannot conceive or represent to ourselves an x as F without not only doing it, that is, consciously taking it as such, but without also in some sense "knowing what one is doing." This peculiar mode of cognitive self-awareness is what Kant terms "apperception." As such, it is not another thing that one does when one judges (a kind of second-order knowing that one is knowing); it is rather an inseparable component of the first-order activity itself.[17]

Apperception, so construed, is contrasted with inner sense, which is the medium through which we can attain to an empirical knowledge of our mental states. Since such knowledge is subject to the transcendental conditions of experience, particularly the form of time, it yields an awareness only of the phenomenal self or the self as it appears to itself. With respect to this self there is no spontaneity. By contrast, apperception, as the consciousness of the act of thinking or, more properly, the self-consciousness built into that very act, is just a consciousness of spontaneity. Thus, in the B-Deduction, Kant describes the representation "I think" (which he identifies with apperception) as itself "an act of spontaneity" (B132), and later, in the Refutation of Idealism, he states, "The consciousness of myself in this representation 'I' is not an intuition, but a merely *intellectual* representation of the spontaneity of a thinking subject" (B278).[18] To be sure, the point of the latter claim is to deflate the pretensions of the Cartesian (problematic) idealist to gain knowledge of the self simply by reflecting on the *cogito*. Self-knowledge, for Kant, requires intuition and, as he argues in the Refutation, ultimately outer intuition. Nevertheless, the fact remains that Kant's account of the understanding commits him not only to the doctrine of the spontaneity of thinking but also to the assumption of a consciousness of this spontaneity that is "merely intellectual" or "intelligible" and that is, therefore, distinguished from self-knowledge, which requires intuition and is based on inner experience.[19]

Similar considerations apply, *mutatis mutandis,* to the faculty of reason insofar as its exercise is construed as the logical activity of inference drawing or reasoning. Although Kant usually has syllogistic reasoning in mind, the main point is simply that any genuinely inferential process (whatever its logical form) involves deriving conclusions from premises in such a way that the premises are taken as justifying the conclusion. In other words, the premises must not only be good and sufficient reasons for asserting the conclusion, they must also be regarded as such. Moreover, as before, this taking as is a spontaneous, inherently self-conscious activity of the subject.

Finally, insofar as reason has a "real use" distinct from that of the understanding, Kant sometimes attributes a distinct, higher level of spontaneity to it in virtue of its total independence of sensibility and its conditions.[20] Kant gives a good indication of what he means by this when, in a previously cited passage, he states that "reason . . . frames for itself with perfect spontaneity an order of ideas" (A548/B576). Translating this into the epistemological context suggests the doctrine, which Kant sketches in the Appendix to the Dialectic, that reason has the capacity to form ideas and to regulate enquiry in accordance with these ideas. Such formation and regulation involve spontaneity because, rather than simply reflecting a pregiven order of nature, reason projects an order of its own "in accordance with ideas," that is, it generates a set of norms and goals of explanation in terms of which scientific enquiry must proceed.[21] This "projection" is, of course, likewise an inherently self-conscious activity.

Given this brief glance at Kant's views on the spontaneity of thought, we are now in a position to determine why Kant insisted on a spontaneity component in his conception of rational agency and why he thought that the inclusion of such a component requires the introduction of the notion of a nonempirical, merely intelligible character. In both cases, the essence of the answer lies in Kant's implicit assumption that to conceive of oneself (or someone else) as a rational agent is to adopt a model of deliberative rationality in terms of which choice involves both a taking as and a framing or positing. Since these activities, as expressions of spontaneity, are themselves merely intelligible (they can be thought but not experienced), it is necessary to attribute an intelligible character to the acting subject, at least to the extent to which one regards that subject's reason as practical.

As presented in the *Critique of Pure Reason,* the distinguishing feature of this model is the virtual identification of rational agency with action on the basis of an *ought*.[22] This identification is, of course, intimately related to Kant's views on moral deliberation and obligation, but it does not involve any conflation of the two. On the contrary, as we have already seen, it is intended to cover both moral and prudential deliberation. In both cases, the essential point is that deliberation involves an appeal to some rule of reason (imperative), which specifies what course of action is "right" or "permissible" in a given situation for an agent, who, as affected by sensible inclination, does not always do what reason dictates ought to be done. Moreover, as the latter point indicates, this model is operative both in the context of deliberation, where it characterizes how one takes oneself qua engaged in a deliberative process, and in the context of appraisal or imputation, where it

38

grounds judgments of praise and blame (including but not limited to the moral variety) on the basis of the actions or "omissions of reason."[23]

The relevance to this model of the notion of taking as, or more precisely, its practical analogue, becomes apparent when we consider how it construes the relationship between rational agents and their inclinations or desires. The key point here is that even in the case of desire-based actions, a rational agent is not regarded as being determined in a quasi-mechanistic fashion by the strongest desire (roughly the Leibniz–Hume model). On the contrary, to the extent to which such actions are taken as genuine expressions of agency and, therefore, as imputable, they are thought to involve an act of spontaneity on the part of the agent, through which the inclination or desire is deemed or taken as an appropriate basis of action. Moreover, much like the conceptual determination of sensible intuition in the epistemic context, this occurs by subsuming the inclination or desire under a practical rule or principle. Thus, even desire-based or, as Kant later termed it, "heteronomous" action involves the self-determination of the subject and, therefore, a "moment" of spontaneity.

Kant hints at this at the very beginning of his discussion of practical freedom in the Dialectic, when he remarks that in considering a free act we are constrained to consider its "cause" as "not . . . so determining that it excludes a causality of our will" (A534/B562). Behind this seemingly paradoxical locution is just the thought that the sensible inclination, which from the point of view of the action's (and the agent's) empirical character is viewed straightforwardly as cause, is, from the standpoint of this model, seen as of itself insufficient to determine the will. Moreover, this insufficiency is not of the sort that can be made up for by introducing further empirically accessible causal factors. The missing ingredient is the spontaneity of the agent, the act of taking as or self-determination. Since this can be conceived but not experienced, it is once again something merely intelligible.

Further indications of Kant's view are contained in a set of *Reflexionen* closely related to the discussion of freedom in the *Critique*.[24] In one of them Kant states that actions are to a large part "induced [*veranlasst*] but not entirely determined by sensibility; for reason must provide a complement of sufficiency" (*ein complement der zulänglichkeit*); in another he speaks of reason using but not being determined by the natural condition of the subject (R 5611 18: 252; R 5612 18: 253). Similarly, in a course of lectures stemming from 1794 to 1795, Kant is recorded as claiming that not merely sensible stimuli but also "the concurrence of the understanding" [*die concurrenz des Verstandes*] is necessary to determine the will (MK$_3$ 28: 1015).[25] In spite of their dogmatic metaphysical flavor, all of these texts may be taken merely to be affirming the model of deliberative rationality in terms of which we must conceive ourselves insofar as we regard our reason as practical.

The same may be said of Kant's fullest and most important published account of his conception of practical spontaneity, which is contained in *Religion within the Limits of Reason Alone*. As he there puts it, "freedom of the will [*Willkür*] is of a wholly unique nature in that an incentive can determine the will to an action *only insofar as the individual has incorporated it into his maxim* (has made it into the general rule in accordance with which he will conduct himself . . .)" (Rel 6: 24; 19). Since this claim, which I call the Incorporation Thesis, underlies virtually everything that Kant has to say about rational agency, we shall return to it throughout this study. For the present, it must suffice to note two features of this thesis that bear directly on our current concerns. First, it makes it clear that for Kant an inclination or desire does not *of itself* constitute a reason for acting. It can become one only with reference to a rule or principle of action, which dictates that we ought to pursue the satisfaction of that inclination or desire. Moreover, as should already be clear from the previous discussion, the adoption of such a rule cannot itself be regarded as the causal consequence of the desire or, more properly, of being in a state of desire. On the contrary, it must be conceived as an act of spontaneity on the part of the agent.

Second, the Incorporation Thesis also enables us to see more clearly the connection, to which Kant himself alludes, between his conception of rational agency and his doctrine of transcendental apperception.[26] Thus, in light of this thesis, one may say that just as it must be possible for "I think" to accompany all my representations in order for them to be "mine," that is, in order for me to be able to represent anything through them, so too it must be possible for the "I take" to accompany all my inclinations if they are to be "mine" qua rational agent, that is, if they are to provide motives or reasons for acting. Again, just as sensible intuitions are related to an object only by being subsumed under concepts, so too sensible inclinations are related to an object of the will only insofar as they are "incorporated into a maxim," that is, subsumed under a rule of action. Finally, and most significantly for the understanding of Kant's conception of intelligible character, the "I take," like the "I think," can be conceived but not experienced. In other words, I can no more observe myself deciding than I can observe myself judging, although in both cases I must be conscious of what I am doing. That is precisely why both activities are merely intelligible in the specifically Kantian sense.

The relevance of the "positing" or "projecting" function of practical reason is likewise apparent. Just as in the theoretical realm the proper, regulative function of reason is to guide enquiry by framing an ideal order involving the systematic connection of phenomena under laws, so too, in the practical realm, its proper function is to guide conduct by framing an order of ends or ought-to-bes. Like its theoretical analogue, this activity is an expression of the spontaneity of reason because it goes beyond what is dictated by the sensible data, which in this case are the desires and inclinations of the agent. Insofar as one x's because one judges that one ought to x (whether for moral or prudential reasons), one x's on the basis of rational considerations. The "necessity" to x is, therefore, a rational necessity stemming from "objective laws of reason" (or at least putative laws), not a causal necessity stemming from antecedent conditions. As such, it is compatible with genuine freedom, since it does not follow from the fact that x-ing is rationally or objectively necessary that one will *x,* whereas it does follow from the fact that it is causally necessary.

In short, both aspects of practical spontaneity are essential to the conception of ourselves as rational agents. I cannot conceive of myself as such an agent without regarding myself as pursuing ends that I frame for myself and that I regard as rational to pursue. Correlatively, I cannot conceive of myself as such an agent without assuming that I have a certain control over my inclinations, that I am capable of deciding which of them are to be acted upon (and how) and which resisted. These are, as it were, necessary presuppositions for all who regard their reason as practical. Kant indicates this in the *Groundwork* by suggesting that we cannot act except under the idea of freedom (Gr 4: 448; 115). In the more metaphysical language of the *Critique of Pure Reason,* this means that we cannot conceive of ourselves as rational agents without attributing to our agency an "intelligible character," capable of determining itself to act on the basis of rational principles, "independently of the conditions of time."

Clearly, it does not follow from the fact (assuming it is a fact) that we are rationally constrained to attribute such a character to ourselves insofar as we regard ourselves as rational agents that we really do possess it. It does follow, however, that we cannot both deny such a character and affirm our status as rational agents. As we shall see in the next chapter, that is precisely why Kant frequently indicates that it remains an open question whether reason has causality.

III. The compatibility of empirical and intelligible character

So far we have considered Kant's conceptions of the empirical and the intelligible character of rational agency separately. We have now to deal with the question of their connection, that is, with the attribution of both characters to a single agent or action. Although the entire account is highly obscure, two passages in particular suggest the air of paradox that Pistorius and so many others have found in Kant's attempt to reconcile causal determinism at the phenomenal level with his incompatibilist conception of freedom.

In the first, after making the previously noted claim that "if we could exhaustively investigate all the appearances of men's wills, there would not be found a single human action which we could not predict with certainty, and recognize as proceeding necessarily from its antecedent conditions," Kant goes on to insist that this does not conflict with the possibility of considering these same actions "in their relation to reason" (A550/B578). Moreover, so considered, they are regarded as actions that ought or ought not to have occurred and, therefore, as free in an incompatibilist sense.[27]

The second is Kant's notorious discussion of a malicious lie, which he describes as an instance of a voluntary action (*willkürliche Handlung*) and treats as an illustration of the "regulative principle of reason" that it is necessary to think of absolutely first beginnings (A554/B582).[28] Faced with such an action, Kant suggests that we first enquire into its "motive causes" (*Bewegursachen*) and then seek to determine the degree to which the action and its consequences may be imputed to the agent; that is to say, we move from the question of explanation to the question of imputation. In considering the former question, the operative assumption is that this concerns the empirical character of the action and that it can be answered in terms of factors such as "defective education, bad company . . . the viciousness of a natural disposition insensitive to shame . . . levity and thoughtlessness" as well as other "occasional causes that may have intervened" (A554/B582). In short, it is assumed that the action can be explained in terms of a combination of environmental factors and character traits. There are, of course, important questions to be raised concerning the interplay and relative weights of these empirical conditions, but Kant is clearly not concerned with such issues. The main point is merely that "although we believe that the action is thus determined, we none the less blame the agent." Moreover, he continues, we do not do so because of his bad disposition or even his previous way of life; rather, Kant suggests,

we presuppose that we can leave out of consideration what his way of life may have been, that we can regard the past series of conditions as not having occurred and the act as being completely unconditioned by any preceding state, just as if the agent in and by himself began in this action an entirely new series of consequences. (A555/B583)

In both passages, then, one and the same action is deemed to be both the causal consequence of antecedent conditions and the beginning of a new causal series, a beginning that is itself unconditioned by anything antecedent to it in the time order. It is further claimed in both that the former is required for the explanation of the action and the latter for its imputation. Of course, we can now see that the former way of considering the action has regard to its empirical and the latter to its intelligible character. But rather than removing the air of paradox produced by the claim, the assignment of the two conflicting descriptions of the same action to two distinct characters seems like a transparent attempt to gloss over a bald contradiction. Or at least that is how it is usually regarded by Kant's critics.

As a first step in dealing with the problem posed by these passages, we note that Kant is not here claiming that it is *always* legitimate to assume that an agent could have done otherwise or, more precisely, that we must regard *every* action as both causally necessitated and free. The claim is rather that the availability of an empirical–causal explanation of an action does not of itself preclude the possibility of assuming that the agent could have done otherwise and therefore of holding the agent responsible. Indeed, if it did, then one could never hold an agent responsible because Kant is committed to the thesis that such an explanation is possible, in principle, for every action, including those motivated by moral considerations. As occurrences in the phenomenal world, even such actions must exhibit an empirical character. As Kant puts it in a *Reflexion*, "virtue as well as vice occurs according to natural laws and must thereby be explained" (R5616 18: 257).

Moreover, far from asserting a doctrine of unqualified noumenal freedom in the *Critique of Pure Reason*, Kant explicitly asserts that since the intelligible character is inaccessible to us, we can never be certain whether, or to what extent, a given action is due to nature or freedom. As he puts it in an important footnote that deals explicitly with the question of moral responsibility but has profound implications for his whole theory of agency:

> The real morality of actions, their merit or guilt, even that of our own conduct, thus remains entirely hidden from us. Our imputations can refer only to the empirical character. How much of this character is ascribable to the pure effect of freedom, how much to mere nature, that is, to faults of temperament for which there is no responsibility, or to its happy constitution (*merito fortunae*), can never be determined; and upon it therefore no perfectly just judgments can be passed. (A551/B579 note)[29]

Unfortunately, this weakening move does not take us very far. The most pressing question, after all, is not whether we are *always* free to act in ways other than we are causally determined to act; it is rather whether we can *ever* regard ourselves as free in that sense. Similarly, even if we reject the possibility of the complete predictability of human actions as incompatible with Kant's denial of nomological status to the empirical generalizations of psychology and anthropology, the problem of causal determinism remains.[30]

Clearly, it is at this point that the two-aspect reading of transcendental idealism becomes central to the interpretation, not to mention the defense, of Kant's position. Equally clearly, however, simply appealing to this reading does not, of itself, suffice to remove the very real and substantive objections to his theory. In fact, far from resolving the problem, the claim that an agent or action can be considered from two "points of view" or, equivalently, be assigned two such distinct characters appears merely to redescribe it in somewhat different terms. Thus, even granting this, we still need to know how these two conflicting points of view or characters can be made compatible. In particular, we need to know how an occurrence can be regarded as causally determined only from a point of view.

The latter difficulty has been sharply expressed by Terence Irwin, who states that "if an event is determined, it is true of it under all descriptions that it is determined, even though only some true descriptions, those referring to the relevant laws, show why it is determined."[31] The clear implication of this, which Irwin proceeds to draw, is that Kant cannot coherently claim that an event is determined under a phenomenal description and free under a noumenal one. The most that he can claim is that the noumenal description prescinds from the phenomenal determining grounds, which brings us right back to compatibilism.

Although he does not spell it out, perhaps because he believes that the point is too obvious to require any amplification, Irwin's objection clearly rests on the assumption that being causally determined is a necessary or essential property of any occurrence of which it is predicated. In the contemporary idiom of possible world semantics, this means that if an occurrence is causally determined in any possible world, it must be causally determined in all. Thus, so the argument goes, Kant cannot limit the property of being causally determined to occurrences in the phenomenal world or, equivalently, to occurrences taken under their phenomenal descriptions.

The first and essential step in the Kantian response to this line of argument is to note that it ignores the basic thrust of transcendental idealism and, therefore, ends up begging the question at issue. This becomes particularly clear if one interprets this idealism in terms of the distinction between epistemic and ontological conditions sketched in the Introduction. Seen in terms of this distinction, Irwin is, in effect, assuming that being causally determined must be taken as an ontological condition. Only so considered, could this property be thought to pertain to events in all possible worlds (including merely intelligible ones). For Kant, however, the concept of causality is merely an epistemic condition, more specifically, a condition of the representation of objective temporal change. Since all experience (including inner experience) is in time, the concept of being causally determined is certainly applicable to any *empirical* description under which an occurrence (including a human action) can be taken. At the empirical level, then, the most that one can do is to say with Irwin that some descriptions of human action, presumably those in terms of reasons, prescind from the causal determinants of the action, which are still assumed to be operative. But it does not follow that this holds also for nonempirical descriptions (if there be such) under which the same action might be taken. Consequently, it does not follow that it holds for all possible descriptions or, alternatively, from all possible points of view.

As interpreted in light of the notion of an epistemic condition, transcendental idealism has primarily a critical or deflationary force, limiting the scope of our legitimate knowledge claims to objects of possible experience. Thus, the claim is not that I only appear to myself and others as causally determined whereas I "really" am free. With respect to my empirical character, which encompasses everything that, strictly speaking, can be known about me as a rational agent, I really am causally determined, just as I really am a spatiotemporal being. This is just the force of Kant's empirical realism. Nevertheless, by treating space, time, and the categories as epistemic rather than ontological conditions, transcendental idealism also opens up a "conceptual space" for the nonempirical thought (although not knowledge) of objects, including rational agents, as they may be apart from these conditions, that is, as they may be "in themselves."

For the most part, of course, this conceptual space remains vacant and the thought of things as they are in themselves therefore reduces to the empty thought of a merely transcendental object, a "something in general $= x$."[32] In the consciousness of our rational agency, however, we are directly aware of a capacity (to act on the basis of an ought) that, for the reasons already given, we cannot regard as empirically conditioned. We have seen that Kant holds open the possibility that we may be deluded in our belief that we possess such a capacity; but the fact remains that insofar as we attribute it to ourselves, we must also attribute an intelligible character, which is thought in terms of the transcendental idea of freedom. Consequently, in attributing the latter to ourselves and our agency, we do not merely prescind or abstract from the causal conditions of our actions, considered as occurrences in the phenomenal world; rather we regard these conditions as nonsufficient, that is, as "not so determining" as to exclude a "causality of our will" since we think of ourselves as initiating causal series through actions conceived as first beginnings.

In addition to the manifestly problematic notion of a "first" or "absolute" beginning, which has supposedly been rescued by the resolution of the Third Antinomy, the major difficulty at this point would seem to be with the mysterious notion of a nonempirical thought, based on an idea of reason (transcendental freedom), of something that is itself empirically accessible and knowable, namely, a human action or agent. Thus, whereas one might be willing to accept transcendental idealism and its conception of epistemic conditions, as long as it is construed solely as a doctrine of epistemological modesty, it becomes quite another matter when such content is given to the vacuous thought of a "something in general $= x$." In fact, by attributing such content to the nonempirical thought concerning rational agents and their activity, Kant would seem to be violating his own critical strictures by transcending, as Strawson puts it, the "bounds of sense."

Nevertheless, the force of this line of objection can be mitigated considerably if we keep in mind that the transcendental idea of freedom, which provides the content to the otherwise empty thought of an intelligible character, has a merely regulative, nonexplanatory function. What it regulates is our conception of ourselves as rational agents. It does so by providing the conceptual basis for a model of deliberative rationality, which includes, as an ineliminable component, the thought of practical spontaneity. Once again, the basic idea is simply that it is a condition of the possibility of taking oneself as a rational agent, that is, as a being for whom reason is practical, that one attribute such spontaneity to oneself. Moreover, as the example of the malicious lie is intended to show, it is likewise a condition of the imputation of actions and, therefore, the assignment of responsibility. Finally, since this spontaneity is merely intelligible, its attribution requires the attribution of an intelligible character. Thus, insofar as we take ourselves and others to be rational agents existing in the world of sense, we are constrained to attribute both an empirical and an intelligible character to our agency.

Although Kant clearly assigns a regulative function to the transcendental idea of freedom, it differs significantly from the function assigned to the other transcendental ideas, for example, God and the soul. In his discussion of this topic in the Appendix to the Dialectic, Kant suggests that each of the latter two ideas guides empirical enquiry, albeit indirectly, by providing a *"focus imaginarius,"* which gives direction to such enquiry. Thus, the idea of God supposedly helps to ground the rationally necessary quest for systematic and purposive unity in nature by enabling us to think of this unity as if it had its origin in a supreme being (A685–8/ B713–16). Similarly, the "I," or soul (the psychological idea), that had been deprived of its metaphysically privileged status in the paralogisms is reinstated as the "schema of a regulative concept" through which reason endeavors to attain systematic unity in the explanation of the appearances of inner sense, that is, in the generalizations of empirical psychology (A682–4/B710–14).

Given all of this, one might expect Kant to claim that the transcendental idea of freedom plays a similar role with respect to pragmatic anthropology. In other words, the claim would be that we introduce systematic order into our empirical account of human behavior by viewing such behavior "as if" it were the product of spontaneous, unconditioned acts of free choice. Clearly, however, Kant could allow no such function since it conflicts with his overriding thesis that there is no room even for the thought of such freedom in connection with the empirical character of rational agents. Thus, if the transcendental idea of freedom is to have a regulative function, it must be broadly practical, although not exclusively morally practical, in nature.[33] Moreover, Kant explicitly claims as much in the Appendix, where he notes that in contrast to the idea of the world, which functions regulatively with respect to the series of empirical conditions (by licensing an indefinite search for further conditions), the idea of freedom is assigned to the practical sphere, where we think of reason as a cause producing actions and, therefore, as functioning outside the sphere of sensible conditions (A685/B713).[34] In its regulative, practical function, then, what this idea licenses is just the thought of nonempirical conditions in light of which actions may be imputed.

Nevertheless, setting these subtleties aside, it is obvious that the overall argument will still not seem convincing to many philosophers since it presupposes the truth of transcendental idealism, which is required to create the necessary conceptual space for this transcendental idea. Unfortunately, this is a difficulty that cannot be overcome, at least not without a full-scale defense of transcendental idealism. Kant's whole treatment of freedom, both in the *Critique of Pure Reason* and in his later writings on moral philosophy, is inseparable from his appeal to the transcendental ideality of appearances. Indeed, in a late *Reflexion* he not only affirms that the ideality of space and time and the reality of the concept of freedom are the two cardinal points around which the system of the *Critique of Pure Reason* turns, which is itself a fairly common claim for Kant, he also contends that one is led analytically from one to the other (R 6353 18: 679). Even if this contention is a bit too strong (as I think it is), it still seems clear that about the best one can do is to try to show that Kant's account of freedom is plausible given the framework of transcendental idealism. This may not seem like much, but it is more than most of his critics will allow.

46

IV. Timeless agency and the causality of reason

The interpretation just presented might also be thought subject to a quite different line of objection, one that concerns its adequacy as a reading of Kant and is therefore quite independent of the truth or coherence of transcendental idealism. The problem is that it is silent with respect to what is usually taken to be the most paradoxical and objectionable feature of Kant's account, namely, the conception of timeless agency it apparently involves. As Allen Wood puts it, "The attribute of timelessness, which some philosophers ascribe to God alone, Kant's theory must ascribe to every one of us insofar as we are transcendentally free."[35] And later: "The temporality of our agency is the necessary ransom that must be paid to the free will problem if our high vocation as moral agents is to be preserved."[36] Wood does not attempt to defend the conception of timeless agency; but he does argue that it is a fundamental feature of Kant's theory of freedom and that given this conception, together with some assumptions concerning causality, Kant did a reasonably good job in showing how free will might be thought compatible with causal determinism.[37]

Quite apart from the question of the cogency of Kant's position on Wood's reading, it is clear that if this truly represents his view in the *Critique of Pure Reason,* then the claim that the conception of an intelligible character plays a necessary regulative role with respect to the conception of ourselves as rational agents must be rejected. Certainly, we need not conceive of ourselves as literally timeless beings in order to regard ourselves as rational agents. On the contrary, our conception of our agency is obviously inseparable from our understanding of ourselves as temporal beings. How, then, could it be claimed that the conception of ourselves as timeless beings is somehow required in order to "model" or regulate our ordinary understanding of ourselves as agents who act and decide in time?

Nevertheless, Kant does seem to require us to regard our agency in just that paradoxical way. For example, after contrasting the empirical character of an action as a "mode of sense" (*Sinnesart*) with its intelligible character as a "mode of thought" (*Denkungsart*) and claiming that the latter must be thought as determined in the former, Kant writes:

The action, insofar as it can be ascribed to a mode of thought as its cause, does not *follow* therefrom in accordance with empirical laws; that is to say, it is not *preceded* by the conditions of pure reason, but only by their effects in the [field of] appearance of inner sense. Pure reason, as a purely intelligible faculty, is not subject to the form of time, nor consequently to the conditions of succession in time. The causality of reason in its intelligible character does not, in producing an effect, *arise* or begin to be at a certain time. For in that case it would itself be subject to the natural law of appearances, in accordance with which causal series are determined in time; and its causality would be nature, not freedom. (A551–2/B579–80)

And again:

But of pure reason [*der Vernunft*] we cannot say that the state wherein the will is determined is preceded and itself determined by some other state. For since reason is not itself an appearance, and is not subject to any conditions of sensibility, it follows that even as regards its causality there is in it no time-sequence, and that the dynamical law of nature, which determines succession in time in accordance with rules, is not applicable to it. (A553/B581)

And finally:

Reason is present in all the actions of men at all times and under all circumstances, and is always the same; but it is not itself in time, and does not fall into any new state in which it was not before. In respect to new states, it is *determining,* not *determinable.* (A556/B584)

To some extent at least, what Kant says in these passages and in similar ones in his other writings can be given an innocent interpretation. Presumably, the idea is that when we regard an action as stemming from "grounds of reason" (an "ought"), we consider it as standing to its reasons as a conclusion to its premises, and this is clearly not a temporal relation. The problem, however, is that although this is part of what Kant had in mind, it is certainly not all. In addition to this unobjectionable thesis, these passages do suggest a picture of reason functioning literally as a timeless causal power. In other words, the notion seems to be that ideas and principles of reason, which are "timeless" in the sense that they hold at all times, themselves have a timeless causal efficacy through which they "determine" the will. Thus, we find Kant speaking of reason as a cause "producing" actions (A550/B578), as having causality in respect of appearance (A551/B579, A552/B580), and even, as we saw in the example of the malicious lie, as a cause that "could have determined, and ought to have determined, the agent to act otherwise" (A555/B583). Moreover, in the *Critique of Practical Reason* and other later writings Kant seems to go even further by referring to a timeless noumenal choice of one's entire character (*Gesinnung*).

Since the latter problem involves issues specifically connected with Kant's moral theory and his conception of moral agency, the consideration of it is reserved for the second part of this study. Thus, our present concern is merely with the timeless agency supposedly involved in acting (or as in the case of the malicious lie, neglecting to act) on the basis of imperatives. Now, as the texts just cited make abundantly clear, the notion of timelessness is closely connected with the idea that in the case of such actions reason directly exercises a causal power, producing effects in the phenomenal world. Accordingly, to attribute to Kant a doctrine of timeless agency is to construe him as a "causal theorist" of a peculiar sort, one who holds that reason's causality is of a special kind, namely, a nonempirical causality of freedom, as opposed to the causality of nature that falls under the principle of the Second Analogy.

Not surprisingly, just such a view is advocated by Wood, although it is hardly unique to him. According to his reading, Kant's incompatibilism differs from the usual variety in that he does not believe that freedom is incompatible with causation in general but only with "natural" causation, that is, with the sort operative in the empirical world.[38] Thus, free actions for Kant are not uncaused but are instead products of a distinct, nonnatural mode of causality, specifically, the causality of reason. As the paradigm case of such causality, Wood cites the Kantian conception of a Holy Will that is determined from within by reason but is nonetheless free.[39] Closely following Kant's language, he also attributes such causality to the intelligible character or noumenal nature of finite rational agents and states that the empirical character is its effect or sensible schema.[40]

Elsewhere, Wood is even more explicit in his causal reading of Kant's doctrine of freedom, going so far as to attribute to him an "essentially causal determinist" theory of action.[41] In attributing such a view to Kant, Wood insists that he is not simply making the noncontroversial point that human actions, considered with respect to their empirical character as occurrences in the phenomenal world, are causally determined. The claim is rather that even free actions are causally determined and not merely considered qua phenomenal occurrences. As Wood interprets Kant, every action is psychologically caused, with the crucial question being whether the cause is inclination or reason. Thus, he states that according to Kant's theory, "every act is seen as arising from a motive either of reason or of inclination, which brings about the act according to a causal law selected by the power of choice."[42]

Much of the language in the texts cited appears to support Wood's reading, and he is certainly correct in insisting that free actions for Kant are caused in a particular way rather than uncaused. Kant does, after all, frequently refer to the causality of freedom. Moreover, at the empirical level, at least, Kant is clearly a causal theorist since he holds that "reasons," in the sense of beliefs, desires, and intentions, are the empirical causes of human actions. In fact, we have seen that this is precisely why Kant's account of empirical character leaves room for a robust form of compatibilism. None of this require us, however, to attribute to Kant either a causal determinist theory of free action in Wood's sense or the conception of timeless agency that goes along with it. Indeed, there are good reasons not to do so.

To begin with, construing free actions as literally caused by reason makes nonsense out of Kant's position and does so quite independently of the question of timelessness. The key point here is that in those places where Kant speaks of a causality of reason, he is referring to actions supposedly based on principles or imperatives, that is to say, actions performed in virtue of the fact that a rational agent takes them as in some sense reasonable, if not obligatory. But although it is common enough to speak metaphorically of the "power" of ideas or reason, it is clear that principles do not of themselves literally have causal efficacy. Such efficacy pertains rather to the *belief* in these principles or, better, to the agents who act on the basis of their beliefs. In other words, reasons can be causes in the sense that beliefs or belief states can be used to explain human actions but not in the sense that the *content* of what is believed (the principle on which an agent acts) is itself a cause. Consequently, even though Kant's language frequently suggests that he is treating reasons as causes in this illicit sense, one should be wary of attributing such a view to him. At the very least, this should be done only if the problematic passages do not admit of an alternative reading.

In addition, there is the problem of reconciling Wood's causal determinist theory of free actions with the freedom of inclination-based or heteronomous actions. If every action is motivated (and therefore presumably caused) by either inclination or reason, then it would seem to follow that inclination-based action cannot be free and, therefore, that such action cannot be imputed. This is a fairly common reading of Kant, but we have also seen that it is radically mistaken. Moreover, Wood himself explicitly rejects it, noting that "although heteronomous acts are motivated by sensuous desires . . . they are not causally necessitated by such desires."[43]

The latter claim is exactly right, but it raises some questions regarding Wood's overall interpretation. First, if all free actions are causally determined and if, as free, heteronomous acts are not causally determined by inclination, by what are they causally determined? Second, if such acts can be motivated without being causally determined by inclination, why cannot we regard acts supposedly motivated by reason as not also caused by reason? For example, with regard to the Holy Will, which Wood correctly presents as the paradigm case of being necessitated by reason, must we construe this necessitation as a species of *causal* necessitation? In short, if Wood is to distinguish between motive and cause in the case of inclination, as he must if he is to preserve the freedom of heteronomous acts, why not carry through that distinction consistently?

Wood's response would no doubt be that free acts for Kant must have causes and that since inclination is ruled out (as incompatible with freedom), the only available candidate is reason. Thus, in the case of rationally motivated or autonomous acts, the cause–motive distinction cannot be drawn. Such acts are both motivated and caused by reason. Similarly, with respect to our first question, the answer must be that even heteronomous actions are caused by reason.[44] Kant's view, then, on Wood's reading, is that all free actions are noumenally and timelessly caused by reason, although only some of these actions (those grounded in moral considerations) are also motivated by reason.

This naturally gives rise to the question of how we are to construe the noumenal activities of reason, particularly in the case of those actions that are not also motivated by reason. Wood's answer appears to be that the causality of reason is to be conceived as operating by means of a single timeless choice of the intelligible character, which is itself the cause of the empirical character and its distinct, temporally appearing actions. Thus, addressing himself to the specter of fatalism raised by the notion of a single timeless choice, he suggests that once one bites the bullet and accepts the idea of timeless agency, there are no "additional" problems in the thought that our timeless choice is simultaneous with each of our temporally discrete acts.[45]

50

Perhaps not, but that is hardly a strong recommendation, particularly in view of the notorious problems involved in the root idea of attributing a timeless agency to temporal beings such as ourselves.[46] In addition, there is the problem that only in the *Critique of Practical Reason* does Kant refer to a choice of character in the way in which Wood indicates. Thus, Wood's reading requires us to interpret the first *Critique* in light of the second.[47] Given these difficulties, it seems reasonable to look for an alternative reading, one that is both in accord with the texts and compatible with the assignment of a regulative function to the conception of an intelligible character.

Any such reading must respect the fact that Kant regards free actions as, in some sense, caused and that he does frequently refer to a causality of reason. The task is to construe all of this in such a way that it does not commit Kant to the view that reason is literally a causal power and to the conception of a timeless noumenal agency, which seems to be inseparable from this commitment. To this end, it may be helpful to consider why Kant might have referred to reason as having causality without intending this to be understood as a claim to the effect that the rational considerations that motivate action are the timeless causes of the action they motivate.

A key to the answer is to be found in Kant's conception of practical reason. To claim that reason is practical in Kant's sense is to claim not merely that it provides rules for action but also that these rules have a motivational force. Similarly, as we shall see in the second and third parts of this study, to claim that pure reason is (or can be) practical, is to claim that it is capable of "determining" the will of itself, independently of inclination. It is certainly tempting, perhaps natural, to think of this force or determination in causal terms, or at least to describe it in such terms, and there is no doubt that Kant sometimes does so.[48] This in turn suggests a picture of agency in which rules or principles function as efficient causes, which can produce or evoke a positive response ("proattitude") in an agent, and even "outweigh" competing desires. Moreover, with this we are well on the way to regarding such rules or principles as Humean causes of a particular sort, namely, intelligible ones.

The Incorporation Thesis, however, suggests a somewhat different picture. According to this picture, which we have already seen to underlie the motive–cause distinction in the case of inclination-based action, incentives (*Triebfedern*) do not motivate by themselves causing action but rather by being taken as reasons and incorporated into maxims. Correlatively, we think of reason as determining the will by legislating to it, that is, by providing the laws or principles ("objective determining grounds") which govern, without causally necessitating, its acts of incorporation or, more simply, its choices. Although reason, according to this picture, is not literally an efficient cause of action, free actions are not regarded as uncaused. It is rather that the act of incorporation is conceived as the genuine causal factor and reason "has causality" only in the Pickwickian sense that it provides the guiding rule.[49] Moreover, since this act is thought (or presupposed) but not experienced, it is in the specifically Kantian sense an intelligible cause. And since this act, as an expression of spontaneity, cannot be regarded as the causal consequence of antecedent conditions, it is thought in accordance with the model of a first beginning.

The Incorporation Thesis also suggests that what must be presupposed as a condition of agency is merely an independence of the "conditions of time" as opposed to a full-fledged timelessness. Although this might seem like a distinction without a difference, it actually points to two quite different readings of Kant's position. More specifically, the former allows, whereas the latter does not, for the possibility of the assignment of a regulative function to the conception of an intelligible character without denying the temporality of our agency. Moreover, the Incorporation Thesis requires the former but is incompatible with the latter.

The former, which is the notion Kant usually emphasizes, consists in an independence from the causal principle of the Second Analogy. That the Incorporation Thesis requires such independence, or at least that Kant takes it as requiring it, should be clear from the earlier analysis. It should also be clear that the notion of such independence involves all of the problems connected with a contracausal conception of freedom. Nevertheless, assuming transcendental idealism, that is, assuming that the causal principle (as an epistemic condition) is epistemologically but not ontologically privileged, it is (at least logically) possible to attribute such independence to an agent with an empirical character that is subject to that principle. As we have seen, this is because this idealism allows for the possibility of considering such an agent from two points of view.

By contrast, actual timelessness must be thought of as a property of a distinct noumenal self or agent and, therefore, not of one with an empirical character. That is why such timelessness, whatever other difficulties it may involve, is incompatible with the Incorporation Thesis. Clearly, this thesis is applicable only to sensuously affected rational agents who are also conscious of standing under imperatives (both hypothetical and categorical) that dictate or prohibit courses of action in the spatiotemporal world. In short, it is applicable only to agents who also have an empirical character and, therefore, not to a timeless noumenal being, which, *ex hypothesi,* could not be sensuously affected.

Finally, we have seen that the Incorporation Thesis requires us to regard the empirical causes (motives) of the actions of sensuously affected and thoroughly temporal rational agents such as ourselves as "not so determining" so as to exclude a causality of the will (A534/B562). As such, it points to the "moment" of spontaneity, or "complement of sufficiency," which must be presupposed in our conception of ourselves as rational agents. Thus, if, as I have argued here, this presupposed moment or complement provides the content for the conception of intelligible character, as it is operative in the *Critique of Pure Reason,* then we should likewise not think of such a character as pertaining to a timeless noumenal agent ontologically distinct from the being who is known only as existing in time.

I shall later argue that despite significant differences similar claims can be made regarding the treatment of intelligible character in the *Critique of Practical Reason* and *Religion within the Limits of Reason Alone*. But that is a separate story, which must be reserved for the second part of this study.

3

Practical and transcendental freedom

The distinction between empirical and intelligible character is only one of two distinctions that play a central role in Kant's first *Critique* account of freedom. The other, and the subject of the present chapter, is the distinction between transcendental and practical freedom. As we shall see, this distinction presents us with a quite different set of problems. Whereas in the first case the issue concerned the coherence of the view that both characters can be attributed to the same agent, the main difficulties now are primarily exegetical. More specifically, there is a need to reconcile the apparently conflicting accounts of the relationship between these two conceptions of freedom contained in the Dialectic and the Canon.

In the present chapter, I shall argue that there is no contradiction between the two accounts and, therefore, no need to invoke the notorious "patchwork theory" in order to reconcile them. I shall also argue, however, that there is an ambiguity in the underlying conception of practical freedom, indeed, one that not only can be found in both the Dialectic and the Canon but also long antedates the *Critique of Pure Reason*. Moreover, I shall try to show that this ambiguity is not, as is usually supposed, between an incompatibilist and a compatibilist conception but rather between two incompatibilist conceptions. In one, practical freedom is regarded as itself a species of transcendental freedom (a kind of first beginning); in the other, it is regarded as a distinct, limited, yet still genuinely incompatibilistic, form of freedom. These are the topics of the first two parts of this chapter. In the third, I shall argue that the latter conception of practical freedom is actually the one dominant in Kant's moral philosophy circa 1781.

I. Freedom in the Dialectic and the Canon

As a first step in dealing with the question of the reconcilability of the accounts of freedom in the Dialectic and the Canon, it is important to realize that the apparent conflict does not concern the characterizations of practical and transcendental freedom taken individually but the manner in which the relationship between them is conceived. Thus, in both places practical freedom is regarded as the kind of freedom corresponding to the "psychological concept" and, therefore, as the kind at issue in the traditional debate regarding human freedom. Correlatively, transcendental freedom, which we have already encountered in the Third Antinomy in its cosmological guise, is treated in both places as a "mere idea."

In the Dialectic, Kant defines freedom in the practical sense as the "will's independence of coercion through sensuous impulses," and he attempts to clarify this by means of the contrast between a "pathologically affected" and "pathologically necessitated" will (*Willkür*). The former includes any will that is affected by sensuous motives (*Bewegursachen der Sinnlichkeit*), and this encompasses the set of finite wills. But not every will that is pathologically affected is similarly necessitated or determined. This holds only of the animal will (*arbitrium brutum*); it does not apply to the human (practically free) will, which is an *arbitrium sensitivum* but nonetheless *liberum* (A534/B562).

In the Canon, Kant describes practical freedom in substantially the same terms. Once again, he distinguishes between *arbitrium brutum,* which is pathologically determined, and *arbitrium liberum,* "which can be determined independently of sensuous impulses, and therefore through motives which are represented only by reason"; he further adds that "everything which is bound up with this will, whether as ground or consequence, is entitled practical" (A802/B830). Apart from this latter addendum, the only difference between this and the formulation in the Dialectic is that Kant here makes specific reference to the determining role of reason with regard to a practically free will. But this difference is merely apparent; for we saw in the last chapter that Kant assigns to reason precisely the same function in the Dialectic. Consequently, both the Dialectic and the Canon operate with a shared conception of practical freedom, which is defined negatively in terms of independence of pathological necessitation (although not affection) and positively in terms of a capacity to act on the basis of reason.[1]

Although perhaps not so obvious, the two texts also operate with the same conception of transcendental freedom. Such freedom is defined in the Dialectic as "the power [*Vermögen*] of beginning a state *spontaneously [von Selbst]*" (A533/B561). As such, it is a pure transcendental idea, which cannot be met with in any experience. Since Kant is explicitly concerned in the Canon with practical freedom, he has little to say about the transcendental variety. At one point, however, he does state that "transcendental freedom demands the independence of this reason – in respect of its causality, in beginning a series of appearances – from all determining causes in the sensible world." In addition, he remarks that such freedom is "contrary to the laws of nature and therefore to all possible experience" (A803/B831). This suggests that the absolute spontaneity and complete independence from everything sensible, which are always the positive and negative defining characteristics of transcendental freedom, are here understood as the spontaneity and independence of reason in determining the will. But since the same thought underlies the discussion of rational agency in the Dialectic, there is likewise no real conflict between the two texts on this point.

It does not seem possible, however, to reconcile the two accounts of the relationship between practical and transcendental freedom so easily. In the Dialectic Kant explicitly states that "the practical concept of freedom is based on this transcendental idea" and that "the denial of transcendental freedom must . . . involve the elimination of all practical freedom" (A535/B562). By contrast, in the Canon he just as explicitly divorces these two conceptions. Since he is there concerned only with practical freedom, he casually states that he will simply set aside "that other transcendental meaning which cannot be empirically made use of in the explanation of appearances, but is itself a problem for reason" (A801–2/B829–30). In addition, he states that "practical freedom can be proven through experience" (A802/B830) and even that "we . . . through experience know practical freedom to be one of the causes in nature, namely, to be a causality of reason in the determination of the will" (A803/B831). Finally, after claiming that reason provides imperatives that can be made into "objective laws of freedom" and that tell us "what ought to happen," he remarks:

Whether reason is not, in the actions through which it prescribes laws, itself again determined by other influences, and whether that which, in relation to sensuous impulses, is entitled freedom, may not, in relation to higher and more remote operating causes be nature again, is a question which in the practical field does not concern us, since we are demanding of reason nothing but the *rule* of conduct; it is a merely speculative question, which we can leave aside so long as we are considering what ought or ought not to be done. (A803/B831)

Although the entire discussion in the Canon is puzzling, this cryptic passage is the main source of the difficulty. At the heart of the problem is the suggestion that the reality of practical freedom is not threatened by the possibility that reason in its legislative capacity ("in the actions through which it prescribes laws") might "itself again be determined by other influences" and, therefore, that "that which, in relation to sensuous impulses, is entitled freedom, may . . . in relation to higher and more remote operating causes, be nature again." Since, presumably, if the latter were the case, we would not be free in the transcendental sense, it does appear that Kant is here indicating that practical freedom (as empirically certified) would remain in place even if there were no transcendental freedom. But this seems both to contradict the Dialectic and to cast doubt on the allegedly incompatibilist nature of practical freedom.

The simplest and the most popular strategy for resolving this problem in the literature consists in an appeal to the patchwork theory. According to this interpretation, the Dialectic and the Canon do contradict one another since the former denies and the latter affirms that practical freedom is possible without transcendental freedom. This, in turn, is understood as a consequence of the fact that the former construes practical freedom in an incompatibilist and the latter in a compatibilist sense. The blatant contradiction between the two texts is then claimed to be the result of the fact that the Canon represents an early, precritical stage of Kant's thought.[2]

Since the patchwork theory can be, and has been, used to account for virtually every textual discrepancy in the *Critique of Pure Reason,* it seems to be a good hermeneutical principle to appeal to it only as a last resort. Moreover, in the present instance there are at least two good reasons to reject it. First, it ignores the fact that practical freedom is described in essentially the same terms in both the Dialectic and the Canon. Although this is hardly decisive, it does make the assumption that they contain two radically different conceptions of this freedom highly implausible. Second, and more important, it requires taking the Canon to be asserting that a "merely comparative," compatibilist conception of freedom is a sufficient foundation for morality. As we shall see later in this chapter, such a view cannot be attributed even to the precritical Kant of the 1770s.

Since it avoids both of these difficulties, the interpretation advanced by Lewis White Beck is far preferable. Beck denies that there is any contradiction between the Dialectic and the Canon because he denies that the latter affirms that practical freedom could stand if there were no transcendental freedom. According to his analysis, Kant is merely making the point that the speculative question of transcendental freedom is not of any relevance to the practical concerns of the Canon.[3] This accords with Kant's statement that the question of transcendental freedom "is a merely speculative question, which we can leave aside so long as we are considering what ought or ought not to be done" (A803/B831). Moreover, it does not entail that Kant is here either presenting a compatibilist conception of freedom or claiming that such a conception is sufficient for morality.

Nevertheless, Beck's is not the only viable alternative to the patchwork reading. The key point, overlooked by Beck, is that the contradiction between the Dialectic and the Canon can be avoided *even* if (as seems at least plausible) we take the latter to be affirming that practical freedom could stand without transcendental freedom. Moreover, Beck's failure to recognize this can be seen as the direct consequence of two assumptions that he shares with the patchwork reading: (1) that the Dialectic unequivocally asserts that practical requires transcendental freedom and (2) that practical without transcendental freedom, that is, "mere practical freedom," would not amount to anything more than the inadequate compatibilist conception. Accordingly, if these assumptions are denied, there is room for an alternative interpretation, one that both takes Kant at his word in affirming the independence of practical freedom and avoids the assumption of a contradiction between the Dialectic and the Canon.

This alternative interpretation turns on two key assumptions of its own. The first is that in the Dialectic Kant is asserting a "conceptual" rather than an "ontological" dependence of practical on transcendental freedom. In other words, Kant is there claiming merely that it is necessary to appeal to the transcendental idea of freedom in order to conceive of ourselves as rational (practically free) agents, not that we must actually be free in the transcendental sense in order to be free in the practical sense. Since this assumption is clearly in accord with the analysis of the last chapter, I shall not argue further for it here.[4] The second, and considerably more controversial, claim is that Kant's conception of practical freedom is ambiguous and that this ambiguity can be found in both the Dialectic and the Canon.

57

Of itself, the claim that Kant's conception of practical freedom is ambiguous is neither new nor controversial. In fact, this very assumption would seem to underlie the patchwork reading. The point to be emphasized, however, is that this ambiguity is between two incompatibilist versions, not, as is usually assumed, between an incompatibilist and a compatibilist version.[5] According to one version, practical freedom just is transcendental freedom, qua applied to the human will. According to the other, it is distinct from transcendental freedom but is still a genuine incompatibilist conception of freedom. More specifically, it is the form attributable to finite, sensuously affected but not determined rational agents such as ourselves. Moreover, although the former conception seems to predominate in the Dialectic and the latter in the Canon, each text at least leaves room for the other conception. This is clear in the case of the Dialectic. Since it asserts merely that the concept of practical freedom presupposes the transcendental idea, it does not rule out the possibility that we might be practically free in the second sense. Admittedly, it is somewhat less clear in the case of the Canon; nevertheless, by analyzing this text in light of Kant's treatment of the contrast between practical and transcendental freedom in his precritical period, I shall endeavor to show in the next section that it too may be regarded as unclear on the question of how practical freedom is to be understood. Before turning to that issue, however, it is necessary to deal with the major obstacle to *any* incompatibilist interpretation of the Canon, namely, Kant's claim that practical freedom can be proven through experience.

In order to understand this puzzling claim, which appears to conflict with what Kant has to say in the Dialectic and many other places,[6] we need to keep in mind both the contrast between empirical and intelligible character analyzed in the last chapter and the practical orientation of the Canon emphasized by Beck. When viewed in light of the contrast between the two kinds of character, Kant can be taken to be claiming that we experience the sensible or empirical side of a capacity that can be partially, although not totally, conceived in empirical terms. This is to be contrasted with the compatibilist (patchwork) reading, according to which we experience a distinct, merely relative kind of freedom. Let us not forget that Kant explicitly states in the Dialectic that the psychological concept of freedom is "mainly empirical," including the transcendental idea as its nonempirical component (A448/B476).[7] Naturally, he emphasizes the nonempirical, transcendental component in the Dialectic and, equally naturally, he emphasizes the empirical component in the Canon. Thus, it is clearly the latter that Kant has in mind when he writes:

For the human will is not determined by that alone which stimulates, that is, immediately affects the senses; we have the power to overcome the impressions on our faculty of sensuous desire, by calling up representations of what, in a more indirect manner, is useful or injurious. But these considerations, as to what is desirable in respect of our whole state, that is, as to what is good and useful, are based on reason. (A802/B830)

This is Kant's fullest statement of the experiential side of practical freedom. Expressed in the language of the Dialectic, what we experience is the "appearance" or "sensible schema" of a capacity to determine ourselves to act on the basis of reason (in light of the recognition of imperatives), independently of any "pathological necessitation." Since he holds that, at bottom, such a capacity is "merely intelligible," Kant can hardly claim that we can certify empirically that we possess it. In fact, elsewhere, presumably with the Leibnizian doctrine of small perceptions in mind, he explicitly points out that we can never prove the negative (independence from pathological necessitation) empirically since the possibility always remains open that there may be unconscious stimuli at work (MM 29: 896–7).

All of this is beside the point, however, given the practical concern of the Canon. Since this concern is merely to determine what we, as putative rational agents, ought to do, speculative questions concerning the nature and limits of our rational agency do not arise. For this purpose, we need only be reminded that we at least *appear* to have rational capacities in virtue of which we attribute to ourselves an *arbitrium liberum*. Moreover, the appeal to the experience of practical freedom suffices for this task even though it is totally incapable of resolving the speculative question.[8]

II. The ambiguous nature of practical freedom

Kant's changing views on freedom during the precritical period is a large and complex topic worthy of a detailed analysis in its own right. But for the purpose of understanding the conception of practical freedom contained in the *Critique of Pure Reason,* the natural point of departure is the metaphysical lectures of the 1770s. Kant there treats practical and transcendental freedom as two quite distinct concepts of freedom and, assigns the former to empirical and the latter to rational psychology.

This early characterization of practical freedom is, in all essentials, quite close to that of the *Critique.* Thus, Kant already identifies it with the psychological concept and introduces it in terms of the contrast between an *arbitrium liberum* and an *arbitrium brutum.* Moreover, as in the *Critique,* the independence from necessitation by sensible stimuli, which is the defining negative characteristic of an *arbitrium liberum,* is correlated with a positive capacity to determine oneself to act on rational grounds. He goes beyond the rather skimpy account in the *Critique,* however, by also suggesting that this freedom gives one the capacity to resist all degrees of torture and by specifying that the only conditions under which this freedom is not operative are early childhood and madness [with extreme melancholy or depression (*Traurigkeit*) being construed as a form of madness] (ML_1 28: 254–7).

Insofar as it bears on the important issue of Kant's views on the limitations of freedom, the latter remark is of considerable significance. For present purposes, however, the most interesting aspect of the whole discussion of practical freedom is the contrast drawn with the transcendental variety. Just as the distinguishing negative mark of the *arbitrium liberum* is its independence from "necessitation" by sensible stimuli, so the distinguishing negative mark of transcendental freedom is its independence from even being sensibly affected. Thus, after distinguishing practical freedom, as the freedom of the person, from physical freedom, or the freedom of condition (the example of Epictetus is cited), he states:

This practical freedom rests on the independence of the will from necessitation through stimuli. But that freedom which is absolutely independent of all stimuli is transcendental freedom, which will be treated in rational psychology. (ML₁ 28: 257)⁹

The clear implication of this passage is that the contrast between practical and transcendental freedom is not between a compatibilist and an incompatibilist conception but between the freedom attributed to an agent that is sensibly affected (although not determined) and that attributed to an agent (if there be such) that is not even sensibly affected. In short, it is between human and divine freedom.¹⁰

The picture becomes a lot murkier, however, when we turn to the actual discussion of transcendental freedom in the section on rational psychology. Such freedom is there defined in positive terms as absolute spontaneity and is contrasted *both* with practical freedom, defined again in terms of independence from necessitation by stimuli, *and* with a merely relative or conditioned spontaneity (*spontaneitas secundum quid* or *automatica*). The latter, in turn, is further characterized as the kind of spontaneity attributable to a body once set in motion or a machine such as a watch or a turnspit. In short, it is the "spontaneity" of an agent whose internal principle of motion must be activated by an external cause (ML₁ 28: 267).

Moreover, in sharp contrast to the *Critique,* Kant not only claims categorically that the former kind of spontaneity pertains to the human soul – "the human soul is free in the transcendental sense" (ML₁ 28: 267) – but also offers a speculative proof of this proposition. As befitting its inclusion within rational psychology, the argument turns on the conception we have of ourselves as egos, that is, as subjects capable of thought and action. As Kant puts it:

If I say I think, I act, etc., then either the word "I" is used falsely or I am free. Were I not free, I could not say: I do it, but must rather say: I feel in myself an impulse to do it, which someone has incited in me. If, however, I say: I do it, this signifies a spontaneity in the transcendental sense. (ML₁ 28: 269)

Kant seems to be claiming here both that the referent of the word "I" must be a genuine subject of thought and action and that such a subject must conceive of itself as free in the transcendental sense. This makes our transcendental freedom inseparable from our selfhood, whether we are regarding ourselves merely as knowers or as agents in the full sense. Moreover, this boldly speculative line of thought is not unique to these lectures. Thus, in one *Reflexion* Kant claims that we know through intellectual intuition that the soul is free in the transcendental sense (R 4228, 17: 467)¹¹; in another he remarks that "transcendental freedom is the necessary hypothesis of all rules, and consequently of any employment of the understanding... the property of a being in whom consciousness of a rule is the ground of its action" (R 4904, 18: 24).[12]

But in spite of such claims, even at that time Kant was far from regarding the self's transcendental freedom as unproblematic. Unlike the *Critique,* however, the problematic aspect of this doctrine is placed in its reconcilability with the ontological status of man as a created, and thus dependent, being rather than with the causality of nature (ML$_1$ 28: 268–70).[13] More precisely, the difficulty is that, on the one hand, transcendental freedom is understood as the kind of freedom attributed to God as *causa sui,* rather than to a finite, created being, whereas, on the other hand, reflection on the conditions of selfhood or agency requires us to attribute such freedom to ourselves. But how can a created being have anything more than the derivative spontaneity of a turnspit, the kind pertaining, for example, to the Leibnizian monad? Kant's "solution" is, in effect, to grasp both horns of the dilemma, insisting that we know that we are free in the transcendental sense while admitting that we cannot conceive how this is possible. Echoing a line of thought prominent in the Inaugural Dissertation, Kant suggests that this latter difficulty is merely subjective and, as such, provides a ground for recognizing the limits of the understanding but not for denying the thing (ML$_1$ 28: 271).

Since transcendental freedom is here contrasted both with practical freedom and with a merely relative spontaneity (*spontaneitas secundum quid*), it might seem reasonable to equate the latter two, which would yield the compatibilist conception of practical freedom. Nevertheless, Kant himself does not make any such equation. On the contrary, in the one place in the discussion of transcendental freedom in which he refers explicitly to the practical variety, he asks how the latter, described as the freedom through which I can act from an inner principle not determined by an outer cause, is possible (ML$_1$ 28: 269). This is, of course, just the problem of transcendental freedom, and Kant proceeds to treat it as such.

The upshot of the matter, then, is that we find in these lectures two competing views of the relationship between practical and transcendental freedom standing next to one another in the text. Moreover, neither of these involves the identification of practical freedom with a merely comparative, compatibilist conception. According to one view, the two conceptions of freedom are distinguished in terms of the nature of the independence from sensibility involved in each (independence from sensible or pathological necessitation vs. independence from sensible affection); according to the other, practical freedom is a kind of transcendental freedom since the latter is regarded as a condition of agency.

In light of the second view, it might be claimed that the compatibilist version of practical freedom is just what we would be left with if transcendental freedom could not be established. But the problem with this is simply that although it is quite clear that for Kant at this time the denial of transcendental freedom entails that human beings, like turnspits, would have

61

merely a relative spontaneity, it is far from clear that he would have been willing to equate such spontaneity with practical freedom.[14] Certainly, there is no suggestion that we are condemned to turnspit spontaneity merely in virtue of the fact that we are sensibly affected.

Finally, we come to Kant's claim that practical freedom is sufficient for morality (ML$_1$ 28: 269). A recent commentator, Karl Ameriks, has expressed puzzlement at this claim and suggested that it is not to be taken literally. On his view, what Kant really meant to say is not that morality requires only practical freedom but rather that the speculative proof of transcendental freedom is only "practically sufficient" because it does not also provide an explanation of the possibility of such freedom.[15]

Ameriks's puzzlement seems to be based partly on the assumption that practical freedom amounts merely to a compatibilist conception and partly on the fact that in the very same context in which Kant affirms this suffi-ciency, he also claims to provide a demonstration of transcendental free-dom.[16] How could Kant claim that a merely compatibilist conception of freedom is sufficient for morality? And why should Kant claim this when he also claims to have proven that we are free in the transcendental sense?

If the interpretation offered here is correct, there is no need for this puz-zlement and no reason not to take Kant at his word. First, Kant is not suggesting that morality requires only a compatibilist conception of freedom (that *would be* puzzling); rather he is noting that morality does not require a conception of freedom distinct from the one presupposed in the conception of ourselves as finite, sensuously affected, rational agents. Second, the spec-ulative proof, which grounds this agency in transcendental freedom, is not needed for moral purposes because from the point of view of practice, the question of the ontological status of our rational agency simply does not arise. In other words, Kant's point is not that the speculative proof is merely practically sufficient; it is rather that it is practically irrelevant.

In addition to the shift of the location of the transcendental problem from rational psychology to rational cosmology, the account of freedom contained in the *Critique of Pure Reason* differs from that of the metaphysical lectures in at least two essential respects. One concerns the locus of the main threat to freedom; in the lectures it is in our ontological dependence on God, whereas in the *Critique* it is in our subjection to the causality of nature. The other, and more significant, is the rejection of the possibility of a speculative proof or demonstration of freedom.

The denial of the possibility of such a proof can, of course, be treated simply as part of Kant's overall critical turn; but it is also possible to locate a more specific basis for his rejection of this particular bit of transcendent metaphysics. The key to his change of mind on the topic is contained in a *Reflexion* in which he distinguishes between "logical" and "transcendental freedom" (R 5442 18: 183).[17] Since logical freedom refers to acts of thought and transcendental freedom to agency, the effect of this distinction is to open up a gap between the spontaneity required for conceptual thinking (epistemic spontaneity) and that required for genuine agency (practical spontaneity). This, in turn, undermines the kind of argument advanced in the metaphysical lectures from the very possibility of the "I think."

But the significance of this distinction reaches even further since it raises the possibility of a global agnosticism regarding rational agency that was blocked by the speculative proof. Moreover, it is not difficult to discern this agnosticism in the Dialectic of the first *Critique,* particularly in those places in which Kant explicitly brackets the question of whether reason has causality. For example, in a key passage cited in the last chapter he states, "That this reason has causality, or that we at least represent it to ourselves as having causality, is evident from the imperatives which in all practical matters we impose upon our executive powers" (A547/B575). Similarly, after completing his sketch of reason's putative causality, he remarks, "Now, in view of these considerations, let us take our stand, and regard it as at least possible for reason to have causality with respect to appearances" (A548/B576). Finally, somewhat later, he concludes, "Thus all that we are justified in saying is that, if reason can have causality with respect to appearances, it is a faculty *through* which the sensible condition of an empirical series of effects first begins" (A557/B582).

Although it is not clear precisely how Kant construed the possibility that reason might not have causality, when viewed in light of the preceding considerations, the most reasonable interpretation is that we might be rational beings, fully capable of conceptual thought and yet lacking in genuine agency or will (practical reason). In other words, it is epistemically possible that our apparent practical spontaneity is ultimately tropistic, the product of some hidden mechanism of nature. We would, if this possibility were realized, be rational *beings* but not rational *agents*; our sense of agency would be illusory.[18]

As Sellars, who is quite sensitive to this issue, puts it, "Kant is leaving open the possibility that the being which thinks might be something 'which is not capable of imputation'. It might, in other words, be an *automaton spirituale* or *cogitans,* a thinking mechanism." Kant, according to Sellars, is certain that we are conscious of ourselves as something more than such a thinking mechanism, but he is also concerned with the possibility that this "more" might be an illusion, a "figment of the brain."[19] Although Sellar's remarks refer to Kant's critique of rational psychology in the paralogisms, they are readily applicable to the account of agency in the Dialectic.

They likewise appear to be applicable to Kant's perplexing suggestion in the Canon that for all that we could ever know, "that which, in relation to sensuous impulses, is entitled freedom, may . . . in relation to higher and more remote operating causes be nature again" (A803/B831). Given what Kant has to say about rational agency in both the metaphysical lectures and the Dialectic, the most natural interpretation of this passage is that he is alluding to the epistemic possibility that our agency might be illusory. Since it was just such a possibility that was supposedly blocked by the speculative proof in the lectures, it would not be surprising to find Kant recalling it at a time when he no longer accepted that proof.

It need not be inferred from this, however, that, lacking such a proof, Kant is now falling back on a surrogate, compatibilist and empirically certified form of practical freedom to save the day by grounding morality. First, there is no reason to believe that Kant regarded a compatibilist conception of freedom as adequate for morality at the time of the composition of the *Critique* any more than he did in the early 1770s. Second, since Kant did not think that the proof was practically necessary when he did accept it, it is reasonable to assume that he would be even more insistent on its dispensability once he abandoned it as a lost cause.

Consequently, if we read the Canon in light of the metaphysical lectures, we need no longer automatically assume that Kant is now claiming that practical freedom would stand if there were no transcendental freedom, that is, if what we call "freedom" really were nature after all. Instead, we can take him to be asserting that from the practical standpoint, where the concern is exclusively with what one ought to do and with reason as the source of this "ought," speculative questions about the transcendental status of our practically free acts simply do not arise. This is, of course, just the interpretation offered by Lewis White Beck, and we now find that it becomes even more plausible when seen in light of the metaphysical lectures of the 1770s.

As already indicated, however, the text also lends itself to another reading, one that does take Kant to be literally claiming that practical freedom could stand without transcendental freedom but that construes such "mere practical freedom" as a genuinely incompatibilist form of freedom. This reading requires that practical be contrasted with transcendental freedom as human to divine freedom or, more precisely, as the freedom of a finite, sensuously affected rational agent to that of an infinite, perfectly rational, nonsensibly affected being.[20] Consequently, it too has a basis in the metaphysical lectures of the 1770s as well as, as we shall soon see, in Kant's moral philosophy at the time of the *Critique*.

In the attempt to develop this alternative reading, it is helpful to begin with the Canon's contrast between practical freedom, as a "causality of reason in the determination of the will," and transcendental freedom, as requiring "the independence of this reason – in respect of its causality, in beginning a series of appearances – from all determining causes of the sensible world" (A803/B828). The analysis of the last chapter indicates that if practical freedom is understood to involve a genuine causality of reason, which is how Kant usually describes it, then it must be taken in an incompatibilist sense.[21] In the language of the metaphysical lectures, a *spontaneitas secundum quid,* a mere turnspit spontaneity, would simply not count as a causality of reason.

Then, however, the puzzle becomes how could there be a genuine causality of reason that falls short of full-blown transcendental freedom, that is, one in which this reason is not independent "from all determining causes in the sensible world?" Presumably, this would be possible only if the dependence of reason on these determining causes were not itself precisely a causal dependence. Although this may appear paradoxical, the recipe for thinking such a state of affairs is already suggested in the Dialectic, where Kant states that practical freedom requires that the phenomenal causes of the action, which are the inclinations and desires of the agent, be "not so determining" as to exclude a causality of the will (A534/B562).

This notion of a noncausal dependence can be further explicated by assuming that the will might require some sensible stimulus to trigger its agency. If this were the case, our sensuous nature would constitute a restricting condition on, but not a causal determinant of, our agency since it would not necessitate us to act in any particular manner. Such a restriction is, of course, incompatible with Kant's mature moral theory since it entails that one could never act from pure respect for the law. Nevertheless, it is perfectly compatible with practical freedom, construed as the kind of freedom attributable to finite, sensibly affected rational agents. Moreover, the assumption that Kant entertained such a possibility at the time of the writing of the first edition of the *Critique of Pure Reason* provides a second viable reading of the perplexing suggestion that "that which, in relation to sensuous impulses, is entitled freedom, may . . . in relation to higher and more remote operating causes be nature again" (A803/B831).

Seen in this light, the distinctive feature of practical freedom is that it involves independence of determination by any particular desire or inclination but not (necessarily) independence of determination by desire or inclination *überhaupt*. Consequently, even without this latter independence, practical freedom would involve a genuine, albeit limited, spontaneity and, therefore, a capacity to act on the basis of imperatives, although the incentives for obeying these imperatives would ultimately be traceable to our sensuous nature. In Sellar's terms, an agent possessed of such a will would be a *"practical automaton spirituale,"* which is to be distinguished from a mere *automaton spirituale* or *cogitans* in that the former, but not the latter, has at least a minimum degree of practical spontaneity.[22] Alternatively, in the terms of Kant's later moral philosophy, such a will would be ineluctably heteronomous.

It must be emphasized, however, that on this reading Kant is not claiming that we are in fact free merely (or at most) in this limited sense; the point is rather that it is epistemically possible that we are free only in this sense, just as it is epistemically possible that we are not rational agents at all. As such, it is in perfect accord with Kant's theoretical agnosticism regarding rational agency, although it does complicate the picture a bit by suggesting that there are three rather than only two alternatives: (1) that we are rational agents possessing practical freedom in the sense in which it is a form of transcendental freedom; (2) that we are rational agents possessing practical freedom in the limited, yet still incompatibilist sense; and (3) that we are not rational agents at all.

Admittedly, Kant should have made these distinctions clear, particularly in the *Critique of Pure Reason*. Nevertheless, it might be noted in his defense that in the practical context of the Canon in which the problem arises, alternative 3 is acknowledged, but dismissed as irrelevant on the grounds that we cannot act on the basis of it; whereas the distinction between 1 and 2, although hinted at, is not made explicit since it is likewise irrelevant to our practical concerns.

Against the latter point, it might be objected that the difference between alternatives 1 and 2 is, indeed, of practical concern since, as noted, 2 entails that the human will is ineluctably heteronomous, which is incompatible with an essential condition of morality as Kant conceives it. Thus, so the objection goes, it is one thing to dismiss as practically irrelevant a speculative doubt regarding agency since we cannot help but regard ourselves as rational agents; it is quite another to dismiss as irrelevant a possibility that is perfectly compatible with our ordinary, nonmoral conception of agency but that conflicts with an allegedly necessary condition of moral agency, namely, the capacity to act from duty alone. This objection rests, however, entirely on the assumption that Kant's moral theory in the *Critique of Pure Reason* is substantially identical with the theory expounded in his later writings in moral philosophy. Moreover, as we are about to see, this assumption is mistaken.

III. Freedom in Kant's moral theory circa 1781

The two main sources for Kant's moral theory at the time of the *Critique of Pure Reason* are the *Critique* itself and the *Lectures on Ethics,* published by Paul Menzer.[23] Accordingly, I shall consider the relevant portions of each of these texts in turn, supplementing the account with references to some *Reflexionen* that presumably stem from roughly this period.

Since Kant maintains in the *Critique of Pure Reason* that the central question of ethics – "What ought I do?" – is practical rather than transcendental and that, as such, it does not constitute a proper topic for a critique of pure reason, it is not surprising that his discussion of morality in this work is extremely sketchy. Nevertheless, the main outlines of his position emerge clearly enough from his discussion of the question "What may I hope for?" which he characterizes as "at once practical and theoretical" (A805/B833). At the heart of this position is the distinction, familiar to all students of the *Groundwork* and the *Critique of Practical Reason,* between moral laws, which command absolutely, and pragmatic laws or rules of prudence, which dictate what is necessary in order to achieve happiness. The former, Kant claims, are known a priori because they are grounded in pure reason and, as such, take no account of human desires or the means to satisfy them. They tell us what we have to do to be worthy of happiness. The latter, by contrast, are based on our empirical nature, that is, on our desires and needs. As such, they are not knowable a priori. Equally familiar is the conception of a moral world, construed as a *corpus mysticum,* in which "the free will of each being is, under moral laws, in complete systematic unity with itself and with the freedom of every other" (A808/B836). This is easily recognized as the "Kingdom of Ends" of the *Groundwork*.

A significant difference emerges, however, when we consider the accounts of the postulates of God and immortality and of the moral incentive. In the *Critique of Practical Reason* and in Kant's subsequent discussions of the topic, God and immortality are postulated as necessary conditions for the realization of the Highest Good, the union of virtue and happiness. Since this Highest Good is itself construed as a necessary object of pure practical reason, it presupposes the validity and emotive force of the moral law (KprV 5: 110–14; 114–18). In other words, Kant's mature doctrine is that it is only because we already assume the reality of moral obligation as a "fact of reason" that we must acknowledge the duty of striving for the realization of the Highest Good.

By contrast, in the *Critique of Pure Reason* the postulates of God and immortality are introduced as props for the moral law itself, not merely as necessary conditions for the attainment of an end commanded by that law.[24] As Kant succinctly puts it, "Without a God and without a world invisible to us now but hoped for, the glorious ideas of morality are indeed objects of approval and admiration, but not springs of purpose and action" (A813/B841).[25] Consequently, in spite of his characteristic emphasis on the purity of the moral law, Kant does not yet draw a sharp distinction between the incentive to be moral and the desire for happiness. Why, after all, should one strive to be "worthy of happiness," which is how Kant here characterizes the virtuous disposition, unless one believes that somehow, someday, happiness will be allotted in proportion to virtue?

It is within the context of what I have elsewhere termed this "semi-critical" moral theory that we must understand the claim that practical freedom is sufficient for morality.[26] Certainly, morality, so construed, requires practical freedom (in an incompatibilist sense) since this is a necessary condition of imputability and of the capacity to take the categorical imperative as one's principle of action. The crucial point, however, is that it does not require more than this since even morally worthy action turns out to be motivated by the prospects of future reward (in proportion to one's worthiness to be happy) rather than by pure respect for the law as such. In other words, although this moral theory requires a genuine causality of reason (practical spontaneity), it hardly requires "the independence of this reason – in respect of its causality, in beginning a series of appearances – from all determining causes of the sensible world" (A803/B828).

The moral theory in the *Lectures on Ethics* is essentially of a piece with that of the *Critique of Pure Reason*. Moreover, as Menzer points out, Kant's discussion of freedom in these lectures is entirely in terms of practical freedom, with no reference to the transcendental variety.[27] The main account of such freedom is contained in the sections entitled: "Moral Compulsion" and "Practical Necessitation" (Ethik 33–41; 27–33). The basis of the analysis is the distinction between two kinds of compulsion or necessitation: subjective or pathological and objective or practical. The former occurs when the will is determined through sensible stimuli. As usual, Kant connects such a state of affairs with an *arbitrium brutum* and insists that it leaves no room for freedom. He cites the example of a dog, which being hungry and in the presence of food is causally determined to eat. This is then contrasted with a person who, possessing an *arbitrium liberum,* can resist the pull of inclination and act on the basis of general considerations (*per motiva*). Moreover, as in the metaphysical lectures, this is illustrated by the capacity to resist torture (Ethik 34; 28).

Of equal, if not greater, relevance to our concerns is the distinction Kant there draws between a principle of moral obligation or discrimination and a principle of performance or execution (*principium diiudicationis* and *principium executionis*). The former refers to the supreme standard or norm of moral evaluation and the latter to the motivating factor, which leads an agent to act on the basis of this standard (Ethik 44; 36). As one might expect, Kant is emphatic about the purely intellectual, a priori nature of the principle of obligation or discrimination. The essence of morality, he insists, is that all our actions are grounded in a general rule that provides the principle or reason for our actions (Ethik 51; 42). Also, although the universalizability test is not formulated with the precision of the later works, it is clearly present. Accordingly, at least with respect to the *principium diiudicationis,* the basic elements of Kant's mature moral theory are already in place. Indeed, although it is not part of our present concerns, it can be argued that Kant had arrived at the intellectual basis of his moral theory and with it at the formula for the categorical imperative by 1765.[28]

The same cannot be said, however, about the *principium executionis,* that is, the moral incentive (*Triebfeder*). To be sure, Kant is quite clear about the problem. "The understanding," he notes, "obviously can judge, but to give the judgment of the understanding a compelling force, to make it an incentive that can move the will to action – this is the philosopher's stone" (Ethik 54; 45). In a similar vein, he also writes: "Man is not so delicately made that he can be moved by objective grounds" (Ethik 56; 46).[29] The point here is that unless we can understand how a purely intellectual principle can affect the sensuous, emotive component of human nature, we cannot understand why the moral law confronts us not merely as a lofty and admirable ideal but also as the source of an unconditional, inescapable demand upon the self.[30]

Unfortunately, Kant's clarity regarding the problem is not matched by a similar clarity in his proposed solution. In fact, it is possible to discern two distinct attempts at an answer, neither of which is compatible with his mature moral philosophy.

The first follows immediately upon the formulation of the problem and consists essentially in the attempt to establish the efficacy (reality) of the moral law by linking the understanding to a moral feeling. Kant's reasoning here is roughly as follows:

1. The understanding repudiates immoral actions on the purely intellectual grounds that they conflict with its own universal rules (immorality as a species of irrationality).
2. The recognition of this conflict somehow produces an emotional reaction in the subject, specifically, a moral feeling of disgust (*Abscheu*).
3. This feeling functions as an incentive or spur to moral behavior.
4. Although not natural or innate (in the manner of the "moral sense" of the British moralists), this feeling can be cultivated so that "a *habitus* which is not natural, but takes the place of nature" is produced (Ethik 56; 46).[31]

In spite of his sharp separation of the understanding and sensibility and his assignment of emotive power to the latter, by means of this analysis Kant thinks that he is entitled to claim that "in a sense an emotive force is embedded in the understanding in virtue of its own nature" (Ethik 54; 45).

As Dieter Henrich has shown, this line of argument is an example of Kant's strategy of providing a "deduction" of morality by deriving the reality of moral obligation directly from theoretical reason.[32] The goal is to demonstrate that the theoretical function of reason applied to the matter of action necessarily produces both a distinctively moral approval or disapproval and an incentive to action. The operative assumption behind this strategy is the existence of an analogy between the functions of the pure concepts of the understanding and the categorical imperative. Just as the former serve as a priori conditions of the unity of the data of consciousness (the manifold of sensibility), so the latter functions as the condition of the unity of the data of the will (the manifold of desire). Correlatively, just as a conflict with the former produces incoherence or absurdity, so a conflict with the latter produces a practical absurdity or impossibility. Henrich also points out, however, that this strategy fails because the analogy breaks down. The categorical demand that the moral law places on the maxims of the will cannot be equated with the intellectual demand for consistency or coherence of thought. Incoherent thinking is simply not of a piece with moral evil. Similarly, the disgust or horror felt toward moral evil cannot be assimilated to the essentially aesthetic response to incoherence.[33]

Kant's second line of argument is more directly relevant to our present concerns. It consists essentially in an appeal to the somewhat peculiar version of theological eudaemonism already encountered in connection with the first *Critique*. Consistent with his intellectualist conception of the moral law, Kant emphatically rejects any attempt to ground either the law itself or its authority in the will of God. Something is not right because God wills it; rather God wills it because it is right. At the same time, however, he also insists upon the necessity of appealing to God as a condition of the obligatory force of the law. As he puts it, "Moral laws can be right without a third being, but in the absence of such a being to make their performance necessary they would be empty" (Ethik 48; 40). And again, "Knowledge of God is, therefore, necessary to make the moral laws effective, but it is not necessary for the mere apprehension of these laws" (Ethik 49; 41).

Just as in the *Critique of Pure Reason,* the reason why God or, more properly, a belief in God (Kant does not mention the postulate of immortality) is required is that such a belief provides an incentive to be moral, that is, to develop a morally pure disposition. Once again, we find that at the heart of his analysis is the correlation between the worthiness to be happy (which is how morality is characterized) and the hope for the attainment of happiness in proportion to one's worthiness. In light of this correlation, Kant insists:

No man can possibly be righteous without having the hope, from the analogy of the physical world, that righteousness must have its reward. He believes in reward on the same ground that he believes in virtue. (Ethik 65; 54)

It is not difficult to recognize the source of the incoherence of this position. It stems from the attempted marriage of an ethic of character, where as in Kant's mature moral theory moral worth is attributed to the purity of disposition, with the theological eudaemonism typical of the enlightenment.[34] If one really must believe that righteousness will have its reward in order to recognize the binding force of the moral law, then, try as Kant does to separate them, our relationship to the law is still mediated by the desire for happiness. For present purposes, however, the important point is not the obvious inadequacy of this position but rather the fact that Kant adhered to it at about the time of the composition of the *Critique of Pure Reason* and that it is perfectly compatible with a neutrality with respect to the question of transcendental freedom.

4

Two alternative interpretations

In this chapter I shall try to clarify further the main features of the account of Kant's first *Critique* theory of freedom sketched in the preceding three chapters by contrasting it with two more or less revisionary interpretations with which it shares considerable common ground but that also reject or explain away a good deal of what has here been claimed to be essential to this theory. These are the well-known interpretation of Lewis White Beck and the suggestive reconstruction of Kant's views in light of Davidson's anomalous monism offered by Ralf Meerbote. In spite of significant differences, both of these authors rely heavily on the strategy of construing the first *Critique*'s account of freedom in light of doctrines developed in the third *Critique* as a way of saving Kant from himself. We shall see that, in both cases, these rescue efforts are misguided.

I. Beck's critique and reconstruction

Although he raises many of the familiar objections, Lewis White Beck's analysis of Kant's theory of freedom is distinguished by its attention to the different conceptions of freedom that Kant advances, its sympathetic treatment of transcendental idealism, at least on the two-aspect reading, and its attempt to provide an alternative account of what Kant could and should have said on the topic, which fits within the framework of this idealism.[1] We shall first consider the critique of the theory as it stands and then the proposed alternative.

Beck's critique is directed almost exclusively against transcendental freedom (one of five different conceptions of freedom that he finds in Kant).[2] His basic complaint is that Kant's attempt to establish the (logical) possibility of this kind of freedom in the first *Critique* and its reality in the second proves both too much and too little. It proves too much because, according to Kant's theory, every phenomenon, not just human actions, has an intelligible or transcendental ground. Consequently, if the appeal to the noumenal licenses the attribution of freedom anywhere, it does so everywhere. As he puts it:

One wants to show that only the empirical, moral, or spontaneously free action [these are three of the five senses of freedom that he distinguishes], and not that just any event, a bodily reflex or an apple falling off a tree, is free.[3]

71

Correlatively, it proves too little because it conflicts with our basic intuitions regarding responsibility and, indeed, agency. These intuitions, according to Beck, preclude us from regarding an agent as at the same time both free and responsible and as causally determined to act in a certain way. If one holds with Kant that all voluntary actions are "before ever they have happened . . . predetermined in the empirical character" (A553/B581), then one cannot also maintain that agents are free to have done otherwise and, therefore, morally responsible. Beck points out that even Kant acknowledges that such judgments "at first appear to conflict with all equity"; but he goes on to insist that the conflict is not only in appearance. As he notes ironically, "We assume the freedom of the noumenal man, but we hang the phenomenal man."[4]

The latter contention is closely connected with Beck's own account of agency, which he develops in his book *The Actor and the Spectator*. As the title indicates, the central feature of this account is the contrast between the "standpoints" of the actor and of the spectator. Each standpoint supposedly has its own distinct mode of explanation; the former is in terms of reasons and the latter in terms of causes. Moreover, just as one can be either an actor or a spectator but not both with respect to the same action at the same time, so too one can explain a given action in terms of either reasons or causes but not both. The main point, in other words, is that there is an exclusive disjunction between these two competing modes of explanation. To apply one is to rule out the other.[5] If this is the case, then, clearly, Kant is not entitled to claim that one and the same action can be both regarded as free and as explicable in causal terms. It is always a matter of either/or, never one of both/and.

In developing this thesis, Beck also insists that there is never any need, for the sake of either science or morals, to make the both/and claim. Thus, Kant's example of the malicious lie as well as its counterpart in the *Critique of Practical Reason,* which are supposedly intended to agree with our prephilosophic intuitions on the subject, are dismissed as misguided.[6] Instead, Beck appeals to the contrast between the wave and particle theories of electrons. "Taken abstractly and schematically," he notes, these two theories "appear to contradict each other." In practice, however, there is no conflict, since it is always a question of which one is applicable in a given explanatory context. Similarly, and more germanely, in the practical sphere:

In no single case does one say: "The criminal behavior of the defendant was caused by a specific brain injury (or a specific physiological state, or the like) and therefore was as unavoidable as an eclipse of the sun; *nevertheless* the defendant acted freely and is therefore responsible for his action."[7]

Given Beck's assumptions, it is clear that Kant's appeal to the phenomenal–noumenal distinction or, equivalently, the contrast between empirical and intelligible character must be seen as an ingenious attempt to solve a pseudoproblem. Since we never have occasion to say of a given action that it is both causally conditioned and yet free, we need no theory to account for the possibility of doing this. At the same time, however, his analysis does suggest a real problem for which transcendental idealism on the two-aspect reading provides the basis for a solution: namely, it must be possible, with respect to any given action, to maintain *either* that it is causally conditioned *or* that it is free. Thus, on Beck's quasi-Kantian account of agency, conceptual space is still required for an incompatibilist notion of freedom. This, in turn, means that there must be two "standpoints" or "points of view" from which actions can be considered (one involving causal determination and the other not), and this is just what transcendental idealism provides.

Beck's revisionary proposal reflects his understanding of transcendental idealism as a two-aspect rather than a two-world theory. Its essential feature, however, is a rewriting of the Third Antinomy in the *Critique of Pure Reason* in light of the antinomy between teleological and mechanistic explanation in the *Critique of Judgment,* that is, as a conflict between alternative regulative maxims, each of which is required for a certain kind of explanation. In support of this proposal, Beck argues that it reflects the actual course of Kant's thought, that by 1790 he had himself come to realize that the causal principle of the Second Analogy must be construed merely as a regulative principle and that this is evident from the Dialectic of Teleological Judgment. Moreover, once this is granted, there is no further difficulty in regarding freedom as likewise a methodological maxim or postulate (Kant's fifth conception of freedom). Finally, this makes it possible to construe the apparent conflict between freedom and the causal principle as an essentially pragmatic or methodological one between alternative maxims or schemata of explanation rather than as an ontological one between competing constitutive principles, the one pertaining to the empirical and the other to the intelligible character.[8] Thus, the latter contrast, which on the interpretation offered here constitutes the focal point of Kant's theory, is dismissed as irrelevant.

The first of Beck's criticisms, namely, that Kant's theory proves too much because it entails that if there is freedom anywhere, there must be freedom everywhere, can be dealt with rather easily. The main point is that although Beck is certainly correct in insisting that according to Kant's "official" theory, every phenomenon has its transcendental or noumenal ground, he is incorrect in inferring from this that every phenomenon (or event) must be regarded as transcendentally free. This would follow only if having such a ground were thought to be equivalent to being transcendentally free. But Kant is committed to no such equivalence. On the contrary, his theory requires us to regard the possession of a transcendental ground merely as a necessary, not also as a sufficient, condition of freedom. In this respect his theory can be compared with that of Leibniz, for whom every occurrence or state of affairs is contingent but not therefore free because contingency is a necessary but not a sufficient condition of freedom.[9]

In addition to having a transcendental ground, an action must be taken as the product of the causality of reason in order to be considered as a candidate for the ascription of freedom.[10] Thus, as we have seen, the problem of freedom is treated in both the Dialectic and the Canon as equivalent to the question of whether reason has causality. Moreover, since it is clearly only with regard to putative instances of rational agency that this question can arise, it follows that only such instances may be thought of as free in the relevant sense. Consequently, although there may be much to object to in Kant's theory, the notion that it entails a "panlibertarianism" should not be included in this category.

Beck's second objection (that Kant's theory of freedom proves too little) raises a number of issues and, therefore, requires a more detailed treatment. The basic point, however, seems to be that just as Kant's ubiquitous noumenalism supposedly requires him to attribute freedom to everything, so now his doctrine that every phenomenon is subject to a naturalistic causal explanation precludes the possibility of marking off a subset of phenomena or occurrences, say the intentional actions of rational agents, that can be considered free. The "conflict with all equity" allegedly arises because it requires us to hold agents responsible for actions that they as empirically knowable, phenomenal beings are causally necessitated to perform.

At the heart of this objection lies Beck's rejection of Kant's characteristic both/and mode of analysis. Consequently, although Beck does not deal with the point, it would seem that if this objection applies to Kant, it must also apply to standard compatibilist accounts, which likewise claim, albeit in a very different sense, that actions can be both causally necessitated and imputed to agents.[11] Leaving that aside, however, it must be admitted that he is certainly correct in pointing out that when we have causal explanations of the kind stipulated, for example, an appeal to a brain injury, we no longer blame the agent since to do so would, indeed, "conflict with all equity." Moreover, Beck is likewise correct in his central contention that we do not, in particular cases, usually employ both the causal principle and the idea of freedom simultaneously.

Nevertheless, this is far from the end of the story. First, as was the case in his first objection, Beck fails to note that the both/and analysis, which he finds so objectionable, is applicable only to the intentional actions of rational agents. If there is no question of such an action, as in the case of a reflex response, then there is no assumption of freedom, no assignment of responsibility, and consequently, no conflict with equity. Presumably, the actions of a person suffering from a brain injury (to use Beck's own example) would also fit into this category, assuming that the injury is serious enough to impair or undermine the person's rational agency. Granted, it is frequently difficult, if not impossible, to decide questions like this with any degree of precision and that is why the law must operate with slippery notions such as "diminished responsibility." But none of this conflicts with Kant; for, as was argued in Chapter 2, he maintains only that the ascription of freedom is not per se incompatible with the availability of a naturalistic causal explanation, not that it is compatible with every kind of such explanation. Moreover, we saw in the last chapter that Kant himself explicitly acknowledges certain empirically accessible conditions under which we would not regard an agent as free, namely, early childhood and madness, with the latter broadly construed to include psychological states such as depression. And lest this be dismissed on the grounds that it stems from Kant's precritical period, it should be noted that substantially the same doctrine is also affirmed in the later writings.[12]

Second, although correct, Beck's claim that we do not in particular cases usually appeal to both the causal principle and the idea of freedom is beside the point as a criticism of Kant. Even worse, it leads him to what, from Kant's point of view, amounts to a conflation of empirical and transcendental level questions. In order to see this, it should suffice to note that for Beck the key issue is what sort of *empirical explanation* is to be offered for a given occurrence, with the alternatives being roughly in terms of reasons or causes. Since he apparently rejects the view that reasons are themselves causes, he quite consistently also rejects the both/and analysis at the empirical level. For Kant, however, the both/and analysis is necessary in cases of rational agency because, in addition to being based on reasons (the causality of reason), tokens of such agency are also occurrences in the phenomenal world and, therefore, subject to the causal principle of the Second Analogy as an epistemic condition. Accordingly, unlike the reason–cause distinction, Kant's distinction between empirical and intelligible character, which underlies the both/and analysis, does not come into play within experience. It functions rather in a transcendental reflection on the conditions of the possibility of experience and the compatibility of such conditions with the conditions of rational agency.

The basic point at issue can be clarified further by noting that, unlike Beck, Kant does not deny that reasons can be causes. On the contrary, as we have already seen, he sides with many contemporary compatibilists (at least at the empirical level) in holding that "reasons," that is, the beliefs and desires of agents, are among the empirical causes of human actions. Thus, just as most compatibilists, Kant would be unwilling to distinguish intentional action from "mere behavior" on the grounds that the former is explicated in terms of reasons and the latter in terms of causes (which is what Beck's position amounts to). At the same time, however, Kant differs from compatibilism in insisting on the necessity of conceiving of rational agents as exercising a certain spontaneity with respect to these reasons, that is, as taking them as such or, equivalently, as "incorporating" them into their maxims. In Beck's terms, he appeals to the concept of freedom as spontaneity (the third of the five concepts of freedom he attributes to Kant). Beck fails to note, however, that this, of itself, entails the both/and analysis to which he objects since it requires the distinction between an empirical and an intelligible character.

Finally, a few words are in order regarding Beck's proposal to revise the Third Antinomy in the first *Critique* in light of the Antinomy of Teleological Judgment in the third.[13] First and most important, we cannot, without doing considerable violence to Kant's thought, replace the causal principle of the Second Analogy with the thesis of this antinomy: "All production of material things and their forms must be estimated as possible on mere mechanical laws" (KU 5: 387; 267). Nor do we have any reason for assuming that Kant himself entertained the possibility of doing so in 1790. The former is a transcendental principle of the possibility of experience (a principle of "determinant judgment" in the language of the third *Critique*), whereas the latter is a maxim of reflection, dictating the kind of explanation one should look for within experience. The difference of scope and level between these principles becomes apparent if we keep in mind that Kant must hold that organic processes, which according to the *Critique of Judgment* are to be "estimated" (*beurteilt*) teleologically rather than explained mechanistically, are still subject to the Second Analogy. The same also applies, *mutatis mutandis,* to the intentional actions of rational agents. In fact, that is precisely why Kant's account of freedom must be grounded in the both/and of a transcendental reflection on the conditions of experience rather than the either/or of reflective judgment within experience.

Moreover, this proposal is based on a questionable interpretation of the antinomy, namely, that its resolution consists simply in declaring that the thesis and antithesis do not conflict because they express regulative rather than constitutive principles. Although Kant does, of course, make that claim, he does so in a section (71) that is explicitly described as "preliminary" to the resolution of the antinomy (KU 5: 388; 269). The actual resolution, like that of all the other antinomies, turns on an appeal to the phenomenal–noumenal distinction and requires conceiving of the latter as the ground of the former (KU 5: 410–15; 294–300).[14] Accordingly, it is not as far removed from the treatment of the Third Antinomy of the *Critique of Pure Reason* as Beck suggests.

II. Transcendental idealism and anomalous monism

The interpretation of Ralf Meerbote is of interest to us here partly for its own sake and partly as a specimen of an interpretive strategy that has become increasingly popular in recent years. This strategy consists in rehabilitating Kant's views on mind and agency by seeing them as anticipations of popular contemporary forms of compatibilism or nonreductive versions of materialism such as functionalism.[15] In the present case, the basis for the rehabilitation is Donald Davidson's anomalous monism. Moreover, in developing his interpretation, Meerbote is following Davidson's own lead since the latter explicitly expresses a sympathy with Kant's reconciliationist approach to the free will problem and notes that for Kant "freedom entails anomaly."[16] But what for Davidson remains a mere hint becomes for Meerbote the basis of a fully worked out interpretation.

The focal point of Meerbote's interpretation is the Kantian conception of the causality of reason.[17] The problem with this conception, as he sees it, is that it suggests a distinct, nonnatural species of causality that is somehow to be integrated into but without interfering with the causal order of nature.

In other words, it suggests the picture assumed by Allen Wood, which was discussed in Chapter 2. His way of dealing with the already noted difficulties connected with such a view differ considerably, however, from that of Wood.

Emphasizing the connection between causality and the "determination" of events on the one hand and causality and "lawfulness" on the other, Meerbote denies that the causality of reason is either determinative or explicable in terms of causal law. Instead, he suggests that to attribute an action to a causality of reason or, equivalently, to characterize it as having an "intelligible cause" is just to describe it as falling under a rationalization requirement. Such descriptions are nondeterminate because they do not involve an appeal to causal laws. (They are, in Davidson's terms, "anomalous.") At the same time, however, Meerbote also insists (again following Davidson) that actions, so described, stand in a token–token identity relation with physical events, which do have determining descriptions because they fall under causal law. By this means, then, transcendental idealism is virtually identified with anomalous monism and Kant emerges as a very contemporary sounding compatibilist on the free will issue.

As should be clear from this brief sketch of his interpretive strategy, Meerbote finds the main textual support for his position in the distinction between determinate and nondeterminate or reflective judgment. Somewhat like Beck, he maintains that the notion of reflective judgment can be used to explicate the regulative function of ideas in the first *Critique* and, therefore, the account of freedom even though Kant officially introduces it only in the third. This move enables him to treat all action descriptions in terms of "reasons" (desires, beliefs, interests, etc.) as instances of teleological judgment, which, as such, are nondeterminate and anomalous (nonmechanistic). Meerbote realizes, however, that this provides only a necessary and not also a sufficient condition for the ascription of freedom; for otherwise animals and perhaps even plants (given Kant's views on teleology) would have to be assigned free will. As he puts it, "Even if causality and teleology are reconcilable, a further step must be taken to explain freedom and to reconcile it with causation."[18]

Actually, Meerbote's account involves at least two distinct further steps, the second of which can be broken down into four substeps. The first major step is the characterization of mental actions as a subset of the activities or processes eligible for noncausal, teleological description. Basing his analysis largely on his reading of section 10 of the *Critique of Judgment,* which he claims contains the essentials of Kant's unified theory of agency, Meerbote suggests that intentional human actions are distinguished from other purposeful, goal-oriented behavior, for example, animal behavior, on the basis of their propositional component. In his terms, mental actions essentially involve "desires or proattitudes of a propositional sort together with beliefs in means–end connections."[19] To specify these propositional components is to "rationalize" the action or, equivalently, to give it a practical reason explanation.

This is, of course, just the familiar belief–desire model of rational agency in its specifically Davidsonian form (the "rationalization model"). Moreover, Meerbote unhesitatingly asserts that this model accurately reflects the Kantian conception of rational agency.[20] Consequently, in the spirit of anomalous monism, the practical reason explanation in terms of proattitudes and beliefs is characterized as noncausal or nondetermining; whereas the whole issue of efficacy is analyzed in terms of the token–token identity between the anomalous mental actions and causally efficacious and determined physical occurrences.

Given this result, the remaining task is to show that the rationalization model likewise captures what is essential to the Kantian conception of freedom. Since he realizes that the notion of spontaneity is the key element in this conception, his strategy quite naturally consists in the attempt to link this notion with the Davidsonian rationalization model of agency that has already been attributed to Kant. As a first step, he characterizes the rationalization model and the Kantian theory of agency supposedly based on it as a model (or theory) of deliberation. Accordingly, the capacity to deliberate, construed in Davidsonian terms as the capacity to arrive at "reasoned preferences regarding competing reasons for action," given an initial set of desires and beliefs in means–end connections, is seen as the defining characteristic of rational agency for Kant.[21]

The second step is to suggest that deliberation, so characterized, and spontaneity share a significant feature, namely, they both at least involve independence from pathological necessitation. By describing their commonality in these terms, Meerbote achieves two results that are crucial for his overall program: (1) He locates deliberation and spontaneity in the same "ball park" and (2) he leaves the door open for a compatibilist account of both. The latter is the case because independence from pathological determination or necessitation, which is how Kant characterizes the independence of an *arbitrium liberum*, is obviously not equivalent to independence from all causal determination.[22]

Moreover, although he thinks that Kant's considered view requires only the former kind of independence, he suggests that even the doctrine of total independence can be given an acceptable sense if it is taken to mean merely that only noncausal, nondetermining descriptions are relevant to the rationalization model.[23] In other words, this model ignores or prescinds from the causal determinants of action, whatever they may be. The main point, however, is that on either reading, ample room is left for nonpathological causally sufficient conditions for free actions, that is, for compatibilism in its usual sense.

The next step is to connect deliberation with transcendental apperception. Appealing to the notion of "epistemic autonomy" as an essential component of any deliberation, including the "heteronomous" means–end variety, Meerbote offers an analysis of deliberation as an apperceptive, self-conscious activity. Since this analysis is in many respects quite close to the one given in Chapter 2, there is no need to consider its details. What is important here is merely that it culminates in the claim that "deliberation has transcendental apperception as a necessary condition."[24]

The fourth and final step is to connect apperception with spontaneity, thereby completing the link between the latter notion and deliberation. This, in turn, enables Meerbote to claim that deliberation is a sufficient condition for freedom. Once again, the argument linking apperception and spontaneity covers largely familiar ground and need not be considered here. What does warrant consideration, however, is the view of freedom that finally emerges from this analysis. In Meerbote's own terms:

> According to Kant to be free is just to be acting in a manner based on self-conscious representations of requisite action-components exemplifying reason-connections. Freedom of an agent consists of his telling himself the appropriate internal story about states of his exemplifying relevant reason-connections, with the telling of the story being one of the components of the overall action.[25]

Apart from its somewhat dense jargon, the first part of this characterization of Kantian freedom seems relatively straightforward and unproblematic. Freedom for Kant is just the capacity for self-conscious rational activity. What is striking is the second part, in which Meerbote claims that this activity consists essentially in an agent "telling himself the appropriate internal story." Such a view of freedom, according to which it is banished to the internal realm of self-consciousness (somewhat like the Stoic freedom analyzed by Hegel in the *Phenomenology*), seems far removed from the Kantian conception, which is supposedly linked to the causality of reason, construed as the capacity for rational agents to effect changes in the phenomenal world. Meerbote is well aware of the seemingly paradoxical nature of this result, however, and as before, his strategy for deflecting such criticism consists in reminding us that this internal story telling, the sequence of mental actions, stands in token–token identity with the sequence of physical occurrences, which are efficacious. Anomalous monism functions, therefore, not only as a convenient device for interpreting Kant's theory of freedom but also as a means for rescuing it from the difficulties to which it is usually thought to fall prey.

At first glance at least, Meerbote's Davidsonian reading of Kant shares a good deal of common ground with the interpretation offered here. To mention only the most salient points: Both attempt to find an acceptable sense for the notion of a causality of reason by suggesting that the expression is not to be taken literally; both see Kant as concerned with providing a unified theory of rational agency rather than merely a theory of moral agency; both regard the essence of this theory as consisting in the appeal to a model involving deliberation; both include spontaneity as an essential component of this model; both interpret this spontaneity in terms of Kant's account of the understanding (epistemic spontaneity); and finally, both contend that an account of intentional actions in light of this model is compatible with a causal explanation of the same actions.

Nevertheless, a closer look reveals even more significant differences. To begin with, our manners of reinterpreting the troublesome notion of the causality of reason are quite distinct. Although my interpretation denies that the claim that reason has a causal power can be taken literally without leading to absurdity (the timeless agency problem), it also leaves room for the notion that such power can be attributed instead to the will (*Willkür*) of a rational agent, with the latter being itself noncausally determined (governed) by reason. By contrast, Meerbote, assuming with anomalous monism that all causation must be explicable in physicalistic terms, makes the much more radical proposal that not even will is to be seen as a genuine causal power for Kant. This, in turn, leads directly to his characterization of Kantian freedom as an agent telling himself "an appropriate internal story."

As already indicated, however, one must stretch things quite a bit to attribute the latter view to Kant, particularly given his insistence on will (if not reason) as a causal power. Admittedly, Kant acknowledges the epistemic possibility that our belief in such a power and, therefore, our belief in the practicality of reason might be illusory; and this could perhaps be described as a scenario in which an "agent," although causally determined by physical factors, nevertheless continues to tell himself "an appropriate internal story." But the point here is surely that this is a scenario in which there is no freedom because there is no rational agency rather than one in which freedom is realized, which is what Meerbote's characterization suggests. In addition, it is difficult to see how freedom, so conceived, could be linked to imputation or responsibility, an issue that is obviously central to Kant and to most accounts of freedom but one that Meerbote, strangely enough, seems to ignore completely.

A second significant difference between the two interpretations concerns the understanding of the model of deliberative rationality attributed to Kant and its connection with the conception of spontaneity. Meerbote, as we have seen, attributes to him the familiar belief–desire model in its Davidsonian form (the rationalization model). He further contends that spontaneity can be explicated in light of this model and, therefore, within a naturalistic, causal framework. Since he recognizes that spontaneity is the essential feature in Kant's account of freedom, the latter move is obviously crucial to his compatibilistic reading.

My interpretation agrees with Meerbote's to the extent that it acknowledges that the belief–desire model roughly expresses the manner in which Kant conceives of rational agency in its "empirical character." It denies, however, that Kant may be read as holding that this model is, of itself, adequate for the conception of rational agency or, what amounts to the same thing, that it is capable of capturing the practical spontaneity (incorporation or concurrence), which is a central feature of this conception. Indeed, if Kant had thought that it was capable of doing this, then there would have been no reason for him to introduce the difficult and problematic notion of an intelligible character and with it the whole apparatus of transcendental idealism.

80

The third and most important difference is a consequence of the preceding two; it concerns the understanding of the nature of Kant's problem and of the kind of reconciliation needed to resolve it. For Meerbote, as for most contemporary philosophers, the potential threat to rational agency and, therefore, to freedom is posed by reductive materialism. Quite naturally, then, he assumes that Kant's main concern, like that of many contemporary compatibilists, is to find some room for the "mental," that is, for belief and desire or, more generally, intentionality, within a universe understood in physicalistic terms. This, in turn, makes it quite tempting to interpret Kant's transcendental account of agency in light of doctrines such as Davidson's anomalous monism or perhaps Dennett's contrast between a "mechanistic," an "intentional," and a "personal stance," which have a certain Kantian ring to them but presuppose a strictly naturalistic framework.[26]

According to the present interpretation, however, this whole approach is fundamentally wrongheaded. Moreover, as is the case for Beck and, indeed, for virtually all interpreters of Kant's theory of agency, the heart of the problem consists in the failure to take seriously Kant's doctrine that the causality of reason, or better, rational agency, exhibits an empirical character. Once the centrality of this doctrine is recognized, it becomes clear that Kant's problem is not, like that of compatibilism, to explain how rational agency can be "naturalized," and therefore that compatibilist solutions (including the Davidsonian version) cannot be attributed to him without doing violence to his thought.

On the contrary, Kant's problematic begins just at the point at which the compatibilist analysis typically ends, namely, with the recognition that rational agency is integrated into the law-governed order of nature. Starting with the assumption that this is true of rational agency in its empirical character, Kant asks how it can be reconciled with the necessity, which stems from our conception of ourselves as rational agents, of also attributing a distinct intelligible character to such agency. Since the latter, *ex hypothesi,* cannot be integrated into the natural order, we are faced with the problem of explaining how one and the same action can be conceived in two such apparently incompatible ways. To return once again to Wood's perspicuous formulation, the task is to show the "compatibility of compatibilism and incompatibilism." Clearly, this is a task, which if it can be accomplished at all, requires extreme measures such as transcendental idealism.

Exegetical questions aside, however, it might still very well be claimed that Meerbote's compatibilist reading makes better sense philosophically. After all, it is widely held that beliefs, desires, and the like can be integrated into nature by a simple appeal to supervenience, whereas noumenal activities remain incomprehensible mysteries. Thus, if in the end, Kant's account of free agency cannot be interpreted at least roughly along the lines indicated by Meerbote, so much the worse for it.

In response to this obvious line of objection, it must here suffice to underscore once again the significance of the Incorporation Thesis and its centrality to Kant's conception of rational agency. If, as I think is the case,

81

Kant is correct in affirming both that the notion of incorporation or concurrence is essential to our conception of ourselves as rational agents and that as something "merely intelligible" this "act" cannot be integrated into a naturalistic framework (such as the belief–desire model provides), then one should not be so quick to dismiss his account as manifest nonsense. On the contrary, in spite of the obscurity and difficulty it involves, Kant's theory of rational agency must be seen as an attempt to come to grips with a dimension of the problem that is simply glossed over in standard compatibilist accounts.

Finally, it is worth noting that the significance of the feature of agency expressed in the Incorporation Thesis has been recognized by a number of thinkers, not all of whom acknowledge its Kantian roots. One of those who does seem to acknowledge it, although he also rejects Kant's conception of a noumenal self as unintelligible, is Thomas Nagel. Essential to what Nagel terms "autonomy" (which as we shall see in the next chapter is not equivalent to Kantian autonomy) is the capacity to "subject all my motives, principles, and habits to critical examination, so that nothing moves me to action without my agreeing to it."[27] Similarly, he suggests that in addition to the external freedom to do as we wish, reflective human beings have, or at least wish to have, a capacity "to stand back from the motives and reasons and values that influence their choices, and submit to them only if they are acceptable."[28] This notion of agreement or acceptance expresses precisely Kant's point about rational agency. Moreover, Nagel is also in agreement with Kant in insisting that the attribution of this same capacity to others is a condition of the assignment of responsibility.[29]

For Nagel these essentially Kantian themes go together with a deep skepticism about the free will problem as well as the already noted rejection of Kant's noumenalism. Thus, he questions the coherence of this very conception of agency that he regards as indispensable on the grounds that it seems incompatible with that other indispensable conception of ourselves, namely, the "objective view," according to which each of us, together with our whole set of beliefs, desires, values, and so on, is just one more item in the world. In this he is perhaps closer to Kant than he realizes, however, for it is an essential feature of Kant's own position that freedom is incomprehensible and, indeed, for very much the same reasons.

II
Moral agency and
moral psychology

5

Rational agency and autonomy

The concern of the first part of this study was chiefly with Kant's first *Critique* conception of rational agency. We saw that according to this conception, rational agents are free in the practical sense, with such freedom being understood negatively as an independence from pathological necessitation and positively as a capacity to act on the basis of imperatives (which includes, but is not limited to, the categorical imperative). We also saw that this must be understood as an incompatibilist form of freedom, even though Kant sometimes distinguishes it from the transcendental variety. Finally, we saw that "mere practical freedom" is all that Kant thought was required for morality circa 1781, because he had not yet arrived at the conception of the autonomy of the will.

The concern of the second part is with the account of moral agency, including the moral psychology, which Kant developed in light of the conception of autonomy in his writings on moral philosophy from the *Groundwork* on. The present chapter is intended to serve as a bridge between the two parts and as the first step in the analysis of Kant's "fully critical" views on moral agency. Although its main focus is on the conception of autonomy, it approaches its target somewhat obliquely by considering this conception in light of the analysis of rational agency in *Groundwork* II. The chapter is divided into three parts: the first analyzes the conception of rational agency; the second investigates the connection between this conception and autonomy, construed as a "property of the will"; the third examines the claim that autonomy functions as the supreme principle of morality.

I. Rational agency in *Groundwork* II

In *Groundwork* I, Kant begins with what he takes to be the ordinary, prephilosophical understanding of morality (as reflected in the idea of a good will as the sole unqualified good) and proceeds analytically from this to the conception of duty and of action motivated by the thought of duty as the locus of moral worth. Then, in *Groundwork* II, he starts from the philosophical conception of rational agency and proceeds, likewise analytically, to the categorical imperative as the rule for dutiful action and from this to the autonomy of the will as the ultimate condition of the possibility of such action. In the reconstruction of his thought, however, it will be helpful to begin with the underlying conception of rational agency, which, as we shall see, is presupposed in Kant's account of moral worth and, indeed, in his

85

moral psychology as a whole. The gist of this conception is expressed in the famous claim:

Everything in nature works in accordance with laws. Only a rational being has the power to act in accordance with the conception [*Vorstellung*] of laws – that is, in accordance with principles – and only so has he a will. Since *reason* is required in order to derive actions from laws, the will is nothing but practical reason. (Gr 4: 412; 80)[1]

Like most significant passages in the Kantian corpus, this one has been interpreted in a variety of ways.[2] Nevertheless, most interpreters, focusing on Kant's equation of action in accordance with the conception of laws with actions in accordance with principles, take Kant to be claiming that the capacity to act on the basis of practical principles is the defining characteristic of rational agency. Moreover, although Kant does distinguish between objective and subjective practical principles, his characterization of the latter, or maxims, as the principles according to which agents actually act strongly suggests that he has primarily these in mind. Thus, we arrive at the view that to act according to the conception of laws is to be understood as equivalent to acting on the basis of maxims.[3]

At first glance, this might appear to conflict with both the *Critique of Pure Reason*, where rational agency is characterized primarily in terms of the capacity to act on the basis of imperatives, and the reference to *law* in the passage under consideration (particularly since Kant distinguishes sharply between maxims and practical laws). We shall see that the conflict with the *Critique* is more apparent than real, however, since rational agents adopt their maxims in light of objective practical principles or imperatives. Moreover, with regard to the second point, it should be noted that, at least on some occasions, Kant does characterize maxims as "subjective laws."[4]

What, then, is a maxim and what is involved in acting on the basis of one? In the *Groundwork*, Kant offers two definitions of a maxim and a number of examples in connection with his attempt to illustrate the application of the categorical imperative as a criterion of maxim selection. The first definition states:

A *maxim* is the subjective principle of a volition: an objective principle (that is, one which would also serve subjectively as a practical principle for all rational beings if reason had full control over the faculty of desire) is a practical law. (Gr 4: 400n; 69n)

In the second he writes, somewhat more expansively:

A *maxim* is a subjective principle of action and must be distinguished from an *objective principle* – namely, a practical law. The former contains a practical rule determined by reason in accordance with the conditions of the subject (often his ignorance or again his inclinations): it is thus a principle on which the subject *acts*. A law, on the other hand, is an objective principle valid for every rational being; and it is thus a principle on which he *ought to act,* that is, an imperative. (Gr 4: 421n; 88n)

On the surface, there appears to be little to choose between these two formulations. Both emphasize the subjectivity of maxims and contrast them with objective practical principles, which are themselves identified with practical laws. Also, both indicate that the primary sense in which maxims are "subjective" is that they are principles according to which an agent actually acts and tends to act in relevantly similar situations. In other words, they express what might be called a generalized intent or policy of action. Correlatively, objective practical principles or practical laws specify how rational agents would act if reason were in full control and how imperfectly rational agents such as ourselves ought to act.

A closer look suggests that although the underlying conception of a maxim is essentially the same, these formulations differ markedly with respect to their characterizations of the relationship between subjective (or maxims) and objective practical principles. The first suggests that objective practical principles could also be subjective and, a fortiori, serve as maxims, at least for that subset of rational agents in whom reason is fully in control. Moreover, as Beck points out, this is in accord with the technical meaning of "maxim" as the first major premise in a polysyllogism (*sententia maxima*).[5]

According to the wording of the second formulation, however, it does not seem possible to regard objective practical principles as maxims. First, the term "maxim" is here explicitly reserved for a specific type of practical principle, namely, one that is subjective in the sense that it involves a particular condition of the subject (e.g., ignorance or inclination). This is a distinct and stronger sense of *subjectivity* than the one operative in the first formulation, where it means simply acted upon by a subject. Second, since it identifies an objective practical principle with an imperative (as well as with a practical law), this formulation rules out the possibility of such a principle serving as a maxim. Imperatives, whether hypothetical or categorical, are of the wrong logical type to be maxims. They are second-order principles, which dictate the appropriate first-order principles (maxims), rather than themselves being maxims. Consequently, according to this formulation, maxims could conform (or fail to conform) to imperatives or practical laws, but they could never themselves become such laws.[6]

The same ambiguity is also present in the account in the *Critique of Practical Reason*. Once again, Kant's concern is to distinguish maxims, as subjective practical principles, from objective practical principles or laws. This time, however, the contrast is presented within the framework of a general account of the nature of practical principles. These are defined as "propositions which contain a general determination [*Bestimmung*] of the will, having under it several practical rules." Maxims are characterized as those principles in which "the condition [*Bedingung*] is regarded by the subject as valid only for his own will" and objective practical principles as those in which "the condition is recognized . . . as valid for the will of every rational being" (KprV 5: 18–19; 17).

If, as seems reasonable, we take the phrase "general determination of the will" to connote a lasting policy on which an agent acts and tends to act in relevantly similar circumstances, that is, a maxim, this formulation implies that both objective and subjective practical principles can be regarded as first-order principles on which agents actually act (or would act if fully rational).[7] In other words, it implies that all such principles are maxims or maxim candidates. This would seem to be in direct conflict, however, with the subsequent characterization of maxims. Like the second formulation in the *Groundwork*, this characterization suggests that maxims are those principles or policies an agent regards as valid only for himself or herself whereas practical laws (objective practical principles) are those the agent regards as valid for all rational agents.[8]

Noting this terminological looseness, Beck suggests that although Kant emphasizes the dichotomy between maxim and law, he is really interested in establishing a trichotomy involving (a) mere maxim, (b) law, and (c) law that is also a maxim.[9] By a "mere maxim" Beck apparently means what Kant sometimes also refers to as empirical, a posteriori, or material maxims and contrasts with a priori, or formal, maxims.[10] The former include all those adopted on the basis of an empirical interest, that is, an interest based on inclination, which, since it reflects the motivational state of the agent, is "valid" for that agent. Kant's concern, as Beck quite correctly notes, is to show that not all maxims are of that nature, that imperfectly rational agents such as ourselves can also act on the basis of a purely formal principle, namely, the moral law or categorical imperative. Since Beck takes this to entail that the law can itself be a maxim, that is, a first-order principle on which an agent actually acts, he arrives at the three-term distinction.

Beck's reading certainly has strong textual support, since Kant does occasionally refer to laws as if they could be maxims and to maxims as suitable to be laws.[11] In addition, there are the previously noted references to a priori, or formal, maxims. Nevertheless, all of this tends to obscure the actual relationship between maxims and objective practical principles that is operative in Kant's thought.

First, it must be reemphasized that *all* maxims are subjective in the sense that they are policies that rational agents freely adopt. They are, in short, self-imposed products of choice (*Willkür*) or, as Kant in one place puts it in the *Groundwork*, self-imposed rules (*sich selbst auferlegten Regeln*) (Gr 4: 438; 105). One does not simply have a maxim, one *makes* something one's maxim.[12]

Second, rather than being construed as maxim candidates, that is, as possible first-order practical principles, objective practical principles are more properly viewed as second-order principles that specify the norms for maxim selection and action. In other words, the relationship between maxims and objective practical principles is analogous to the relationship in the theoretical realm between empirical concepts as first-order rules for the unification of the sensible manifold and the pure concepts or categories as second-order rules governing the formation of empirical concepts.[13]

The crucial point here is that as products of practical reason all maxims are subject to the objective criteria of reasonableness expressed in the objective practical principles.[14] This can be either an intrinsic reasonableness, that is, a reasonableness under all conditions, which is the kind that maxims conforming to the categorical imperative are supposed to possess, or a reasonableness under a certain condition, which is specified by the agent's interests, capacities, circumstances, and so on.

The distinction between two kinds of reasonableness reflects the distinction between objective practical principles in general and the subset thereof that are practical laws. As we have seen, Kant tends to equate these two when he is contrasting objective practical principles with maxims; but he does distinguish sharply between the corresponding types of imperative. The basic idea here is that every objective practical principle expresses a "necessitation of the will," that is, an *ought* that applies universally. If the principle presupposes some condition of the subject (an inclination or empirical interest), then its universality is limited to the sphere of those agents that are subject to that condition, and the corresponding imperative is hypothetical; it dictates the proper policies or maxims to be adopted by an agent given this condition. Correlatively, if the principle applies universally and unconditionally to all agents independently of their empirical interests, then it has the status of a practical law and the corresponding imperative is categorical.[15] Kant's concern in the *Critique of Practical Reason* is to prove that there is such a law and that it is the moral law as he defines it. His success (or lack thereof) in this endeavor will be the subject of the third part of this study.

Our present concern, however, is still with maxims, and the previous discussion has suggested that there is an intimate connection between maxims and interests. Moreover, Kant himself emphasizes this connection in the *Critique of Practical Reason* when he states that the concept of a maxim rests on that of an interest (KprV 5: 79; 81). Accordingly, if we are to arrive at a proper understanding of the nature of maxims, it is necessary to consider, at least briefly, the associated concept of an interest.

Interests, like maxims, are products of practical reason. One has an interest in something (as opposed to a mere inclination) only insofar as one spontaneously *takes* an interest, and this necessarily involves the projection of some end as in some sense desirable. For the most part the interest is based on inclination, in which case it is an empirical or "pathological" interest in the object; but Kant also asserts the existence of a "pure" moral interest in a course of action as intrinsically right.[16] Leaving moral considerations aside for the present, however, the main point is simply that interests and maxims constitute the two subjective poles of practical reason. A minimally rational agent is one who forms interests on the basis of some kind of reflective evaluation of inclination and adopts policies on the basis of these interests.[17] Such policies are termed maxims and an agent that behaves in this way can be said to act "in accordance with the conception of laws, that is, in accordance with principles."

In light of these considerations, a maxim may be characterized as a self-imposed, practical principle or rule of action of the form: When in S-type situations, perform A-type actions. Implicit in this schematic rendering, however, are a number of features that need to be specified if we are to have an understanding of Kant's view of maxims and of their place in his conception of rational agency.

First, since maxims are self-imposed rules, one cannot make something one's maxim without in some sense being aware of it as such, or at least without the capacity to become aware of it. As in the earlier account of practical spontaneity (Chapter 2), the analogy with apperception is instructive. A maxim I could never be aware of as mine, like a representation to which I could not attach the "I think," would be "nothing to me" as a rational agent. It might function as an unconscious drive or *habitus* governing my behavior, but it would not be a principle on which I act as a rational agent.

This does not entail, however, either that we possess a "Cartesian certainty" regarding our motivation (which Kant, of course, denies) or that we must explicitly formulate our maxims to ourselves before acting. The point is rather a conceptual one: namely, that I cannot act on a principle (according to the *conception* of law) without an awareness of that principle, although I need not be explicitly aware of myself *as* acting on that principle. Moreover, it must be possible in subsequent reflection to discover and articulate (albeit not in an indefeasible way) the maxims on which one acts, if not the "ultimate subjective ground of the adoption" of these maxims. At least this must be assumed to be possible if the whole project of the evaluation of maxims (as opposed to actions) is to have a point.

Second, as rules dictating action types rather than particular actions, maxims, like concepts, are general with respect to the number of possible items (actions) falling under them. Accordingly, there are always (in principle at least) a number of distinct ways in which an agent can act upon a maxim, just as there are a number of different ways in which one can attempt to realize an end that one has chosen for oneself.[18] This indeterminacy leaves scope for practical judgment, both in deciding whether action on the maxim is appropriate in given circumstances and in determining how best to carry out the general policy in a particular situation.

Third, as we have seen, every maxim reflects an underlying interest of the agent, which provides the reason for adopting the maxim. Consequently, a reference to this interest is implicit in every maxim, constituting, as it were, part of its "deep structure"; but it need not be and, in fact, usually is not made explicit. One example of a maxim in which it is made explicit is Kant's own notorious formulation of the suicide maxim: "From self-love I make it my principle to shorten my life if its continuance threatens more evil than it promises pleasure" (Gr 4: 422; 89). This is to be contrasted with the false-promising example: "Whenever I believe myself short of money, I will borrow and promise to pay it back, though I know that this will never be done" (Gr 4: 422). The latter maxim is quite explicit in the sense that it specifies a particular course of conduct in a particular type of situation, but there is no mention of the end or interest.[19] Nevertheless, since it is clear that this policy is adopted as a means to the attainment of money, one could say that the interest of the agent is implicit in the maxim.

Finally, also implicit in every maxim is the assumption that the selected action type is, under the particular circumstances (the existence of an S-type situation), the best available means for the attainment of the chosen end.[20] Once again, this is a consequence of the assumption that maxims are products of practical reason and, as such, subject to a rationality requirement. If the agent did not both believe the end or interest worth pursuing and the proposed plan of action the best strategy, all things considered, for attaining the desired end, there would be no reason to adopt the maxim. Rational agents can, of course, adopt foolish or immoral maxims, but they cannot adopt maxims without taking them to be, in some sense, justified (although this may very well rest on self-deception).

Although much of the preceding account of maxims is relatively noncontroversial, it is in at least partial conflict with a line of interpretation that has gained considerable support in the recent literature. Central to this alternative reading is the thesis that maxims constitute merely a subclass of the broad class of subjective rules on which rational agents supposedly act. The motivation for this narrow construal of maxims stems primarily from Kant's moral theory rather than his theory of agency. In particular, it is thought to provide a means for defending Kant's analysis of the categorical imperative against the familiar objections of excessive formalism and rigorism. The situation is complicated, however, by the fact that this reading is found in two closely related, yet distinguishable forms. Thus, it will be helpful to consider them separately.

According to the view of Otfried Höffe and Rüdiger Bittner, only the most general self-imposed rules or practical principles under which an agent acts are to be regarded as maxims. More specifically, they claim that the term "maxim" should be reserved for the most basic "life rules" (*Lebensregeln*) that express what sort of a person one is by specifying a way of living.[21] This reading is based largely on two considerations: (1) the importance of distinguishing between genuine maxims, which leave scope for practical judgment, and inflexible rules or precepts (*Vorsätze*), such as "I shall begin each day with 20 push ups" or "I shall never drink hard liquor before sundown," which do not leave such scope, and (2) Kant's assignment of maxims to the class of practical propositions "which contain a general determination of the will, having under it several practical rules." Although not made fully explicit, the operative assumption seems to be that the subordinate practical rules are *Vorsätze* rather than maxims.[22]

Similarly, in her recent work Onora O'Neill emphasizes the distinction between the specific intentions of an agent manifested in particular actions and the underlying intention "by which the agent orchestrates his numerous more specific intentions."[23] Only the latter on her view is to be regarded as a maxim. To cite O'Neill's example, an underlying intention to make a visitor welcome could generate a more specific intention, say to offer her a cup of tea, which in turn involves a host of "ancillary intentions" such as warming the pot, offering sugar, and the like. The basic idea is that the underlying intention or maxim is the proper locus of moral evaluation, since it is this that is expressed in the more specific intentions, which, as relative to a particular situation, could change completely while the underlying intention remained the same. Thus, as O'Neill suggests, if one were an ancient Athenian, one might express the same intention to make visitors feel welcome by offering wine or conversation. (Certainly one would not offer tea!) She also insists, however, that these underlying intentions need not be construed as longer-term intentions (and, therefore, presumably not as *Lebensregeln*), since we remain free to change them.[24]

In addition to illustrating its fruitfulness as a tool for countering the familiar objections and counterexamples to the conception of the categorical imperative as the determinant of the moral status of particular rules,[25] O'Neill provides two main arguments in support of her account of maxims. (1) We are usually aware of our specific intentions, but Kant insists that we are never able to determine with certainty the real morality of our actions. Taking the latter claim to mean that we can never be certain about the maxim on which we act, she concludes (reasonably enough) that this entails a distinction between maxims and specific intentions. (2) Not all our acts are preceded by specific intentions, yet Kant maintains that apart from mere reflex action we always act on some maxim. For example, negligent action (as in Kant's example of the person who neglects to develop his talents) is clearly subject to moral assessment for Kant and must, therefore, be based on some maxim, which cannot be equated with the specific intention of the action. In addition, she notes that most actions or sequences of actions involve many distinct specific intentions although there is supposedly only a single maxim.[26]

With respect to the Höffe–Bittner line of interpretation, it must be acknowledged that the distinction between genuine maxims and mere *Vorsätze* is an important one and that it helps to avoid many common misunderstandings and criticisms of Kant's moral theory. For example, it is frequently noted that principles like "I shall play golf every day at 3 pm" cannot, without contradiction, be conceived as universal laws, although the kind of behavior they enjoin is morally permissible. Objections such as this, which are all too familiar in the literature, can be dismissed out of hand once it is realized that principles of this sort are mere *Vorsätze,* falling under maxims, rather than themselves being maxims.

Of itself, however, this distinction hardly entails that maxims be construed merely as *Lebensregeln,* since it does not follow that the *Lebensregel–Vorsatz* dichotomy is exhaustive. On the contrary, although clearly distinct from mere *Vorsätze,* many of Kant's own familiar examples of maxims fall considerably short of qualifying as *Lebensregeln.* The example of the maxim of borrowing money knowing that one will not be able to repay is a case in point. Far from itself being a *Lebensregel,* this would seem to be a relatively specific rule, applicable only to a specific type of situation. Clearly, however, this does not prevent Kant from regarding it as a maxim.

Similar considerations also apply, *mutatis mutandis,* to O'Neill's analysis, which likewise does not square very well with some of Kant's examples.[27] Moreover, the specific arguments O'Neill advances in support of her interpretation are inconclusive at best. First, Kant's agnosticism regarding the real morality of our actions need not be taken as an agnosticism about our maxims. One might be aware of the fact that one is acting on a maxim, say of treating people fairly, without being sure whether one is doing this from duty or self-interest. In that case, then, it becomes necessary to distinguish, as Kant does in *Religion within the Limits of Reason Alone,* between the maxim itself and the "ultimate subjective ground" of the adoption of the maxim (Rel 6: 25; 20). To be sure, Kant there goes on to state that this ground is itself a maxim, and this raises fundamental problems with which we shall be concerned later. For the present, however, we need only note that this complication hardly supports O'Neill's claim that *only* the underlying intention can be regarded as a maxim.

Second, one might very well quarrel with her claim (at least as a reading of Kant) that although every act is based on some maxim, not every act embodies a specific intent. This would follow only if we take the latter to require that the act be preceded by an explicit decision, but this is clearly too strong a condition. In fact, in her earlier work she provided a subtle and interesting analysis of intentional action, construed as action on a maxim, in which this condition is explicitly denied.[28]

Finally, it has been noted by Robert B. Louden that there is a tension between O'Neill's conception of maxims as underlying intentions that determine what kind of a person one is, morally speaking, and her insistence that underlying intentions not be equated with "longer-term" intentions.[29] As Louden points out, this move seems motivated, at least in part, by O'Neill's recognition that not all of Kant's examples of maxims can be regarded as long-term or lifetime commitments (which is the same problem faced by the *Lebensregel* interpretation). As Louden also points out, however, by denying that underlying intentions need be long term, O'Neill tends to undermine the plausibility of the connection, on which she also insists, between such intentions and the sort of person one is.

These considerations, together with the earlier analysis, strongly suggest that Kantian maxims come in various degrees of generality and that some, but by no means all, may be characterized as *Lebensregeln* or as underlying (as opposed to specific) intentions. This further suggests that the "several practical rules" falling under a maxim might include other, more specific maxims and not simply mere *Vorsätze* and/or specific intentions that are not themselves maxims. On this reading, one might think of maxims, in analogy with concepts (considered intensionally), as arranged hierarchically, with the more general embedded in the more specific, like genera in species.[30] Correlatively, although it reopens problems involving the application of the categorical imperative, one might even regard *Vorsätze* and very specific intentions of the kind indicated by O'Neill as limiting cases of maxims, the bottom rung of a continuum of practical principles. But even if this suggestion is rejected, the fact remains that, important as the distinction may be for Kant's moral philosophy, the line between maxim and *Vorsatz,* like that between underlying and specific intention, is not always an easy one to draw.[31]

Admittedly, this interpretation of maxims appears to conflict with their status as the major premises in bits of practical reasoning as well as with Kant's account of the universalizability test, both of which entail that an action can be brought under only a single maxim. This difficulty can be met, however, if we distinguish between the maxim on which an agent actually acts and other, more general principles, likewise maxims, that are implicit in the operative maxim as "background conditions" without being explicit factors in the decision. On this view, the relatively specific maxims on which agents usually act, for example, the maxim of false promising, presuppose more general principles in the sense that a commitment to the maxim entails a commitment to the more general principle (although not vice versa).

Such an interpretation accords with much of the spirit of O'Neill's analysis, since it underscores the fact that the person who "makes it his maxim" to promise falsely to repay debts likewise makes it his maxim to disregard the truth when it suits his purposes and, more generally still, to treat others in a manipulative manner. Sometimes, as in the case of false promising, the relatively specific intention, which could still have more specific intentions concerning the manner in which one promises falsely, falling under it, is the morally relevant factor, whereas at other times, such as the case of negligence, it is necessary to look deeper to the underlying intention.[32] Admittedly, this complicates considerably the relatively straightforward testing procedure that Kant sketches in *Groundwork* II. Nevertheless, it, or something very much like it, seems to be required by the fact that Kantian morality is concerned with both the rightness or wrongness of particular action types and the goodness or badness of the underlying disposition.[33] Moreover, as we shall see in subsequent chapters, this hierarchical view of maxims is presupposed by Kant's conceptions of *Gesinnung* and radical evil, which rest on the assumption of a fundamental maxim underlying the choice of more specific maxims.

II. Autonomy as a property of the will

With the analysis of rational agency sketched in the preceding section as our backdrop, we are finally in a position to approach the central conception of autonomy, which Kant introduces near the end of *Groundwork* II. Our task is greatly complicated, however, by the ambiguity of his account. Part of the problem stems from the fact that the term is used to refer both to a property or character (*Beschaffenheit*) of the will and to a moral principle. In addition, the account of autonomy as a principle is itself ambiguous, since

Kant treats it both as the supreme condition of the possibility of the categorical imperative and as itself a formula for this imperative. These complexities make a two-step treatment necessary; and since the analysis of
autonomy as a property of the will is clearly the basis of the analysis of it as
a principle, we shall consider the former aspect in the present section and
the latter in the next.

Kant defines the autonomy of the will as "the property the will has of
being a law to itself (independently of every property belonging to the objects
of volition)" (Gr 4: 440; 108). This is contrasted with heteronomy, according
to which "the will does not give itself the law, but the object does so in
virtue of its relation to the will" (Gr 4: 441; 108). At the beginning of the
third part of the *Groundwork*, Kant identifies autonomy as a property of the
will with the positive conception of freedom and states that it "springs from"
(*fliesst aus*) the negative conception. The latter, in turn, is described as the
property of the causality of the will of rational beings of "being able to work
independently of *determination* by alien causes" (Gr 4: 446; 114). In addition to linking autonomy explicitly with an incompatibilist conception of
freedom, this also entails that autonomy (positive freedom) must be attributed to every will that is negatively free.[34]

Kant also links autonomy directly with the moral law. In fact, he goes so
far as to claim that "a free will [one with the property of autonomy] and a
will under moral laws are one and the same [*einerlei*]" (Gr 4: 447; 114).
This claim together with the identification of will with practical reason and
the characterization of natural necessity as a "heteronomy of efficient causes"
(Gr 4: 447; 114) have led many commentators to assume that Kant, at least
in the *Groundwork*, equates autonomy and, therefore, freedom with obedience to the moral law. On this reading, then, the will is free only insofar as
it is motivated by respect for the law. In all other instances, that is, in all
inclination-based agency, the will is not only heteronomous but also causally
determined. More precisely, since will is practical reason, all nonmorally
motivated actions are ultimately nothing more than "mere bits of behavior,"
not genuine products of will at all.[35]

Given the obvious absurdities to which such a doctrine leads, many of the
same interpreters who attribute it to Kant in the *Groundwork* also maintain
that he abandoned it in his later writings, with the introduction of the *Wille–
Willkür* distinction. On the basis of this distinction, it is argued, Kant can
explain what he could not with his earlier view, namely, how freedom to do
evil and, indeed, choice between morally indifferent alternatives are possible.
He can do so because, according to this new view, even heteronomous willing
turns out to involve a certain kind of autonomy. In short, Kant is taken as
having abandoned the analytic connection between autonomy and moral willing that is characteristic of the *Groundwork* (and even the *Critique of Practical Reason*), introducing instead a premoral or morally neutral conception
of autonomy.[36]

By contrast, if one understands by the autonomy of the will primarily a
capacity for self-legislation or self-determination, then it seems possible to

find a morally neutral conception of autonomy already at work in the account of rational agency in *Groundwork* II. In fact, such a conception seems to be implicit in the analysis of action on the basis of maxims, which, as we have seen, Kant himself describes as "self-imposed rules." Once again, the point is that if I decide to make something my maxim, say to borrow money without any intention to repay it, it is I who make it my rule of behavior, and this always involves an act of self-legislation. To be sure, such a rule reflects my inclinations and needs, but it is never determined solely by them. Consequently, it might be argued that even in the case of desire-based or "material" maxims, the "law" stems from the will rather than from some "property belonging to the object of volition." If it did not, the "action" would be a mere conditioned response to a stimulus rather than an expression of rational agency. As Rüdiger Bittner, the main advocate of this interpretation of the *Groundwork* correctly notes, there is, for Kant, no receptivity of practical reason.[37]

These interpretations share the assumption that Kant's theory of agency requires a morally neutral conception of autonomy; they differ only with respect to the question of whether this conception is to be found in *Groundwork* II. I shall argue, however, that both are incorrect, because both fail to distinguish properly between practical freedom and autonomy. Nevertheless, of the two, the second is clearly preferable. In addition to avoiding attributing to Kant the view that only morally motivated action is free, with all of the well-known difficulties that this involves, it makes the analysis of rational agency in *Groundwork* II internally consistent as well as compatible with the account in the *Critique of Pure Reason*.

The major problem with this second view is that it undermines the distinction between autonomy and heteronomy, since all rational agency is "autonomous" in *this* sense. Moreover, for that very reason it also makes it difficult to see how, as one commentator correctly notes, the "discovery" of the principle of autonomy "marks a decisive turn in the development of Kant's thought."[38] Otherwise expressed, if as this interpretation implies, autonomy is to be equated with the practical spontaneity that we have already seen to be the essential feature of the first *Critique* theory of rational agency, then its "discovery" could not have led to a break with the "semi-critical" moral theory of the *Critique* outlined in Chapter 3, a theory that, as we have seen, is "heteronomous" according to the standards of the *Groundwork*.

The problem, then, is to understand the distinction between autonomy and heteronomy in such a way that even heteronomous action is free in the sense previously discussed. This, in turn, requires that the introduction of the notion of autonomy be seen as compatible with the general conception of rational agency considered so far, yet as also refining it in some significant respect. In short, the attribution of autonomy as a property of the will of rational agents must be understood as complementing rather than conflicting with the analysis of agency in the earlier portions of *Groundwork* II.

In light of the preceding discussion, let us return to the definition of autonomy as "the property the will has of being a law to itself (independently of every property belonging to the objects of volition)" (Gr 4: 440; 108). Up to now we have assumed that for the will to have the property of being a law to itself, it must have the capacity to impose "laws" in the sense of maxims upon itself, that is, to make something its maxim. But the parenthetical clause, which we have thus far ignored, suggests that this is only a necessary and not also a sufficient condition. Giving this clause its due weight, it now seems that it is also necessary that in imposing maxims upon itself the will functions "independently of every property belonging to the objects of volition." Thus, it is essential to determine just to what this independence condition amounts. As is so often the case with Kant, this can best be accomplished by considering the excluded alternative, namely, a self-imposition lacking such independence, one in which "the will does not give itself the law, but the object does so in virtue of its relation to the will" (Gr 4: 441; 108).

To begin with, by "object" in this context must be understood an object of practical reason, that is, some possible state of affairs regarded by an agent as in some sense good.[39] Such an object can be said to "give the law to the will" just in case an agent is moved to act by an inclination or desire for the realization of that state of affairs. This being "moved to act" should not be understood in a causal sense, however, since actions resulting from such motivation are still genuine intentional actions based on maxims rather than mere bits of behavior causally conditioned by stimuli. The point is rather that as based on inclination these maxims reflect the agent's needs as a sensuous being, needs that are themselves explicable in terms of laws of nature. Accordingly, it must be because these needs provide the only sources of motivation or reasons to act, not because they are the causal determinants of behavior, that the heteronomous agent is, qua agent, subject "only to the law of nature – the law of his own needs" (Gr 4: 439; 106).

Correlatively, a will with the property of autonomy is just one to which this limitation does not apply. Thus, the defining characteristic of autonomy is not independence from causal determination by one's needs as a sensuous being (since such independence pertains to the very concept of an *arbitrium liberum*). Nor is it a total freedom from these needs (since only a divine or holy will is thought to be free of these needs). It is rather a motivational independence, that is, a capacity for self-determination independently of, and even contrary to, these needs. Positively expressed, a will with the property of autonomy is one for which there are (or can be) reasons to act that are logically independent of the agent's needs as a sensuous being.

Since "needs" in the preceding functions essentially as a place holder for desires and inclinations, this means that an autonomous will is one with the property (or capacity) of being motivated independently of the latter. As Thomas Hill has noted, however, such a characterization of autonomy seems open to two diametrically opposed objections, each stemming from a particular understanding of the key terms.[40] On the one hand, if we take "desire" (and related terms such as "inclination") in the broadest sense to refer to whatever happens to motivate an agent, then the notion of a non-

97

desire-based motivation becomes a contradiction in terms. But if, on the other hand, we take it in a narrow sense to refer to some sort of immediate urge or strong feeling, then it is noncontroversially true that rational beings such as ourselves have this capacity (Hume's "calm passions" are a case in point), and we need not appeal to any special property of the will in order to account for it. In fact, we have seen that even heteronomous agency involves desire independence in *this* sense.

As Hill also notes, the way out of this dilemma lies in the understanding of desire (and similar terms) as referring to any *empirical* motivation. This includes desires in the narrow sense but also any preference or aversion and the like (including, as we shall soon see, nonegoistic one's), which rational agent's might have as a result of their sensuous nature. Kant's essential claim, then, is that the latter does not encompass all conceivable sources of motivation, reasons for action, or in Kant's terminology, "determining grounds of the will." In addition to the familiar panoply of empirical determining grounds, there is also a nonempirical determining ground, a "pure interest." At least this must be the case if the will is to have the property of autonomy.

Moreover, it is clear from the preceding what this alternative, nonempirical source of motivation must be, namely, practical reason itself or "pure practical reason." In other words, to attribute the property of autonomy to the will is to attribute to it the capacity to be moved to action by a rule of action (practical principle) that makes no reference to an agent's needs or interests as a sensuous being. Kant, of course, identifies this rule with the moral law; but this identification is not itself part of the analysis of the concept of autonomy as a property of the will of rational agents. Consequently, we can see, even apart from this identification, that a will with the capacity to be so motivated, and only such a will, could be said to be a law to itself, indeed, "independently of every property belonging to the objects of volition." In this sense, then, the concept of autonomy is "morally neutral."

In a deeper sense, however, it is not morally neutral; for it is only the moral law that gives it any standing. In other words, were it not for the demands of morality, there would be no reason to attribute such a capacity to the will, although there would be good reasons to attribute to rational agents such as ourselves the capacity for self-legislation involved in acting on a maxim. Moreover, this is the key to the understanding of Kant's otherwise puzzling claim in the *Critique of Practical Reason* that the moral law is the "*ratio cognoscendi* of freedom" (KprV 5: 4n; 4n). Taken, as it sometimes is, as claiming that apart from our awareness of moral obligation we would have no basis for regarding ourselves as free agents at all, this is both counterintuitive and in blatant contradiction with the doctrine of the first *Critique*. If, however, it is taken to refer specifically to freedom positively defined as autonomy, it is both true and compatible with (although going beyond) the earlier doctrine.

Finally, although we do not yet know whether a will with this peculiar property is possible (Kant deals with this issue in *Groundwork* III), it is at least clear that this conception of the will as a law to itself presupposes not merely a causality of reason, that is, a capacity to be motivated by general rules or principles, but also "the independence of this reason – in respect of its causality, in beginning a series of appearances – from all determining causes of the sensible world." In other words, it presupposes not merely practical but also transcendental freedom.[41] The question is why Kant now thinks that morality presupposes the latter sort of freedom whereas he held the contrary view in the *Critique of Pure Reason* and the *Lectures on Ethics*. This is equivalent to the question of why morality requires the peculiar property of autonomy as its "supreme condition"; and it is to this topic that we now turn.

III. From property to principle

The thesis that the autonomy of the will is the supreme principle of morality is the culmination of the analytic or regressive argument of the first two parts of the *Groundwork*. As such, it presupposes the accounts of duty, moral worth, and of course, the specification of the categorical imperative: *"Act only on that maxim through which you can at the same time will that it should become a universal law"* (Gr 4: 421; 88). It is also primarily a claim about what must be presupposed if morality, as characterized up to that point, is to be possible. In other words, the thesis is that a will and only a will with the property of autonomy is capable of acting on the basis of a categorical imperative. Consequently, only a moral theory that attributes such a property to the will is able to account for the possibility of morality.

Kant's argument for this thesis presupposes a basic dichotomy between autonomy and heteronomy, construed as all-inclusive and mutually exclusive models of volition. In other words, if there is such a thing as volition or, more generally, rational agency (action "in accordance with the conception of laws"), then either the will gives the law to itself, in which case we have autonomy, or the law is somehow given to the will from without, in which case we have heteronomy. Since Kant holds that all moral theories must presuppose one of these models of volition, he likewise thinks that there is a corresponding dichotomy at the level of moral theory. Thus, the class of moral theories (both actual and possible) may be divided on the basis of their commitment (or lack thereof) to the principle of autonomy, with all those that lack this commitment being classified under the principle of het-eronomy or, more simply, as heteronomous. Kant's procedure here consti-tutes a precise parallel to his procedure in the *Critique of Pure Reason*. Just as he there subsumed all noncritical positions under the generic label "tran-scendental realism," to which he juxtaposed his own transcendental idealism, so now in the *Groundwork* and the *Critique of Practical Reason,* he subsumes all opposing moral theories under the label "heteronomy" and contrasts them all with his own conception of "autonomy."[42]

The structure of the argument is also quite similar to what one finds at many key junctures in Kant's work. It attempts to show that heteronomy in its various forms fails to account for the possibility in question and that its opposite, autonomy, succeeds. Assuming, as Kant does, that the autonomy–heteronomy disjunction is exhaustive, this amounts to the claim that morality is possible if and only if the will is autonomous in the sense previously indicated. In analyzing this argument, it will be convenient to begin with the "only if" portion, which consists in the attempt to prove that no heteronomous moral theory can account for the possibility of morality (conceived of as grounded in a categorical imperative).

The argument in the *Groundwork* for "the failure of heteronomy"[43] is concise and highly reminiscent of the famous depiction of his "Copernican revolution" that Kant describes some two years later in the preface to the second edition of the *Critique of Pure Reason*. Just as it is impossible in the epistemological context to explain the possibility of a priori knowledge, if one assumes that our knowledge must conform to objects, so too, in the practical context, one cannot explain the possibility of a categorical imperative, or more generally, an a priori practical principle with the requisite universality and necessity, if one assumes that an object (of the will) must be source of moral requirements. As Kant puts it:

Whenever an object of the will has to be put down as the basis [*Grund*] for prescribing a rule to determine the will, there the rule is heteronomy; the imperative is conditioned, as follows: '*If*, or *because*, you will this object, you ought to act thus or thus'; consequently it can never give a moral – that is, a categorical command. (Gr 4: 444; 111)

This indicates that, at bottom, Kant's charge against all heteronomous moral theories, that is, all theories except his own, is that they necessarily reduce the categorical to a hypothetical imperative. Since, *ex hypothesi*, some interest (desired object of the will) must always be presupposed as a condition for accepting moral principles as binding, these principles derive their obligatory status from this interest. Thus, implicitly at least, all such theories regard moral requirements as having the form: "I ought to do something *because I will something else*" (Gr 4: 441; 111). Moreover, since this interest, whether sensuous (e.g., in one's own happiness) or rational (e.g., in ontological perfection) reflects the "natural constitution" of the subject, Kant once again asserts that in all such cases it is "strictly speaking . . . nature which would make the law" (Gr 4: 444; 112).

The corresponding argument in the *Critique of Practical Reason,* (Theorem IV) is quite similar, although it is based on the distinction between the form and matter of a practical principle. By the former, Kant understands the universalizability of a principle, that is, its suitability as a universal law. By the latter, he understands its object, that is, the end or state of affairs intended in an action falling under that principle. Heteronomy of choice (*Willkür*) arises whenever the matter or object "comes into the law as a *condition of its possibility*" (KprV 5: 33; 33–4), that is, whenever it must be presupposed as an incentive to adopt the principle. As in the *Groundwork*, Kant notes that, under this scenario, "the will does not give itself the law but only directions for a reasonable obedience to pathological laws" (KprV 5: 33; 34). Similarly, he argues that this model of volition cannot account for the possibility of a categorical imperative. In a remark added to the main argument, however, Kant goes beyond the explicit doctrine of the *Groundwork* and claims that, in the end, all heteronomous principles, without exception, "revolve about the principle of one's own happiness" (KprV 5: 34; 34).

Since the antiheteronomy argument in both works presupposes the account of morality as based on a categorical imperative, its overall cogency cannot be determined independently of an evaluation of this account. In short, if morality does not rest on a categorical imperative, then the whole critique of heteronomy loses its point. Moreover, critics of Kantian morality are very often critics of the very idea of a categorical imperative.[44] Nevertheless, even setting aside that larger issue, there are at least two features of this critique that call for further discussion.

The first is the central claim that heteronomy, in all its forms, necessarily transforms moral requirements into hypothetical imperatives. At first glance, it might seem that the line of argument sketched in the preceding can show at most that heteronomous moral theories are incapable of accounting for moral worth (assuming Kant's understanding of such worth), since they must presuppose some extramoral interest or incentive; but this is quite distinct from being incapable of accounting for the possibility of a categorical imperative. In fact, as we have seen, Kant himself affirmed the categorical imperative as the principle of morality long before he arrived at the conception of the autonomy of the will.

This possible line of objection rests on a failure to understand what the categorical imperative, and therefore morality, in Kant's view requires. This imperative requires not merely that we adopt maxims that are in fact universalizable, that is, suitable as universal laws, but also that we choose our maxims precisely *because* of their suitability for universal law or, in the language of the *Critique of Practical Reason,* in virtue of their "legislative form." Consequently, if we choose maxims with the proper form, yet only do so because of some interest or, equivalently, because of the "matter" of the maxim, then it is clear that we are not fulfilling the dictates of the law. It is also clear that under this scenario we are treating moral requirements as hypothetical imperatives, since they are regarded as necessary means for the attainment of a presupposed end rather than as intrinsically obligatory.

A second, more complex problem concerns the claim that all competing moral theories, or at least all those known to Kant, fit the picture he provides of heteronomy. Given the sketchiness of his account and the great variety of moral philosophies that Kant tries to force into a single mold, this claim is problematic on the face of it.[45] Thus, a problem arises in the practical sphere that is the direct counterpart of the problem generated in the first *Critique* by Kant's assumption that all positions other than transcendental idealism may be regarded as varieties of transcendental realism.[46]

It becomes particularly problematic if one includes in this picture the

101

previously noted claim in the *Critique of Practical Reason* that all heteron-omous principles, without exception, "revolve around the principle of one's own happiness" and the theorem "All material practical principles are, as such, of one and the same kind and belong under the general principle of self-love or one's own happiness" (KprV 5: 22; 20). These claims suggest that Kant holds that the extramoral interest supposedly assumed by all the-ories not based on the principle of autonomy is necessarily a form of self-interest (understood in hedonistic terms as the maximization of pleasure or satisfaction). Additional support for this view is provided by Kant's noto-rious denial of any qualitative distinction between different kinds of pleasure in Remark I attached to this theorem (KprV 5: 23; 21) and his characteristic insistence on the connection between inclination and inclination-based action and feelings of pleasure and pain. Moreover, this would explain both why Kant thought that all such theories can appropriately be grouped together under the generic label "heteronomy" and why they are incapable of ac-counting for the possibility of morality.

It is at this point that we must deal with the claim, already touched upon in Chapter 2 in connection with his theory of freedom, that Kant's analysis rests on a crude, hedonistic view of nonmoral motivation. Thus, even though it has been shown that Kant's attachment to this view cannot account for his rejection of a compatibilistic conception of freedom, the preceding con-siderations suggest that he does, in fact, hold such a view and that it underlies his global critique of all competing moral theories. As T. H. Green, the originator of this line of criticism, puts it, "Kant's error lies in supposing that there is no alternative between the determination of desire by the an-ticipation of pleasure and its determination by the conception of a moral law."[47] Once this error is pointed out and a more accurate and nuanced view of motivation introduced, then the argument for autonomy as the sole prin-ciple of morality collapses. Or so it would seem.

Although this reading of Kant is widely accepted and appears to have a good deal of textual support, a closer consideration indicates that it does not represent his considered view. To begin with, following the lead of Andrews Reath, we can note that the linkage between inclination and feel-ings of pleasure and pain that Kant asserts is causal rather than inten-tional.[48] That is to say, Kant is committed to the doctrine that such feelings play a causal role in the genesis of our inclinations; but this is quite distinct from the hedonistic thesis that the end or object of all incli-nation-based (and therefore heteronomous) action is the attainment of pleasure or the avoidance of pain. As Reath suggests, we can think of in-clinations (which for Kant are essentially habitual desires[49]) as having complex causal histories, involving both genetic and environmental fac-tors, as a result of which the pleasant or painful sensations that helped produce the initial desire bear little or no resemblance to the satisfaction felt in the attainment of the object of that inclination.

Moreover, we need not assume Kant thought that if an action is "from inclination," its aim or object is the satisfaction of that inclination. A case

102

in point is Kant's "friend of man" or naturally sympathetic person, with whom we shall be concerned at some length in the next chapter. As the context makes clear, this person's concern is with the well-being of others rather than his own. Thus, whereas helping others in need provides him with satisfaction and he would not act in that way unless it did so, the end he has in mind is nevertheless the improvement of the lot of others and not the satisfaction of his own needs. Similarly, as we shall see in later chapters, conscientious moral agents, who act "from duty," are concerned with the attainment of some morally required end because it is morally required, not merely with doing duty for duty's sake. In fact, the parallel between these two cases is highly instructive, since it suggests that both the objection that Kant is committed to a crudely hedonistic psychology and the objection that his conception of action from duty is vacuous rest on the same foundation, namely, a failure to distinguish between the end or object of an action and the ground or reason for adopting such an end.

The same distinction, which is rooted in the Incorporation Thesis, also enables us to understand Kant's connection of heteronomy with the principle of happiness or self-love. As Reath has likewise noted, what is crucial here is that this is the *principle* on which heteronomous agents act and, according to heteronomous moral theories, on which all agents must act, not the *end* or *object* of their action.[50] To say that it is the principle on which heteronomous agents act, or in Kant's terms, "the determining ground of the will," is to say that it provides the ultimate norm or criterion governing choice. In other words, Kant's central claim, which is really only made explicit in the *Critique of Practical Reason,* is that all heteronomous theories are committed to a model of choice or deliberation in which the maximization of satisfaction (however that be construed) is the standard in terms of which specific maxims or courses of action are to be judged. Since this model is compatible with the pursuit of any number of ends, it hardly commits one to hedonism. On the contrary, it includes even explicitly nonegoistic or self-regarding theories such as the moral sense theory of Francis Hutcheson.[51]

Seen in this light, then, it does seem reasonable to take heteronomy as the "moral equivalent" of transcendental realism and to claim that it represents a model of choice, which, implicitly at least, is adhered to by all non-autonomy-based moral theories. Moreover, for the reasons already given, it also seems reasonable to claim that this model is not capable of accounting for the possibility of a categorical imperative.

But the global critique of heteronomy is only the first step in the overall argument for autonomy as the principle of morality. The next step (the "if" portion) requires demonstrating that the unacceptable consequence of such theories (the reduction of moral requirements to hypothetical imperatives) is avoided if we attribute to the will the property of autonomy as described earlier in this chapter. Consequently, one would expect this part of the argument to take roughly the following form:

1. The analysis of morality as based on a categorical imperative has shown that we are required to adopt maxims in virtue of their suitability as universal law or "legislative form."
2. But this presupposes a capacity to determine oneself to act independently of, and sometimes even contrary to, one's interests as a sensuous being with needs.
3. A will with the property of autonomy has this capacity.
4. Therefore, morality (as based on a categorical imperative) is possible if the will has the property of autonomy.

Although Kant does argue in roughly this way in the *Critique of Practical Reason*,[52] the argument in the *Groundwork* takes a different, more convoluted course. Thus, after completing his analysis of the second formula (the "formula of humanity" or of rational beings as ends in themselves), Kant makes the very point that has been here emphasized repeatedly, namely, that the exclusion of interest as an incentive (*Triebfeder*) is an essential feature of a categorical imperative in both forms. This is, of course, just the premise needed to argue for autonomy as property. But rather than drawing the obvious conclusion, he suggests that what is needed is a new formula that makes explicit the interest independence implicit in the very idea of a categorical imperative. This, he claims, is accomplished in the third formulation of the principle, which he characterizes as "the idea of the will of every rational being as *a will which makes universal law*" (Gr 4: 432; 99).

Since, as characterized, the presumed "formula" is not even in imperatival form, it is difficult to see how it could count as an expression of the categorical imperative. This difficulty is easily remedied, however, if we substitute the presumably canonical form of the principle of autonomy: "Never to choose except in such a way that in the same volition the maxims of your choice are also present as universal law" (Gr 4: 440; 108). To choose in this way is to select maxims in light of the idea of oneself (and every rational agent) as a maker of universal law or, as Kant now terms it, as "supreme lawgiver." What Kant must therefore show is that this way of viewing moral obligation helps to bring out the independence from interest supposedly implicit in the categorical imperative. To this end he argues:

Once we conceive a will of this kind [one which makes universal law], it becomes clear that while a will *which is subject to law* may be bound to this law by some interest, nevertheless a will which is itself a supreme lawgiver cannot possibly as such depend on any interest; for a will which is dependent in this way would itself require yet a further law in order to restrict the interest of self-love to the condition that this interest should itself be valid as a universal law. (Gr 4: 432; 99)

The chief difficulty posed by this all too brief argument lies in the notion of the will as "supreme lawgiver." If a will is thought to function in this way simply in virtue of the fact that it makes its own maxims and in this sense imposes "laws" upon itself, then the conclusion that a will, considered as such, "cannot possibly . . . depend on any interest" hardly follows. It does follow, however, if we take it as equivalent to the notion of a will as a "law to itself (independently of every property belonging to the objects of volition)." Indeed, since as we have already seen, a will can be said to function

104

as (or be) a "law to itself" just in case it determines itself to act on the basis of principles that make no reference to the agent's interests, it follows analytically.

The analyticity is perhaps more obvious if, as Kant clearly intends, we equate the will as supreme lawgiver with the will as making universal law through its maxims. To conceive oneself as acting in this way is just to regard oneself as motivated by purely universal considerations, that is, as acting on the basis of principles that hold for all rational agents. Not only is this precisely what the categorical imperative requires, but also it involves acting independently of one's own interests in the sense that universal interests become the primary consideration in determining what one ought to do.

Admittedly, Kant expresses the point somewhat obscurely by suggesting that if the will were dependent on interest, it would need a further law "in order to restrict the interest of self-love to the condition that this interest should itself be valid as a universal law." Nevertheless, we can understand this if we take him to be not only ruling out self-interest as the ultimate ground of the maxims of a will functioning as supreme lawgiver but also indicating that action from self-interest may itself be "lawful" if it is compatible with a possible universal law. In other words, although self-interest cannot ground a categorical imperative, self-interested action is morally permissible, subject to the limiting condition that it does not conflict with universal interests. We shall explore further some of the implications of this in later chapters.

As has been frequently noted, Kant regards autonomy as the principle of morality not only in the sense of being a necessary condition of its possibility but also in the sense of being one of the formulas of the categorical imperative and, therefore, as itself a first-order ethical principle.[53] Indeed, he moves from the former to the latter as if it were completely unproblematic. Thus, immediately after defining autonomy as a property of the will, he writes: "Hence the principle of autonomy is 'Never to choose except in such a way that in the same volition the maxims of your choice are also present as universal law'" (Gr 4: 440; 108). At the end of the same paragraph, after claiming that the status of the principle of autonomy as the "sole principle of ethics" (presumably understood as necessary condition of its possibility) follows from the analysis of the concepts of morality undertaken in the *Groundwork* up to that point, he states, "For analysis finds that the principle of morality must be a categorical imperative, and that this in turn commands nothing more or less than precisely this autonomy" (Gr 4: 440; 108). Autonomy therefore seems to be at once both a condition of the possibility of a categorical imperative and the content of what is commanded by such an imperative.

Although Kant is certainly to be faulted for failing to distinguish sharply in the *Groundwork* between autonomy as a property of the will and as a formula of the categorical imperative, it is fairly easy to see why he did not bother to do so. The essential point is simply that autonomy *is* both a property of the will that must be presupposed, if action on the basis of a categorical imperative is to be conceivable, and an expression of what this imperative requires. This is because what such an imperative requires is just to act reflectively in light of the property the will has of being a law to itself. Moreover, it is precisely the conception of the will as making universal law through its maxims that brings this out and, therefore, makes it clear why autonomy as property is necessary. Thus, it is neither surprising nor inappropriate that Kant introduce his revolutionary conception of autonomy as a property of the will by means of this formula. The formula of autonomy does not add anything to the other formulas by way of specifying further the criteria of dutiful action, but it does characterize the regulative idea under which rational agents ought to act.

6
Duty, inclination, and respect

Having analyzed Kant's conception of agency in *Groundwork* II and seen how the introduction of autonomy modifies the earlier, first *Critique* conception, we are finally in a position to consider his moral psychology. Although this psychology underwent a significant development in the writings from the *Groundwork* to the *Metaphysics of Morals,* its basic elements are already in place in the former work. Thus, it is here that we find the familiar, yet frequently criticized account of a good will as one motivated by the thought of duty alone, with the consequent disparagement of inclination as a potential source of moral worth. Closely related to this is the doctrine of reverence or respect (*Achtung*) for the law as the only genuine moral motive, which Kant sketches in the *Groundwork* and develops in much greater detail in the *Critique of Practical Reason.* These are the topics of the present chapter, which is therefore divided into two parts.

I. A good will and moral worth

Groundwork I begins with Kant's famous proclamation that "it is impossible to conceive anything at all in the world, or even out of it, which can be taken as good without qualification except a *good will*" (Gr 4: 393; 61). This claim, which Kant himself presents as an expression of the universal judgment of ordinary human reason, has been frequently criticized[1]; but our concern is not so much with the cogency of the claim itself as with the analysis of the goodness of a good will. As an unqualified or unconditioned good (something that is good in all respects and in all possible contexts), it must be an intrinsic good, which Kant takes to mean that its goodness must lie in its mode of willing rather than in anything it might accomplish in the world.[2] In an effort to delineate this mode of willing, Kant introduces the concept of duty, which, he tells us, "includes that of a good will, exposed, however, to certain subjective limitations and obstacles." Moreover, he adds, "these, so far from hiding a good will or disguising it, rather bring it out by contrast and make it shine forth more brightly" (Gr 4: 397; 65).

One of the puzzling features of Kant's account is that immediately upon completing his paean to the good will and indicating its connection (in its human, or nonholy, form) with the idea of duty, he turns to a discussion of moral worth, which pertains to particular actions rather than to an enduring will or character. The central claim is that moral worth is to be attributed to actions if and only if they are from duty (*aus Pflicht*). Since by a "good will" (again under human conditions) Kant obviously means one that is in some sense motivated by duty, this suggests that his view is that we can be said to have a good will just in case we act from duty alone or, equivalently, just in case our actions possess moral worth.

Although this is perhaps the most natural and certainly the most prevalent reading, there are at least two respects in which it is misleading.[3] First, following the lead of Barbara Herman, we shall see that it is necessary to distinguish between two ways in which duty can motivate, only one of which yields actions that are in Kant's sense "from duty" and therefore possess moral worth, whereas both are characteristic of a good will. In other words, a good will is manifested, but not exclusively, in actions possessing moral worth. Second, in his later writings, particularly *Religion within the Limits of Reason Alone* and *The Doctrine of Virtue*, Kant attributes a good will to agents who are lacking in virtue. In fact, he maintains that having a good will is compatible with radical evil (Rel 6: 36, 44; 32, 39). A discussion of the second of these problems is best reserved for Chapters 8 and 9, where the focus is specifically on Kant's doctrine in these works. I hope to shed some light on the first in the present chapter, however, by means of an analysis of the *Groundwork* account of moral worth.

Central to Kant's account of moral worth and, indeed, to his moral psychology as a whole, is the contrast between duty and inclination as two competing sources of motivation. Although Kant twice distinguishes between inclination and fear, the operative assumption is that every action is motivated by either inclination or the thought of duty, that is, every action is either *aus Neigung* or *aus Pflicht* (Gr 4: 398, 401n; 66, 69). Presumably, inclinations constitute the "subjective limitations and obstacles" to which a potentially good will is exposed. Presumably also, it is by bringing out the contrast between action *aus Neigung* and action *aus Pflicht* that the essential goodness of the latter is made to "shine forth more brightly."

In the *Groundwork,* Kant defines *inclination* as the "dependence of the faculty of desire [*Begehrungsvermögens*] on sensations," and he remarks that the presence of an inclination always indicates a need (Gr 4: 413n; 81). Elsewhere, as noted in the last chapter, he defines it as "habitual desire" (MS 6: 211; 9 and Anthro 7: 251; 119). Moreover, on occasion, he not only contrasts inclination with desire (*Begierde*) that is not habitual but also with passion (*Leidenschaft*). By the latter is understood a particularly powerful inclination, one that a rational agent is capable of overcoming only with great difficulty, if at all (Anthro 7: 251; 119 and Rel 6: 29n; 24). These complexities indicate that, strictly speaking, inclination is merely one species of desire and, therefore, that action *aus Neigung* is itself only one species of desire-based action.

Nevertheless, it is clear that insofar as Kant assumes a dualism of inclination and duty as the sources of motivation, "inclination" must be construed in a broad sense to refer to any stimulus to action that stems from our sensuous, as opposed to our rational, nature. So construed, inclination encompasses momentary desires, instincts, passions, fears, and disinclinations

108

(*Abneigungen*), all of which pertain only to sensuously affected beings. Given this broad conception of inclination, it turns out that not only courses of action for which one has an immediate liking (inclination in the narrow sense) but also those that, although not in themselves desirable, are nonetheless deemed necessary for the enhancement of one's long-term self-interest are or, better, can be from inclination.

Kant's illustrations involve the contrast between the broad and narrow senses of inclination, but his appeal to this distinction serves only to obfuscate his account. Starting with the assumption, itself questionable, that actions performed from duty cannot, objectively speaking, be contrary to duty, he proposes to limit his consideration to actions that are at least in agreement with duty (*pflichtmässig*).[4] He also proposes to neglect the subset of these for which there is no *immediate* inclination but that the agent is motivated to perform by some other "mediate" inclination. Not surprisingly, these turn out to be actions motivated by self-interest or prudential considerations (inclinations in the broad sense). The reason offered for their neglect is that in their case, in contrast to actions for which there is an immediate inclination, it is easy to determine whether the action is merely in accordance with or actually from duty. This claim is supposedly illustrated by the example of the honest shopkeeper who treats his customers fairly because he perceives it to be in his self-interest rather than because of either a sense of duty or love. Although Kant does not develop the point, the clear implication is that if the shopkeeper were motivated by love, then the moral status of his behavior would be more difficult to determine.[5]

This explicitly self-interested behavior is then contrasted with the endeavor to preserve one's life, which is based on immediate inclination. Given what Kant has just said about the two types of motivation, one would naturally expect the point of the contrast to be to show that since life-preserving behavior is based on immediate inclination, it is more difficult to distinguish from genuine moral activity (action from duty) than the behavior of the shopkeeper. But this is patently false. Indeed, Kant himself suggests as much with his description of the circumstances in which the effort to preserve one's life can be thought to be motivated by a sense of duty rather than the natural love of life. As he puts it:

When . . . disappointments and hopeless misery have quite taken away the taste for life; when a wretched man, strong in soul and more angered at his fate than faint-hearted or cast down, longs for death and still preserves his life without loving it – not from inclination or fear but from duty; then indeed his maxim has a moral content. (Gr 4: 398; 65–6)

The real basis of Kant's distinction does become somewhat clearer, however, with the next and most important example, namely, that of people blessed with a naturally sympathetic temperament, who, "without any further motive of vanity or self-interest . . . find an inner pleasure in spreading happiness around them and can take delight in the contentment of others as their own work" (Gr 4: 398; 66). Admittedly, Kant once again muddies the

109

waters by stipulating that such people take delight in the well-being of others "as their own work" (*so fern sie ihr Werk ist*). This suggests that what motivates them is not so much a disinterested concern with the well-being of others as it is the desire to be the source of this well-being. But this runs directly contrary to Kant's purpose with the example, which is to depict an action type that in contrast to that of the prudent shopkeeper is not motivated by self-interest and, therefore, on the surface at least, appears to be a ready candidate for the attribution of moral worth. Accordingly, he explicitly denies that an action of this kind, "however right and however amiable it may be," possesses genuine moral worth. On the contrary, he insists:

It stands on the same footing as other inclinations – for example, the inclination for honor, which if fortunate enough to hit on something beneficial and right and consequently honorable, deserves praise and encouragement, but not esteem; for its maxim lacks moral content, namely, the performance of such actions, not from inclination, but *from duty*. (Gr 4: 398; 66)

In order to drive this point home, Kant contrasts the *initial* state of such a "friend of man" with a *subsequent* state in which, as a result of personal misfortune, all sympathetic feeling has been extinguished. Then, and only then, Kant suggests, "when no longer moved by any inclination, he tears himself out of this deadly insensibility and does the action without any inclination for the sake of duty alone" (*lediglich aus Pflicht*), does the action possess moral worth (Gr 4: 398; 66).

Finally, varying the situation once again, Kant asks rhetorically whether if this, or any, man had been born with little or no natural sympathy, being in all other respects an honest person, "would he not still find in himself a source from which he might draw a worth far higher than any that a good-natured temperament can have?" As expected, Kant answers this affirmatively, noting that "it is precisely in this that the worth of character begins to show – a moral worth and beyond all comparison the highest – namely, that he does good, not from inclination, but from duty" (Gr 4: 398–9; 66).

Generations of commentators and critics have taken Kant here to be claiming, or at least implying, that an action cannot have moral worth if, at the time of its performance, the agent has an inclination to perform it. Indeed, this reading can be traced back to Kant's contemporary Schiller, who, in the following well known-lines, jokingly ridicules the Kantian view:

Gladly I serve my friends, but alas I do it with pleasure.
Hence I am plagued with doubt that I am not a virtuous person.
To this the answer is given:
Surely, your only resource is to try to despise them entirely,
And then with aversion do what your duty enjoins you.[6]

The standard strategy for dealing with the objection implicit in these lines is to point out that Kant is here practicing his so-called "method of isolation."[7] In other words, he is merely trying to describe situations in which the moral worth of actions becomes apparent, not claiming that actions can only possess such worth in the absence of inclinations.

Recently, Barbara Herman has gone beyond this general point and challenged the reading of the text underlying the standard criticism. Rather than contrasting the moral status of the actions of two distinct individuals, one with sympathetic feeling and the other without it, she notes that Kant is actually contrasting the moral status of the benevolent actions of a single individual in two quite distinct psychological states. So construed, Kant's point is merely that the actions of *this particular individual* only attain moral worth when the duty motive takes the place of inclination. And this, of course, is quite different from the claim that moral worth requires the absence of inclination.[8]

Herman's reading is correct. In fact, Kant never claims that an otherwise morally praiseworthy act loses its moral significance if an agent has an inclination to perform it. His claim is rather that such an act lacks moral significance if the agent performs it only because of the inclination.[9] Thus, the distinction between an act being accompanied by inclination (*mit Neigung*) and being motivated by or from inclination (*aus Neigung*) is an essential component of Kant's moral psychology.[10] Admittedly, Kant does not make this as explicit as he might have; nevertheless, this distinction is certainly implicit in his suggestion, at the very beginning of the analysis of moral worth, that the determination of whether an action is from duty is "far more difficult when the subject has in addition an *immediate* inclination to the action" (Gr 4: 397; 65). Unless it is assumed that an action can be accompanied by inclination without being from inclination, this would be easy to determine, since the mere presence of inclination would be enough to resolve the matter.

It is clear, however, that this distinction is only a first step in the analysis of the Kantian conception of moral worth and does not suffice to resolve all of the problems. One must also explain exactly why actions from inclination are lacking in moral worth. Moreover, granting that actions from inclination *alone* are lacking in such worth and that the duty motive must somehow be operative, it seems to be quite a jump from this to the claim that actions must be from duty *alone* in order to possess moral worth. Is it not more plausible to think of actions as motivated by *both* the thought of duty and inclination? And is it not more in accord with our moral intuitions to attribute moral worth to actions so motivated? These, then, are the issues that must be dealt with if one is to make any sense out of Kant's conception of moral worth as delineated in *Groundwork* I.

In considering these issues, it must be kept in mind that although they reflect the needs of the agent as a sensuous being, inclination-based actions are nonetheless expressions of the agent's practical spontaneity. Accordingly, the denial that such actions can possess moral worth is not predicated on the assumption that they are mere bits of behavior or products of nature. On the contrary, it assumes that they are genuine, imputable actions and attributes their lack of moral worth to the fact that they stem from maxims that lack moral content (*moralischen Gehalt*) (Gr 4: 397–8; 65–6). To say that

111

a maxim lacks moral content is to say that the moral appropriateness of a proposed course of action is not the reason for its adoption. Consequently, although such a maxim and the ensuing action may accord with what is morally required, this accord is merely contingent.

In spite of the significant differences between them, the general point is clear enough from Kant's examples. Consider first the case of the honest shopkeeper. Since he is motivated by self-interest rather than a sense of duty, it follows that his scrupulous treatment of customers will continue only so long as it is perceived to be in his self-interest. This suggests that the problem with the shopkeeper's behavior is merely that it is unreliable, since, as conditioned by the profit motive, it can be expected to continue only so long as the honest treatment of all customers is thought to be more profitable than, say, selective cheating. Although certainly correct, it would be a mistake to regard this as the *whole* story with regard to the shopkeeper example. For even if circumstances and the empirical character of the shopkeeper were such that his behavior could be relied on with as much confidence as one can rely on a shopkeeper motivated by a sense of duty, his behavior would still be a function of nonmoral factors that are themselves contingent. Thus, it would remain a purely contingent matter that his conduct accords with the dictates of the moral law.[11]

Since it involves not only a different type of motivation than the preceding example (immediate inclination rather than calculating self-interest) but also a different kind of obligation, the example of the person who acts beneficently because of a sympathetic nature rather than from moral considerations introduces another dimension into the account. The difference stems from the fact that the shopkeeper's obligation not to cheat his customers is for Kant a perfect duty, indeed, a duty of justice. As such, it both enjoins a particular kind of behavior (honest dealing) and allows for no exceptions. Correlatively, the duty of beneficence, which is under consideration in the second example, is an imperfect duty, more specifically a duty of virtue. As such, it is both of "wide obligation" (allows for exceptions) and enjoins the adoption of a general policy or "maxim of ends" (helping others in need when possible) rather than particular actions.

Admittedly, the distinction between perfect and imperfect duties, as drawn in the *Groundwork*, and its relation to the distinction between duties of justice and duties of virtue, which is central to the *Metaphysics of Morals*, are complicated and controversial topics and raise a number of important issues that shall be with us for the remainder of this study.[12] For present purposes, however, we need note only that since he is acting in accordance with a perfect duty (more precisely, a duty of justice), the shopkeeper's behavior at least conforms to the law (has "legality"), even if it is totally lacking in moral worth. By contrast, the person of sympathetic nature can, although acting on the basis of that inclination, actually violate the moral law.[13] This is because such actions can violate both duties of justice (as in the case of someone who steals from the rich in order to give to the poor)

112

and even perfect duties to oneself (if one totally neglects one's own real needs out of an overly zealous concern with the needs of others).

The comparison of these two cases suggests a distinction between two senses in which an action can agree only contingently with the dictates of the moral law, each of which suffices to deny moral worth to the action. First there is the contingency that stems from the need for a nonmoral motive, or more simply, "motivational contingency." This is the sense that Kant usually emphasizes, and it applies to both the self-interested honest shopkeeper and the "friend of man" (in his premoral stage). Both act in morally correct ways for morally irrelevant reasons. Thus, the shopkeeper can be counted on to be honest only as long as honesty is perceived to be the best policy and the friend of man to help others in need only as long as he is sufficiently moved by sympathetic feeling.

Second, there is the contingency with respect to whether the action itself, so motivated, agrees with the law, or "agreement contingency." This applies to the friend of man but not to the honest shopkeeper. To be sure, the latter may change his behavior if he perceives it to be in his interest to do so; nevertheless, the fact remains that as long as he perceives it to be in his best interests to treat his customers honestly, it is not a contingent matter that his conduct agrees with the law (he may treat his customers unsympathetically but not unjustly). As we have just seen, however, this is not at all the case with the friend of man. Remaining well-disposed, he can quite easily violate the rights of others and even, as Kant would put it, the "rights of humanity in his own person."

Contingency in the first of these senses is clearly absent in the case of actions from duty; for then the agreement of the action with the dictates of morality is not a function of either the perceived self-interest or the current psychological state of the agent. It could still be argued, however, that contingency in the second sense has not been eliminated, at least as long as the possibility remains open that an action done *from* duty might not, objectively speaking, accord *with* duty. As already noted, Kant dismisses such a possibility in the *Groundwork,* although he does recognize it elsewhere.[14] Given this recognition, it seems appropriate to revise Kant's account so as to require that an action be both from and in accordance with duty as a condition of its possessing moral worth.[15] If both conditions are met it is, of course, analytic that the agreement of the action with the law is not contingent.

The preceding analysis has shown that acting from duty alone (assuming that the actions also accord with duty or are "dutiful") is a sufficient condition for the attribution of moral worth. It does not, however, suffice to show that it is also a necessary condition. One possibility, as yet unexplored, is that there are actions motivated by both duty and inclination and that such actions possess moral worth. In other words, actions possessing moral worth might be overdetermined. To cite the example suggested by Richard Henson,

Kant's own behavior as university lecturer could have been motivated by a number of factors, including the fact that he enjoyed lecturing and that he recognized lecturing as a moral duty.[16] The point, of course, is that this overdetermination would not diminish the moral worth of Kant's activities as a lecturer.

Henson maintains that Kant neglected such a possibility in the *Groundwork* because he there assumed a "battle citation" model of moral worth. This turns out to be the familiar (and I hope by now discredited) view that an action can possess moral worth only if it is performed in opposition to inclination or at least without any inclination in support of it. Thus, we can reject this part of his claim without further discussion. He also suggests, however, that Kant advanced a different, "fitness report" model of moral worth in the *Metaphysic of Morals* and that, although Kant apparently never realized it, this model is capable of accommodating overdetermined actions. According to this second model, one might claim that a dutiful act was done from duty and thus had moral worth "provided that respect for duty was present and would have sufficed by itself, even though (as it happened) other motives were also present and might have sufficed."[17]

Before attempting to deal with this issue, it is important to become clear regarding exactly what is meant by "overdetermination" in this context. Given the previously noted distinction between an action being performed with and from inclination, it is apparent that the mere presence of an inclination is not enough to characterize an action from duty as overdetermined. If this label is to fit, the action must be both from duty and from inclination. Moreover, this point is recognized (at least in part) by Henson. Thus, he acknowledges the possibility of an agent having a motive to act in a certain way and actually acting in that way, although not from that motive; nevertheless, he also insists that he has in mind a situation in which the nonmoral as well as the moral motive is operative and not merely present.[18]

Henson's analysis has been challenged by Barbara Herman, who focuses her attention on his fitness report model of moral worth. According to Herman, this model can be construed in either a weak or a strong sense, neither of which is capable of providing an adequate account of moral worth.[19] Taken in the weak sense, it amounts to the claim that the moral motive was "sufficient if alone," that is, sufficient to produce the act even if the other cooperating motives were not operative. Taken in the strong sense, it maintains that what is required is that the moral motive would have been sufficient even if other, conflicting motives had also been present.

The problem with the weak reading, according to Herman, is that it neglects the possibility that in different circumstances the very same nonmoral motives that supposedly cooperate with the moral motive in overdetermining the action might move the agent in the opposite direction. For example, the profit motive that, in the case of the shopkeeper, happens to favor the policy of honest dealing might very well favor the opposite policy under different circumstances. Since, *ex hypothesi,* the action was motivated by both a sense of duty and a desire for profit, it would remain possible that it was merely an accident (due to favorable circumstances) that the agent did what duty requires; and this is incompatible with the attribution of moral worth.

Herman notes that the strong reading avoids this difficulty, but she insists that it does so only at the cost of denying moral worth to actions to which we should normally attribute it. This is supposedly because it requires us to deny moral worth to an action if we assume that had circumstances been different the agent would not have been able to perform it (since in that event the moral motive would not have sufficed). Against this, she argues that the fact that an agent would not be able to act dutifully in radically different circumstances does not undermine the worth of an action dutifully performed in less trying circumstances. As she puts it:

> Even if circumstances tomorrow are such that the alignment of moral and nonmoral motives breaks down, and the dutiful action is as a result not done, it is surely possible that the dutiful action that *is* done today, when the motives are aligned, has moral worth.[20]

Herman is correct in insisting upon this possibility. Certainly, there are cases in which it would be inappropriate to deny moral worth to an action in a given set of circumstances simply because it is assumed that the agent would not have acted in similar fashion had the circumstances been different. Typically, these are cases where what is at issue is the agent's strength of will. For example, we would hardly deny moral worth to the action of a person who heroically resisted torture for two hours on the grounds that the person would have succumbed had the torture been continued an hour longer.

Herman is incorrect, however, in suggesting that a consideration of what an agent might have done in different circumstances is *never* relevant to the determination of the moral worth of an action.[21] On the contrary, counterfactual assumptions about what someone would have done had circumstances been different often affect (and properly so) our judgments of moral worth. Moreover, this follows from the very principle emphasized by Herman in her critique of the weak reading of Henson's fitness report model: If an action is to possess moral worth, it must be noncontingently dutiful. To claim that an action is noncontingently dutiful is to claim that its dutifulness is not a function of circumstances, which means that it still would have been performed had circumstances been different. Accordingly, by insisting that assumptions about how an agent might have acted in different circumstances have no bearing on judgments of the moral worth of a particular action in given circumstances, it appears that Herman makes the possibility of acting from duty (at least partly) a function of circumstances after all, thereby reintroducing an element of contingency or luck into the moral situation.[22]

Herman anticipates this line of criticism and attempts to counter it by drawing a sharp distinction between moral worth, which pertains to particular actions, and moral virtue, which pertains to character. Given this distinction, she, in effect, admits the role of chance but denies that it affects the question of moral worth because it concerns only those to whom virtue (strength of character) is to be attributed. Thus she writes:

The effect of chance . . . is on *who* is able to act in a morally worthy way. It poses a distributive problem that belongs to the theory of moral virtue and not to moral worth. And although it may be only a matter of luck *whose* actions have moral worth, what moral worth expresses is the relation of a motive to an action (through its maxim). When an agent does act dutifully from the motive of duty, when his maxim of action has moral content, it is not a matter of luck that the *action* has moral worth.[23]

This response is not, however, very satisfying. Certainly, Herman is correct in claiming that *when* an agent acts dutifully from duty, it is no accident that the action possess moral worth. But that is really beside the point, since it expresses an analytic judgment (an action has moral worth just in case it is both dutiful and from duty). In other words, the issue is not whether it can be accidental that an act possesses moral worth when an agent acts dutifully from duty; it is rather whether it can be an accident (function of circumstances) *that* an agent acts in this manner.

In dealing with this issue, it is important to recall the fact that the notion of moral worth is introduced within the context of a discussion of a good will. Although it was noted earlier that Kant, somewhat misleadingly, suggests that a will is good just in case its actions possess moral worth, it is certainly his view that goodness of will is a *necessary* condition of the actions of an agent possessing such worth. But clearly the goodness of a good will is itself a function of its character, that is, the permanent structure of its motives or, equivalently, its disposition (*Gesinnung*) to act on the basis of morally appropriate maxims.[24] Put simply, a good will can be characterized as one whose enduring maxim is to conform to the dictates of the moral law.[25] Equally clearly, the kind of character one has, that is, the kind of person one is, is not (at least for Kant) a matter of luck. Consequently, it cannot be *only* a matter of luck that the actions of a given agent have moral worth.[26]

The conclusion to be drawn from this, however, is that Herman's critique is somewhat misdirected, not that she is incorrect in rejecting the claim that acts possessing moral worth can be overdetermined in the sense stipulated by Henson. In reality, the problem is not so much with the fitness report model of moral worth as it is with the assumption that this model, on its strong reading, is compatible with overdetermination in the stipulated sense. Moreover, there are two reasons why the true nature of the problem has escaped notice. (1) Henson's own example of Kant's lecturing clearly suggests the weak version of the model, which, as already indicated, does assume overdetermination. (2) Neither Henson nor Herman consider the question in connection with Kant's theory of agency, that is to say, in connection with the question of how motives motivate.

In order to see the relevance of both points, we need only consider briefly what the overdetermination thesis amounts to on the strong reading of Henson's model. Continuing with his own example, we imagine Kant motivated to lecture by both the thought of duty and the sheer love of lecturing. *Ex hypothesi,* each of these motives is sufficient of itself; but the duty motive is of such strength that it would have sufficed even if, for some reason, Kant had come to detest lecturing or, to make the situation less extreme, had a strong inclination to do something else at a time when he was scheduled to lecture – say work on the *Critique of Pure Reason.* So far, there is nothing implausible in this hypothetical scenario. In fact, assuming, as Kant's critics frequently do, that motives or incentives are distinct psychic forces that can move an agent either singly or in cooperation with one another, it is also reasonable to assume that Kant was moved by both and that the duty motive had the superior strength.

The problem is that Kant does not conceive of motives or incentives in that manner. On the contrary, as has been noted repeatedly, he maintains that an incentive can determine the will only if it is "taken up into a maxim." Consequently, in order to deal with Henson's example in terms of the Kantian account of agency, it is necessary to consider the maxim on which the hypothetical overdetermined Kant is supposed to act. Since Henson insists that his Kant actually acts on both incentives (otherwise the act would not be overdetermined), the maxim must be a complex one, incorporating both incentives. Moreover, since it is difficult to see how both these incentives could be incorporated into a single maxim except as joint conditions of the action, it can be assumed that the maxim will be roughly of the form: I shall lecture whenever I am both obligated and feel inclined to do so.

It is clear, however, that this will not do, since to act on the basis of such a maxim is, in effect, to make the performance of one's duty dependent upon the presence of an inclination. Moreover, this, as we have seen in the last chapter, is to convert the categorical into a hypothetical imperative and, therefore, to undermine completely the notion of duty. That is why, in the *Critique of Practical Reason,* Kant insists first that it is "risky" (*bedenklich*) even to let other motives "cooperate" (*mitwirken*) with the law (KprV 5: 72; 75) and later that no empirical determining grounds of the will should be incorporated with the law into one's maxim as a "condition," since "this would destroy all moral worth just as surely as any admixture of anything empirical in geometrical axioms would destroy all mathematical certainty" (KprV 5: 93; 96–7).

In response to such criticism, it might be countered that the maxim has been misdescribed. The correct way to characterize the maxim, so the rejoinder goes, is not in terms of a conjunction but rather in terms of a disjunction of motives. Thus, it should read: I shall lecture whenever I am either obligated or feel inclined to do so. Not only does this formulation avoid the consequences of the first one, it is also more in accord with the operative assumption that each of the motives "suffices of itself."

The problem with this response is simply that the proposed disjunctive maxim is not really a single maxim at all. It is rather a combination in one formula of two distinct maxims: I shall lecture whenever duty requires me to and I shall lecture whenever I have the opportunity and feel so inclined. Thus, it becomes legitimate to ask on which maxim the agent acted. Kant admits, of course, that such a question cannot be answered with certainty, since we can have no indefeasible knowledge regarding the ultimate sources of our motivation; but this does not undermine the meaningfulness of the question or its relevance to the determination of moral worth.[27]

This should not be understood as ruling out the notion of a disjunctive maxim altogether, however, but merely what might be termed a "motivational disjunction." For example, I could very well make it my maxim to accept invitations to lecture only when they are either tendered by a prestigious university or involve a sufficiently large stipend. This disjunction concerns the conditions under which an agent adopts a certain course of action, which are just the conditions under which that agent takes the proposed course of action to be reasonable, all things considered. Since these conditions all reflect the same underlying ground or motive, namely, self-interest or inclination in the broad sense, there is no reason why they cannot be disjunctively connected in a single maxim. By contrast, in the example at issue, the proposed disjunction concerns the possible ultimate grounds for adopting a course of action (duty and inclination); and these cannot be disjunctively combined as the ground of a single maxim. In short, whereas one can lecture either from duty or from inclination (or even from both), one cannot lecture from "either duty or inclination" (taking this as a single, complex motive).

In the end, then, it would seem that the possibility of overdetermination, at least of the kind envisaged by Henson, does not provide a cogent rejoinder to Kant's claim that being from duty alone is a necessary condition for the ascription of moral worth to an action. If, on the one hand, the cooperation of inclination is deemed necessary to determine the will, then the action is not really from duty in the appropriate sense and is, therefore, lacking in moral worth. If, on the other hand, the assumption is that duty alone would have sufficed, then it is not a genuine case of overdetermination. The action is properly described as *with* but not *from* inclination. One simply cannot have it both ways.

There is also, however, another possible challenge to Kant's claim that actions possessing moral worth must be from duty alone. Moreover, it is precisely this challenge that points to the need to distinguish the class of actions possessing moral worth from the class of actions stemming from a good will. Although she does not herself mount it, the basis for both the challenge and the distinction is provided by Barbara Herman, who focuses on the role of the duty motive in morally permissible but not obligatory actions. She notes that since such actions are from self-interest, they cannot be motivated directly by the thought of duty. Nevertheless, such actions might still be viewed as motivated by a sense of duty in an extended sense, and therefore as expressions of a good will, insofar as the conscientious moral agent appeals to the moral law in order to determine whether a desired course of action is morally permissible. In such cases, then, the idea of duty functions as a kind of secondary motive, or limiting condition, that is brought to bear on the consideration of the primary motive without itself directly determining the agent to act.[28]

Appealing to a similar account of acting from duty presented by Marcia Baron,[29] Paul Benson has suggested that the principle underlying Herman's analysis might be extended to obligatory or dutiful actions.[30] Thus, just as merely permissible actions are governed by moral considerations in an indirect manner, so one might regard obligatory actions as governed in essentially the same way. The intent of this proposal is to preserve the intuition that in order to possess moral worth, an action must be governed by an agent's moral concern to do what is right but to separate it from the overly restrictive requirement that this concern be itself the directly motivating factor. Such direct motivation, on his view, might, but need not, be present. As he puts it, "knowing that an action must be performed can authoritatively govern conduct while non-moral concerns directly motivate it." And, again, we can view morally worthy acts as "prompted by non-moral interests" yet "ruled by an overriding critical moral capacity." As was the case with Herman, the crucial factor is "the distinction between motives functioning to prompt action directly and those functioning as constraints on the operation of other motives."[31]

To begin with, Kant clearly allows for the possibility that morally worthy actions might be *prompted* by nonmoral motives such as sympathy. In fact, that is why he argues in the *The Doctrine of Virtue* that we have an indirect duty to cultivate our sympathetic feelings (MS 6: 457; 126). As we shall see in more detail in Chapter 9, the point there is that the more we develop these feelings, the more sensitive we will be to the needs of others and, therefore, the better able to practice the duty of beneficence. It does not follow from this, however, that the agent is to be thought of as motivated directly by a feeling of sympathy or, in Kantian terms, as acting from sympathy. On the contrary, the difference between the conscientious, yet sympathetically disposed moral agent and the friend of man of the *Groundwork* is just that the former acts *with* but not *from* inclination. Moreover, the reason for this is, as Benson suggests, that moral considerations provide the overriding determinant of action. Thus, if duty were to require the withholding of aid from someone in need, the conscientious agent would withhold such aid in spite of sympathetic feeling, whereas the friend of man would not.

This in turn suggests that it is precisely by providing the ultimate norms governing conduct that moral considerations motivate at all. In other words, to act from duty in the Kantian sense is just to act in light of the recognition of the moral law as supremely authoritative or, equivalently, as unconditionally binding. To that extent Benson is on solid Kantian ground in emphasizing this role for the moral law. Where his account is lacking is in the implication (never quite made explicit) that this does not coincide with what Kant himself means by acting from duty and in the claim (made against

119

Herman) that this analysis entails the rejection of a sharp distinction between the function of the duty motive in merely permissible and obligatory actions.[32] In fact, what Benson's analysis really shows is not the untenability of the sharp distinction between the two functions for the duty motive but rather the need to distinguish between the acts of a good will *überhaupt* and the subset of those acts possessing moral worth.

The first issue will be discussed at length in the next section, where we consider Kant's account of action from duty as action from respect for the law; the second can be dealt with briefly now. The main point is simply that although a conscientious moral agent grants supreme authority to the moral law in the determination of both the permissible and the obligatory, the mere fact that a course of conduct is permissible is not a sufficient reason to choose it. There must also be some nonmoral reason or interest that is ultimately traceable to the agent's sensuous nature. In such cases, then, it is appropriate to characterize the action as from inclination, albeit governed by moral considerations. Since it is from inclination rather than directly from duty, the action cannot be said to possess moral worth; but since it is governed by moral considerations, it is nevertheless the action of a person with a good will. By contrast, in cases of obligatory action, the mere fact that an action is obligatory is, of itself, sufficient reason to perform it.[33] Accordingly, if moral considerations are to govern at all in the case of obligatory actions, they must do so by serving as sufficient reasons, which is just to say that the action must be from duty. In such cases, then, goodness of will is exhibited only in actions directly from duty or, equivalently, in those possessing moral worth. Thus, although not all the actions of a good will must be directly from duty, all dutiful actions must be. As we have seen, however, this is perfectly compatible with the possibility that the agent also has an inclination to perform the action and even that the agent is "prompted" by that inclination.

II. Respect

The argument up to this point has attempted to show that an action possesses moral worth if and only if it is performed from duty alone. But what is involved in acting from duty? How are we to understand this unique species of motivation, in which the mere dutifulness of a course of action can serve as a sufficient incentive to adopt it, independently of and even contrary to one's other interests as a sensuously affected rational agent? This is precisely the problem of the *principium executionis,* which, as we have seen in Chapter 3, Kant posed sharply in his lectures without being able to answer adequately. His new, fully critical attempt to answer this question is contained in his account of respect for the law as the only legitimate moral incentive.

In the *Groundwork,* where he first deals with the topic, respect is introduced at the end of the discussion of moral worth. After arguing that actions can have moral worth only if they are done from duty and that the worth of such actions stems from the maxim on which they are based rather than from the end at which they are directed, Kant claims that it can be inferred from this that *"duty is the necessity to act out of respect for the law"* (Gr 4: 400; 68).[34] The argument, such as it is, is by elimination. Having eliminated inclination and with it every object of the will as a possible ground of obligation, Kant concludes that "there is nothing left able to determine the will except objectively the *law* and subjectively *pure respect* for this practical law" (Gr 4: 400; 68–9). The actual account of respect as a feeling that is "self-produced from a rational concept" and, therefore, qualitatively different from other feelings, which stem entirely from our sensuous nature, is then relegated to a single, dense footnote (Gr 4: 401n; 69).

Since the contents of this note are expanded into the central topic of a lengthy chapter in the *Critique of Practical Reason* ["The Incentives of Pure Practical Reason" (KprV 5: 71–89; 74–92)], we shall focus primarily on the latter in expounding Kant's doctrine of respect. Before turning to the text, however, it will be helpful to place it within the overall argument of the "Analytic of Pure Practical Reason." In particular, it is important to realize that as the third chapter of the Analytic it follows both the exposition of the moral law and the establishment of its validity as a "fact of reason." Thus, it presupposes that Kant has already shown that pure reason is practical, that is, that reason, of itself, independently of inclination, is sufficient to determine the will (KprV 5: 14–15; 14–15).[35] Given all of this, the main job of the chapter is to explore the effects of the consciousness of the (valid) law on agents such as ourselves, who have a sensuous as well as a rational nature. In other words, Kant provides what could be termed a "theory of moral sensibility," which is intended to play a role in the second *Critique* analogous to that of the Transcendental Aesthetic in the first.[36]

Fortunately, although it is necessary to have this background in mind in order to follow the argument of the chapter, it is also possible to "bracket," as it were, the underlying presupposition of the validity of the moral law and to regard the discussion of respect essentially as a phenomenology of moral experience.[37] Considered as such, it can be taken as complementing the account of moral worth offered in the *Groundwork* without denying the possibility that, for all we know, morality might be nothing more than a "phantom of the brain" (*Hirngespinst*), which is the methodological assumption of the first two parts of the latter work.[38] Accordingly, this is the approach to be followed here and, indeed, in the remainder of this portion of the study. As already indicated, the whole question of the adequacy of Kant's attempt to ground morality is reserved for the third part.[39]

Kant defines an incentive (*Triebfeder*) at the very beginning of the discussion as "a subjective determining ground of a will whose reason does not by its nature necessarily conform to the objective law" (KprV 5: 72; 74). In the terms of Lewis White Beck, it is the "conative or dynamic factor in volition," the actual impetus to action, whereas the objective determining ground is the rule or principle governing the action.[40] The qualification "whose reason does not by its nature necessarily conform to the objective law" serves to preclude the attribution of an incentive to a divine or holy will. Since such a will obeys the law by its very nature, and since there is no countervailing motivation, no temptation to transgress the law, it does not stand in need of an incentive (KprV 5: 72, 79, 82, 84; 74, 81, 84, 86).[41] That is why the law does not take the form of an imperative for such a will and why one cannot speak of it as having duties. Although Kant does not deal explicitly with the matter, it is also clear that irrational beings possessed of an *arbitrium brutum* likewise cannot have an incentive, since they are lacking the capacity to recognize the law.

Accordingly, the notion of an incentive to morality is in place only for finite rational agents such as ourselves, who stand between the beasts and the gods.[42] Like the beasts, we are subject to sensuously conditioned needs and desires; like the gods, we are free rational agents, capable of recognizing and, presumably, following the dictates of morality. With regard to the capacity for morality, however, the crucial feature of our finitude does not seem to be simply the fact that we are creatures of needs and desires; it is rather that because of this we can misuse our freedom in that we do not necessarily choose to do what is objectively required. As Kant himself puts it, a finite rational agent requires an incentive because "the subjective character of its choice [*Willkür*] does not itself agree with the objective law of practical reason" (KprV 5: 79; 82). That is also why the law confronts us as an imperative and why moral requirements take the form of duties.

The obvious problem with this is that by claiming that we need an incentive to do what duty dictates, Kant would seem to be regressing to the heteronomous moral theory of his "semi-critical" period, thereby contradicting his whole account of autonomy and moral worth. Kant's strategy for avoiding this dilemma is to insist that although we need an incentive, the moral law itself functions as this incentive, indeed, as the sole incentive to morality (KprV 5: 72; 74). The basic idea here is familiar enough, namely, that if we perform a dutiful act for any reason other than that it is our duty, our performance lacks all moral worth (it has legality but not morality). What is puzzling is how the *law*, which specifies what our duty is, can also serve as an incentive for doing it, how the *principium diiudicationis* can be at the same time the *principium executionis*. This seems more like a relabeling of the old problem than a fresh attempt to resolve it.

As a first step in dealing with this puzzle, we must take Kant to be claiming that it is the *consciousness* of the law, not the law itself, that functions as the actual moral incentive.[43] This is only a first step, however, since this claim itself is puzzling. The implication is that the mere consciousness of the law of itself produces something like a "proattitude" toward the law in the agent, which in turn constitutes the conative factor in action from duty. The problem with this picture is not that it is totally incorrect, but rather that it is far too crude and invites misunderstanding. This is particularly true if it is taken as suggesting that the moral law exerts a kind of attractive force on the psychological state of an agent, so that one, as it were, comes to desire following its dictates. Far from advocating such a view, Kant explicitly dismisses it as "moral fanaticism" and insists that our relationship to the law must be defined in terms of duty rather than "spontaneous inclination" [*freiwilliger Zuneigung*] (5: 84; 87).[44]

Kant's characteristic insistence on duty makes it clear that if the moral law is to function as an incentive, it must be in virtue of the fact that it commands rather than that it attracts. In short, respect for the law consists simply in the recognition of its supremely authoritative character, which is to be taken to mean that it provides a reason for action that outweighs or overrides all other reasons, particularly those stemming from one's desires.[45] As Kant puts it in the *Groundwork*, "What I recognize immediately as a law for me, I recognize with respect, which means merely consciousness of the *subordination* of my will to a law without the mediation of external influences on my senses" (Gr 4: 402n; 69).

This immediately raises the question of in what sense such consciousness or recognition can serve as an *incentive,* and it is in his attempt to answer this that Kant provides what amounts to a phenomenology of respect. Denying the possibility of showing *how* such consciousness can function as an incentive on the grounds that this would be equivalent to showing how a free will is possible, he starts with the "fact" (itself an aspect of the fact of reason, as we shall see in Chapter 13) that it does function in this way and endeavors to show "what it effects (or better, must effect) in the mind, so far as it is an incentive" (KprV 5: 72; 75). What it effects is a feeling of a peculiar sort, with both a negative and a positive aspect. Respect itself is, therefore, a complex phenomenon, having both an intellectual and a sensible component. Consequently, it is to Kant's account of the interrelations of these components that we must turn if we wish to understand his conception of respect and its function in the moral life.

Although in general agreement with the brief treatment in the *Groundwork,* the account in the second *Critique* fine-tunes and modifies it in several significant ways. First, whereas he had previously characterized respect as "the awareness of a value which demolishes my self-love," Kant now distinguishes between self-love (*Selbstliebe*) or selfishness (*Eigenliebe*) and self-satisfaction (*Wohlgefallens*) or self-conceit (*Eigendünkel*) and claims that the consciousness of the law has a distinct effect on each (KprV 5: 76; 78). Second, in distinguishing between the negative and the positive aspects of the feeling of respect in his earlier treatment, Kant had suggested that the former has some analogy with fear and the latter with inclination (although he also insisted, of course, that they are not to be equated). Now, however, he describes the negative side of the feeling component as pain and connects it with humiliation, whereas the positive side, although distinguished sharply from pleasure, is connected with self-approbation (*Selbstbilligung*) (KprV 5: 76, 80–1; 78, 81–2). Finally, he adds the claim, totally lacking from the account in the *Groundwork,* that both aspects can be known a priori as the necessary consequences of the effect of this consciousness on sensuously affected rational agents such as ourselves (KprV 5: 79; 82).

Self-love and self-conceit are presented by Kant as the two species of self-regard (*Selbstsucht*) (KprV 5: 73; 75–6). The latter is an umbrella term encompassing the sum total of inclinations, the satisfaction of which is entitled happiness. Self-love, or more precisely, selfishness, is defined as "a predominant benevolence toward one's self (*philautia*)." In essence, it is the natural desire or propensity to seek one's own happiness, insofar as it gives rise to principles of action. Presumably, this is also Kant's point in characterizing it as a "propensity [*Hang*] to make the subjective determining grounds of one's choice into an objective determining ground of the will in general" (KprV 5: 74; 76–7). Since an "objective determining ground of the will" is the rule or principle governing the agent's choice of maxims, the basic idea here would seem to be that self-love is to be understood as the tendency to find a reason to act in what promises satisfaction. As such, it is a natural tendency in all finite rational beings.

Kant initially describes self-conceit simply as "self-satisfaction" (*arrogantia*) and states that it arises from self-love when this propensity "makes itself legislative and an unconditional practical principle." A few lines later, he remarks that it "decrees the subjective conditions of self-love as laws" (KprV 5: 74; 76–7). The extreme crypticness of this characterization of self-conceit makes interpretation difficult to say the least. Nevertheless, the general tenor of the account suggests that Kant takes it to be an attitude that has its basis in self-love but that goes beyond the latter by making the satisfaction of one's desires, which is naturally aimed at by self-love, into a matter of principle or right. In other words, self-conceit inflates the satisfaction of desire, which self-love already tends to regard as providing a reason for action, into an unconditional principle or "law" capable of overriding all other claims.[46]

This relationship, in turn, explains both the difference in the moral status of these two attitudes and the difference in the effect that the consciousness of standing under the moral law has on each.[47] Since it claims merely that satisfaction of desire provides a reason for action (as opposed to an overriding or unconditionally valid reason), self-love does not necessarily conflict with the moral law. As such, it needs only to be controlled or limited, not eliminated. Indeed, as a natural propensity, it cannot be eliminated. Kant expresses this by remarking that the consciousness of standing under the moral law merely "checks selfishness," transforming it into "reasonable self-love," that is, into a rational pursuit of self-interest limited by moral constraints. By contrast, since self-conceit rejects any constraints on the requirements of inclination, treating their satisfaction as a matter of right or law, it is in direct conflict with the moral law. Consequently, Kant insists that it must be not merely limited or constrained but "struck down" or "humiliated" (KprV 5: 73; 75–6).

The consciousness of the moral law produces this result because in making us aware of a genuine unconditioned practical law, it unmasks, as it were, the pretensions of sensibility (really of sensibly conditioned practical reason) to be itself the source of the supreme norm governing conduct or, equivalently, of all reasons for action.[48] The direct effect of all of this on the psychological state of an agent is a sense of humiliation, which, as such, is painful. Nevertheless, the law itself, as the source of this humiliation, is an object of respect.

The latter point is also the key to the positive side of Kant's account and, therefore, to the description of the process whereby sensuously affected rational agents such as ourselves come to take a pure, that is, nonsensuously conditioned, interest in morality. Once again, Kant's account is extremely cryptic, but it does seem possible to distinguish at least three aspects of it. First, Kant argues that in striking down self-conceit, the capacity of the will to submit itself to the dictates of pure practical reason is increased proportionally. This is a straightforward application of the principle that "any diminution of obstacles to an activity furthers this activity itself" (KprV 5: 79; 82). Second, since this increased capacity of the will would obviously be of little significance unless there were some interest in exercising it, Kant also contends that the recognition of the superiority of the moral law to the claims conditioned by our sensuous nature creates an esteem for this law and, therefore, an interest in obeying its dictates. Kant expresses both points in several places, perhaps the clearest of which is the following:

Since the idea [*Vorstellung*] of the moral law deprives self-love of its influence and self-conceit of its delusion [*Wahn*], it lessens the obstacle to pure practical reason and produces the idea of the superiority of its objective law to the impulses of sensibility; it increases the weight of the moral law by removing, in the judgment of reason, the counterweight of the moral law which bears on a will affected by sensibility. (KprV 5: 75–6; 78)[49]

The third and final positive aspect of respect is its connection with a sense of self-worth or self-approbation. Kant's basic claim is that the constraint or limitation of our sensuous nature and its pretensions, which supposedly results from the awareness of the authoritativeness of the moral law, is at the same time an elevation (*Erhebung*) of our rational nature and produces a feeling of self-approbation that is the positive counterpart of the negative feelings of pain and humiliation (KprV 5: 80–1; 82–3). As Kant makes clear, this is because the constraint is self-imposed, that is, imposed by one's own legislative reason. Consequently, the consciousness of this constraint is also a consciousness of oneself as an autonomous moral agent, and it is this consciousness that is "elevating" and produces a feeling of self-approbation. Moreover, in producing such feeling, the consciousness of the moral law likewise produces a pure moral interest and even, as Kant at one point suggests, a sense of "the sublimity of our own supersensuous existence" and "higher vocation" (*höhere Bestimmung*) as autonomous moral agents (KprV 5: 88; 90).

The latter claim makes it clear that Kant viewed his account of respect as the incentive to morality to be intimately connected with his conception of autonomy, and the same thought is also present in the *Groundwork,* where, as already noted, he describes the feeling as "self-produced from a rational concept." Similarly, in the *Critique of Practical Reason,* he insists that the feeling of respect is unique in being "practically" rather than "pathologically affected" and, therefore, as the product of an "intellectual" or "intelligible cause" (KprV 5: 73–5; 75–7). Accordingly, what we strictly speaking respect, on this view, is the autonomy of pure practical reason in ourselves and, by extension, in all rational agents.[50]

It is also the case, however, that much of Kant's language, for example, his reference to the removal of obstacles and to weights and counterweights, as well as his emphasis on the opposition between inclination and the law as competing "determining grounds of the will" reinforce the view that he conceives of the moral life as essentially one of conflict between psychic forces in which the human will is playing field and prize rather than autonomous arbitrator. On this reading, it is by weakening the opposing forces of inclination (through a process of humiliation) that the feeling of respect prepares the way for the ultimate victory of the law as the superior force. Moreover, this lends fresh credence to Henson's view (supposedly discredited) that Kant sometimes operates with a "battle citation" model of moral worth, which has the unacceptable implication that an action can have moral worth only if it results from the victory of the duty motive (now specified as respect for the law) in its battle with inclination.

Nevertheless, further consideration shows that, appearances to the contrary, Kant does not adopt a conflict-of-forces conception of agency in his account of respect. Central to such a conception is the assumption that inclinations directly determine the will by exerting an affective force on it. Given this assumption, it certainly seems to follow that if the law is to determine the will instead (as morality requires), it can do so only by exerting a stronger and contrary affective force. But we have already seen that inclinations do not determine the will in this manner. On the contrary, they do so only by being "incorporated into a maxim," that is, by being taken by the agent (at least implicitly) as sufficient reasons for action. Thus, as has been emphasized repeatedly, the spontaneity and rationality of the agent are involved even in heteronomous or inclination-based agency.

The relevance of this conception of agency to Kant's account of respect has been clearly shown by Andrews Reath. Appealing to the Incorporation Thesis (which he calls the "principle of election"), Reath suggests that the appropriate metaphor for picturing how the moral law confronts the claims of inclination in the consciousness of the moral agent is not that of a conflict of forces but rather "that of a struggle between two parties for something like legal authority or political legitimacy."[51] Although some of the details of Reath's analysis may be questionable, his central claim is both correct and illuminating.[52] The conflict is not between psychic forces but between principles, each of which claims to be the supreme ground for the selection of maxims. Indeed, this becomes clear once one realizes that it is self-conceit, not inclination or even self-love, that is opposed to the moral law and that this is because it makes the satisfaction of inclination into a matter of unconditioned right, thereby affirming a principle that is contrary to this law.

It is also important to realize that the principle of self-conceit entails a certain view about justification, namely, that a maxim is justified (reasonable to adopt) if and only if acting upon it serves to maximize the satisfaction of one's inclinations. By contrast, the moral law is a principle according to which the requirements of inclination, although not intrinsically evil, must nevertheless be subordinated to the dictates of an impartial rational norm, which itself serves as the ultimate ground of the justification of maxims. Consequently, the conflict is, indeed, between two principles or standards of justification.

Seen in this light, Kant's phenomenology of respect can be regarded as his account of the psychological effects on the "human faculty of desire" of this act of recognition. In both its negative and positive aspects, respect is produced by the consciousness of a rationally compelling value or norm (the moral law), not by the conquest of a weaker by a superior psychic force. Moreover, this enables us to see more clearly why Kant can characterize respect as the incentive to morality. If, as indicated, to respect the law is just to regard it as the ultimate norm governing one's choice of maxims, then, clearly, to respect it is to have a sufficient reason (although not a desire) to obey it. Finally, since this law is (or is at least taken to be) the self-imposed product of pure practical reason, we can also see more clearly why Kant holds that the consciousness of its applicability to oneself is, at one and the same time, both humiliating and elevating.

These considerations are likewise relevant to the assessment of the influential and essentially Hegelian critique of Kant's theory of respect mounted by Dieter Henrich. This critique falls into two parts. First, it is alleged that because of his dualistic, undialectical conception of the self, Kant is incapable of accounting for respect as a unitary phenomenon of the ethical consciousness. This, according to Henrich, is because Kant not only is forced to treat the two aspects of respect (the striking down or humiliation and the elevation) as two distinct acts, but he must assign them to two distinct faculties. Of these, only the former relates directly to sensibility, generating the feeling of pain. The latter, Henrich argues, cannot relate to sensibility because sensibility cannot be elevated. Consequently, it is merely a matter of the relation of practical reason to itself and, as such, involves only the intellectual side of the ethical consciousness. Second, on Kant's view, respect for the law is based merely on the awareness of its negative effect on sensibility (its coercive power), not on the recognition of its intrinsic rationality and authority. According to Henrich, this runs directly counter to the dictates of the ethical consciousness.[53]

In light of the preceding analysis, this critique can be easily shown to be wrong on both counts. First, the so-called direct effect of the law on sensibility (the feeling of pain arising from humiliation) is itself mediated by judgment. As we have seen, it results from the *recognition* (an intellectual act) of the superiority of the law, as a product of pure practical reason, to the "delusion of self-conceit," which consists in the granting of unconditional validity to the claims of reason in the service of inclination. Thus, the effect

127

is not direct at all. Second, since respect arises from the recognition of the superiority "in the judgment of reason" of one principle over another rather than from the awareness of its coercive force over sensibility, it does, indeed, have regard to the intrinsic rationality and authority of the law. The failure to recognize this, like the analogous failure to recognize how actions possessing moral worth can be with but not from inclination, stems from the failure to recognize the connection between Kant's moral psychology and his conception of rational agency.

7

Wille, Willkür, and Gesinnung

In the preceding two chapters we were concerned respectively with the change in Kant's conception of agency brought about by the introduction of the concept of autonomy and with the basic elements of his moral psychology as these are presented in the *Groundwork* and the *Critique of Practical Reason*. If we were to stop here, however, we would be left with a very incomplete view of Kant's conception of moral agency and, therefore, of his theory of freedom. In order to complete the picture, it is necessary to focus on elements of his theory that, although implicit in these earlier writings, are fully developed only in the major writings of the 1790s, namely, *Religion within the Limits of Reason Alone* and the *Metaphysic of Morals*.

The most important of these elements are the distinction between *Wille* and *Willkür* and the conception of *Gesinnung*. The former constitutes a much needed qualification, although not an abandonment, of the *Groundwork*'s account of will as practical reason; whereas the latter, which refers to the underlying disposition or character of a free agent, provides the basis for a further clarification of the conception of a good (and, indeed, an evil) will. We shall also see that it leads to a significant modification of the first *Critique*'s conception of an intelligible character. These, then, are the concerns of the present chapter, which, accordingly, is divided into two parts.

I. The *Wille–Willkür* distinction

Kant uses the terms *Wille* and *Willkür* to characterize respectively the legislative and executive functions of a unified faculty of volition, which he likewise refers to as *Wille*. Accordingly, *Wille* has both a broad sense in which it connotes the faculty of volition or will as a whole and a narrow sense in which it connotes one function of that faculty.[1] Needless to say, this together with the fact that *Willkür* and both senses of *Wille* can be rendered in English as "will" create major problems for the translator.[2] There are two main strategies in the standard English translations for dealing with this problem. One is to render *Wille* as "will" and *Willkür* as "choice"; the other is to render the former as "will" and the latter as "will^w."[3] For the most part I have simply followed the relevant translation, adding the German term when it helps to clarify. In order to avoid confusion and undo complexity in the present discussion, however, I shall simply keep to the German terms.

Although it is already operative in the *Critique of Practical Reason* and plays a major role in *Religion within the Limits of Reason Alone*, Kant first officially formulates this crucial distinction in the Introduction to the *Metaphysic of Morals*. Moreover, as if to emphasize its importance, he presents it in two separate places (MS 6: 213–14, 226; 10–11, 26–7). In the first, Kant is attempting to move from a general account of the faculty of desire (*Begehrungsvermögen*) to an analysis of human volition. In the second, he is concerned explicitly with the nature and grounds of obligation. Not surprisingly, this results in certain terminological differences. For example, in the first formulation *Wille* and *Willkür* are introduced as distinct aspects of the faculty of desire, whereas in the second such a characterization is completely absent. But since these differences do not reflect any inconsistency in doctrine, there is no need to consider the two formulations separately. Nevertheless, we shall see that there are some significant differences between the published account and the formulations contained in the unpublished *Vorarbeiten* (23: 248–9, 379, 383–4).

To begin with, all of the formulations agree in equating *Wille,* or will in its legislative function, with practical reason. Considered as such, *Wille* is the source of the laws that confront the human *Willkür* as imperatives. Although Kant is silent on the point, it seems clear that this must include both the categorical and hypothetical imperatives or, more generally, moral and prudential principles. Both are higher-order rules governing our selection of maxims and both are products of practical reason. Both, therefore, must be attributed to *Wille.*[4] Correlatively, it is *Willkür,* or will in its executive function, that can be said to act, that is, to decide, choose, and even wish under the governance of *Wille.*

In the second formulation, Kant states that laws stem from *Wille* and maxims from *Willkür.* The attribution of maxims to *Willkür* conflicts with the suggestion in the *Vorarbeiten* that they come from *Wille,* which Kant there defines as the "faculty of maxims" (*das Vermögen der Maximen*) (23: 378).[5] Nevertheless, it certainly reflects Kant's considered view. *Willkür,* after all, is the faculty or power of choice, and choice, for Kant, involves not merely particular actions but also maxims. Moreover, as we have seen, rational agents do not simply have maxims in the sense in which they have inclinations; rather they "make something" their maxim, and this always involves the spontaneity of *Willkür.*

Presumably, Kant's main motivation for introducing this distinction into his account of rational agency is to clarify his conception of the will as *self-determining* and, ultimately, as autonomous. In the *Groundwork,* Kant not only defines the will as practical reason, he also speaks of reason as determining (or failing to determine) the will. This locution, which is certainly not unique to Kant, presupposes a certain duality of function within the will, and the *Wille–Willkür* distinction provides just what is required in order to articulate this duality within unity. Thus, it is *Wille* in the narrow sense that provides the norm and *Willkür* that chooses in light of this norm. Similarly, this distinction allows us to speak of the will as giving the law to, or even as being the law for, itself, since this is just a matter of *Wille* giving the law to, or being the law for, *Willkür.* Strictly speaking, then, it is only

Wille in the broad sense that has the property of autonomy, since it is only *Wille* in this sense that can be characterized as a law to itself.[6]

Although this increased complexity does not constitute a major change of doctrine, it does shed light on some points that were unclear in the earlier works. One of these is the contrast between maxims and practical laws or, more generally, objective practical principles. In spite of some of Kant's language and the views of highly respected commentators such as Beck, it was argued in Chapter 5 that this is best taken as marking a contrast between first- and second-order practical principles. On this reading, it will be recalled, laws can never become maxims and vice versa; rather, maxims can conform (or fail to conform) to laws. This is necessary to preserve the normative character of laws vis-à-vis maxims. The assignment of laws to *Wille* and maxims to *Willkür* serves to reinforce this reading.

The correct interpretation of this distinction also helps to correct some of the ambiguities in Kant's theory of freedom. In the *Critique of Pure Reason,* Kant discusses freedom in terms of the human *Willkür.* Correlatively, in the *Groundwork* and to a considerable extent in the *Critique of Practical Reason,* the focus is on the freedom of *Wille,* construed in the broad sense as the entire faculty of volition. Also, freedom as a condition of rational agency was construed essentially as spontaneity and as a capacity to act from duty alone as autonomy. What is lacking in all of this is any attempt to link freedom, in its various senses, with the different aspects of volition. Kant makes this attempt in connection with his presentations of the *Wille–Willkür* distinction. Unfortunately, the interpretation of Kant's considered views on the matter is complicated by the discrepancies (or at least tensions) between the published account and some of the statements in the *Vorarbeiten.*

Much of the interpretive problem concerns *Wille* and its freedom or lack thereof. Although it is *determining* and not *determined,* Kant affirms unequivocally in the published text that only *Willkür* can be regarded as free and that *Wille,* which relates to nothing but the law (*der auf nichts anderes, als bloss auf Gesetz geht*), can be termed neither free nor unfree. The reason for this is simply that it is not concerned with actions but with the legislation for the maxims of actions (which is why it is identified with practical reason). As such, Kant contends it functions with absolute necessity and, yet, is not capable of being necessitated (MS 6: 226; 26).

By contrast, in the *Vorarbeiten,* Kant is far from consistent on this issue. In one passage, which closely parallels the published account, he affirms that only *Willkür* can be termed free (23: 248). Elsewhere, however, he characterizes *Wille* as "absolute practical spontaneity in the determination of *Willkür*" (23: 248). Moreover, in another passage, after characterizing the freedom of *Willkür* in terms of spontaneity, he remarks that *Wille* is free in another way (*ist auf eine andere Art frei*) because it is law giving and not law following. As such, he remarks, it is a positive capacity, not to choose, since with respect to its legislation there can be no question of choice, but rather "to determine the subject with respect to the sensible action" (*das Subject in Ansehung des sinnlichen der Handlung zu bestimmen*) (23: 249).

131

Finally, in yet another passage he states unequivocally that *Wille,* as practical reason, is free in itself (*ist an sich frei*) in the sense that it is not determined in its legislation by natural impulses (23: 383).

Taking these last two statements from the *Vorarbeiten* as our guide, we are led naturally to the conclusion that *Wille* is free in the sense of being autonomous. Accordingly, it is not surprising to find Lewis White Beck suggesting that autonomy pertains to *Wille* and spontaneity to *Willkür,* thereby correlating the two aspects of Kant's conception of freedom with the two functions of will.[7] Unfortunately, things are not quite that simple.[8] As already indicated, it is only *Wille* in the broad sense (the whole faculty of volition) that can be spoken of as autonomous, since *Wille* in the narrow sense (the legislative faculty) is not a law to itself but to *Willkür.* Given this, the most reasonable course seems to be to accept at face value the claim in the published text that *Wille* (in the narrow sense) can be described as neither free nor unfree. Alternatively, if we wish to attribute a sense of freedom to *Wille,* it can consist only in the negative property of not being subject to necessitation.

In light of what we have already learned about his conception of rational agency, Kant's account of the freedom of *Willkür* contains few surprises. In fact, it closely parallels the accounts of practical freedom in the *Critique of Pure Reason* and the *Lectures on Ethics.* Thus, human is distinguished from animal *Willkür,* or *arbitrium brutum,* on the grounds that although the latter is determined solely by inclination or impulse, the former can be determined by pure reason and, therefore, is affected but not determined by impulse. This is simply another way of making the by now familiar point that the freedom of *Willkür* is its practical spontaneity; even in acting on impulse, it is not causally determined by that impulse.

Admittedly, the situation is complicated by the fact that Kant distinguishes between a negative concept of the freedom of *Willkür,* which is just independence from determination by sensuous impulses, and a positive concept, which is characterized as the "capacity of pure reason to be of itself practical" (MS 6: 213–14; 10). This calls to mind the similar contrast drawn in the *Groundwork,* where the positive conception of freedom is identified with autonomy (Gr 4: 446–7; 114). Moreover, since the claim that pure reason is practical is equivalent to the claim that the will is autonomous, it suggests that Kant is here contrasting spontaneity and autonomy as the negative and positive conceptions of the freedom of *Willkür.*

Given what we have already seen, however, this cannot be correct, since the freedom of *Willkür* consists in spontaneity rather than autonomy. Nevertheless, Kant does invite such a misunderstanding by characterizing the positive concept in the way in which he does. What he should have said is rather that the positive concept of the freedom of *Willkür* is its capacity to act on the basis of the dictates of pure reason or, equivalently, pure *Wille.* To say this is to say that it has the capacity to select its maxims in virtue of their conformity to universal law, which is, of course, precisely what the categorical imperative requires. Insofar as it does so, pure reason is practical

132

and *Wille* (in the broad sense) autonomous; but the basic point is that this is the result of the spontaneity of *Willkür* being exercised in a particular way.

This understanding of the contrast between the negative and positive aspects of the freedom of *Willkür* is also operative in a controversial passage in which Kant responds to criticisms of his earlier formulations, specifically to that of Reinhold. In the second volume of his *Letters on the Kantian Philosophy* (*Briefe über die Kantische Philosophie*), Reinhold, like many subsequent critics, objected to Kant's identification of will with practical reason and freedom in the positive sense with autonomy on the grounds that it makes it inconceivable how one could freely violate the moral law. In order to account for such a possibility, Reinhold suggests that freedom be understood as a capacity for self-determination either in accordance with or contrary to the dictates of the law.[9] Apparently in response to this Kant writes:

Some have tried to define freedom of *Willkür* as the power to choose between the alternatives of acting with or against the law (*libertas indifferentiae*). But freedom of *Willkür* cannot be defined in this way, although choice as *phenomenon* gives frequent examples of this in experience. For we know freedom (as it is first made known to us through the moral law) only as a *negative* property in us: the property of not being *necessitated* to act by any sensuous determining ground. But we cannot explain *theoretically* freedom in its positive aspect, as it *exercises necessitation* on the sensuous *Willkür* – that is, freedom as *noumenon,* as the power of man viewed merely as an intelligent being [*als Intelligenz betrachtet*]. We can say only this: that while our experience of man as a *sensible being* shows that he can choose to act *against* the law as well as in *conformity with* it, his freedom as an *intelligible being* cannot be *defined* by this, since appearances cannot explain a supersensible object (like free *Willkür*). . . . For it is one thing to admit this proposition (on the basis of experience) and another thing to make it into the *principle that defines* the concept of free *Willkür* and serves as the universal criterion for distinguishing it (from *arbitrio bruto s. servo*). Merely to admit a proposition on the basis of experience is not to say that the characteristic so admitted belongs *necessarily* to the concept, but to define the concept in terms of this characteristic does imply this. – Only freedom with regard to the inner legislation of reason is really a capacity: the possibility of deviating from legislative reason is an incapacity. How, then, can this possibility be used to define freedom? (MS 6: 226; 25–6)

Soon after the publication of the *Metaphysic of Morals,* Reinhold responded with a vigorous reaffirmation of his previous position and critique of Kant's account of freedom, particularly as it is expressed in the passage just cited. Referring with approval to Kant's account of moral evil in terms of freedom in *Religion within the Limits of Reason Alone,* which appeared at virtually the same time as the second volume of his *Letters on the Kantian Philosophy,* he claims to find Kant's new account in terms of the *Wille–Willkür* distinction either unintelligible or untenable. Reinhold accepts Kant's basic premise that the morally relevant concept of freedom must be derived from our consciousness of the moral law, but he rejects his positive formulation of this concept in terms of the legislation of pure reason or, as he puts it, the spontaneity (*Selbststätigkeit*) of reason.

133

According to Reinhold, there are two possible alternatives: Either the only conception of freedom derivable from the moral law is that of the spontaneity of reason, in which case the presumed "capacity" to act immorally is not merely an incapacity but an impossibility, or freedom is construed as the capacity of the *person* for self-determination, either in accordance with or contrary to the dictates of reason, in which case the "capacity" to act immorally would not be a mere incapacity but rather the very same capacity without which moral action cannot be thought.[10] By treating immoral action as an expression of a mere incapacity, empirically accessible but not conceivable in terms of freedom, Kant is opting for the former alternative, thereby making it impossible to regard morally evil actions as products of freedom. This can be accomplished only by accepting the second alternative; but it has as its consequence the rejection of the inseparability of freedom and practical reason, which is the hallmark of the Kantian view.

Recently, Gerold Prauss has advanced a somewhat modified version of the Reinholdian critique. Prauss agrees with Reinhold that the source of the difficulty with Kant's position lies in the allegedly analytic connection between freedom, practical reason, and autonomy, since this leaves inexplicable the possibility of freely acting contrary to the dictates of morality. He likewise concurs with Reinhold in affirming the superiority (although not the adequacy) of the explanation of the possibility of morally evil actions in *Religion within the Limits of Reason Alone* to that contained in the *Metaphysic of Morals*. In fact, he even goes further in suggesting that the latter amounts to a regression to the totally inadequate standpoint of the *Groundwork*.[11] At the same time, however, he also claims that Reinhold went too far in separating freedom completely from practical reason. By advocating what amounts to a complete divorce between these conceptions, Reinhold, as Prauss sees it, effectively threw out the baby (morality understood in terms of autonomy) with the bath water (the will defined in terms of a morally practical reason).[12] Thus, in lieu of Kant's analytic connection and Reinhold's total separation, Prauss suggests a third view, according to which the connection between freedom and moral autonomy is regarded as synthetic.[13]

Kant's account of moral evil in *Religion within the Limits of Reason Alone* will be analyzed in the next chapter and the problem of the analyticity of the connection between freedom and the moral law (what I term the Reciprocity Thesis) will be among the central topics of the third part of this study. Even apart from these matters, however, there are some things to be said in response to the Reinhold–Prauss line of criticism, particularly as it relates to the passage currently before us. Moreover, since much of the ground for this response has been prepared by previous discussions, it is possible to be fairly brief.

To begin with, we can readily acknowledge the essential agreement of the account of freedom in this passage with that of the *Groundwork* while denying the negative implications drawn by Prauss from this agreement. As we saw in Chapter 5, already in the *Groundwork* Kant assumes a conception of freedom as practical spontaneity (a capacity to act in accordance with the conception of law), according to which even actions on desire-based or material maxims are free. Moreover, we also saw that this conception of freedom is neither equivalent to nor incompatible with the attribution of autonomy. Thus, although the issue is not specifically addressed in the *Groundwork,* the conceptual basis for an understanding of actions not motivated by respect for the law as free and imputable is already in place.

With regard to the account in the *Metaphysic of Morals,* the locus of the difficulty is Kant's positive characterization of freedom as the "power of reason to be itself practical." Reinhold apparently took this to mean that freedom just is the capacity of reason to determine the will; and if this were true, it would certainly follow that freedom to disobey the law has not been established. In fact, it would also follow, as Reinhold himself suggests, that the *Wille–Willkür* distinction itself is groundless, since free *Willkür,* on this view, reduces to *Wille.*[14]

Admittedly, Reinhold has a point here. Even setting aside the material from the *Vorarbeiten,* to which Reinhold presumably had no access, Kant's formulations of the *Wille–Willkür* distinction are hardly models of philosophical lucidity. Moreover, we have already seen that Kant should not have defined the freedom of *Willkür* as the "power of reason to be itself practical," since this pertains to *Wille* in the broad sense (the unified faculty of volition). We also saw, however, that this positive characterization of freedom presupposes a capacity of *Willkür* to be motivated by and to act according to the dictates of *Wille* in the narrow sense, or practical reason. Thus, properly construed, Kant's positive characterization of freedom is perfectly compatible with his overall conception of freedom and does not entail the collapse of the *Wille–Willkür* distinction.

Although perhaps not immediately obvious, it is also compatible with the possibility of freely acting contrary to the dictates of the moral law, which is the main point of the Reinhold–Prauss critique. The key to Kant's account is his reference to the "power" or "capacity" (*Vermögen*) of *Willkür.* As pertaining to *Willkür,* this must be understood as a power of the agent to be motivated by and act from respect for the law rather than as a power of reason to impose a law and to provide an incentive (to generate a feeling of respect). In the language currently before us, it is the capacity of *Willkür* to act according to the dictates of pure *Wille.* But clearly the possession of such a capacity is perfectly compatible with the failure to exercise it, and Kant does not deny this. Nor, Reinhold and Prauss to the contrary, does he deny that such failure is itself an expression of freedom.

What Kant does deny, and with good reason, is simply that a "capacity" for such failure, or in Reinhold's terms, a capacity either to accept or reject the dictates of pure practical reason, be included in the *definition* of freedom. To cite his own formulation, he denies that it can be regarded as the "universal criterion" for distinguishing free *Willkür,* or *arbitrium liberum,* from *arbitrium brutum.* Granted, an *arbitrium brutum* does not have the capacity to disobey the moral law or, more generally, the dictates of practical reason; but this is obviously only because it does not have the capacity to obey them either.[15] Kant's claim, then, which is certainly a reasonable one, is that only a being with freedom, positively construed as the capacity for self-determination on the basis of rational grounds (the capacity to act according to the conception of law), can be meaningfully conceived to have a corresponding capacity to deviate from the dictates of reason. In a word, only a being with freedom, positively construed, can be regarded as capable of misusing that freedom. Nevertheless, deviation from the law constitutes a misuse of such freedom rather the absence of it because, as we have seen repeatedly, even our heteronomous actions involve the spontaneity of *Willkür*.[16]

II. Kant's concept of *Gesinnung*

We move from the conception of *Willkür* to that of *Gesinnung* when we raise the question of the ground of the specific acts of the former, including acts involving the misuse of freedom. In other words, the conception of *Gesinnung* refers to the enduring character or disposition of an agent, which underlies and is reflected in particular choices.[17] In Kant's terms, it is "the ultimate subjective ground of the adoption of maxims" (Rel 6: 25; 20). Although Kant first explicates this conception in *Religion within the Limits of Reason Alone*, in connection with his account of radical evil, it is already at work in the *Critique of Practical Reason* and is a key ingredient in his later account of virtue in *The Doctrine of Virtue* as well. Nevertheless, we shall here be concerned with the analysis of the general features of this important conception, saving the specific discussion of its role in Kant's accounts of evil and virtue for the next chapters.

Even apart from a consideration of the latter topics, the need for such a conception should be apparent from the preceding discussion of Kant's moral psychology. For example, the *Groundwork*'s focus on the moral worth of particular actions might create the impression that Kant conceives of these actions as grounded in free-floating, isolated decisions (for the law or inclination) that stand in no connection with an enduring moral agent with a determinate nature and interests. To be sure, we saw that this impression is incorrect because the central concept of a good will, which the introduction of the notion of moral worth was intended to clarify, refers precisely to the underlying character or disposition of the agent. Nevertheless, the fact remains that since Kant never really discusses this underlying character or disposition or explicates its relationship to the particular actions that possess or fail to possess moral worth in the *Groundwork*, the moral psychology of that work remains seriously incomplete.

The missing element is provided by the conception of *Gesinnung* as described in the preceding discussion. By introducing it, Kant makes it clear that he recognizes that the choices of rational agents, or in his terms, the maxims they adopt, must be conceived in relation to an underlying set of intentions, beliefs, interests, and so on, which collectively constitute that agent's disposition or character. Otherwise these choices and maxims could be neither imputed nor explained; they would have to be regarded as completely arbitrary expressions of a "liberty of indifference," without any "sufficient reason." In this respect, then, Kant's doctrine of *Gesinnung* may be assigned the systematic purpose of saving the rationality of decision.[18] In addition, by enabling us to regard a person's specific acts and decisions as expressions of an underlying set of intentions or pattern of willing, which can itself be the object of a moral evaluation, it provides a means for thinking about the moral life of a person as a whole.[19]

So far, then, there is nothing particularly novel or paradoxical in Kant's conception of *Gesinnung.* On the contrary, it reflects his partial agreement with a tradition in moral psychology that stretches at least back to Aristotle and that includes, in addition to Leibniz and Hume, contemporary thinkers who insist that moral responsibility presupposes that actions be connected with the character of the agent. Where Kant breaks with this tradition and where problems begin to arise is with his insistence that, like the specific maxims adopted on the basis of it, an agent's *Gesinnung* is itself somehow chosen. In insisting on this point, Kant appears to go well beyond the widely shared intuition that, to some extent at least, we are responsible for our characters as well as for our deeds and to affirm a paradoxical, if not totally incoherent, doctrine of a timeless act of self-constitution. At least that is how it has seemed to many commentators.

Moreover, such a reading appears to be confirmed by the *Critique of Practical Reason,* where Kant provides the metaphysical underpinnings for his conception of *Gesinnung.* For example, while speaking of a subject's intelligible existence as thing in itself, he remarks:

In this existence nothing is antecedent to the determination of his will; every action and, in general, every changing determination of his existence according to the inner sense, even the entire history of his existence as a sensuous being, is seen in the consciousness of his intelligible existence as only a consequence, not as a determining ground of his causality as a noumenon. (KprV 5: 97–8; 101)

And in discussing repentance:

For the sensuous life is but a single phenomenon in the view of an intelligible consciousness of its existence (the consciousness of freedom), and this phenomenon, so far as it contains merely manifestations of the disposition [*Gesinnung*] which is of concern to the moral law (i.e., appearances of character [*Charakter*]), must be judged not according to natural necessity which pertains to it as appearance but according to the absolute spontaneity of freedom. (KprV 5: 99; 102)

And, again, in explaining how one might be justified in holding persons responsible for criminal acts, even though they give evidence of a fixed and hopelessly depraved character (*Denknungsart*) from early childhood, he writes:

This could not happen if we did not suppose that whatever arises from man's choice [*Willkür*] (as every intentional act undoubtedly does) has a free causality as its ground, which from early youth expresses its character [*Charakter*] in its appearances (its actions). These actions, by the uniformity of conduct, exhibit a natural connection. But the latter does not render the vicious quality of the will necessary, for this quality is rather the consequence of the freely assumed evil and unchangeable principles. (KprV 5: 100; 103)

Finally, in *Religion within the Limits of Reason Alone,* in discussing the sense in which a *Gesinnung* can be regarded as innate, he writes:

To have a good or an evil disposition [*Gesinnung*] as an inborn natural constitution does not here mean that it has not been acquired by the man who harbors it, that he is not the author of it, but rather, that it has not been acquired in time (that he has *always* been good, or evil, *from his youth up*). The disposition, i.e., the ultimate subjective ground of the adoption of maxims, can only be one and applies universally to the whole use of freedom. Yet this disposition itself must have been adopted by free choice (*Willkür*), for otherwise it could not be imputed. (Rel 6: 25; 20)

In Chapter 2 it was argued that Kant's claims about the intelligible character and its noumenal activities in the *Critique of Pure Reason* need not be construed in the metaphysically objectionable way in which they usually are. In particular, it was claimed that the contrast between empirical and intelligible character is not between two ontologically distinct characters, which are somehow causally related, but between "two points of view," representing two models of agency, in terms of which the activity of a rational agent can be construed. So interpreted, the conception of intelligible character really reduces to the thought of practical spontaneity (the Incorporation Thesis), which functions regulatively in the conception of ourselves as rational agents with an empirical character. Moreover, it was noted that this conception involves the idea of an independence of "the conditions of time" (the causal principle of the Second Analogy) but not an actual timelessness.

Even if all this be granted, however, it does not appear that a similar analysis can be given to the passages cited in the preceding. In these and similar texts, Kant certainly seems to be committed to something like a full-fledged doctrine of noumenal agency, that is, to the conception of a merely intelligible subject that creates its own character, together with its phenomenal manifestations, through an unconditioned timeless activity. According to this doctrine, the intelligible character stands to the empirical character of the same agent in roughly the same relation as God stands to his creation in traditional Judeo–Christian theology.

Moreover, on any such interpretation, Kant is vulnerable to many of the objections prevalent in the literature. To begin with, if we take literally the notion that one chooses one's intelligible character, which in turn serves as the transcendental cause or ground of one's empirical character, then it apparently becomes impossible to keep the attribution of responsibility within intuitively plausible limits. This is because, according to Kant's empirical realism, one's empirical character is itself a causally conditioned and conditioning item in the phenomenal world. Consequently, in choosing one's character, one is also choosing a causal history that reaches indefinitely into the past and future. Indeed, it seems difficult, on this view, to avoid the con-

138

clusion that one is choosing and, therefore, is responsible for the entire phenomenal world.[20]

Furthermore, since the foundational choice, itself outside time, supposedly determines the temporally appearing empirical character in its entirety, and since this empirical character, together with certain "contributing causes," is the causally sufficient condition of all of the specific phenomenal actions of rational agents, it seems to follow that our freedom is limited to a single "intelligible act" in which we choose our character. On this reading, then, Kant's position reduces to a variant of the Platonic myth of Er, in which each soul (noumenal self) freely chooses whom to be in a deterministic universe.[21] Quite apart from whatever metaphysical difficulties such a position involves, it obviously entails a denial of the possibility of attributing freedom in the ordinary sense of a capacity to do otherwise to rational agents within the world. To be sure, Schopenhauer, who attributes just such a view to Kant, takes this consequence as the sign of the profundity of the Kantian view.[22] Nevertheless, it seems reasonably clear that Kant could not accept such a consequence, particularly in light of his emphasis on moral progress and on the possibility of a radical conversion.[23]

Finally, and perhaps most significantly, it might be argued that the very idea of a choice of *Gesinnung* is incoherent. The notion of *Gesinnung* was introduced in the first place to ground the rationality of choice and the imputability of action. It supposedly does this by linking discrete acts of *Willkür* with an enduring agent possessing a set of beliefs, interests, intentions, and the like. How, then, can one assume a choice of *Gesinnung* without opening up the possibility of either an infinite regress or, equally unacceptable, a choice for which no ground or reason is available? In short, if choice presupposes *Gesinnung,* then it cannot be claimed that *Gesinnung* is itself chosen. Correlatively, if, as Kant also maintains, we are always free with respect to our past character, then it would appear that *Gesinnung* neither guarantees the needed continuity of personality nor provides an adequate basis for understanding and imputing actions. In both respects, then, it would seem that the conception of *Gesinnung* not only fails to do the job for which it is intended but also leads one quickly into paradox and incoherence.

These latter considerations further suggest that the problem with Kant's conception of *Gesinnung* may be that it attempts to combine two incompatible requirements, both of which are regarded as conditions of agency. One is the need for an enduring character, with reference to which choice can be understood; the other is the need (stemming from the presuppositions of morality) to regard this character as itself something for which an agent is responsible and that can be radically transformed by an act of freedom. Reflecting on this tension, a recent critic has suggested that rather than being a coherent conception, *Gesinnung* reduces under analysis to an unstable combination of the Aristotelian *hexis* and the Sartrean *"projet fondamental."*[24] Underlying this criticism is the view that the continuity of personality supposedly provided by *Gesinnung,* understood in the Aristotelian sense as a fixed and determinate character, is incompatible with the radical freedom built into Kant's conception of agency. Kant needs but cannot have it both ways. Or so it would seem.

In dealing with these problems, we must begin by acknowledging that the introduction of the conception of *Gesinnung* marks a significant deepening of the first *Critique* theory of freedom and that the notion of intelligible character operative in the second *Critique* cannot be equated with that of the first. Moreover, these changes are to be understood as concomitant to the changes in Kant's moral theory brought about by the introduction of the principle of autonomy. Given this principle, we have seen that Kant could no longer remain sanguine about the possibility that "that which, in relation to sensuous impulses, is entitled freedom, may . . . in relation to higher and more remote operating causes be nature again" (A803/B831). Thus, Kant found it necessary in the *Critique of Practical Reason* to insist that morality requires transcendental freedom (KprV 5: 97; 100–1) and even to redefine practical freedom, so as to make it accord with the kind of freedom presupposed by autonomy (KprV 5: 93–4; 96–8). This in turn required a modification of the original conception of an intelligible character.

This modification takes the form of a thickening. Rather than being limited to the bare idea of practical spontaneity or "incorporation," it now encompasses the specifically moral nature of the agent (the moral quality of the will). As such, it is a "character" not simply in the first *Critique* sense of a "law of causality" but also in the anthropological sense of a way of thinking or "cast of mind" (*Denkungsart*).[25] The subsequent account of *Gesinnung* in *Religion within the Limits of Reason Alone* only makes fully explicit what is already implicit in the second *Critique,* namely, that this character or disposition is to be construed as an agent's fundamental maxim with respect to the moral law.[26]

Nevertheless, these changes are best understood as modifications of the original conception of rational agency brought about by the already mentioned developments in Kant's moral theory rather than as an abandonment of this conception. Thus, in spite of first impressions, it remains possible (indeed, necessary) to take Kant's later claims about intelligible character and *Gesinnung* in a regulative rather than a straightforwardly ontological sense. Moreover, by this means we can once again avoid having to saddle Kant with the conception of a timeless noumenal agent making a timeless choice of its empirical character. The difference is simply that what is now being "regulated" or "modeled" is not just the conception of ourselves as rational agents *überhaupt* but rather the conception of ourselves as autonomous moral agents subject to the requirements of the categorical imperative. In short, the practical regulative idea of the first *Critique* becomes the morally practical regulative idea of the second.

The morally practical, as opposed to dogmatically metaphysical, nature of Kant's claims in the problematic passages cited earlier emerges from a closer attention to their language. Thus, although Kant does refer to a subject's "intelligible existence" and "causality as noumenon," (KprV 5: 97–8; 101) it seems clear from the context that he is not propounding a noumenalistic metaphysics but simply describing how subjects, qua responsible moral agents, must take themselves. Similarly, when, in his discussion of repentance, he states that "the sensuous life is but a single phenomenon" that must be "judged . . . according to the absolute spontaneity of freedom," (KprV 5: 99; 102) he is not positing a timeless noumenal choice of one's entire character but merely indicating that we remain responsible for all our deeds and, therefore, cannot, as it were, outgrow our need to repent for past transgressions. Such a doctrine may be objectionable on moral grounds, but it is not a bit of wild metaphysics. Finally, Kant provides an important clue regarding his understanding of the notion of a choice of intelligible character or *Gesinnung* when he suggests that it consists in the adoption of "unchangeable principles" (KprV 5: 100; 103).

The latter point is absolutely crucial and receives further explication in *Religion within the Limits of Reason Alone,* where, as already noted, Kant states that an agent's *Gesinnung,* or the "ultimate subjective ground," of the adoption of maxims is itself a maxim. This result is the logical consequence of Kant's most fundamental assumptions. The only other possible candidate that he recognizes for ultimate subjective ground is a natural impulse, and this is dismissed on the grounds that it is incompatible with freedom (Rel 6: 21; 17).[27] If one is to avoid regarding an agent's *Gesinnung* as a product of nature rather than freedom, which would effectively undermine morality by reducing goodness or badness of will to a matter of constitutive moral luck, then it is necessary to consider it as itself chosen. But as chosen, this *Gesinnung* must itself be conceived as a maxim, albeit one of the highest order, that provides a direction or orientation for the moral life of the agent viewed as a whole.

We shall be returning to this difficult notion of a fundamental maxim in the next chapter in connection with the analysis of Kant's account of radical evil. For the present, the main point is simply that given this characterization of the choice of a *Gesinnung,* it cannot be identified with the choice of one's character or nature in the full Aristotelian sense. Indeed, the latter, for Kant, is to a large extent a function of factors such as temperament or "way of sensing" (*Sinnesart*), over which a person has relatively little control.[28]

The relevance of this to the criticisms cited earlier is direct and obvious. Implicit in these criticisms and in many of the standard attacks on Kant's conception of freedom is the assumption that in choosing a *Gesinnung* one is, in effect, choosing a phenomenal self in toto, or at least a "character" in the usual sense of a relatively fixed nature, construed roughly along the lines of the Aristotelian *hexis.* This in turn is taken to entail both that one must also choose (or at least be responsible for) the causal chain (or chains) in which this self or character participates and that once this chain is chosen and the agent's character fixed, there is no room for any further exercise of freedom. If in spite of this Kant still insists on such freedom, it can be viewed simply as a further indication of the incoherence of his position.

But if Kant is not committed to the view that we are totally responsible for our natures as sensuous beings, then clearly he is not committed to the absurd view that in "choosing ourselves," we are also choosing the entire causal chain of which the actions of our phenomenal selves form a part. The latter is a metaphysical reading of Kant's claims that ignores their practical context, that is, the fact that he is concerned explicitly with the moral quality of the will (for which we must somehow be responsible). The exclusively practical force of Kant's views on this matter is well expressed in his dictum that "man *himself* must make or have made himself into whatever, in a moral sense, whether good or evil, he is to become" (Rel 6: 44; 40). The key here is the qualifying expression "in a moral sense," since it makes clear that only with respect to their fundamental principles may persons be thought to choose or constitute themselves.

Similar considerations apply to the objection that Kant's doctrine limits free agency to a single primordial choice through which our character is fixed. Although this consequence seems to follow from an understanding of a choice of *Gesinnung* as something like a choice of a disposition or character in the full-blown psychological sense, it does not follow if it is taken merely as the choice of a fundamental maxim or set of principles, that is, of a *Denkungsart*. Since the relationship between a maxim as a "general determination of the will" and the more specific practical rules and particular actions falling under it is logical rather than causal, the relationship between the fundamental choice of *Gesinnung* and the particular choices that rational agents make in light of their *Gesinnung* is likewise broadly logical rather than causal.[29] Accordingly, the particular actions of a rational agent are not to be regarded, in Leibnizian or Humean fashion, as the causal consequences of that agent's *Gesinnung*.

But neither are they to be regarded as deductive consequences of it, which is why the relationship must be characterized as "broadly" logical. Practical reasoning, as Kant conceives it, is not a rigid, quasi-mechanical process. On the contrary, as we saw in Chapter 5, a major difference between genuine maxims and mere *Vorsätze* is that the former, unlike the latter, leave scope for practical judgment, that is, for a determination by the subject whether and how to act on a maxim in a particular situation. Since a *Gesinnung* or fundamental maxim is, by definition, a practical principle of the utmost generality, dictating a basic orientation of the will rather than a particular course of action, the same presumably applies to it as well. Thus, properly construed, Kant's conception of *Gesinnung* does not entail that there is, strictly speaking, only one free act.

Although it once again raises issues that are best considered in the next chapter, the understanding of a *Gesinnung* as a fundamental maxim also helps to mitigate considerably, if not totally remove, the apparent incoherence in the idea that one chooses one's own *Gesinnung*. First, as an act of *Willkür*, it presupposes the dictates of *Wille*, that is, it presupposes objective practical principles, both the moral law and the principle of one's own happiness or self-love, and (as we shall see in the next chapter) consists in a ranking or prioritizing of these principles and the requirements stemming from them. Thus, in spite of what was suggested earlier, the Kantian choice of *Gesinnung* differs decisively from the Sartrean *projet fondamental*. Second, and this point will be developed further shortly, since we are dealing with a regulative, morally practical model, we no more need regard this choice as a psychological or, worse, metaphysical occurrence than we need regard the social contract as a historical occurrence. On the contrary, just as in the case of the social contract, it is precisely by regarding it as an idea of reason rather than as an actual event that its morally practical force is preserved.[30]

Nor may it be claimed that by allowing for the possibility of a change of *Gesinnung*, Kant is either undermining or trivializing this conception. As we shall see in subsequent chapters, Kant holds open the possibility of a "conversion" from evil to good principles as well as a "fall" from good to evil ones. Since it involves a change of principles or of a fundamental maxim rather than the miraculous casting off of a full-fledged nature or Aristotelian *hexis*, such a change is conceivable given the Kantian conception of freedom. But since it is a change of a fundamental maxim and, therefore, a reorientation of one's moral life, it can hardly be regarded as an everyday event. Thus, the bare possibility of such a revolution in one's cast of mind does not undermine the continuity of personality or the rationality of decision, which the conception of a *Gesinnung* was introduced to secure in the first place. Moreover, it secures these in a way that is compatible with Kantian freedom by providing a direction or orientation for the will, a kind of meta-reason or supreme value with respect to which we decide on particular courses of action rather than by functioning as a fixed *habitus* that causally conditions our subsequent choices.

In response, it might be argued that the preceding remarks side-step rather than address the major difficulties raised by Kant's doctrine. The problem is that in trying to make sense of Kant's account by stressing the analogy between a *Gesinnung* and ordinary maxims, we have ignored the significant difference between them. Indeed, Kant himself calls attention to this difference by insisting that, although acquired, a *Gesinnung* is not acquired in time or, as he later puts it with respect to the propensity (*Hang*) to evil, its origin is not in time but in "rational representation" (Rel 6: 39–40; 35). How, then, are we to understand this seemingly paradoxical notion of a timeless acquisition?

Since what is allegedly acquired is not simply a *Gesinnung* but a radically evil one, the full treatment of this topic must await the discussion of radical evil in the next chapter. Fortunately, however, it is possible to sketch the basic outlines of the Kantian response to the timeless acquisition problem without considering the specifics of his theory of evil. Once again, the key is the specifically ethical or practical context in which the claim arises. Taken in this context, the conception of an acquisition that is not in time reflects the foundational role of this acquisition in the moral life, its inseparability from the conception of ourselves as moral agents, rather than an appeal to a metaphysical doctrine of pre- or nontemporal choice. Such a role is clearly indicated by Kant in the passages cited earlier, when he remarks that this *Gesinnung* is expressed "from early youth" or "from . . . youth up." Similarly, in his account of radical evil, he accepts the characterization of guilt as "innate" on the grounds that "it may be discerned in man as early as the first manifestations of the exercise of freedom" (Rel 6: 38; 33). This explicitly temporal language would seem out of place if Kant were affirming some kind of pre- or nontemporal origin for *Gesinnung*. It is perfectly appropriate, however, if the claim is merely that one's *Gesinnung* is coextensive with one's moral personality, that is, coextensive with the operation of freedom.[31]

The main point can be clarified by comparing Kant's characterization of the mode of acquisition of *Gesinnung* with the appeal in his theoretical philosophy to the juridical notion of an "original acquisition" (*acquisitio originaria*) in order to explicate the origin of the representations of space, time, and the pure concepts of the understanding.[32] Rejecting the view that these representations, as opposed to the "law of the mind" or its capacity to form them, are innate, Kant nonetheless insists, in virtue of their function as conditions of the possibility experience, that they cannot be derived from experience. His solution is to offer a third alternative, namely, that they are original acquisitions, meaning thereby that their genesis can be traced to the very operations of the mind through which experience is constituted.[33] As such, they are conceptually but not temporally prior to experience.

Although Kant does not use the expression, the acquisition of a *Gesinnung* may likewise be regarded as "original" because it is inseparable from and constitutive of our nature as moral agents or, equivalently, of our moral personality. Similarly, it can be claimed that it is not acquired "in time," meaning thereby in the course of moral or "spiritual" development, because it is a precondition of the very possibility of such a development or, indeed, of a life conceivable in terms of moral categories (just as space, time, and the categories are preconditions of the possibility of experience).

The upshot of the matter, then, is that by asserting that a person's *Gesinnung* must be thought of as acquired, but not in time, Kant is making a conceptual claim rather than offering a metaphysical explanation. This claim, in turn, is grounded in a reflection on the conditions of the possibility of imputation, which for Kant is equivalent to the conditions of the possibility of personality in the moral sense.[34] Starting with the fundamental principle that "man *himself* must make or have made himself into whatever, in a moral sense, whether good or evil, he is to become," Kant is led by his understanding of the moral requirement to act from respect for the law to extend the scope of this principle from particular acts to the general orientation of the will. We shall see shortly that this move likewise underlies Kant's notorious "rigorism" and his analysis of radical evil.

The interpretation of Kant's account of *Gesinnung* as a conceptual claim or, more precisely, an interlocking set of such claims is similar to the treatment given to the first *Critique* account of an intelligible character in Chapter 2. The difference stems from the explicitly ethical context of the present discussion. In the former case, it was argued that the attribution of an intelligible character conceived in terms of the transcendental idea of freedom functions as a necessary condition of the conception of ourselves as rational agents. Thus, although the epistemic possibility that we may be complex mechanisms rather than genuine agents was acknowledged, it was claimed that we can act only under the latter assumption and that this suffices to secure a firm regulative status for the idea of freedom. In the present case, however, we are concerned with the presuppositions of the conception of ourselves not simply as rational agents but also as autonomous moral agents capable of acting from respect for the law and, therefore, subject to imputation. Consequently, the cogency of this conception of a *Gesinnung,* like most of the conceptions dealt with in this part of the study, rests ultimately on Kant's grounding of the moral law.

8
Radical evil

As indicated in the last chapter, the conception of *Gesinnung* cannot be understood fully apart from a consideration of the uses to which Kant puts it. Since the most explicit and best known of these uses is in the account of radical evil in *Religion within the Limits of Reason Alone,* the present chapter is devoted to an exploration of this difficult, yet intriguing, text. The discussion is divided into three parts. The first analyzes Kant's conception of radical evil and its connections with other features of his moral theory, particularly his rigorism. It also maintains that the roots of this conception are to be found in the *Groundwork.* The second considers the claim that there is a propensity (*Hang*) to evil in human nature and, therefore, that radical evil is universal. It argues that in spite of Kant's tendency to present it as an empirical generalization, this doctrine is best understood as a postulate of morally practical reason and, therefore, as a synthetic a priori claim. As such, it stands in need of a deduction, and the attempt is made to provide one for him. The third examines Kant's distinction between stages or degrees of radical evil and his claim that such evil is compatible with a good will. Its focal point is the connection between radical evil and self-deception.

I. Radical evil and rigorism

Kant's discussion of radical evil is deeply perplexing. In the process of finally providing the much needed account of the connection between freedom and moral evil, he raises a whole set of new problems with the claim that there is a propensity to evil in human nature or, more simply, that "man is evil by nature" (Rel 6: 32; 27). Thus, just as critics of his earlier writings in moral philosophy have attacked Kant for his apparent identification of free action with action motivated by respect for the law, so the worry now is that the doctrine that mankind is radically evil or evil by nature is incompatible with the basic principles of his moral philosophy, not to mention our moral intuitions. How can we be both autonomous agents capable of acting from respect for the law and radically evil? And if we are evil "by nature," how can this evil be imputed to us at all? Indeed, given Kant's conception of freedom, what can it mean to claim that we are evil by *nature*?

Confronted with these problems, it is tempting to follow the lead of Schiller and Goethe (among others) and to dismiss Kant's whole account of evil as an unfortunate concession to Christian orthodoxy, thoroughly at variance with the "critical" spirit of his moral philosophy.[1] Moreover, in support of this view, one can note that the doctrine appears only in *Religion within the Limits of Reason Alone,* a work in which Kant is concerned to provide what today might be called an attempt at a "rational reconstruction" of Christian theology.

In spite of the very real difficulties presented by Kant's discussion and the conciliatory tone adopted toward Christian theology, such a negative reaction is not warranted. Since many of the difficulties concern the conception of *Gesinnung* analyzed in the last chapter, a beginning has already been made in addressing them. On the basis of this analysis, I shall now attempt to show that Kant's doctrine of radical evil is not only in accord with but also a consequence of the basic principles of his moral philosophy. Admittedly, such a result is far from a defense of the doctrine itself; but it does help us to gain a deeper understanding of Kant's overall conception of moral agency. We shall also see in the next chapter that it enables us to understand crucial features of Kant's accounts of virtue and the pursuit of holiness as a moral ideal, both of which presuppose the doctrine of radical evil.

To begin with, it is important to keep in mind that by "radical evil" Kant does not mean a particular, especially perverse, form of evil but rather the root or ground of the very possibility of all moral evil. Moral evil itself, clearly enough, must consist for Kant in the adoption of maxims contrary to the law. Consequently, radical evil must be the "subjective ground" (itself a maxim) of the possibility of the adoption of immoral maxims. Kant's operative assumption is that without such a ground, which he characterizes as a propensity, moral evil would be impossible.

An underlying premise of Kant's account, and the source of a good deal of the dissatisfaction with it, is his ethical "rigorism," which he contrasts with "latitudinarianism." By the former, he understands the position that holds that with respect to both morally relevant actions and character, there is no moral middle ground, that is, every action to which moral categories are applicable at all and every moral agent must be characterizable as either good or evil. By the latter, he understands the contradictory of this, that is, the position that allows for the possibility of a moral middle ground in the case of both actions and character. Although he admits that the latter is suggested by experience, he insists that the former is required by sound moral philosophy (Rel 6: 22–3; 18–19).

Rigorism, so construed, is clearly already implicit in the accounts of moral worth and of respect as the sole moral incentive in the *Groundwork* and the *Critique of Practical Reason.* In presenting his argument for rigorism, however, Kant relies heavily on the Incorporation Thesis (which is here formulated). Starting with the premise that respect for the law is an incentive, Kant reasons that since the freedom of the will (*Willkür*) entails that an incentive can determine the will only if it is "taken up" into a maxim, it follows that the failure to make it one's incentive, that is, the failure to make the thought of duty or respect for the law the sufficient motivation for one's conduct, must be regarded as resting on the adoption of an alternative principle of action. But since the adoption of an alternative principle involves an

147

explicit deviation from the law, such an act must be characterized as "evil." Correlatively, since the adoption of a deviant principle or maxim itself reflects the *Gesinnung* of the agent, the agent must likewise be regarded as evil (Rel 6: 23–5; 18–20). Thus, Kant argues for both act and agent rigorism, although it is clearly the latter that is his focus of concern.

In illustrating both forms of rigorism, Kant appeals to his favorite contrast between a "real opposition" or contrariety and a merely logical opposition or contradiction. The point is that it is precisely because the moral law provides a motivating force that the failure of an agent to act according to its dictates cannot be regarded merely as the result of the law's failure to motivate (serve as an incentive). On the contrary, it must be seen as the consequence of a real opposition of *Willkür*, an opposition that is expressed in the adoption of a deviant maxim, which in turn reflects an evil *Gesinnung* (Rel 6: 23n; 18).

This uncompromisingly bivalent account of the moral life has struck many critics as both unduly harsh and incompatible with our moral intuitions, which seem to support a more nuanced view, allowing room for gradations of virtue as well as gradual moral improvement.[2] We shall see later in this chapter and in the next that Kant does, in fact, have room for a more nuanced view with respect to both evil and virtue. Our present concern, however, is still with the connection between Kant's rigorism and his doctrine of radical evil. In order to clarify this connection, it is first necessary to consider Kant's brief account of the "predispositions" (*Anlagen*) to good. Since this account constitutes his version of the Christian (and Rousseauean) doctrine that man is created good, it provides the indispensable backdrop for understanding his conception of the "Fall."

According to Kant, there are three such predispositions or, more precisely, a single and original predisposition to good that can be divided, with respect to function, into three elements. Each of these, Kant notes, can be considered a distinct element in the determinate nature (*Bestimmung*) of the human race. At the end of his account, he indicates that the force of characterizing them (or it) as "original" is to underscore their status as necessary ingredients in human nature. In short, they are fundamental and essential capacities without which a truly human existence is inconceivable (Rel 6: 26–8; 21–3).

The first is the predisposition to "animality." It concerns man taken as a "living" being and encompasses the prerational, instinctual basis of human nature. More specifically, it involves three fundamental impulses (self-preservation, sexual propagation, and community), all of which are included under the general label "physical or *mechanical* self-love." The second is the predisposition to "humanity." It concerns man taken as a "rational" animal and basically involves the capacity to use reason in the service of inclination. The third is the predisposition to "personality." It concerns man not simply as a rational animal but also as a moral or "accountable" being, that is, a being for whom reason is practical of itself.

Although he notes that the first two can be used contrary to their ends,

148

Kant insists that they are all good, not merely in the negative and weak sense that they are compatible with morality but also in the positive and strong sense that they are "predispositions *toward good* (they enjoin the observance of the law)" (Rel 6: 28, 23). Kant does not explain what he means by the latter claim, but his point is apparently that even the first two predispositions are the source of moral obligations. Thus, in *The Doctrine of Virtue* he argues that we have duties to ourselves insofar as we are mere animal or living beings and as rational animals as well as moral beings.[3]

Kant's inclusion of the first two of these predispositions among the predispositions to good is indicative of the more positive attitude toward the inclinations expressed in *Religion within the Limits of Reason Alone*. We have already seen that Kant never held that an action lacks moral worth simply because it is performed with inclination, and his account of agency (particularly the Incorporation Thesis) certainly entails that inclinations themselves are not the source of moral evil. Nevertheless, in a notorious passage in the *Groundwork* he states that "inclinations themselves, as sources of needs, are so far from having an absolute value to make them desirable for their own sake that it must rather be the universal wish of every rational being to be wholly free of them" (Gr 4: 428; 95–6). Moreover, lest this be considered an aberration, it should be noted that the same sentiment is also expressed in the *Critique of Practical Reason* (KprV 5: 118, 122). By contrast, in *Religion within the Limits of Reason Alone* he affirms that "natural inclinations, *considered in themselves,* are *good,* that is, not a matter of reproach, and it is not only futile to want to extirpate them but to do so would also be harmful and blameworthy" (Rel 6: 58; 51).

The key aspect of Kant's account of the predispositions is, however, the predisposition to personality, which is just the capacity to be motivated by respect for the law. Since it is in virtue of this capacity that we are moral agents, capable of either good or evil, it is noteworthy that Kant regards this as a separate predisposition, distinct from the predisposition to humanity. In so doing, he affirms that our status as persons in the full sense, that is, as moral agents, cannot be derived from our status as rational animals. As Kant puts it in a highly significant footnote that is intended to explain the significance of the distinction between these two predispositions:

For from the fact that a being has reason it by no means follows that this reason, by the mere representing of the fitness of its maxims to be laid down as universal laws, is thereby rendered capable of determining the will unconditionally, so as to be "practical" of itself; at least, not so far as we can see. The most rational mortal being in the world might still stand in need of certain incentives, originating in objects of desire, to determine his choice. He might, indeed, bestow the most rational reflection on all that concerns not only the greatest sum of these incentives in him but also the means of attaining the end thereby determined, without ever suspecting the possibility of such a thing as the absolutely imperative moral law which proclaims that it is itself an incentive and, indeed, the highest. (Rel 6: 26n, 21)

As we shall see in the third part of this study, this much neglected passage is crucial for a correct understanding of Kant's attempt to ground the moral law, since it indicates that our subjection to this law cannot be derived from a reflection on our status as rational agents (animals with rationality or practical reason). Our immediate concern, however, is still with the question of how this and, indeed, all the predispositions to good help to determine the nature of radical evil. To anticipate, the account of the predispositions to good rules out two traditional ways of construing such evil and points the way to a more adequate alternative.

The first view to be ruled out is the familiar doctrine that evil has its source in our sensuous nature, particularly our inclinations. As we have just seen, far from regarding the inclinations as inherently evil, Kant includes them in the predisposition to good. Moreover, since they are aspects of our biological nature (the predisposition to animality), we are not responsible for their existence. Accordingly, they can hardly be regarded as the ground of something for which we are preeminently responsible, namely, moral evil (Rel 6: 35; 30).

The second view to be ruled out is that the ground of evil is to be located in "a *corruption* of the morally legislative reason" (Rel 6: 35; 30). As Kant construes such a scenario, it amounts to the assumption of a "malignant reason," that is, a thoroughly evil will (*Wille*). Without providing much in the way of argument, Kant rules out such an extreme immoralism as absurd, a form of reason (the source of the moral law) attempting to deny itself. Accordingly, in a famous passage he writes:

Man (even the most wicked) does not, under any maxim whatsoever, repudiate the moral law in the manner of a rebel (renouncing obedience to it). The law, rather, forces itself upon him irresistibly by virtue of his moral predisposition; and were no other incentive working in opposition, he would adopt the law into his maxim as the sufficient determining ground of his will [*Willkür*]. (Rel 6: 36; 31)

Because of this and similar passages, Kant is sometimes taken to be claiming that deliberate defiance of the moral law is a kind of psychological impossibility. Given such a reading, it is not surprising to find Kant's claim criticized on the grounds that the defiant rejection of the law "is an ineradicable fact of human experience."[4] As Allen Wood has pointed out, however, this reading and criticism stem from the failure to consider Kant's claim in light of his conception of a moral predisposition (to which he refers in the passage just cited). So considered, it is not a dubious psychological assertion but rather a claim about the conditions of the possibility of being accountable beings at all. More specifically, the claim is that in order to be accountable and, therefore, in order to be *either* good or evil, it is necessary to recognize that the moral law (in the form of the categorical imperative) makes valid claims. Since a being who lacked this recognition and the concomitant feeling or respect would not be morally accountable, such a being could hardly be said to have a diabolical will. On the contrary, such a being would have to be regarded as an unfortunate product of nature, lacking the defining characteristic of personality.[5]

Given these results, we can now proceed to determine the nature of radical

150

evil. First, since its source can lie neither in sensuous inclination nor morally practical reason or *Wille,* it must lie in *Willkür.* Second, since neither the moral incentive nor the incentive stemming from inclination or self-love can be removed (both are predispositions and, therefore, inextirpable), and since both must be incorporated into our maxims (we cannot renounce our natural desire for happiness any more than we can renounce the law), it follows that this ground can be located only in a tendency of *Willkür* to give priority to the nonmoral incentive or, equivalently, the principle of happiness, even in those cases where it conflicts with the dictates of morality. Apart from such a tendency there would be no basis for adopting maxims that are contrary to the law and, therefore, no possibility of evil.

Since we have already seen that this tendency must be regarded as a maxim of the highest order, it can be more properly described as the fundamental or ruling maxim to license exceptions in one's own case to moral requirements ("moral holidays," as it were) while still acknowledging the general validity of these requirements.[6] In Kant's terms, "the proposition, man is evil, can mean only, he is conscious of the moral law but has nevertheless adopted into his maxim the (occasional) deviation therefrom" (Rel 6: 32, 27). As he puts it, with reference to the distinction between good and evil,

the distinction between a good man and one who is evil cannot lie in the difference between the incentives which they adopt into their maxim (not in the content of the maxim), but rather must depend upon *subordination* (the form of the maxim), *i.e., which of the two incentives he makes the condition of the other.* Consequently man (even the best) is evil only in that he reverses the moral order of the incentives when he adopts them into his maxim. (Rel 6: 36; 31)

Admittedly, the expression "radical evil" does not appear in the text of the *Groundwork;* nevertheless, the basis for this doctrine is already present in that work. Perhaps the clearest evidence of this is provided by a passage near the end of Part 1, where Kant writes:

Man feels in himself a powerful counterweight to all the commands of duty presented to him by reason as so worthy of esteem – the counterweight of his needs and inclinations, whose total satisfaction he grasps under the name of "happiness." But reason, without promising anything to inclination, enjoins its commands relentlessly, and therefore, so to speak, with disregard and neglect of those turbulent and seemingly equitable claims (which refuse to be suppressed by any command). From this there arises a *natural dialectic* – that is, a propensity [*Hang*] to quibble with these strict laws of duty, to throw doubt on their validity or at least on their purity and strictness, and to make them, where possible, more adapted to our wishes and inclinations; that is, to pervert their very foundations and destroy their whole dignity – a result which in the end even ordinary human reason is unable to approve. (Gr 4: 405; 73)[7]

What Kant here terms a "natural dialectic" and also characterizes as a "propensity" (*Hang*) is precisely what he later calls a "propensity to evil." It consists, Kant suggests, in a tendency to challenge ("quibble with") the supremely authoritative or unconditioned status of moral principles in the

name of the claims of need and inclination. To do so is, in effect, to subordinate the former to the latter. Accordingly, the "dialectic" is between
principles competing for supremacy in the practical judgment of the agent
rather than between reason and inclination as psychic forces or psychological causes. By characterizing this conflict as a dialectic, Kant treats it as a
problem in moral theory (albeit one of great practical import), which can
be resolved only by a step into practical philosophy and ultimately a critique of practical reason.[8] By contrast, in *Religion within the Limits of
Reason Alone,* it is viewed as an existential problem, calling for a radical
conversion or reorientation of the will on the part of the agent. Those differences aside, however, this passage shows that the conceptual apparatus
for articulating the doctrine of radical evil was already in place in 1785.
In addition to making all of this fully explicit by focusing on it themati-
cally for the first time, what Kant does in the later work is to explain how
the attribution of a propensity to evil is compatible with freedom (no
small task) and to argue that this propensity is universal. It is to these
topics that we now turn.

II. The propensity and its universality

The basic problem here is simply that a propensity, like a predisposition, is
not the sort of thing for which an individual is normally held responsible.
On the contrary, a propensity is usually construed as a physiological condition, an inherited tendency to behave or react in certain ways.[9] Moreover,
initially at least, Kant's own account seems to be in accord with this view.
"By *propensity* (*propensio*)," he tells us, "I understand the subjective ground
of the possibility of an inclination (habitual craving, *concupiscentia*)" (Rel
6: 28; 23–4). And in a note attached to this definition, he cites as an illustration the propensity of all savage people for intoxicants (Rel 6: 28n; 24).

Kant's example may be highly questionable on empirical grounds, but it
is at least in accord with what is normally understood by a propensity. After
stating this, however, he proceeds to claim that "a propensity is distinguished
from a predisposition by the fact that although it can indeed be innate, it
ought not to be represented as such; for it can also be regarded as having
been *acquired* (if it is good) or *brought* by man *upon himself* (if it is evil)"
(Rel 6: 29; 24). Since it affirms a possible connection between a propensity
and freedom, this move enables Kant to distinguish between physical and
moral propensities and to speak of a propensity to evil. Unfortunately, it is
just this hybrid notion of a freely chosen propensity that seems problematic.

Kant was, of course, aware of the difficulty, and he poses it in the form
of a dilemma. The dilemma stems from the fact that, on the one hand, only
an agent's acts, as expressions of freedom, may be imputed, whereas on the
other hand, a moral propensity of the will is, qua moral, imputable and, qua
propensity, a "subjective determining ground of *Willkür* which *precedes all
acts* and which, therefore, is not itself an act" (Rel 6: 31; 26). Thus, it
would seem to be necessary either to give up the principle that only acts

may be imputed or to abandon, as self-contradictory, the notion of a propensity with a moral value (whether good or evil).

Kant's solution consists in the introduction of a distinction between two meanings of the term "act" (*That*). One signifies the exercise of freedom through which the supreme maxim with respect to the moral law is adopted, the other the ordinary actions (*Handlungen*) of human beings in accordance with that maxim. The former is characterized as "intelligible action, cognizable by means of pure reason alone, apart from every temporal condition," the latter as "sensible action, empirical, given in time." Not surprisingly, Kant also claims that the propensity to evil is an act in the first sense and "at the same time the formal ground of all unlawful conduct in the second sense" (6: 31; 26).

Kant cannot, of course, be taken as literally identifying a propensity with an act, even an intelligible one, since propensities are things we have whereas acts are things we perform. Presumably, then, Kant's point is that this particular propensity is acquired by means of such an act, or at least that it must be represented as having been so acquired. Admittedly, this still leaves us with the problematic notion of an acquired propensity, which was the source of the trouble in the first place; but we can begin to understand what Kant is getting at here if we keep in mind the account of *Gesinnung* sketched in the last chapter.

As we saw there, the distinctive features of the Kantian conception of *Gesinnung* are that it is acquired, although not in time, and that it consists in the fundamental or controlling maxim, which determines the orientation of one's *Willkür* as a moral being. Given this, we can now see that this *Gesinnung* is precisely what Kant means by a moral propensity. Moreover, this realization puts us in a position to gain a somewhat deeper understanding of the grounds for identifying a *Gesinnung* or moral propensity with a maxim and of the alleged "timelessness" of its acquisition.

With regard to the first point, what is important is that this propensity is a *deliberative* tendency and, as such, quite distinct from a natural impulse or the like. Accordingly, by a "propensity to evil" is to be understood a tendency to allow, at least under some conditions, nonmoral considerations stemming from inclination to outweigh moral ones. As such, it functions as a subjective practical principle, a kind of "permissive law" for a limited immorality. Such a principle is itself obviously evil for the reasons already given, and as Kant puts it, this evil is radical because "it corrupts the ground of all maxims" (Rel 6: 37; 32).

To be sure, it is also a very peculiar sort of principle or maxim, since it is not to be thought of as explicitly and self-consciously adopted by an agent. One does not, after all, one day deliberately resolve to "make it one's maxim" to allow moral holidays under certain conditions. It is rather that one finds that this is how one has been behaving all along. Nevertheless, since this behavior is that of a rational agent (or at least is regarded as such), it must be thought of as involving action based on the "conception of law" and, therefore, a maxim.

153

The peculiarity of this maxim mentioned in the preceding also provides the key to the understanding of Kant's insistence on the timelessness of its acquisition or, equivalently, the "intelligible" nature of the act through which it is adopted. Such an act is timeless or intelligible, not in the sense that it must be regarded as occurring in some timeless noumenal world but rather in the sense that it is not to be viewed as performed at a specific point in one's moral development. On the contrary, as we have just seen, this propensity to give undue weight to the nonmoral incentive and, therefore, to reverse the proper ordering of principles is already at work when moral reflection begins. Consequently, the adoption of the maxim underlying this propensity must be presupposed by, rather than revealed in, moral reflection. That is why Kant claims that this "intelligible act" of adoption is "cognizable by means of pure reason alone, apart from every temporal condition." In effect, the assumption of such a propensity functions as a postulate of morally practical reason; something that must be presupposed both as a condition of the possibility of evil and, as we shall see in the next chapter, of the possibility of the attainment of virtue.[10]

Even assuming the intelligibility of the idea of a freely chosen moral propensity as a postulate of morally practical reason, it still remains unclear why we must postulate a propensity to *evil* (rather than to good) and why this propensity must be regarded as universal. Both the thesis that there is a propensity to good in human nature and the intuitively more plausible view that some people have a propensity to good and others to evil would seem to be compatible with Kant's conception of *Gesinnung* and his rigorism. The latter, in particular, merely requires us to assume that each individual is either good or evil in a fundamental way. But this is quite distinct from the doctrine that the human race, taken collectively, is fundamentally either good or evil, not to mention the view that it is fundamentally evil. Nevertheless, Kant insists not only that there is a propensity to evil but that it is "rooted in humanity itself" and, therefore, universal. What grounds, we may ask, does Kant offer for this apparently audacious claim?

Kant's official answer to this obvious question is quite disappointing and, indeed, seems to conflict with the preceding account of the propensity as a postulate. Instead of offering a "formal proof" of the universality of the propensity to evil, he simply asserts that the necessity for such a proof is obviated by "the multitude of crying examples which experience *of the actions* of men put before our eyes" (Rel 6: 33; 28). In short, he seems to treat it as an unproblematic empirical generalization.[11] But clearly, even if for the sake of argument one accepts Kant's appeal to some rather selective anthropological evidence, the *most* that this evidence can show is that evil is widespread, not that there is a universal propensity to it.[12] Moreover, since Kant insists that this propensity concerns only the ultimate subjective ground of one's maxims and is perfectly compatible with a virtuous empirical character, it is difficult to see what could conceivably falsify his claim. Consequently, it is also difficult to take seriously the suggestion that it is intended as an empirical generalization.[13]

The claim, then, is to be taken as a priori; indeed, as a postulate, it must be synthetic a priori. Consequently, it requires some sort of deduction or justification; and since Kant fails to provide one, we must attempt to do so for him.

The key to this deduction is the impossibility of attributing a propensity to good to finite, sensuously affected agents such as ourselves (either to the race as a whole or to particular individuals). This impossibility, together with rigorism, entails the necessity of attributing a universal propensity to evil to agents relevantly like ourselves. And since, as we shall see, the impossibility at issue is not logical (the notion of a propensity to good is not self-contradictory for Kant), the conclusion has synthetic a priori status.

As a first step in developing this analysis, it is necessary to determine what a propensity to good would be like if, *per impossibile,* a human being could possess one. Although Kant does not describe it in so many words, it is clear from his characterization of the propensity to evil that it must be conceived as the disposition, itself based on a maxim, to subordinate the incentive of self-love to the moral incentive. In other words, a propensity to good would consist in a kind of spontaneous preference for the impersonal requirements of morality over one's own needs as a rational animal with a built-in desire for happiness. Since this preference must itself be based on a maxim and, therefore, consist in a settled policy, it might seem inappropriate to characterize it as "spontaneous." The point, however, is that for such an agent the moral incentive would, as a matter of course, always outweigh the incentive of self-love. Consequently, for an agent blessed with such a propensity, there would be no temptation to adopt maxims that run counter to the law and, therefore, no thought of the law as constraining. Within the Kantian framework, this means that the law would not take the form of an imperative and moral requirements would not be viewed as duties.

Interestingly enough, the belief that some people either have or are capable of acquiring such a disposition or propensity corresponds precisely to what Kant terms "moral fanaticism," a point of view that he criticizes in the latter portions of his account of respect in the *Critique of Practical Reason* (KprV 5: 84–6; 86–8). Although, strictly speaking, moral fanaticism includes any position that places the moral incentive and disposition in something other than respect for the law, the text makes it clear that Kant is really concerned with positions that advocate a "higher" form of morality than that of bare duty. More specifically, he is concerned with positions that locate the moral disposition in love, a "ready willingness" (*bereitwillige Ergebenheit*) or, equivalently, a "spontaneous inclination" (*freiwilliger Zuneigung*) that is unfettered by any thought of obligation or constraint (KprV 5: 84; 86–7).

As the text also makes clear, the problem with these positions is not that the concept of such a higher form of morality is self-contradictory (which would make the claim that finite rational agents cannot possess such a disposition analytic); it is rather that it reflects an ideal of moral perfection that is unobtainable by finite, sensuously affected agents such as ourselves. In fact, such a disposition, which is equivalent to a propensity to good, characterizes what Kant terms "holiness," that is, the "complete accordance of the disposition [*völlige Angemessenheit der Gesinnung*] to the moral law" (KprV 5: 122; 126).[14] Against the assumption that holiness is obtainable by human beings, Kant insists that "the stage of morality on which man (and, so far as we know, every rational creature) stands is respect for the moral law." And, again, "The moral condition which he can always be in is virtue, i.e. moral disposition [*Gesinnung*] in conflict, and not holiness in the supposed possession of perfect purity in the intentions [*Gesinnungen*] of the will" (KprV 5: 84; 87).

The reason for the unattainability of this ideal stems from our sensuous nature, yet not in such a way as to make this nature of itself directly responsible for our moral failings. For the perfectly good or holy will of the *Groundwork*, there is no possibility of a conflict between inclination and morality and, therefore, no possibility of impure intentions because, *ex hypothesi*, such a will (or agent) is not sensuously affected. By contrast, finite, sensuously affected rational beings such as ourselves are not only autonomous moral agents but also creatures of desire and inclination, which, as resting on natural causes, are neither completely in our control nor necessarily in agreement with the dictates of morality (KprV 5: 84; 86). Obviously, this does not mean that we are incapable of subordinating our sensuously based needs to moral considerations and, therefore, incapable of virtue. It does mean, however, that we are never beyond the possibility of temptation and the need for moral constraint. And this means that we cannot be thought to have a propensity to good.

Kant regards this inescapable need for moral constraint as equivalent to the impossibility of acting from duty gladly (*gern*), which in turn is equivalent to the impossibility of exhibiting the "ready willingness" to follow the law that is characteristic of a holy will. We can, to be sure, on occasion do dutiful acts gladly, as in the case of someone who helps others from a sympathetic feeling; but such actions, as we have seen, are not *from* duty and are lacking in moral worth. Similarly, we can have an inclination to perform an act that we in fact perform from duty. Moreover, in such circumstances, we can be glad that our duty does not conflict with our inclination. Nevertheless, insofar as we act from duty we act on the basis of the recognition of a moral constraint and, therefore, not gladly.

In the last analysis, then, it is this impossibility of acting from duty gladly that explains why Kant rejects the possibility of attributing a propensity to good to finite rational beings such as ourselves. Assuming rigorism, the inference to a universal propensity to evil follows from this result. Put simply, if the *Gesinnung* or moral quality of every *Willkür* must be characterizable as either good or evil and if the former is ruled out for the reasons just given, then the latter is necessarily the case. Baldly stated, however, this conclusion does not seem very satisfying; for it strongly suggests that Kant's

156

doctrine of radical evil, which initially appeared so paradoxical, reduces in the end to the rather unremarkable claim that the human will is not capable of holiness. Accordingly, in attempting to make Kant's account of the universality of a propensity to evil coherent, we have succeeded only in trivializing it. Or so it would seem.

Clearly, what is needed at this point in order to put some bite back into the doctrine that there is a universal propensity to evil is a reason, apart from the general principle of rigorism, for regarding the lack of a propensity to good as equivalent to, or at least as entailing, an actual propensity to evil. Fortunately, although Kant never spells out his position with sufficient clarity, the basis for an explanation is provided by the previous analysis. The essential point is that the very fact that we only obey the law reluctantly (*ungern*) indicates not merely a lack of holiness but also an actual propensity to subordinate moral considerations to our needs as sensuous beings, that is, a tendency to let ourselves be tempted or "induced" by inclination to violate the moral law even while recognizing its authority.[15] More precisely, since this openness to temptation is not a mere consequence of the fact that we have a sensuous nature but reflects an attitude that we take toward this nature or, better, a value we place on its requirements, it may be imputed. And since this evaluation stems from a concern with our well-being that is inseparable from our nature as *rational* animals, it is "rooted in humanity itself" (the predisposition to humanity) and is, therefore, universal.

III. Degrees of radical evil

Kant notes that as a mere propensity to reverse the proper order of incentives, radical evil need not lead to actions contrary to the law, much less to vice, which he defines as a propensity to perform such actions (Rel 6: 37; 33).[16] Thus, although the latter two are impossible without the former (since radical evil is precisely the ground of the possibility of evil), the converse does not hold. Of itself, this provides the basis for a more nuanced account of evil than his rigorism might suggest. A further basis for such an account as well as some fresh puzzles are provided by Kant's brief, yet highly suggestive discussion of various degrees of radical evil. As his initial treatment of the topic makes clear, these are to be understood as three successive stages (*Stufen*) in the realization of the original propensity to evil, which Kant now equates with an "evil heart" (Rel 6: 29; 24).

The first of these stages is characterized as "weakness of the heart" or "frailty" (*Gebrechlichkeit*) in the observance of adopted maxims. Kant finds this alluded to in St. Paul's lament, "What I would, that I do not!" (Romans, VII, 15). In his gloss on this, he suggests that the point is that the good, which objectively considered is an inexpugnable (*unüberwindliche*) incentive, subjectively considered, that is, with respect to its actual motivational force, turns out to be the weaker in comparison with inclination. The second is impurity or insincerity (*Unlauterkeit*). It consists in the propensity to mix a nonmoral with the moral incentive. At this stage, the good is still intended, but the objective goodness (or rightness) of what morality requires is not a sufficient incentive. One stands in need of an extramoral inducement, a bribe, as it were, in order to do what duty dictates. The third stage, or wickedness (*Bösartigkeit*), consists in the propensity to adopt evil maxims. Given Kant's rejection of the possibility of a diabolical will, this cannot be understood as a policy of choosing evil for the sake of evil but rather as one of neglecting totally the moral incentive (which is always present) in favor of those stemming from inclination. At this stage, then, the proper ordering of incentives is explicitly reversed, even though the agent's actual conduct may continue to conform to the law (Rel 6: 29–30; 24–5).

Later in his discussion of radical evil Kant returns to this notion of an "evil heart" and states that such a heart "may coexist with a will [*Willen*] which is in general [*im Allgemeinen*] good" (Rel 6: 37; 32). In addition, he now characterizes the first two stages of evil as "unintentional" (*unvorsätzlich*) and the third as deliberate or intentional (*vorsätzliche*) guilt, indicating a "radical perversity of the human heart," even when it does not result in actual vice or conduct directly opposed to the moral law. Finally, and most significantly, Kant suggests that a fundamental feature of this third stage is a kind of systematic self-deception. The idea here is that one tells oneself that one is doing all that mortality requires as long as one's overt behavior agrees with the law. Accordingly, Kant notes that this stage may coexist with a certain ungrounded moral self-satisfaction, which stems from the fact that one has simply been fortunate in avoiding those circumstances that would have led to actual immoral behavior (Rel 6: 38; 33).

This account of various stages in the development of the propensity to evil certainly provides some much needed additional content to the claim that this propensity is universal or, equivalently, "rooted in human nature," but it also suggests new difficulties, which in turn might be thought to cast further doubt on the coherence of Kant's whole conception of radical evil. Moreover, these difficulties concern each of the three stages or degrees of radical evil.

First, with respect to the initial stage, it seems difficult to see how, given Kant's conception of freedom (particularly the Incorporation Thesis), he could have any room for the notion of moral weakness or, more generally, "unintentional guilt." Second, even granting such a possibility, it remains unclear why this weakness should count as *moral* evil. According to Kant's official doctrine, such evil consists in the adoption of (or the propensity to adopt) evil maxims. Here, however, the assumption is that the maxims are good, with the moral failure consisting simply in the agent's inability to live up to them.

Although it is lumped together with frailty as a species of unintentional guilt, the second stage, or impurity, suggests the opposite problem: How can an impure "heart" be regarded as in any sense morally good? As we have already seen, Kant is adamant in his insistence that any reliance upon an extramoral incentive as a condition of the performance of duty undermines all moral worth.[17] This is, however, precisely what he now claims occurs in the case of impurity. Finally, the same considerations make it still more perplexing how Kant could maintain that even wickedness, the third degree of the propensity to evil, is compatible with a good will.[18]

In dealing with these problems, it is essential to keep in mind that three degrees of radical evil correspond to three stages in the subordination of the moral incentive to the incentive of self-love, which constitutes the original propensity to evil. Accordingly, Kant's analysis attempts to show how the reversal of the proper ordering of incentives can be thought to manifest itself progressively. If one is to make sense of this analysis, however, it is also necessary to assume that the self-deception, which Kant only mentions in connection with the third degree, or intentional guilt, is operative from the beginning and, indeed, is an essential ingredient in the propensity to evil.[19]

To begin with, what Kant terms the "frailty of human nature" or the "weakness of the human heart" can be seen as compatible with both his conception of freedom and his account of evil if one equates it with the bare propensity to evil itself. As such, it is both freely adopted and evil for the reasons previously given. The root idea here, which is already implicit in the earlier account of the propensity, is that the susceptibility to temptation, now characterized as weakness, is the direct result of the original primacy granted to the claims of one's sensuous nature. Otherwise expressed, the so-called lack of sufficient strength to follow moral principles when they conflict with the claims of inclination reflects the lack of a full commitment to these principles in the first place. Thus, self-deception enters the picture at the very beginning, depicting what is in reality a free evaluation on one's part as a "weakness" for which one is not responsible.[20] So construed, Kant's account does not appear unreasonable as a bit of moral psychology. In any event, it does not involve any fresh difficulties beyond those connected with the very notion of a propensity to evil.

Impurity, like frailty, must be understood as a propensity. It involves self-deception in the sense that an impure heart goes together with the false belief that one is motivated by the thought of duty alone. Thus, part of the propensity would be a tendency to hide this impurity from oneself, just as at the level of frailty one excuses oneself by an appeal to weakness. Since Kant insists that we can never be certain about our own motivation, this should not be surprising. What is surprising, at least to a student of the *Groundwork*, is the previously noted claim that such a propensity is compatible with a "will which is in general good." This is, of course, primarily a general problem regarding the compatibility of the doctrine of radical evil with the conception of a good will, but it involves impurity as a special case. What is needed, then, is an account of how an agent may be said to have both a propensity to evil, or more specifically an impure heart, and a good will.

It can hardly be claimed that Kant provides such an account in *Religion within the Limits of Reason Alone* (or elsewhere for that matter). Nevertheless, he at least shows a keen awareness of the problem. This awareness is reflected both in his contrast between an evil *heart* and a good *will* and in the characterization of the latter as "in general good," as opposed, one assumes, to a will that is wholly good. In addition, Kant insists that although the propensity to evil is inextirpable by human powers, "it must be possible to *overcome* it, since it is found in man, a being whose actions are free" (Rel 6: 37; 32).

The latter claim points to Kant's conception of virtue and, therefore, to the central topic of the next chapter. In fact, we shall see that it is only in light of Kant's doctrine of radical evil that we can fully understand his conception of virtue. Nevertheless, even prior to this consideration, we must note two points that bear directly on the problem currently before us. First, as a propensity, radical evil in general and impurity in particular can be struggled against, and even combatted successfully, if not completely eradicated. This is, of course, just the point Kant is making in the passage cited in the previous paragraph, and it leaves room for the notion of a good will, understood as one sincerely committed to the struggle. Second, with respect to impurity, it is clear that in spite of the need for an extramoral incentive, such impurity is compatible with a considerable degree of moral commitment. Thus, Kant speaks of the maxims as good ones (objectively speaking) and of the intention as moral, if not purely moral (Rel 6: 29–30; 24–5). The problem is simply that, as in the case of frailty, this commitment is not total, although there is a tendency to tell oneself that it is.

When we come to wickedness, the third degree of radical evil, the situation seems quite different and the difficulties involved in showing the compatibility of such evil with a will that is *in any sense* good much more severe. Not only does Kant characterize this as intentional guilt, suggesting that it is something more than a mere propensity, he also notes that it is marked by a complete neglect of the moral incentive. One is satisfied and thinks oneself virtuous so long as one's actions do not conflict with the law. Moreover, as we have seen, it is at this stage that self-deception is most fully developed and the moral incentive completely rejected. Accordingly, it is here that we find the full expression of the reversal of the proper ordering of incentives implicit in the propensity from the beginning.

It is obviously crucial for Kant, however, that even here there is not a complete abandonment of moral considerations. The self-deception and hypocrisy of wickedness is, as the saying goes, "the compliment which vice pays to virtue."[21] Thus, there remains at least a concern to maintain legality and, presumably, to justify one's immoral actions as allowable exceptions to a law, which is recognized as generally valid even in its breach. If this were not the case, there would hardly be grounds for moral self-satisfaction, even of a spurious sort. This in turn provides a possible basis for understanding how, in spite of his rigorism, Kant could insist that we can still speak about a good will in connection with this degree of radical evil.

Essential to this understanding is the conception of the predispositions to good, particularly the predisposition to personality. Since this, like all the predispositions, is itself inextirpable, it follows that a germ of goodness remains in the worst of sinners (Rel 6: 28; 23). Kant is committed to such a view in virtue of both his rejection of a diabolical will and his insistence on the possibility of a conversion of someone with a "corrupt heart." It is perhaps significant in this regard that Kant refers explicitly in this context to a good *Wille,* not *Willkür* or *Gesinnung.* This suggests that he has in mind the "goodness" of morally legislative reason, which is just the predisposition to personality.

At first glance at least, this conception of a good will might appear to be far removed from the conception originally advanced at the beginning of *Groundwork* I. That good will, it will be recalled, was one that acted from duty alone. Moreover, it was not only good in itself but also good without qualification. By contrast, the good will of *Religion within the Limits of Reason Alone* is infected by radical evil. As such, it seldom, if ever, acts purely from duty and is engaged in an ongoing project of self-deception.

Further consideration, however, suggests that the two conceptions are quite close after all. First, already in the *Groundwork* Kant contrasts a will that is good under human conditions, that is, an imperfectly good will with a perfectly good or holy will (Gr 4: 414; 81). In addition, he refers on occasion to an absolutely (*schlecterdings*) good will, meaning, thereby, not a holy will but merely one that consistently acts on the basis of the categorical imperative (Gr 4: 437, 447; 104, 115).[22] This, of itself, leaves room for the notion of a will that is good but not absolutely good. Finally, in appealing to the two standpoints as part of the attempted "deduction" of morality in *Groundwork* III, Kant contrasts the "good will," which pertains to one as a member of the intelligible world, with the "bad will," which pertains to one as a member of the sensible world (Gr 4: 455; 122–3). Since he also asserts that the former constitutes a law for the bad will, he is here using the notion of a good will in precisely the same way as, I have suggested, he later uses it in connection with the wicked will. Thus, the ambiguity in Kant's treatment of the good will in *Religion within the Limits of Reason Alone* is already to be found in the *Groundwork*.

9
Virtue and holiness

> In the moral development of the predisposition to good im-
> planted in us, we cannot start from an innocence natural to us
> but must begin with the assumption of the wickedness of
> *Willkür* in adopting its maxims contrary to the original moral
> predisposition; and, since this propensity is inextirpable, we
> must begin with the incessant counter-action against it. (Rel
> 6: 51; 46)

As the above passage from *Religion within the Limits of Reason Alone* indicates, the doctrine of radical evil not only defines our moral condition but
also sets the moral agenda for finite, imperfect beings such as ourselves,
namely, to struggle to the best of our ability against an ineliminable reluctance to subordinate the requirements of our sensuous nature to the dictates
of morality. Since this reluctance is ineliminable, we can never attain holiness; but since we can struggle against it and even succeed in the subordination of our sensuous to our moral selves, we are capable of virtue. Kant's
account of virtue is complicated, however, by his insistence that although
holiness is unobtainable, we have a duty to strive after it and, indeed, that
this striving or commitment is an essential feature of a virtuous life. Accordingly, the present chapter, which completes our analysis of Kant's conception of moral agency, is divided into two parts. The first sketches Kant's
conception of virtue and considers its connections with the theory of radical
evil; the second analyzes the presumed connection between virtue and the
pursuit of holiness and Kant's various attempts to explain how we can be
morally required to pursue an unobtainable ideal.

I. The nature of virtue

Kant's discussion of virtue as a character trait in *The Doctrine of Virtue*,
which contains his fullest treatment of the topic, is largely embedded in his
attempt to delineate and justify a set of duties of virtue or ethical duties.
Together with juridical duties (the subject matter of *The Doctrine of Right*),
they constitute the two types of duty considered in the *Metaphysic of Morals*.
Both types of duty rest on the categorical imperative, and the difference
between them turns mainly on the type of legislation or constraint appropriate for each. Juridical duties, such as the duty to keep a contract, can be
externally legislated, and one can be compelled to fulfill them. Duties of
virtue or ethical duties, such as the duty of beneficence, by contrast, are self-
imposed or, in Kant's terms, enjoined by "inner legislation," and the only
kind of constraint they involve is self-constraint (MS 6: 218–22; 16–21).
Kant also recognizes, however, that ethical or inner legislation likewise en-

joins the fulfillment of juridical duties, so that such duties, and indeed all duties, are at least "indirectly ethical" (MS 6: 221; 20–1).

Closely connected with this difference in the mode of legislation is a difference in what is enjoined by the two types of duty. The former enjoins (or prohibits) specific types of action, whereas the latter enjoins merely the adoption of certain ends.[1] Accordingly, a central concern of *The Doctrine of Virtue* is to justify the claim that there are in fact obligatory ends, that is to say, ends that are also duties. In particular, Kant claims that there are two such ends: one's own perfection and the happiness of others. The first of these yields a set of duties to oneself (including, as we shall see, the duty to pursue holiness); the second yields a set of duties to others. Together they constitute the duties of virtue. But just as Kant holds that we have an ethical obligation to fulfill juridical duties, even apart from external constraints, so he also maintains that virtuous activity is not limited to the fulfillment of duties of virtue. As Kant puts it, "what it is virtuous to do is not necessarily a *duty of virtue* in the proper sense" (MS 6: 394; 55).

In *The Doctrine of Virtue* and elsewhere, Kant defines virtue, considered as a character trait, in a number of different ways, almost all of them involving a contrast with holiness and some notion of self-constraint or self-mastery based on moral principles. Typically, he uses terms such as "ability" or "capacity" (*Fertigkeit*), "courage" or "fortitude" (*Tapferkeit*) and "strength of mind," "soul" or "maxims" to describe it. Perhaps the most helpful of these is his characterization of it as "self-constraint according to a principle of inner freedom, and so by the mere thought of one's duty in accordance with its formal law" (MS 6: 394; 54).[2]

As a form of self-constraint or self-mastery, virtue involves strength of character, which consists in an actual ability to control one's inclinations insofar as they conflict with moral requirements. We shall consider the Kantian response to some familiar criticisms of this view in the next chapter. For the present, it must suffice to note that this control of inclination does not amount to a total suppression. As we have already seen in *Religion within the Limits of Reason Alone,* Kant includes the inclinations as part of the predisposition to good and, in general, holds that it is only insofar as inclinations lead us to neglect our duty that they need be held in check. Moreover, Kant frequently insists that the virtuous disposition, the "state of moral health," is marked by a cheerfulness in the performance of duty.[3]

Given the analysis of moral worth in the *Groundwork* as well as Kant's denial that we do our duty gladly, this claim might seem quite surprising. As Karl Ameriks has pointed out, however, it is precisely what is required by his conception of freedom.[4] Properly construed, this conception yields a picture of a virtuous character, according to which the truly virtuous person, the one with genuine self-control, is to be conceived as someone who feels little or no temptation in the first place rather than someone who is engaged in a constant and heroic struggle with temptation. It is in turn this lack of openness to temptation to do otherwise that makes it possible to be cheerful in the performance of duty.

The roots of this view have already been explored in Chapter 8 in connection with the analysis of radical evil. As we saw there, what was initially regarded as straightforward weakness in the face of temptation turned out, on further analysis, to be an expression of freedom, more specifically, an evaluation placed on certain ends of inclination. Consequently, if as free agents we are tempted, it is only because we, as it were, allow ourselves to be. In short, in Kant's model of rational agency (the Incorporation Thesis) "yielding" to temptation is not to be conceived as being overcome by a superior psychic force but rather as a kind of inner voting in favor of certain ends, a taking of these ends as one's own. The fact that we seldom regard it in this light is, as we have seen, explained in terms of self-deception.

Kant's account of virtue as involving a cheerful demeanor in the performance of duty is a direct consequence of this view of temptation as self-imposed. Given this, it follows that the truly virtuous are those who do not allow themselves to be tempted or, more properly, since no finite agent is beyond the possibility of temptation, those who do not allow themselves to be tempted by the things that are irresistible to the rest of us. Kant makes this explicit in *The Doctrine of Virtue,* where, while noting that the strength of virtue can be measured only by the greatness of the obstacles that it overcomes (which suggests Henson's "battlefield model"), he also states that these are obstacles "man creates by his inclinations" (MS 6: 405; 67).[5] The point, of course, is not that one creates one's inclinations but rather that one allows them to become obstacles to morality by placing a higher value on their satisfaction than is placed on the fulfillment of duty. Self-control, then, must be understood as control over this propensity rather than merely over the inclinations themselves. Given the inclusion of the inclinations in the predisposition to good, this is just what one should expect.

Also central to Kant's conception of virtue is the distinction between actual strength of character or self-control and the mere capacity (*Vermögen*) for it. The latter is possessed by all rational agents, no matter how weak or evil, in virtue of their moral autonomy; the former must be acquired through a process of self-discipline. As such, it is attained only by a few, although Kant does insist that we all have an obligation to attain it, since we all have the capacity to do so (MS 6: 397; 58). This difference between capacity and control is just the difference between the *autonomy* of practical reason (which is possessed by all moral agents), and its *autocracy,* by which is understood its power to master inclinations when they run counter to the law (MS 6: 383; 41–2).[6] Virtue, for Kant, requires the latter, although this is only possible on the basis of the former. Since a holy being, by definition, has no competing inclinations, such a being has no need for autocracy and therefore no need for virtue. As we have already seen, however, Kant holds that virtue is the highest moral condition that finite beings such as ourselves can hope to attain.

But self-control or self-mastery is merely a necessary and not also a sufficient condition of virtue. What distinguishes virtue from other forms of self-control for Kant is that it is based on a "principle of inner freedom," that is to say, a moral principle freely adopted by the agent. Thus, neither the self-control based on purely prudential considerations, of which even a criminal is capable, nor that produced by mere habit, without conscious direction through principles, would count as virtue in the Kantian sense. Moreover, the latter is the case even if the agent is habituated to act in morally commendable ways. As Kant puts the matter in an important passage:

For unless this habit [*diese*] results from considered, firm, and continually purified principles, then, like any other mechanism of technically-practical reason, it is neither armed for all situations nor adequately insured against the changes that new temptations could bring about. (MS 6: 383–4; 42)[7]

In this and similar passages, Kant is objecting to a kind of moral tropism, such as would be produced by a merely habitual training in "goodness," which did not develop the capacity for independent moral judgment on the basis of firmly held principles.[8] As the text indicates, the claim is that without such a capacity one would not be prepared either for new situations requiring moral decisions or fresh temptations, which one had not been already trained to resist. Thus, Kant once again insists that virtue requires correct principles and consists essentially in a disposition (*Gesinnung*) or way of thinking (*Denkungsart*) that has thoroughly internalized these principles. This internalization is then reflected in a relative lack of susceptibility to temptation.

Although it is not part of our concern here to deal with the details of Kant's moral theory, it must be noted that this passage also shows how far he is from regarding moral principles as rigid rules, which one applies in a mechanical fashion in order to determine the right course of action in given circumstances. A tropism of rules would be as bad as one of habit and for the same reasons. Thus, rather than being governed by such rules, the virtuous agent is committed to broad principles (maxims to pursue obligatory ends), which leave considerable scope for practical judgment in their application.[9]

Finally, as should be clear from our entire discussion up to this point, virtue involves not merely power over one's inclinations through a firm commitment to principles (a principled self-control) but also, and indeed primarily, a disposition or enduring maxim to act from duty alone or, equivalently, to make respect for the law the supreme norm governing one's behavior. This is directly expressed in what Kant terms the "universal ethical command": "Do your duty from the motive of duty" (*handle pflichtmässig aus Pflicht*) (MS 6: 391; 52). It also underlies Kant's claim that although there are many duties of virtue, there is only one "obligation of virtue" (*Tugendverpflichtung*), since there is only *"one* virtuous attitude of will [*Gesinnung*], as the subjective ground determining us to fulfill our duty" (MS 6: 410, 73).[10]

The situation is complicated, however, by the vastly more complex moral psychology contained in Kant's later writings. Thus, although continuing to insist on the necessity of the duty motive, he also assigns a morally significant, if subordinate, role to certain inclinations, such as love, which from the standpoint of the *Groundwork* would seem to be without any moral significance at all.[11] Although this added complexity makes Kant's later position more appealing than that of the earlier work, by bringing it closer to our intuitions regarding human "goodness," it also raises fresh questions about the coherence of his overall doctrine.

The problem was already touched upon in Chapter 6, where it was noted that in *The Doctrine of Virtue* Kant claims that we have an indirect duty to cultivate our sympathetic feelings (which includes an obligation to visit scenes of human misery such as hospitals and debtors' prisons). In dealing with this claim, which seems to stand in blatant contradiction with the *Groundwork* account of moral worth, I there suggested that this indirect duty should be understood as a requirement to increase our sensitivity to human suffering so as to be better able to fulfill the duty of beneficence. This thesis itself requires further clarification, however, since it can be taken in at least two different ways, between which Kant does not bother to distinguish.

Perhaps the most natural way to take it is simply as the claim that we have an obligation in our better moments to prepare for our worst ones, so that when duty does not itself move us, we will at least be able to do what duty requires. On this reading, the duty motive functions directly only in the preparation (we cultivate our sympathetic feelings from duty), not in the actual dutiful actions, which are motivated by the developed sympathetic feelings. This accords with Kant's remark that the feeling of sympathy is "one of the impulses which nature has implanted in us so that we may do what the thought of duty alone would not accomplish" (MS 6: 457; 126). It likewise accords with Kant's often noted claim in "The End of All Things" that love, defined as "the free reception of the will of another person into one's own maxim," is "an indispensable complement [*Ergänzungstück*] to the imperfection of human nature" (8: 338).

But this is not the only way in which the moral function of feelings such as sympathy and love can be understood. It is also possible, and I believe more in accord with Kant's views, to regard them as facilitating our ability to act from duty rather than as replacing, or even supplementing, the duty motive. In order to see this, however, it is necessary to reconsider the whole question of moral motivation against the backdrop of Kant's conception of imperfect duties or duties of wide obligation as duties to adopt certain ends rather than to perform specific actions and the doctrine of radical evil. Since the former is merely noted in passing and the latter not considered at all in the *Groundwork,* it is not surprising that Kant's later account of moral motivation is more complex than the initial picture leads one to believe.

Let us consider briefly the duty of beneficence, that is, the duty of promoting, according to one's means, the happiness of others in need without hope of gaining anything in return (MS 6: 453; 122–3). As a duty of wide obligation, it does not, except perhaps under certain limiting conditions, require us to perform any particular act of assistance. Thus, it is left up to the agent to determine when, to whom, to what extent, and at what personal cost such aid is to be offered. Clearly, the virtuous person is fully committed to this end and, therefore, regards it as a duty to do as much as possible in the way of helping others, consistent with other moral requirements. The problem is that to be required to do as much as possible is not to be required to do anything in particular; and it is just at this point, that is, in the move from the general requirement to particular actions, that the extramoral feelings come into play. In the case of sympathetic feelings, it is a matter of increasing our sensitivity to the suffering about us by making us both more aware of this suffering and more capable of being moved by it. This in turn enhances our ability to act beneficently.

But why does the virtuous person need to be moved by sympathy (or love, for that matter), and how is such need compatible with the overriding requirement to act from duty alone? In order to explain this, it is necessary to bring in the doctrine of radical evil. As we have seen, the essence of such evil lies in our ineliminable susceptibility to temptation, with the latter understood as self-imposed in the manner previously explained. This susceptibility applies, of course, to both perfect and imperfect duties. One can be tempted to break a valid contract or to refuse to help someone in need. Nevertheless, precisely because of their indeterminateness, we are particularly susceptible to temptations to neglect imperfect duties such as beneficence. Since, on most occasions at least, there is no guilt or demerit involved in the neglect of an opportunity to offer help to someone in need, it is relatively easy to justify such neglect to oneself.[12]

It is therefore against just this propensity that the truly virtuous need be on guard, and it is here that supportive feelings come into play. Very roughly, the idea is that such feelings, when properly cultivated, provide an important counterweight to the self-regarding inclinations that we tend to allow to tempt us into taking moral holidays. For example, to the extent to which I truly sympathize with someone's plight I am less inclined to pursue my own legitimate ends when I can help that person instead. On this reading, then, it is as weapons against the propensity to evil rather than as directly motivating factors that these feelings enter into the moral life as Kant conceives it. Correlatively, it is in this sense that they enable us to do "what the thought of duty alone would not accomplish."

Finally, although it would take us well beyond the confines of this study to develop the point adequately, this is analogous to the instrumental value with regard to the development of a moral disposition that Kant attributes to the sensitivity to the beautiful (in nature) and the sublime in the *Critique of Judgment*.[13] It is not that the possession of such sensitivity is equivalent to the possession of a virtuous disposition, much less that it is an acceptable surrogate for it (any more than sympathy or love as motives are acceptable surrogates for respect); it is rather that the heightening of this sensitivity increases our actual ability (as opposed to our mere capacity) to abstract from the influence of inclination and to adopt the universalistic perspective required by morality. In this sense, then, aesthetic feeling is likewise a valu-

167

able weapon in the struggle against the propensity to evil. Perhaps this in turn helps to explain Kant's claim that "we require from everyone as a duty, as it were [*gleichsam als Pflicht*], the feeling in the judgment of taste" (KU 5: 296; 162).[14]

In order to understand Kant's conception of virtue, it is also necessary to consider the conditions to which it is opposed. There are two such conditions, namely, vice (*Laster*) and the mere lack of virtue (*Untugend*), and in *The Doctrine of Virtue* Kant distinguishes sharply between them. Thus, appealing to the same analogy he used in the explication of his rigorism in *Religion within the Limits of Reason Alone,* Kant states that the lack of virtue, which he also characterizes as moral weakness, is related to virtue as its logical opposite or contradictory, whereas the former is related to it as its real opposite or contrary (MS 6: 384; 42).

Since, logically speaking, the negation of virtue or nonvirtue (the contradictory) must include vice within it, this formulation is somewhat misleading. Nevertheless, Kant's point is clearly that simply to lack virtue, understood as strength of character or resoluteness in obedience to the law and the self-mastery that stems from it, is not equivalent to being actually vicious or wicked. The latter, unlike the former, is not only a deliberate but also a *principled* violation of one's duties. This does not mean that not doing one's duty is itself made into a principle (that would be the mark of a diabolical will), but rather that the vicious person is firmly committed to immoral principles (MS 6: 390; 50–1).

Actually, Kant has relatively little to say about vice; but perhaps the clearest statement of his views on the topic is contained in a passage devoted to a critique of the Aristotelian characterization of virtue as a mean between two extremes. The problem with this view, as he sees it, is that:

what distinguishes *avarice* (as a vice) from thrift (as a virtue) is not that avarice carries thrift *too far* but that avarice has an entirely different principle (maxim): that of economizing, not for the sake of *enjoying* one's wealth, but merely for the sake of *possessing* it, while denying oneself any enjoyment from it. (MS 6: 404n; 65)

Although Kant may have been unfair to Aristotle in suggesting that he regarded virtue as produced by mechanical habituation and in failing to acknowledge the role of practical reason in his predecessor's account,[15] he does succeed in calling attention to the essential difference in their views on the virtues and vices. If, with Aristotle, we construe virtues essentially as habitual desires conducive to human flourishing, then it perhaps makes sense to regard a virtue as a mean condition and a vice as an extreme. Given the Kantian conception, however, it makes no sense to regard virtues and vices in this manner. Desires can be excessive or insufficient but maxims cannot. Similarly, one cannot be excessive in following one's maxims, although one can, of course, adopt maxims calling for excessive behavior.

From Kant's standpoint, then, what distinguishes virtue from vice is not the degree to which one follows a certain maxim but the nature of the maxim that one follows. This is nicely illustrated by the example of avarice, which shows that what makes avarice a vice is that the avaricious person sets the mere possession of wealth as the ultimate end and makes it a matter of principle, as it were, that nothing is to be permitted to interfere with the pursuit of that goal. Such a principle is immoral because it leads necessarily to the violation of duties, both to others and to oneself.

By contrast, mere lack of virtue or moral weakness is compatible with good maxims and even, as Kant suggests at one point (echoing *Religion within the Limits of Reason Alone*), with "the best will" (*dem besten Willen*) (MS 6: 408; 69). It is manifested particularly in a failure to fulfill (at least to the degree that one might) the duties of virtue. Unlike the vicious person, who actually "makes it his principle not to submit to these duties," the unvirtuous or morally weak person recognizes the general obligation to pursue the ends dictated by these duties: to help others and to cultivate one's own perfections. In that sense, then, such a person has the correct maxims. The failure consists in a lack of sufficient resolve to act on these maxims (MS 6: 391; 51–2). Such a person is easily sidetracked in the fulfillment of his duties, in Kant's terms, "letting himself be ruled by his feelings and inclinations" (MS 6: 408; 70). Once again, however, as Kant's locution indicates, such "weakness" is itself an expression of freedom and therefore imputable.

We have noted on several occasions the connection between Kant's conception of virtue and his doctrine of radical evil. This connection is also apparent in the account of moral weakness. Although it operates at a different level, since it is concerned with the actual neglect of duty rather than a mere propensity to neglect it, this account closely parallels the analysis of fragility or weakness as the first degree of radical evil.[16] As was emphasized at the very beginning of the chapter, however, the key to the connection between virtue and radical evil lies in the claim that the moral life begins not in innocence but in the struggle with wickedness.

That is why in *Religion within the Limits of Reason Alone*, Kant insists that the pursuit of virtue involves not merely a "change of practices" (*Sitten*) but also a "change of heart," that is, a revolution or radical change in one's *Gesinnung* (Rel 6: 46–7; 42–3).[17] Admittedly, this line of thought is not as prominent in *The Doctrine of Virtue*, but it is not entirely absent. Thus, in a passage in which his main theme is that virtue is acquired only through cultivation and practice, Kant concludes:

> But the *resolution* [*Entschliessung*] to practice virtue must be made all at once and in its entirely, since the intention [*Gesinnung*] (*animus*) of surrendering at times to vice, in order gradually to break away from it, would in itself be impure and even immoral. Consequently this attitude could also produce no virtue (in so far as virtue is based on a single principle). (MS 6: 477; 149)

As the passage makes clear, Kant's point is that a mere reform in one's behavior is perfectly compatible with the continuance of an evil disposition.

169

In fact, if it is *merely* such a reform, it leaves the propensity to evil intact and therefore cannot lead to genuine virtue. Similarly, the attempt to achieve virtue gradually, much as one might attempt to quit smoking in stages, is inherently self-defeating because the project presupposes a continued attachment to nonmoral incentives, which is just what the propensity to evil amounts to in the first place. Thus, the first step on the road to virtue must be a firm resolution to break with this propensity and to restore the order of incentives to their original and proper ranking. Since this resolution involves a break with one's previous disposition, it amounts to a dispositional change or revolution in one's cast of mind (*Denkungsart*). Moreover, since the disposition with which one breaks is evil, Kant insists that this revolution must consist in the adoption of the opposite maxim of holiness (Rel 6: 47–8; 43–4).

This conception of a revolution in one's cast of mind, which Kant describes in the biblical language of a "rebirth" and a "new creation," is perhaps the most perplexing feature of Kant's whole discussion of the moral life. Indeed, it calls to mind all of the difficulties already noted in the initial discussion of *Gesinnung* (Chapter 7) and gives them an additional poignancy. Put simply, the basic problem is that the very radical evil, which makes such a revolution necessary as a precondition of the attainment of virtue, would also seem to make it impossible.[18] At the very least, such an attitudinal change would seem to require a bootstrap operation of heroic proportions. Moreover, Kant himself is of little help, as he admits its inexplicability while insisting that it must be possible since it is required (Rel 6: 47, 50; 43, 46).

Nevertheless, the air of paradox surrounding this claim can be mitigated somewhat, if not totally removed, by considering it in light of Kant's conception of radical evil. To begin with, we must keep in mind that this conception hardly amounts to a doctrine of total depravity. On the contrary, the predisposition to good and therefore the capacity to be motivated by respect for the law is presupposed as still operative. Moreover, what is required is not a shift from a propensity to evil to a propensity to good; that would be impossible, according to Kant, since it would require becoming holy. It is rather that we are required to struggle against this propensity, which remains inextirpable, instead of yielding to it by means of the self-deceptive strategies noted in Chapter 8. To commit oneself to this struggle, which amounts to taking the moral life with full existential seriousness, is to reverse the order of incentives and to adopt a maxim of holiness. Assuming transcendental freedom, itself obviously a large assumption, such a commitment is at least conceivable, which is all that Kant claims.

It is equally true, however, that to make such a resolution, even in all sincerity, is not yet to be virtuous. It is also necessary to strive continually to progress in the actual exercise of virtue, that is, in the performance of one's duties from duty. Thus, whereas the moral life, as Kant conceives it, is in one sense an all-or-nothing affair, requiring a "change of heart" or "rebirth," apart from which particular virtues are nothing more than "splendid vices"; in another sense it is a matter of degree, of a continued effort to approximate an ideal. As Kant puts it in a particularly noteworthy passage in *The Doctrine of Virtue:*

Virtue is always in *progress* and yet always beginning *from the beginning.* It is always in progress because, considered *objectively,* it is an ideal which is unobtainable, while yet our duty is constantly to approximate to it. That it is always beginning anew has a *subjective* basis in human nature, which is affected by inclinations under whose influence virtue can never settle down in peace and quiet, with its maxims adopted once and for all – unless it is climbing, it inevitably sinks. (MS 6: 409; 71)

II. Holiness as a moral ideal

The conception of virtue sketched in the preceding section not only presupposes a revolution or radical reorientation of the will (*Willkür*) as a condition of its possibility but also requires us to conceive this revolution as the adoption of a maxim of holiness. Thus, although Kant defines virtue in opposition to holiness, claiming that the former is the highest stage of morality possible for imperfect, finite rational beings such as ourselves, he also insists that the life of virtue involves, as an essential component, the pursuit of holiness. Needless to say, this creates a fresh problem, which threatens the coherence of Kant's whole account of virtue.

The problem does not lie in understanding why Kant should think it necessary to adopt a maxim of holiness rather than, say, one of becoming more virtuous, of trying harder, or some such less extreme principle. Given the doctrine of radical evil, it is clear that a genuine resolution to break with evil, that is, to cease yielding to that inextirpable propensity, must consist in a resolution to seek holiness, understood as a perfect purity of disposition. To settle for anything less would amount to a capitulation to evil, and this is incompatible with virtue (MS 6: 446; 113).[19]

Even granting this, however, it is by no means clear how we can be obligated to adopt such a maxim; and herein lies the problem. Since one cannot sincerely adopt any maxim without acting according to it, one cannot adopt a maxim of holiness without striving with all one's power to realize this ideal. Any less zeal is incompatible with the sincere adoption of the maxim (one cannot pursue perfection halfheartedly). But holiness, as we have seen, is unattainable by finite beings. We can struggle against our propensity to evil but we cannot extirpate it. Accordingly, it turns out that we are morally required to pursue an unattainable goal; and this seems absurd. Since Kant is famous for insisting that ought implies can, he was obviously well aware of this difficulty. In fact, he attempts to deal with it in the *Critique of Practical Reason, Religion within the Limits of Reason Alone,* and *The Doctrine of Virtue.* I shall consider each attempt in turn.

1. In the *Critique of Practical Reason,* Kant treats the problem in connection with the account of immortality, which, together with the existence of God (and freedom), is postulated as a necessary condition of the realization of the Highest Good. This good is defined as the union of virtue and happiness, with the former "wearing the trousers" in the sense that it is the

171

condition under which happiness is to be allotted. As usual, the operative assumption is that since we are morally required to do all in our power to realize the Highest Good, it must be assumed to be possible of attainment. Since the distribution of happiness in exact proportion to virtue is beyond human capacity or, more precisely, is not something that can be assumed to occur according to the laws of nature, it is left to God to accomplish this task. Accordingly, our task is to supply the required virtue. At least that is what one would naturally assume.

In arguing for the necessity of postulating immortality, however, Kant describes the supreme (moral) condition of the Highest Good not simply as virtue but as "the complete fitness of intentions [*die völlige Angemessenheit der Gesinnungen*] to the moral law." Moreover, as he proceeds to note, such complete fitness is precisely holiness, "which is a perfection of which no rational being in the world of sense is at any time capable" (KprV 5: 122; 126). Accordingly, our part in the realization of the Highest Good is redefined as the achievement of holiness.

Since a complete fitness of the will to the law, or equivalently holiness, is something of which no rational being "in the world of sense" is capable at any point in time, Kant stipulates that it "can be found [*angetroffen*] only in an endless progress to that complete fitness." He also asserts the necessity of regarding such progress "as the real object of our will." This in turn leads to the postulation of immortality as the sole condition under which the required progress is possible. As Kant puts it, "This infinite progress is possible... only under the presupposition of an infinitely enduring existence and personality of the same rational being" (KprV 5: 122; 127).

The most obvious and frequently cited difficulty with Kant's "moral proof" of immortality concerns the intelligibility of the idea of a "future" life outside time involving endless progress.[20] I am not sure that anything very useful can be said in defense of Kant at this point, and in any event, I shall not attempt a defense here. Nevertheless, even leaving that issue aside, serious problems remain.

To begin with, there is the previously noted shift from virtue to holiness as the required moral component in the Highest Good. Clearly, this shift is needed to get the argument for postulating immortality off the ground, since Kant could hardly claim that we need an eternity to become virtuous. Unfortunately, Kant supplies absolutely no explanation for it; so that one is left with the strong impression that the whole account is artificial in the extreme.[21]

If the previous analysis of virtue is correct, this problem can be partially resolved by providing an account of virtue (something that Kant does not do in the *Critique of Practical Reason*). Since this would show that virtue consists in the resolute pursuit of holiness, it would at least explain why the *pursuit* of holiness is necessary. This does not resolve the problem completely, however, because what is supposedly required for the realization of the Highest Good is not simply the pursuit of holiness, or even genuine progress in this pursuit, but rather its actual attainment. Moreover, it is clear that the postulation of immortality is of no help here, since the most that it allows for is the possibility of endless progress. Thus, in his effort to justify this postulate, it appears that Kant shifts unannounced first from virtue to holiness and then from holiness to unending progress in the pursuit of it. Initially, at least, this seems very much like the kind of illicit shift or dissemblance (*Verstellung*) that Hegel ridiculed in his famous critique of Kant's doctrine of the postulates in the *Phenomenology*.[22]

Admittedly, this is not completely fair to Kant because, as noted, he does state that holiness is met with in this endless progress. If this is the case, then holiness is attainable after all, which entails that it can be regarded as a condition of the Highest Good and the pursuit of it can be required. Nevertheless, this ploy serves merely to shift the locus of the difficulty. Since, as Allen Wood points out, Kant can hardly mean that holiness is actually attained at a particular point *within* or at the *end* of this endless progress, he can only mean that some condition, feature, or counterpart of this endless progress is to somehow count as holiness.[23] Moreover, this is precisely what his claim amounts to. After acknowledging that endless progress from lower to higher stages of moral perfection is the most that is possible for a finite rational being, Kant suggests that "the infinite Being, to whom the temporal condition is nothing, sees in this series . . . a whole conformable to the moral law; holiness . . . is to be found in a single intellectual intuition of the existence of rational beings" (KprV 5: 123; 127).

As the subsequent discussion makes clear, this "whole," accessible to God through an intellectual intuition, turns out to be the "immutable *Gesinnung*" of the agent, that is, the resolute disposition to achieve holiness. Consequently, Kant's position, at least in the *Critique of Practical Reason,* ends up being that in the eyes of God this disposition, as exemplified in a life of moral earnestness, is equivalent to holiness itself. But since the problem of the reasonableness of the requirement to pursue holiness only arose in the first place because of the allegedly unbridgeable gap between the disposition to holiness and holiness itself, it would appear that this "solution" begs the question at issue.[24]

2. In *Religion within the Limits of Reason Alone,* Kant takes up this theme again, this time in connection with a discussion of the ideal of moral perfection, which in Christian terms is equivalent to the ideal of a humanity pleasing to God. As before, the realization of this ideal is considered as the supreme condition of the Highest Good, and likewise as before, Kant both insists that we have a duty to realize it and acknowledges the impossibility of full compliance because of the disparity between disposition and deed. Moreover, the proposed solution is once again that for God the purity of disposition counts as the deed. Consequently, those who have undergone the required spiritual transformation, that is, sincerely adopted the maxim of holiness or, as he now puts it, striven to follow the archetype of moral perfection, have reason to hope that they will become well pleasing to God (Rel 6: 60–6; 54–60). Unlike the *Critique of Practical Reason,* however, Kant here at least raises the essential question by asking: "How can a dis-

position count for the act itself, when the act is *always* (not universally, but at each instant of time) defective?" (Rel 6: 67, 60).

Unfortunately, Kant's answer is not very helpful. In fact, it consists in little more than a slightly qualified reiteration of the doctrine of the second Critique. Thus, he remarks that in spite of our unavoidable confinement to time conditions, which requires us to conceive of the moral life as a series of discrete, imperfect acts, that is, as a progression, we may nonetheless think of it as "being judged by Him who knows the heart, through a purely intellectual intuition, as a completed whole, because of the disposition, supersensible in its nature, from which this progress itself is derived" (Rel 6: 67; 60).[25] In addition to not really answering the question, this "solution" has the defect of suggesting that the moral struggle, and therefore whatever progress we make, is itself something "merely phenomenal" and, as such, becomes irrelevant when the moral life is viewed *sub specie aeternitatis*. According to this view, there would be no difficulty in allowing the disposition to count as the deed, but only because the very distinction between them, which generates the problem in the first place, is relativized to our finite, human perspective.

In a footnote attached to the text, Kant qualifies the claim that the disposition can count for the deed by suggesting that it does not compensate for all moral imperfections but only "for that failure which is inseparable from the existence of a temporal being as such, the failure, namely, ever wholly to be what we have in mind to become" (Rel 6: 67n, 61). This helps somewhat, since it eliminates an obvious objection; but it hardly addresses the main question.

In spite of this, Allen Wood has argued that Kant does provide an answer to this question, indeed a successful one, in *Religion within the Limits of Reason Alone*. Reduced to its essentials, Kant's answer, according to Wood, is that the disposition counts as the deed because of divine grace.[26] In other words, God not only grasps the disposition through an intellectual intuition but also allows this disposition to compensate for the moral deficiencies that are inseparable from finitude. Since this is done only in the case of those who have made a genuine commitment to the pursuit of holiness, it has a moral basis; but since it grants something that, strictly speaking, is undeserved, it is nonetheless an act of grace. In support of this interpretation, Wood cites Kant's claim:

Here, then, is that surplus . . . over the profit from good works, and it is itself a profit which is reckoned to us by *grace*. That what in our earthly life (and possibly at all future times and in all worlds) is ever only a *becoming* (namely, becoming a man well pleasing to God) should be credited to us exactly as if we were already in full possession of it. (Rel 6: 75; 70)[27]

As Wood recognizes, Kant actually makes this appeal to grace in response to a different difficulty, namely, that of explaining how even those with a good disposition can be well pleasing to God, since the propensity to evil (original sin) remains. In other words, Kant's appeal to divine grace is intended as the basis of a rational reconstruction of the Christian conception of the vicarious satisfaction rather than as a solution to the problem of how the disposition can count as the deed.[28] Nevertheless, Wood insists that it is equally relevant to the latter problem.

But even granting the correctness of Wood's exegesis, it is not at all clear that the proposed solution is much of an improvement. Quite apart from the problems involved in any appeal to divine grace, if we really have done all that we can (which must be assumed if we are to be deemed "worthy" of grace in the first place), then we have done all that can reasonably be expected of us. On this assumption, then, there remains no gap to be filled by grace. Interestingly enough, however, the same problem does not arise with respect to the explicit purpose to which Kant puts the concept of grace. Since with respect to that purpose a genuine gap remains (due to the propensity to evil) even after we have done all that we can, there is still a need for justification and therefore a conceptual space for divine grace.

3. In *The Doctrine of Virtue,* the obligation to holiness is treated within the context of a discussion of duties to oneself as a moral being. Moreover, Kant here distinguishes explicitly, as he previously had not, between holiness and moral perfection. The former concerns the subjective element in morality, the purity of one's disposition; so the command "be holy" expresses the requirement to make duty alone the motive of one's actions. The latter concerns the objective element, the extent of one's obligations; so the command "be perfect" expresses the requirement to perform all one's duties (MS 6: 446; 113). Although Kant does not discuss the point, it seems reasonable to assume that the latter requirement does not merely stipulate that we should never violate the moral law, that is, never lie, steal, cheat, and so on (that would be gratuitous), but rather enjoins us positively to perfect all of the particular virtues associated with the various duties of virtue.

In addition, Kant now classifies both duties as imperfect or of wide obligation. In the case of holiness, which is the main focus of our concern, this means simply that we are required to strive to the utmost of our ability after purity of motive without the expectation that we shall ever attain it. Now, one might think that this is not really anything new, since Kant consistently affirms the unattainability of holiness. Nevertheless, we have seen that he also struggled with the pseudoproblem of how something less than holiness could count as the attainment of it; and once it is recognized that our duty is merely to strive after holiness, not to attain it, that issue disappears. Moreover, with it goes the need for the postulate of immortality, God's intellectual intuition and grace (at least insofar as they are relevant to that concern).

As is so often the case, however, this development brings with it fresh problems. The major new difficulty is that the obligation to holiness (and the same can be said *mutatis mutandis* of perfection) does not seem to fit the paradigm of imperfect duties. As we have seen, such duties are of wide obligation, which means that they enjoin the pursuit of certain ends or, more precisely, the adoption of maxims to pursue certain ends, rather than the performance or prohibition of specific actions. To be sure, holiness does not require specific actions, but it does require a disposition that is in complete accordance with the law or, as Kant here puts it, that always acts from duty. Moreover, this is clearly a demand that allows no latitude. A disposition to be as holy as possible or holy in general is not a disposition to be holy at all.

Kant himself shows a keen awareness of the problem, since he states that although the duty is "*narrow* and perfect . . . in its quality," it is "wide and imperfect in its degree." He further states that this is due to the "*frailty* (*fragilitas*) of human nature" (MS 6: 446; 113). Unfortunately, the distinction between quality and degree is clearly an ad hoc device, designed to deal with the anomalous nature of the duty of holiness (and perfection). Similarly, the frailty of human nature should have no bearing on the question of whether a duty is perfect or imperfect, since it cannot justify any latitude in the rule. Indeed, if it could, then all duties would be imperfect.

The situation is further complicated by the fact that Kant offers a second but equally irrelevant justification for the imperfect nature of the duty to pursue holiness, namely, the familiar doctrine of the ineliminable uncertainty regarding our own motivation. Given this uncertainty, Kant suggests that no one is ever in a position to know whether one has acted from duty alone or "whether there are not many other impulses of sensuous origin, co-operating with it – motives that look to advantage (or to avoiding disadvantage) and that, in other circumstances, could just as well serve vice" (MS 6: 447; 114). In short, Kant's argument seems to be that because we can never, in any given instance, be certain whether we have acted from duty alone, our duty to seek holiness (understood as complete purity of motive) must be imperfect, enjoining merely the adoption of the maxim to strive to the best of our ability after it (MS 6: 392; 52–3).[29]

This line of argument raises a number of serious questions. The first is its compatibility with key elements of Kant's moral theory. Kant usually contrasts holiness, of which we are not capable, with acting from duty or respect for the law, of which we are capable. In the present instance, however, he seems to have virtually identified them, thereby also raising doubts about the possibility of acting from duty alone. Second, like the appeal to human frailty, it is irrelevant to the point at issue. Why, after all, should our incapacity to know with complete certainty whether we have fulfilled an obligation affect the degree of the obligation itself? Third, it only displaces the problem; for we would seem to be equally incapable of knowing with certainty whether we have tried as hard as we can. Finally, even if all of these problems can be dealt with successfully, it remains the case that the duty to pursue holiness still fails to meet the official criteria for imperfect duties.

The first point can be handled fairly easily. Thus, although it is true that, as it stands, Kant's claim virtually identifies a holy will with a pure will, that is, one that acts from duty alone in all morally relevant contexts, it can be reformulated so as to avoid that difficulty. Suitably reformulated, it becomes the claim that regardless of one's present and past success in the moral

176

struggle, one can never be certain that one is not susceptible of temptation, that one's virtuous activity was not a matter of moral luck (not encountering what would truly tempt one).[30] This accords both with Kant's conception of holiness and with the possibility of acting from duty alone.

The appeal to an ineliminable uncertainty regarding one's motivation can also be defended if, as seems reasonable, the duty to pursue holiness is taken to include moral self-evaluation. In fact, at one point Kant explicitly refers to the duty of "valuing the worth of one's actions not merely by their legality but also by their morality (attitude of will [*Gesinnung*])" and claims that *this* duty is only of wide obligation (MS 6: 393; 53). Clearly, if we can never attain certainty regarding our own motivation, then the most that we can be expected to do is to be as conscientious as possible in our moral self-examination.[31] Given what we have already seen about the connection between radical evil and self-deceptive strategies of justification, we can readily understand why Kant regarded such self-examination as an absolutely vital part of the moral life.[32]

Moreover, although the same epistemological limitations do apply to our ability to know if we have tried as hard as we can, this does not undermine the requirement of moral self-evaluation because it does not amount to a radical skepticism regarding self-knowledge.[33] Clearly, there are many instances in which we are aware that we have not been as scrupulous as we might have been, or at least in which we could have been aware had we bothered to reflect. Accordingly our lack of certainty regarding our own motivation together with our propensity to develop self-deceptive strategies create a justifiable suspicion concerning any appearance of purity; but they neither rule out the possibility of such purity (construed as action from duty alone) nor render the process of moral self-examination otiose. On the contrary, the latter is precisely what gives this process its moral significance.

Admittedly, it remains the case that the duty to strive for holiness does not allow for the kind of latitude that is supposedly characteristic of imperfect duties; but this should neither surprise us nor be used as a pretext for the complete rejection of Kant's account. With regard to the first point, it is clear that holiness is not the only duty that does not fit neatly into the Kantian schema. In fact, it is notorious that Kant's account suffers from his desire to force the distinctions between perfect and imperfect duties, juridical and ethical duties, and duties to oneself and duties to others into a single, rigid, conceptual framework. For example, a large part of *The Doctrine of Virtue* is concerned with a set of perfect duties to oneself, thus of duties that presumably combine the incompatible properties of requiring specific actions or omissions (as perfect) and of requiring only the adoption of maxims (as duties of virtue).[34]

In light of this fact, the reasonable course seems to be to acknowledge the anomalous nature of the duty to pursue holiness and to consider whether a good case can be made for granting it imperfect status.[35] The key point here (and the same applies to moral perfection) is that this duty concerns the moral life as a whole, not simply one particular sphere of action. As such, it concerns the orientation of one's existence as an ethical being. But the requirement to orient one's life in a certain direction, namely, toward an ideal, is one that can never, in principle, be completable; it is in this sense that it is "imperfect."

It is, of course, true that there is a legitimate sense in which no obligations are completable. For example, there never comes a point (short of the moment of death) at which one may claim that one has been sufficiently truthful. No matter how truthful one has been in the past, one is still under the obligation to be truthful in the future, and the same holds, *mutatis mutandis*, for all "perfect" duties. Nevertheless, there is still a significant difference in that in the case of truthfulness there is a determinate degree (complete truthfulness) that is required of us; whereas in the case of holiness there is no maximum, no achievable degree that satisfies the requirement and with which we may be content. In short, no matter how hard we try, there is always room for improvement. Thus, to be satisfied with a certain level of virtue (or holiness) is to violate one's duty.

Against this, it might be argued that the entire discussion of holiness up to this point has ignored the central issue. The concern has been to show that the duty to strive after holiness is imperfect; but perhaps the real question is whether there is any such duty at all. Indeed, it has been maintained by W. D. Ross that the claim that we have such a duty or, more generally, the claim that we have a separate duty to act from duty involves Kant in an infinite regress. The point here is simply that if in connection with every duty we also have a further duty to do it from duty, then that principle must apply to that further duty *ad infinitum*.[36] Or alternatively, if one thinks that this objection is unfair to Kant or that he can reformulate his position so as to avoid it, it might still be argued that his doctrine rests on his failure to distinguish adequately between his theories of moral praise and of moral obligation. An action may be morally praiseworthy only if it is done from duty, but it hardly follows from this that we have a distinct obligation to perform praiseworthy acts.[37]

Since the issue is inexorably intertwined with some of the most controversial topics in Kant's moral theory, including the conception of a duty to oneself and the doctrine of the Highest Good, I cannot hope to deal adequately with it here. Nevertheless, certain things can be said in defense of Kant's claim that we have such a duty. To begin with, the duty to seek holiness is the obligation to strive toward a well-defined state of moral perfection. As such, there is no infinite regress, although there is, to be sure, an infinite task. For similar reasons, the requirement cannot be dismissed as the product of a confusion of the conditions of moral praise and moral obligation. It is not that one is obligated to strive toward the goal of being worthy of moral praise; it is rather that such praise is appropriately awarded on the basis of the strength of character (virtue) that one manifests in the pursuit of that goal. Moreover, since holiness represents a specific kind of moral perfection, the justification of the claim that we have a duty to strive toward it must be of a piece with the justification of the claim that we have a duty to develop any of our capacities or "perfections." In other words, it must consist essentially in an argument to the effect that to neglect to develop these capacities is to deny "humanity in oneself" and therefore one's status as an end in oneself, an autonomous moral agent.[38]

Finally, although Kant develops this general line of argument in *The Doctrine of Virtue* independently of and without explicit reference to his doctrine of radical evil, it acquires additional significance when seen in connection with the latter doctrine. As we have already seen, Kant holds that because of our self-imposed propensity to evil, the path to virtue must begin with a revolution or radical change of disposition and this revolution consists in the adoption of a maxim of holiness. Accordingly, to fail to adopt this maxim, that is, to fail to strive toward holiness, is to rest content with one's radical evil. But to do this is to opt out of the moral struggle, to choose freely to content oneself with (at best) conformity to the letter of the law; and this is, indeed, to deny one's status as a moral agent. For these reasons, then, the claim that we have an imperfect duty to strive after the unobtainable ideal of holiness is not an eliminable addendum to Kant's moral theory but rather an essential component of it.

10
The classical objections

Although many objections to various aspects of Kant's conception of moral agency and moral psychology have been considered in the preceding four chapters, we have not yet dealt explicitly with a line of objection that deserves to be termed "classical" because of its long and distinguished history. This line can be traced back to some of Kant's most important contemporaries and immediate successors, most notably Schiller and Hegel, and it reappears in the work of influential present-day writers such as Bernard Williams. Thus, it seems appropriate to conclude this portion of the study with a consideration of its essential features and the formulation of a possible Kantian response.

This consideration must be prefaced, however, with two large caveats. First, since this line reflects the criticisms of thinkers with quite different overall philosophical commitments, who attack Kant from quite different points of view, it would require a separate book (and a lengthy one at that) to deal adequately with all of the points at issue and to consider the differing nuances of the various criticisms. Accordingly, I shall limit myself to the attempt to express the main thrust of this line of objection as it is reflected in the criticisms of Schiller, Hegel, and Williams, followed in each case by a brief sketch of a possible (in the case of Schiller, at least in part, an actual) Kantian rejoinder. Second, since much of Kant's account of moral agency and his moral psychology presuppose the objective reality of the moral law, and since Kant's attempt to ground morality as he conceives it has not yet been considered, the defense mounted on his behalf at this point necessarily has a provisional status. Nevertheless, where the present provisional analysis fails to convince, it is hoped that it will at least help clarify the issues.

I. Schiller's critique

Schiller's major challenge to Kant's moral psychology is not contained in the famous joke discussed in Chapter 6 but in his seminal essay, "On Grace and Dignity."[1] This challenge is largely indirect, however, since Schiller ostensibly criticizes Kant's rhetoric or mode of presentation rather than his doctrine. Expressing basic agreement with Kantian principles, particularly the critique of eudaemonism and the grounding of the moral law in reason alone, he nonetheless complains that because of the manner in which Kant and his followers ordinarily express these principles, an impression is created that "inclination can never be ... otherwise than a very suspicious companion, and pleasure a dangerous auxiliary for moral determinations."[2] Schiller's self-imposed task, then, is to correct the unduly harsh picture that Kant paints of the moral life by emphasizing the proper role in this life of the sensuous, emotive side of human nature. In terms of Schiller's governing metaphor, he must show how dignity is complemented and perfected by grace.

Even though Kant himself took Schiller at his word in acknowledging an agreement in principle, it is generally recognized that there are fundamental differences separating the two thinkers and that these concern mainly the moral significance attributed to sensibility.[3] As the passage cited in the previous paragraph indicates, Schiller grants a much more positive role to sensibility than does Kant. In this spirit, he characterizes virtue as involving an "inclination to duty" and suggests not merely that it is possible to perform one's duty with pleasure but also that one "ought to establish between them this accord," one "ought to obey...reason with a sentiment of joy."[4] In addition, Schiller criticizes Kant's insistence on the imperatival form of the law with respect to human beings and suggests that in spite of the principle of autonomy this gives to the law the "appearance of a foreign law, a positive law," through which reason tyrannizes over the sensuous side of the self.[5] It is with the latter point in mind that he asks: "If in the moral realm the sensuous nature were only the oppressed and not a contributing party, how could it participate with all the ardor of its sentiments in a triumph which would be celebrated only over itself?"[6]

Finally, it is clear that this critique reflects not merely a difference of emphasis but a radically different conception of the state of moral health. For Kant, this state is one in which reason controls and limits (but not really suppresses) the inclinations; for Schiller, it is one in which the two coexist in perfect harmony, with each directed toward the same end. An individual in whom this harmony is present is called by Schiller a "beautiful soul" (*schöne Seele*), and for such an individual morality allegedly becomes a "second nature" rather than an onerous obligation.[7]

In dealing with the much discussed topic of the Kantian response to Schiller, we have the advantage of Kant's own words on the subject. These are to be found in a long note in *Religion within the Limits of Reason Alone* and in a brief discussion in the *Vorarbeiten* to that work, which did not find its way into the published text.[8] In addition, there are the remarks about virtue in *The Doctrine of Virtue*, which were considered in the last chapter. Although Kant does not there refer explicitly to Schiller, his characterization of the demeanor of the virtuous person closely parallels that of the earlier work and was undoubtedly written with Schiller's critique in mind.

Unfortunately, these materials are of only limited value, since they themselves require a good deal of interpretation. The direct response, particularly in its published form, is quite conciliatory and accepts at face value Schiller's contention that the difference between them is largely one of presentation. Similarly, the remarks about virtue stress Kant's partial agreement with Schiller while ignoring their deep differences. As Gerold Prauss has suggested, however, perhaps the most important text for reconstructing the full Kantian response to Schiller is the *Critique of Practical Reason,* particularly the discussion of moral fanaticism considered in Chapter 8.[9] Thus, Kant's own failure to refer back to this important but generally neglected portion of the second *Critique* should not deter us from doing so on his behalf.

In the published response, which maintains the highly conciliatory tone, Kant's strategy is to acknowledge the truth of Schiller's complaint that in emphasizing the dignity of the idea of duty he dissociated it from "the graces" while denying its significance. To this end, he states simply that "the idea of duty involves absolute necessity, to which grace stands in direct contradiction," and that "when duty alone is the theme, they [the graces] keep a respectful distance" (Rel 6: 23n; 19). The main point here is the familiar one that duty requires obedience to the impersonal dictates of pure practical reason, not following one's inclinations. Consequently, the whole "aesthetic" side of morality, that is, the question of inclination as opposed to principle (or grace as opposed to dignity in Schiller's terms), must be ignored or abstracted from when one is considering the nature and grounds of moral obligation.

At the same time, however, Kant also acknowledges that what Schiller refers to as the "graces" come into play in connection with virtue, defined as "the firmly grounded disposition strictly to fulfill our duty." In other words, he admits that a virtuous person will exhibit something like the qualities that Schiller regards as essential to the moral life. As he puts it:

Now if one asks, what is the *aesthetic character* [*Beschaffenheit*], the *temperament,* so to speak, *of virtue,* whether courageous and hence *joyous* or fear-ridden and dejected, an answer is hardly necessary. The latter slavish frame of mind can never occur without a hidden *hatred* of the law. And a heart which is happy in the *performance* of its duty (not merely complacent in the *recognition* thereof) is a mark of genuineness in the virtuous disposition. (Rel 6: 23–24n; 19–20)

In this apparent "concession" to Schiller, Kant is expressing his view that the genuinely virtuous person is cheerful in the performance of duty. But since he fails to indicate his reasons for holding this view, he creates the impression that there is more agreement than is in fact the case. Given his conception of virtue, Kant can certainly agree with Schiller that the moral life is not one of perpetual self-flagellation; that there is a deep sense in which "virtue is its own reward"; and that this is exhibited in the positive attitude of the genuinely virtuous person. For Kant, however, this is the result of the discipline of inclination or, more properly, of the propensity to yield to inclination, rather than of a spontaneous, undisciplined, "goodness" of character.

When considered in this light, perhaps the most significant feature of the passage is Kant's characterization of the joyous attitude merely as a "mark" (*Zeichen*) of virtue. By describing it in this way, Kant is implicitly distancing himself from Schiller, for whom the graces are not merely adornments or even signs of virtue but partially constitutive of it.[10] Moreover, if this difference had been brought out, Kant would have been able to claim that Schiller had conflated the question of moral motivation with the question of the comportment and attitude of the virtuous person. And with this, the battle lines would have been drawn.

Although he does not really offer any explanation, Kant goes further in the *Vorarbeiten* and dismisses as conradictory Schiller's claim that we have a duty to do something gladly and from inclination (*gern und aus Neigung*). In the same context, he also makes the important and previously noted distinction between doing something dutiful (*pflichtmässige*) with pleasure (*mit Lust*), which is perfectly possible, and doing something *from* duty with pleasure (*mit Lust aus Pflicht*), that is, taking pleasure in acting from duty, which presumably is impossible (23: 100).

As previously suggested, however, the full extent and the true grounds of Kant's disagreement with Schiller only become apparent when we supplement his direct response (in both its published and unpublished forms) with the critique of moral fanaticism. As noted in Chapter 8, Kant understands by moral fanaticism any view that locates the moral incentive in something ostensibly "higher" than respect for the law, but he particularly has in mind positions that ascribe to the virtuous disposition a "ready willingness" or "spontaneous inclination," unfettered by any thought of obligation or constraint, to fulfill the dictates of morality. Even from our brief sketch of Schiller's position, it is clear that his conception of an "inclination to duty" falls within that category and, therefore, that his ideal of a beautiful soul represents a species of moral fanaticism.

Given this, it is relatively easy to fill in the gaps in Kant's direct response to Schiller. The essential point is that by raising the possibility for human beings of a form of morality that can dispense with the thought of obligation, Schiller is in effect forgetting our ontological status as finite, sensuously affected beings. Since our form of morality is grounded in this ontological status, its characteristic feature of constraint cannot be eliminated or overcome through the development of a good disposition or the right desires.

This emphasis on human finitude likewise accounts for the radical gulf separating Kant's problematic conception of holiness from Schiller's superficially similar conception of a beautiful soul. Reduced to its essentials, the difference consists in the fact that whereas the latter is conceived as a moral condition attainable by human beings through a moralization of the inclinations (the development of an inclination to duty), holiness is a purely regulative idea to be approached asymptotically but never attained by a finite rational agent. Accordingly, when Kant speaks, as he does in the *Critique of Practical Reason,* of "practical love" toward God as "liking" to do His commandments (*seine Gebote gerne tun*) and of such love toward one's neighbor as liking to practice all duties toward him (*alle Pflicht gegen ihn gerne ausüben*), he must be taken to be referring to the unobtainable, yet pursuable ideal of a pure will, not to a state in which we have something like Schiller's inclination to duty.[11]

Moreover, the claim that our finitude does not enable us to transcend the

183

standpoint of duty does not entail, as Schiller (and later Hegel) thought, that the law must be conceived as confronting us as an alien burden that tyrannizes over our sensuous nature. The point is rather merely that the moment of rational constraint, the ought, is never *entirely* absent, even for the best of us. If it were, we would be beyond the possibility of temptation and therefore holy rather than merely virtuous beings. Accordingly, from Kant's point of view, Schiller (and Hegel after him) could be accused of conflating the "discipline of reason," which is an ineliminable component of the moral life for a finite rational agent,[12] with a tyranny thereof, which, far from being a mark of genuine virtue, is symptomatic of what Kant terms "fantastic virtue."[13]

Finally, this also enables us to understand Kant's claim in the *Vorarbeiten* that Schiller's contention that we ought to do our duty gladly (in the sense of from inclination) is contradictory. As we have already seen, the claim is not that the very idea of a "ready willingness" to conform to the moral law is contradictory or otherwise incoherent (since this is precisely how a holy will is characterized). Nor is it that we cannot have an inclination to perform the very same act or pursue the very same end that we have a duty to perform or pursue. It is rather that we cannot have an inclination to do something *because* it is our duty to do it (an inclination to duty). If we did, then the moral requirement would not be represented as a duty because the law would not take the form of an imperative. And since the latter is necessary for unholy beings such as ourselves, so too is the moment of moral constraint.

II. Hegel's critique

As a critic of Kantian moral theory, Hegel is perhaps best known for his contention that this theory amounts to nothing more than an "empty formalism." Reduced to its essentials, the familiar objection is that the categorical imperative, at least in the universal law formula, is incapable of providing either a principle from which specific duties can be derived or even a criterion by means of which the moral correctness of maxims can be tested. The former is the case because Kant is allegedly forced to import gratuitous empirical assumptions in order to arrive at particular obligations and the latter because the only available criterion, noncontradictoriness, can be met by any properly formed maxim, even the most immoral.[14] This line of argument is then used as the basis for the replacement of the abstract, formal, and individualistic conception of morality (*Moralität*), which is best exemplified by Kant's theory, with a concrete, social ethos (*Sittlichkeit*), wherein moral norms and principles are embodied in the institutions of a society.

Although the issues are still controversial, a number of Kant sympathizers have argued quite persuasively that the entire line of criticism is misguided, since it rests upon an extremely implausible reading of Kant's position.[15] In addition, it can be argued that the Hegelian conception of *Sittlichkeit* involves significant difficulties of its own.[16] Recently, however both Andreas

Wildt and Allen Wood, while acknowledging the force of the Kantian reply to the "emptiness" objection in its standard form, have attempted to resurrect the Hegelian critique by arguing that its main target is not the categorical imperative at all but rather Kant's account of moral motivation and worth.[17] It is also this aspect of Hegel's Kant critique that both reflects the influence of Schiller and anticipates the criticisms of contemporary thinkers such as Williams.

Hegel first gave expression to this line of criticism in his youthful essay, "The Spirit of Christianity and Its Fate," where he contrasts the spirit of Judaism, which is based on the Mosaic law and which he regards as antithetical to freedom, with the spirit of Christianity, which is based on love. Within this framework, he links Kantian ethics with the former and contrasts both with the moral teaching of the Sermon on the Mount. Moreover, from the standpoint of an essentially religious ethic of love and reconciliation, he criticizes sharply what he takes to be Kant's reduction of the biblical injunction to love God first and one's neighbor as oneself to the moral imperative.[18] Thus, echoing Schiller, he remarks that the difference between those who are subjected to positive religion (which for Hegel includes the Tungu Shaman, the European prelate, the Voguls, and the Puritans) and the Kantian autonomous moral agent ("the man who listens to his own command of duty")

is not that the former make themselves slaves, while the latter is free, but that the former have their lord outside themselves, while the latter carries his lord in himself, yet at the same time is his own slave. For the particular – impulses, inclinations, pathological love, sensuous experience, or whatever else it is called – the universal is necessarily and always something alien and objective.[19]

The main point in this passage is that Kantian morality, particularly its central conception of autonomy, involves a kind of self-imposed tyranny of the universal (rational) over the particular (sensuous) part of the self. Consequently, it produces a diremption within the self rather than the desired harmony or integration. This self-diremption then requires healing by means of the religious ethic of love, which is the young Hegel's counterpart of Schiller's ideal of a beautiful soul. Although the mature Hegel rejected much of his early religious romanticism, he continued to assign a crucial role to love and reconciliation as stages in the dialectic of "Spirit." Moreover, he also continued to locate the main problem with Kantian morality in its inability to connect properly the universal (rational goals and principles) and the particular (the interests and inclinations of individuals). Nevertheless, the thrust of this critique shifts from an emphasis on what might be termed the existential implications of the Kantian requirement to the alleged incoherence of the underlying theories of agency and of moral motivation. This in turn leads naturally to the familiar charges of hypocrisy (in connection with the Postulates) and of positing an unbridgeable gap between is and ought.

According to Allen Wood's reconstruction of the Hegelian critique, the

185

alleged incoherence stems from the incompatibility of the requirement that an action be motivated by duty alone if it is to possess moral worth, with the conditions of the possibility of the agency. As Hegel himself puts it in his critique of the "moral view of the world" in the *Phenomenology*:

> According to this latter view, I act morally when I am *conscious* of performing only pure duty and nothing else but that; this means, in fact, when I do *not* act. But when I really act, I am conscious of an 'other,' of a reality which is already in existence, and of a reality I wish to produce; I have a *specific* purpose and fulfill a *specific* duty in which there is something else than the pure duty which alone should be intended.[20]

As Wood indicates, Hegel's essential claim in this passage is that to pursue any determinate end or, equivalently, to act on the basis of any nonvacuous principle is necessarily to act from something other than pure duty, and this other can only be the particular interests, desires, or inclinations of the agent.[21] It follows from this that the requirement to act from duty alone is incoherent in the sense that the attempt to meet it, that is, the attempt to preserve the purity of one's disposition, prevents one from acting at all. It also follows, according to Wood, that the moral worth of an action is not diminished by the fact that it is motivated by inclination, "since it is an inevitable fact about agency that this be so."[22]

Since Kant recognizes as clearly as Hegel that every action, including those supposedly performed from duty alone, necessarily aims at some determinate end, this suggests that the central issue separating the two thinkers, at least with respect to the question of rational agency, is whether the motive of an action must necessarily coincide with its end or intention. Kant, who holds that an agent can adopt a given end, say to alleviate suffering, from either duty or inclination, obviously must deny that motive and end necessarily coincide; otherwise, he would be forced to deny the possibility of autonomous action. By contrast, Hegel, for whom there can be no action without passion, that is, without the particular interest of an agent, affirms the opposite.[23]

Wood suggests that Hegel's position on this issue should be viewed in light of his tendency to analyze actions in terms of internal reasons rather than motives. To explain an action, on this view, is to provide the reason why the agent acted as he or she did, with this reason always being some intention or purpose to be realized by the action. Presumably, this is to be contrasted with providing a motive (in the sense of a psychic force) which "causes" the agent to act in a certain way (or adopt an intention). In fact, Wood states that "motivation proper plays virtually no role in Hegel's theory of action."[24]

At the same time, however, he also maintains, somewhat incongruously, that Hegel does not completely neglect the question of motivation, at least in moral contexts. Nevertheless, in his reconstruction of Hegel's position, which is based primarily on materials from the lectures of 1821–2 that were not incorporated into the published text of the *Philosophy of Right,* it turns out that the motive for an action is nothing other than a certain aspect of an intention, "namely its 'particular' side." In other words, a motive for Hegel is a fact about an agent's psychological makeup or character, specifically, the fact that the agent has an interest in the action. Moreover, even in the case of unselfish actions of universal import, this interest necessarily reflects the agent's basic needs and personal attachments, which constitute the moment of "particularity."[25] Given *this* conception of agency, it should be clear that there is no room for the Kantian notion of an action from (motivated by) duty alone. Since, *ex hypothesi,* such an action would not reflect any interest of the agent, it would be one the agent has no (internal) reason to perform.

Wood further suggests, reasonably enough, that this difference in the conception of agency leads to a different conception of moral worth. Thus, for Hegel, the relevant "subjective" side of an action, which is the locus of its moral worth, consists in the intention manifest in it. This intention need not be selfish and it can even be universal in import, for example, the alleviation of suffering; but is must always express an "interest" of the agent, that is, be something the agent has an internal reason to adopt. From this point of view, then, it would seem that the distinctively Kantian question concerning the grounds for the adoption of a particular maxim or end (is it duty or inclination?) simply does not arise.[26]

Finally, it should be clear from the preceding account that the Hegelian critique of Kantian morality is essentially a protest against its location of supreme value (a good will) in an inner realm of "purity" that is divorced from the real "objective" world of actions and events. The self for Hegel, as for twentieth-century existentialists, is what it does. It is in terms of its deeds that it is both recognized and judged. This does not make Hegel into a consequentialist of the usual stripe, since what is central for him is the intention of an agent. Nevertheless, intentions count only insofar as they are actualized. Moreover, from this standpoint (a standpoint shared by many thinkers who have little sympathy with Hegel's metaphysical views), Kant's alleged location of the moral self and its struggle for purity in an inaccessible noumenal world is seen as the logical consequence of a misguided subjectivism in moral psychology, which in turn reflects an alienated form of human existence. As Wood eloquently puts it:

Hegel's fundamental concern in rejecting the Kantian conception of the good will is to prevent our conceiving of the good will as an essentially alienated form of human existence, cut off both from its own sensuous nature and from the real world in which it acts. Just as the Kantian picture of a struggle of motives in the intelligible world alienates our practical reason from our self-satisfaction, so in Hegel's view the Kantian idea that the moral worth of willing and acting does not depend on their results alienates moral agents from their existence in the real world and from their concerns with it. This idea makes us regard the essence of our moral action itself as occurring in an alien world, a beyond, so that our noblest actions and accomplishments in the real world are made to seem to us at best as by-products of moral willing, whose worldly splendor may always be nothing more than the dazzling costume which cloaks a bad will.[27]

As the citation from Wood indicates, underlying Hegel's critique of Kant's moral psychology is his wholesale rejection of the metaphysics of transcendental idealism and the associated doctrine of transcendental freedom. Since the latter issue is the concern of the study as a whole, I do not intend to deal with it here. Nor shall I consider further Hegel's critique of the postulates, which was touched upon in the last chapter. Instead, the focus of the present discussion will be almost exclusively on the issues regarding agency and motivation, which are emphasized by Wood and are also the issues of greatest interest to Kant's contemporary critics.

From what we have already seen, it is clear that the main issue here concerns the relationship between the motive and the end or intention of an action. Given Hegel's view (as interpreted by Wood) that end and motive necessarily coincide or, more precisely, that by "motive" is meant nothing more than the particular side of an intention, that is, an interest that an agent has in intending a state of affairs, all of the previously mentioned criticisms of the Kantian theory follow. For example, on this view, the Kantian requirement to act *from* (in the sense of being motivated by) duty alone is reasonably construed as the requirement to do duty purely for duty's sake, thereby ruling out, as morally illegitimate, all other intentions, including supposedly morally worthy ones such as the alleviation of suffering. Moreover, that this is in fact how Hegel saw the matter is clear from the previously cited passage from the *Phenomenology* (see note 20), where the governing assumption is that for the Kantian position it is pure duty "which alone should be intended" (*die allein beabsichtigt werden sollte*).

The obvious problem with this whole line of criticism is simply that it is based on an assumption that Kant rejects, namely, the identification of motive and intention.[28] In fact, Wood (apparently following Hegel) seems to assume this conception of the relation of intention and motive and to argue from it against Kant rather than to argue directly for it. Thus, as noted, he connects it with Hegel's tendency to explain actions in terms of intentions (construed as internal reasons) rather than in terms of motives (construed as psychic forces). This certainly advances our understanding of Hegel's critique of Kant by linking it to his own conception of agency; but of itself it hardly amounts to a cogent argument against the Kantian position (particularly since, as we have seen, Kant likewise rejects the conception of motives as psychic forces).

What is needed, then, is a critique of the distinction between motive and intention that supposedly underlies Kant's account of moral worth. Although Wood does not directly provide such a critique, he does so indirectly by depicting the distinction as a consequence of Kant's adherence to what he terms an "essentially causal determinist" theory of action, according to which free actions are casually determined by reason. It is, Wood claims, precisely because Kant holds such a theory that he is led to distinguish between "having something as my end and being motivated by having it as my end," which is tantamount to the distinction in question.[29] Moreover, in arguing in this way, he also claims to be following Hegel, whose rejection of Kant's theory of moral worth, he suggests, can "from one point of view . . . be understood as a rejection of the psychological determinism on which Kant's theory is based."[30]

Whether this truly reflects Hegel's view of Kant's theory need not concern us here. Nor is it necessary to belabor the obvious point that it does not follow from the fact (assuming it is a fact) that the grounds on which a distinction is drawn are inadequate that the distinction itself must be rejected. The crucial point is simply that as we have already seen in Chapter 2, Kant does not have a causal determinist theory of action in the sense intended by Wood. Consequently, Kant's adherence to such a theory, which is presumably itself untenable, cannot be used to undermine his account of moral worth.

On the contrary, it must be insisted once again that the centerpiece of Kant's conception of rational agency is the Incorporation Thesis, that is, the claim that an incentive (or, in Wood's terminology, "motive") can determine the will only insofar as it has been incorporated into a maxim. As we have seen at length, this means that an incentive (or motive) is denied any causal efficacy apart from the adoption of a maxim by an agent to act on the basis of that incentive. This holds whether the source of the incentive is pure reason or sensuous inclination. Moreover, as an expression of the practical spontaneity of the agent, this act of adoption or incorporation is not itself causally conditioned. Thus, insofar as we are moved by inclination, it is because we, as it were, allow ourselves to be so moved. This thesis is obviously not without its difficulties; although its plausibility increases if, as I have in effect argued, one treats it as part of a model of practical rationality rather than as a bit of introspective psychology. For present purposes, however, what is important is not its plausibility but merely the fact that Kant held it and that, in so doing, he explicitly rejected the view of agency attributed to him by Wood.[31]

Focusing on the Incorporation Thesis and the conception of practical spontaneity that is inseparable from it also makes it clear that the relevant Kantian distinction is not between motive and end or intention but rather between the intention in the sense of purpose (*Absicht*) and the ground or reason for making that purpose one's own.[32] To be sure, the latter can also be termed a motive but in the sense of *Bestimmungsgrund* rather than *Triebfeder*.[33] In other words, it is a principle on the basis of which an agent decides to pursue a particular end, not a cause (noumenal or otherwise) of either the decision or the ensuing action. This in turn supports the intuition (central to Kant's moral theory) that we can adopt a given maxim for a number of distinct reasons, not all of which are of equal moral significance. To return to Kant's example of the honest shopkeeper, he can treat his customers honestly either from self-interest (the recognition that honesty is the best policy, in which case the principle of his action is a hypothetical imperative) or from duty (in which case it is the categorical imperative). But it is not the case that in the former instance inclination and in the latter reason is the efficient cause of the behavior.

189

Wood's putatively Hegelian analysis of this very example is highly instructive. According to him, both its long-term profitability and its accordance with duty are features of the policy of honest dealing that recommend it to the hypothetical shopkeeper. Assuming, then, that the shopkeeper with both of these interests chooses to act honestly, we have what Wood, speaking for Hegel, describes as "an exhaustive report of the morally relevant facts of the case." Moreover, he adds significantly that "they are sufficient for the shopkeeper to have a good will and his act to have moral worth.[34]

At first glance, this seems very much like the overdetermination thesis discussed in Chapter 6. Further consideration, however, shows that it is far more radical. As Wood's subsequent analysis makes clear, the main point is not simply that a morally worthy act can be overdetermined (that it *must* be overdetermined is assumed) but rather that questions such as "which of the two motives caused the shopkeeper to act according to duty" or "which motive was the strongest in producing it" are to be dismissed as morally irrelevant. In short, Hegel is depicted as wielding a psychological version of Ockham's razor against Kant, thereby undercutting any appeal to noumenal grounds. Thus, after emphasizing Kant's own admission of the unanswerability of such questions, Wood writes:

Hegel merely draws the quite sensible conclusion that if such matters are necessarily nothing to us, they cannot possibly concern us as moral agents and we have no business of building our concept of moral worth upon them. Consequently, the moralist's anguish about whether he has "done the right deed for the wrong reason," together with the whole grand Kantian struggle of duty with inclination in the shopkeeper's soul, carried on somewhere in the intelligible world with God as the sole witness to the combat . . . this entire drama is a fiction, a fantasy, simply a product of the moralist's unhealthy imagination.[35]

The alternative conception of moral worth that Wood attributes to Hegel, namely, that an action has moral worth if its moral goodness is *one* of the reasons why the agent performs it, is problematic enough in its own right, since it allows no distinction between a situation in which this is a mere afterthought, as when Nixon added to his prudential considerations the infamous "And it would be wrong," and one in which it is the central consideration.[36] Leaving that issue aside, however, the problem with this account as a critique of Kant is that it conflates the question of the *principle* on which the shopkeeper acts with that of the *cause* of his action. Indeed, this is evident from Wood's shift from talk of motives causing the shopkeeper's behavior to talk of the reasons for it. Granted, Kant himself is guilty of this conflation on Wood's reading; but having rejected this reading (the "causal determinist" theory of free agency), we need not follow him here. Consequently, we need not infer the moral irrelevance of the principle on which an agent acts from the irrelevance of the cause of that action.

Finally, this puts us in a position to deal with the claim that the Kantian requirement to act from duty alone is equivalent to the (absurd) requirement to make the performance of duty itself, rather than the attainment of any determinate end, the goal of one's action, which as we have seen is the basic

premise underlying the entire Hegelian critique. Given the distinction between the end or purpose intended by an action and the ground or reason
for adopting such an intention, it becomes clear that it simply does not follow
that someone who is ostensibly interested in helping others because of the
recognition of a moral obligation to do so is not really interested in helping
others but merely in the doing of duty for duty's sake. On the contrary, such
a person is genuinely concerned to help others, just as much as another
might be who behaves in a similar way from inclination. The difference
between them is not the genuineness of the concern but rather its rational
ground. Correlatively, this genuineness of concern is not incompatible with
the "purity" of intent. Thus, although it may well be the case, as Kant
himself admits, that no one has ever acted purely from duty alone, this is
not, as Hegel claims, because such action is incompatible with the pursuit
of a determinate end.

III. Williams's critique

Although the rhetoric is somewhat different, a substantially similar line of
criticism is prominent in the recent literature. The most influential repre-
sentative of this "neo-Hegelian" movement (if it can be called such) is undoubtedly Bernard Williams. Williams's critique, like that of Hegel's, with
which it has deep affinities, is quite complex and takes somewhat different
directions at different times.[37] Nevertheless, its focal point is clearly the claim
that, at least in certain circumstances, the dictates of an impartial morality
(such as the Kantian or utilitarianism) can conflict with the conditions of an
agent's integrity and that in these circumstances it is unreasonable, if not
absurd, to require the agent to conform to these dictates.[38] As a result, moral
requirements have, at best, a relative legitimacy, not the unconditional status
insisted upon by Kant and other moral theorists.[39]

Underlying this critique is a conception of character and motivation that
reflects the influence of Hume (and perhaps Aristotle), although it is also
reminiscent of Hegel, particularly as interpreted by Wood. According to this
conception, a person's character is constituted by certain "categorical desires"
or "ground projects" (Williams seems to regard these as equivalent). Like
Hegelian intentions and interests, these can be altruistic and "universal" as
well as selfish or parochial. Consequently, they can include commitments to
moral ideals and principles. Whatever their specific character in a given case,
however, the crucial point is that they make one the person one is in the
sense that they serve as the ultimate source of meaning, motivation, and
justification. Indeed, Williams suggests that they are what gives one a reason
for living.[40]

The actual critique of Kantian-type moral theories follows directly from
this conception. The fundamental complaint is that such theories require us
to adopt an impartial, impersonal standpoint, which in turn can lead to a
dissociation from our deepest concerns and commitments ("particularity" in
the Hegelian terminology). This is the point of the claim that adherence to

191

the dictates of such theories can involve the loss of one's "integrity" or, alternatively, an "alienation" from one's true self. It is also, of course, implicit in this that the moral requirements stemming from these theories cannot be justified, since, as already noted, an individual's ground projects or categorical desires are the ultimate source of justification. In short, what these theories require is both destructive of personality and without any rational justification.[41]

Much as in the case of its Hegelian antecedent, the Kantian (if not the proponent of a contemporary Kantian-type theory) could reply that this critique is question-begging, since it rests on a conception of agency explicitly denied by Kant. Williams is not oblivious to the possibility of such a response, however, and in *Ethics and the Limits of Philosophy* he mounts a fresh critique directed at just this point. Although he makes the common mistake of assuming that for Kant all actions not motivated purely by moral considerations are to be regarded as causally determined and expresses the usual dismissive attitude toward "the more extravagant metaphysical luggage of the noumenal self," he does recognize that the deep issue between Kant and himself concerns the nature of rational agency.[42] According to his analysis, the central point of contention is the Kantian picture of the self as standing in judgment on its own desires from what seems like a detached, impersonal standpoint or, as he nicely puts it, the conception of the self "as a citizen legislator in a notional republic."[43]

The gist of Williams's critique of this Kantian picture of agency is that it conflates the standpoints of theoretical or factual and practical deliberation, both of which are seen (by Kant) as involving the exercise of rational freedom. The assumption is that Kant is basically correct in his account of the former, namely, that it requires us to conceive of ourselves as reasoning to conclusions rather than as being caused to have them and that this reasoning process involves a detachment from one's initial beliefs, an impartial consideration of the evidence, a commitment to impersonal, intersubjectively valid rules of inference and standards of evidence. Kant's great mistake, according to Williams, was to think that this same model is also applicable in the context of practical deliberation. Whereas the former is impartial, impersonal, disinterested, the latter is, in every respect, the precise opposite. In Williams's own terms, practical deliberation is "first-personal, radically so, and involves an I that must be more intimately the I of my desires than this account allows."[44]

By this line of reasoning, which amounts to a repudiation of the Incorporation Thesis, Williams reinforces his original contention that Kantian morality is alienating, since it requires us to negate what is most truly ourselves, namely, our desires. In addition, he argues that Kant's whole program of providing a rational foundation for morality is vitiated by a single but fundamental mistake, which he describes as the equation of reflection and detachment.[45] Because of this mistake, the Kantian erroneously assumes that reflecting on what is required according to universal rules of equity will, of itself, produce "the motivations of justice," that is, an incentive to do what is required even when it conflicts radically with one's desires, just as reflection on the inadequacy of one's beliefs leads one to modify or abandon them. This assumption is erroneous, according to Williams, because we stand in a radically different relationship to our desires than we do to our beliefs.

Finally, in addition to this argument from the nature of agency, which in its latest formulation is directed specifically against Kant, Williams also argues that if given unconditional status, the requirements of impersonal morality can conflict with our deepest attachments to other people. In short, he maintains that the requirements of an impersonal morality alienate us from others as well as from ourselves. In his well-known discussion of this issue, Williams appeals to the example, borrowed from Charles Fried, of a man who, after a shipwreck, is in a position to rescue only one of a number of drowning survivors that includes his wife. The assumption is that the husband decides (appropriately) to save his wife, but only after first determining that it was morally permissible to act accordingly in such circumstances. Commenting on this hypothetical scenario, Williams writes:

> But this construction provides the agent with one thought too many: it might have been hoped by some (for instance, by his wife) that his motivating thought, fully spelled out, would be the thought that it was his wife, not that it was his wife and that in situations of this kind it is permissible to save one's wife.[46]

Although the particular "construction" to which Williams refers is a rule utilitarian one (the dutiful husband deciding on the grounds that "in situations of this kind it is best for each to look after his own"), it is clear that the example is intended to apply as well to the Kantian who consults the categorical imperative. The main point is simply that general moral considerations (whatever their precise nature) are not only irrelevant in such situations, since saving one's wife because one loves her needs no justification from principles, but also intrude in an unhealthy way upon our deepest personal attachments.

In a similar vein, other contemporary critics have resurrected the old Hegelian attack on the very idea of acting from duty. For example, it is argued that to help a friend *because* one believes it to be a duty is quite different from helping a friend because she is a friend and is perceived to be in need of help. In the former case, one's relationship to one's friend is mediated by the requirements of an abstract principle rather than being based on the direct emotional link that is constitutive of friendship. Consequently, to the extent to which one is motivated by the demands of morality rather than concern for one's friend, one is necessarily alienated from one's friend. Or so it is argued.[47]

As in its earlier incarnations, the root intuition underlying this familiar line of criticism is that there is something morally unsatisfactory (if not actually repugnant) in an act motivated by the mere thought of duty without any accompanying emotive component such as love or sympathy. Such an act, so it would seem, aims at fulfilling the requirements of an abstract principle rather than at providing aid to a person in need. Correlatively, an agent so motivated would seem to be more concerned with the worthiness of his own conduct than the good of the person standing in need of help. This seems offensive in general, but particularly so when the person in need is a friend or loved one. Thus, although it takes a somewhat different route, this line of objection ends up in agreement with Williams's contention that an impartial morality such as Kant's can alienate one from those to whom one has deep personal attachments.

Many aspects of this multifaceted critique have been discussed at length in the recent literature, although, on the whole, these discussions have been more concerned with the vindication of Kantian-type moral theories than with the actual views of the historical Kant. Without attempting to be exhaustive, they feature the following strategies: (1) an emphasis on the role of the categorical imperative as a limiting condition, which (properly) rules out some ground projects as illegitimate without violating the conditions of the integrity of character; (2) the suggestion that Kantian morality itself defines a sense of self by presenting an ideal of what a person ought to be, namely, a member of a community of autonomous agents bound by relations of mutual respect; (3) an insistence that an agent can, without any loss of integrity, take a *personal* interest in ethical principles (an interest in morality in Kant's sense), as distinct from merely having nonegoistic interests, which Williams himself allows; (4) the drawing of a sharp distinction between an impartial and an impersonal standpoint together with the charge that Williams conflates them and the claim that morality requires only the former, whereas only the latter is "alienating"; and (5) the attempt to show that criticisms focusing on the alleged "repugnance" of acting from duty and similar themes are based on radical misunderstandings and distortions of the Kantian or, more generally, deontological position.[48] Roughly speaking, the first four of these strategies constitute different ways of making the point that Kantian morality is compatible with the conditions of character integrity as stipulated by Williams, whereas the fifth can be described as an attempt to vindicate the "morality" of Kantian morality, that is, its accordance with our deepest intuitions on the matter.

These are all reasonable strategies for responding to Williams and other like-minded critics; but they fail to deal adequately with the deep issues regarding agency. At least with respect to the historical Kant, the central question is whether Kant's account of agency involves, as Williams contends, a conflation of the theoretical and practical standpoints, of reflection and detachment. Not only does this objection get to the heart of the matter, it also has a prima facie plausibility. Kant does *seem* to assume, without argument, the same detachment from desire of the moral agent that can reasonably be expected of the knower with respect to beliefs; indeed, this would seem to be a consequence of the close kinship between epistemic and practical spontaneity discussed in Chapter 2. Moreover, Williams is undeniably correct in defining the difference between the theoretical and the practical standpoints in the way in which he does.

194

Nevertheless, closer consideration suggests that it may not reflect an accurate reading of Kant's position after all. To begin with, it should be recalled that Kant himself was concerned with the very conflation alleged by Williams during his late precritical period. This is evidenced by his sharp distinction between logical and transcendental freedom and his rejection of the attempt to derive the latter from the former; his worries about how a purely intellectual principle could motivate (the problem of the *principium executionis*); and finally his eventual rejection of the strategy (prevalent in the *Reflexionen* of the late 1770s and early 17780s) of providing a deduction of the moral law from the nature of theoretical reason. (See Chapter 3 for a discussion of these points.) Admittedly, none of this shows that the critical Kant is not in fact guilty of the conflation alleged by Williams; but by making it clear that Kant was very much aware of the problem, it at least casts some doubt on the charge.

Perhaps more to the point, the critical Kant's doctrine that the recognition of what is morally required brings with it an incentive to do what is required, even when it conflicts radically with one's desires, does not stem from the conflation of the theoretical and practical standpoints. On the contrary, the account of respect (see Chapter 6) makes it clear that Kant holds that we have a consciousness of the moral law as supremely authoritative for us; that this consciousness brings with it an incentive to follow its dictates that is totally independent of inclination or desire (a pure moral interest); and that both of these are rooted in the consciousness of the law as the self-imposed principle of one's own practical reason. In other words, the view of oneself as "a citizen legislator in a notional republic" (to use Williams's description) is built into the first-person conception of oneself as an autonomous agent, not produced by the illicit extension into the practical domain of the third-person conception of oneself as a detached surveyor of the evidence.

Granted, this response does not suffice to meet Williams's deeper objections to the Kantian project and conception of agency, since by assuming an unconditional, supremely authoritative status for the law and the nonillusory nature of the consciousness of autonomy (in the specifically Kantian sense), it begs the main points in question. Nevertheless, it also shows once again that the issues are far more complex than Williams's facile critique might suggest, and it points ahead to the doctrine of the fact of reason as the basis on which Kant's position must ultimately rest.

In the meantime, there is still more to be said in response to Williams's conflation objection that does not rely, at least not directly, on the difficult and problematic doctrine of the fact of reason. Of particular significance in this regard is Kant's conception of interest. As we have seen, Kant links interest specifically with practical reason and maxims. To have an inclination or desire is not yet to have an interest or, equivalently, to be interested. The latter requires that one *take* an interest, which involves the projection of an end as desirable, either in its own right or as a means to some further end. This projected end may be simply the realization of a desired state of affairs, but the fact remains that is is not deemed *desirable* simply because

195

it is *desired*. A practical judgment is required, a certification by practical reason, as it were, even if merely prudential considerations or "empirical interests" are involved.

Although it might at first glance be thought to support Williams's view, this conception of interest actually makes it clear that Kant is not guilty of the conflation in question. The key point here is that being interested is for Kant the distinguishing characteristic of the practical (including the morally practical) standpoint. Thus, far from simply conflating the theoretical and practical standpoints, Kant begins with a clear recognition of their difference, and in light of this difference, he endeavors to show how reason can have a practical function.

This also suggests that the major difference between the two thinkers with respect to the question of agency can be expressed in terms of their radically different conceptions of interest. Williams does not use the term in a technical sense, but it seems reasonable to assume that he would equate having an interest with having a desire. Kant, however, takes seriously the conception of practical spontaneity and therefore distinguishes between having a desire, which is a matter of nature, and being interested, which is (at least partly) a matter of freedom. This may be mistaken, perhaps even deeply mistaken (certainly both Spinoza and Hume would have thought so); but Williams has done nothing to show that it is.

Since the "one thought too many" objection is based on somewhat different considerations, it requires separate discussion. The main thrust of the objection, it will be recalled, is that the requirements of impartial morality (whether construed in a utilitarian or Kantian fashion) can, in certain limiting situations, conflict with our deepest personal attachments. Since adherence to these requirements in such situations would, *ex hypothesi,* involve giving up a significant part of that which makes life worth living in the first place, it supposedly follows that they lose their hold on us. It supposedly also follows that by worrying about whether saving his wife's life in the situation described is morally permissible, the husband indicates that he does not have such a deep attachment to her after all. That is why his worry is one thought too many.

But is it really? The answer depends on how one fills in the gaps in the picture. In particular, we need to distinguish between a husband who, regarding all the drowning passengers equally, coolly decides that saving his wife is the most reasonable course of action under the circumstances (perhaps on rule utilitarian grounds) and one who, loving his wife deeply and desperately wishing to save her, nonetheless recognizes that in certain circumstances love of itself is not a sufficient reason. Much of the rhetorical force of Williams's account stems from a blurring of the differences between these two pictures. In the first, the husband clearly has one thought too many and by treating his wife as a counter in a utilitarian calculation shows that his affection for her does not run very deep. In the second, however, the genuineness of the husband's feeling for his wife is a given, and the assumption is that moral considerations still have a crucial role to play as sanctioning (or perhaps prohibiting) a course of action based on love.

Perhaps the simplest way to bring out the viability of the second picture is to sketch an alternative scenario in which an agent, acting solely on the basis of a deep personal attachment and not giving any weight to moral considerations, could be justly blamed for having one thought too few. For example, following the lead of Barbara Herman, let us assume that in order to save his wife the husband had to throw a child overboard.[49] Here is a situation (and one can easily imagine many others) in which a deep personal attachment could lead to actions that conflict with the rights of others. Would we not want to say that an agent who in such a situation takes this attachment as of itself sufficient reason for an action is guilty of having one thought too few?

Clearly, this is the Kantian position, which, with respect to the issue before us, can be characterized in terms of its adherence to the second picture. In other words, Kantian morality does not require us to disregard our deepest personal attachments, to consider them as counting for nothing in the determination of the right course of action. Rather, it requires an openness to the *possibility* of overriding moral considerations, a sensitivity to the rights and feeling of others, which would lead an agent to reflect, when the occasion warrants it, on the permissibility of actions motivated by even the deepest personal attachments. As we have seen, such openness or sensitivity is one of the essential marks of a virtuous disposition as conceived by Kant.

Granted, in certain circumstances (perhaps of the kind envisaged by Williams) truly heroic virtue would be required to do the morally correct thing; but this does not entail, as Williams seems to suggest, either that moral considerations become irrelevant or that in continuing to recognize their force one is led to deny one's deepest personal attachments. On the contrary, it is precisely because both the moral requirements and the personal attachments are still in place that such situations are sources of anguish and tragic conflict.

Similar considerations apply, *mutatis mutandis,* to those contemporary critics, mainly proponents of "virtue ethics," who attack Kantian-style deontic moral theories under the banner of the "repugnance" of acting from duty. To begin with, it has been noted in the literature that much of the argument for this alleged repugnance assumes a conception of acting from duty that is radically at variance with Kant's or, indeed, that of any serious defender of a deontic position.[50] According to this conception, to act from duty is to act grudgingly, without any interest in the action or its outcome, simply because one feels that somehow one "must," that it is expected according to the ruling social norms or for some such reason. Clearly, such an action is not a fitting candidate for the attribution of moral worth; but equally clearly, it would not be regarded as such by Kant. Like Schiller before them, critics who opt for this line of attack misconstrue the nature of moral constraint as it is understood by Kant.

Finally, it cannot be maintained that insofar as one acts from duty, one's interest is in producing a dutiful act, come what may, perhaps in order to enhance one's own moral worth or self-esteem, as opposed, say, to helping another human being. As we have already seen in discussing this objection in its Hegelian form, it rests upon the fallacious assumption that if one wants to bring about x because one believes it to be morally right, then what one really intends is not x but "rightness." Once again, this is fallacious because it conflates the intention of an action, which is always the attainment of some end, with the grounds for adopting a maxim to pursue that end. Thus, to the extent to which the contemporary critique of the notion of acting from duty is based on the contrary assumption, it is, like its Hegelian predecessor, without foundation.

III
The justification of morality
and freedom

11
The Reciprocity Thesis

The second part of this study has been devoted to an analysis of the concept of freedom as it is operative in Kant's major writings in moral philosophy. Starting with a consideration of the introduction of autonomy as a property of the will in the *Groundwork* and the modifications in Kant's first *Critique* theory of agency that this involves, it has explored various aspects of Kant's views on moral agency and moral psychology as well as some of the major and persistent criticisms of these views. In so doing, however, it has bracketed the question of the grounding of morality itself, thereby following the analytic method of the first two parts of the *Groundwork*. Accordingly, for all that we have seen so far, the possibility remains open that as Kant himself suggests near the end of *Groundwork* II, morality may be a "chimerical idea," a mere "phantom of the brain" (Gr 4: 445; 112).

The task of the third and final part of this study is to analyze and evaluate Kant's efforts to remove this specter by establishing the objective reality of the moral law and/or categorical imperative.[1] Since Kant insists that it is only by way of practical reason and from a "practical point of view" that we are warranted in assuming the reality of freedom, success in this project is obviously crucial for his theory of freedom as well as for his moral theory.

Unfortunately, our task is complicated by the fact that Kant's attempts to ground morality and freedom as he conceives them take markedly different forms in *Groundwork* III and the *Critique of Practical Reason*. In the former, Kant provides what purports to be a deduction of the moral law on the basis of the necessity of presupposing the idea of freedom. By contrast, in the latter he explicitly denies the possibility of any deduction of the moral law and claims instead that this law as a "fact of reason" can serve as the basis for a deduction of freedom. Although the issue is quite controversial, I believe that Karl Ameriks is correct in characterizing this change as a "great reversal."[2] Moreover, by analyzing the reasons for the failure of the deduction in the *Groundwork*, I hope to show why this reversal was necessary and what it consists in.

But before we are in a position to analyze this issue, we must consider a thesis that is common to both the *Groundwork* and the *Critique of Practical Reason* and that constitutes the first step in the Kantian justification of morality. This is the claim that morality and freedom are reciprocal concepts, henceforth termed the "Reciprocity Thesis." Its significance stems from the fact that it entails that freedom of the will (transcendental freedom) is not only a necessary but also a sufficient condition of the moral law.[3] We shall see in the present chapter that this is a crucial, yet generally neglected feature of Kant's moral theory and in the final two chapters that it figures prominently in both of his attempts to ground morality and freedom.

The present chapter is divided into four parts. The first considers Kant's formulations of the Reciprocity Thesis and the problems they raise. The second and third parts deal with two stages in an extended argument needed to establish the reciprocity between freedom and an unconditioned practical law, which is how Kant expresses this thesis in the *Critique of Practical Reason*. The fourth part attempts to provide an argument capable of taking us from the bare idea of such a law to the moral law as Kant defines it.

I. The formulations of the thesis

The best known of Kant's formulations of the Reciprocity Thesis is at the beginning of *Groundwork* III. After defining will (*Wille*) as a "kind of causality belonging to living beings so far as they are rational" and freedom (negatively construed) as "the property this causality has of being able to work independently of determination by alien causes," Kant offers his positive conception of freedom, which presumably "springs" (*fliesst*) from this negative one:

The concept of causality carries with it that of *laws* [*Gesetze*] in accordance with which, because of something we call a cause, something else – namely, its effect – must be posited [*gesetzt*]. Hence freedom of will, although it is not the property of conforming to laws of nature, is not for this reason lawless: it must rather be a causality conforming to immutable laws though of a special kind; for otherwise a free will would be self-contradictory. Natural necessity, as we have seen, is a heteronomy of efficient causes; for every effect is possible only in conformity with the law that something else determines the efficient cause to causal action. What else then can freedom of will be but autonomy – that is, the property which will has of being a law to itself? The proposition "Will is in all its actions a law to itself" expresses, however, only the principle of acting on no maxim other than one which can have for its object itself as at the same time a universal law. This is precisely the formula of the categorical imperative and the principle of morality. Thus a free will and a will under moral laws are one and the same. (Gr 4: 446–47; 114)

Kant also argues for the same thesis in §6 of the *Critique of Practical Reason*. After contending on the basis of an analysis of the concept of a practical law (§1) that such a law much be formal in the sense that it could only impose the formal condition of lawfulness on the maxims of a rational agent (§4) and that only a will that is free in the transcendental sense could have its "determining ground" in such a law (§5), he then (§6) poses the problem: "Granted that a will is free, find the law which alone is competent to determine it necessarily" (KprV 5: 29; 29). The proposed solution exploits the dichotomy between the form (lawfulness or universality) and the matter (desired object or end) of a practical principle developed in §2–4. Kant claims that since (1) a free will (by definition) must be independent of all "empirical conditions," which includes the "material" element of practical principles, and (2) a free will must nonetheless be "determinable" (presumably according to some law), then (3) "the legislative form, insofar as it is contained in the maxim, is the only thing which can constitute a determining ground of the [free] will." On this basis, Kant concludes at the very beginning of the Remark following the analysis that "freedom and unconditional practical law reciprocally imply each other" (KprV 5: 29; 29–30).

The argument at this point is completely hypothetical and consequently does not involve any claims concerning the reality of either freedom or an unconditional practical law. Nevertheless, given the identification of an unconditional practical law with the moral law (§7), it is but a short step to the conclusion that "it [the moral law] would be analytic if freedom of the will were presupposed" (KprV 5: 31; 31).[4] Admittedly, this last claim is somewhat strange. How, one might ask, could the presupposition of freedom convert a synthetic proposition into one that is analytic? The most reasonable explanation is that analyticity is to be attributed to the hypothetical, "If freedom then the moral law," and to its reciprocal. Kant clarifies his position near the end of the Analytic of Pure Practical Reason when he remarks:

> If [per impossibile] we saw the possibility of freedom of an efficient cause, we would see not only the possibility but also the necessity of the moral law as the supreme practical law of rational beings, to whom freedom of the causality of their will is ascribed. This is because the two concepts are so inextricably bound together that practical freedom could be defined through the will's independence of everything except the moral law. (KprV 5: 93–4; 97)[5]

Although these formulations of the Reciprocity Thesis differ significantly, they reflect a common underlying argument with roughly the following form: (1) As a "kind of causality" the will must, in some sense, be law governed or, in the language of the second *Critique,* "determinable" according to some law (a lawless will is an absurdity); (2) as free, it cannot be governed by laws of nature; (3) it must therefore be governed by laws of a different sort, namely, self-imposed ones; and (4) the moral law is the required self-imposed law.

A compatibilist would certainly object to step 2 and perhaps to 3, but the major difficulties we need consider here concern steps 1 and 4. Apart from the passage from the *Groundwork* cited at the beginning of this section, which seems to be little more than a dogmatic assertion, Kant does not appear to offer any argument in support of the claim that a free will must be law governed or determinable. In fact, the account in the second *Critique* suggests that this essential question is simply begged.

Moreover, step 4 appears to be equally problematic; for even if we assume that a free will must be law governed in some nontrivial sense and that its law must be self-imposed, it does not seem at all obvious that the moral law as defined by Kant is the only viable candidate for such a law. In fact, many commentators criticize Kant's attempt to derive a nonvacuous moral principle from the bare notion of conformity to universal law, and this step would seem to require a move of just that sort. We shall see that this move can be negotiated successfully with the assumption of transcendental freedom (a point Kant indicates in the *Critique of Practical Reason*); but before dealing with that problem, we must consider the fundamental claim that "freedom and unconditional practical law reciprocally imply each other." Presumably, this result would be of some significance even if it turned out to be impossible subsequently to identify this law with the moral law.

II. Freedom and practical law: a first attempt

Given Kant's account of rational agency, it is trivially true that a free will must be law governed in some sense. As we saw in Chapter 5, the defining feature of such agency is the capacity to act in accordance with the conception of law, with this understood as equivalent to action on the basis of maxims. Moreover, since we also saw that maxims are themselves sometimes described as "subjective laws," it follows that a free will cannot be without laws of at least that sort. But since, as we further saw, Kant distinguishes sharply between maxims and objective practical principles or laws, and since an unconditional practical law is clearly a principle of the latter type, this is not sufficient for our purposes. What we still need is an argument linking a free will with practical law in the strong sense.

The argument that comes immediately to mind at this point is a familiar one, and so too is the objection to it. Although frequently taken to be Kant's main argument linking rational agents with the moral law, we shall see that, properly construed, it is merely the first step in an extended Kantian argument. We shall also see that when viewed in this manner, the familiar objection loses its force.

In the endeavor to sketch this argument or, more accurately, argument segment, it will be helpful to return to the analysis of maxims sketched in Chapter 5. For present purposes, the essential point is that as products of practical reason an agent's maxims are subject to criteria of reasonableness. This holds whether maxims are limited merely to *Lebensregeln* or, like many of Kant's examples, include relatively specific policies to act in a given way in situations of a certain type. In either case, maxims, as the policies on which agents actually act (subjective practical principles), are taken by the agent to express a policy that, at least given the interests, situation, and capacities of the agent, is rational. Consequently, rational agents must regard their maxims as in some sense rationally justifiable or, equivalently, their reasons for acting in a certain way as "good ones," although as we have seen, this belief may well rest on self-deception.

Once this justification requirement (loosely formulated so as to encompass both prudential and moral justification) is granted, the argument proceeds relatively smoothly. The next step is to note that in claiming that one's reason for acting in a certain way is a "good" in the sense of justifying reason, one is, implicitly at least, assuming its appropriateness for all rational beings. The intuition behind this is simply that if reason R justifies my x-ing in circumstances C, then it must also justify the x-ing of any other agent in similar circumstances. As Marcus Singer, paraphrasing Sidgewick, remarks, "A reason in one case is a reason in all cases – or else it is not a reason at all."[6] To be sure, there is a perfectly legitimate sense in which I might claim that something is "right for me" and not for others; but this must be construed as an elliptical way of stating that there is something peculiar about my circumstances (which can include, among other things, my desires and capacities). Thus, I might claim that a course of action, say going to the race track to relax, is justifiable for me because of my superior ability as a handicapper, great wealth, or luck, and so on, whereas it is not justifiable for others who lack these attributes. What I may not do is to claim that the possession of these attributes justifies my action but not that of other similarly inclined and endowed agents. In roughly this way, then, the universalizability of one's intention, maxim, or plan of action seems to be presupposed as a condition of the possibility of justifying one's action, even when this justification does not take an explicitly moral form.

Moreover, it is argued, rational agents cannot simply refuse to play the justification game, that is, refuse to concern themselves with the question of whether the reasons for their actions are "good" reasons, at least in a non-moral sense of good. This is, of course, not to say that such agents always act on the basis of good and sufficient reasons or that, in retrospect, they must always believe themselves to have done so. The point is rather the familiar one that agents for whom the whole question of justification is irrelevant, who never weigh the reasons for their actions, who act without at least believing at the time that their reasons are good reasons, would not be regarded as rational.

But since as we have just seen, to regard one's reason for acting in a certain way as good is to assume its legitimacy for all rational beings in similar circumstances, it would seem, so the argument goes, that rational agents cannot reject the universalizability test without, at the same time, denying their rationality. This in turn means that the universalizability test functions as the ultimate standard governing one's choice of maxims or, equivalently, that it has the status of a practical law. Finally, since the universalizability test is just the requirement expressed in the categorical imperative ("Act only on that maxim through which you can at the same time will that it should become a universal law"), it follows not only that a rational agent cannot deny being subject to a practical law in the strong sense intended by Kant but also that this law takes the form of the categorical imperative.

This line of argument, which has here been sketched in bald terms and adapted to the exigencies of the Kantian terminology, is too familiar to require further elaboration; and so, too, is the objection to it. The fundamental problem is simply that one cannot move from the claim that all rational agents must regard their principles of action as universalizable in the sense that they are willing to acknowledge that it would be reasonable for every other agent in relevantly similar circumstances[7] to adopt the same principles or even that such agents ought to adopt them (where the "ought" is the ought of rationality) to the desired conclusion that the agent ought to be able to will (as a universal law) that every rational agent act on the basis of the principle in question. Rational egoists, for example, might very well be willing to admit that the maxims on which they act in pursuit of their own perceived self-interest are also those on which all other rational agents "ought" to act (and would act if sufficiently enlightened). It hardly follows from this, however, that the rational egoist is committed (on pain of self-contradiction) to will that all other rational agents behave likewise.[8]

Although there can be little doubt about the cogency of this line of objection, considered as a response to the project of somehow deducing morality conceived in Kantian terms from the concept of rationality, there are serious questions about its relevance to Kant's own procedure. The reason why it is generally thought to provide a decisive criticism of Kant can no doubt be attributed to his misleading claim that since moral laws hold for rational beings as such, they ought to be derived from the "general concept of a rational being as such" (Gr 4: 412; 79). Quite understandably, this has led innumerable commentators and critics simply to assume that what Kant is offering us as the foundation of his moral theory is something like the argument sketched in the preceding.

Closer consideration, however, indicates that Kant intends this methodological stricture on the grounding of morality to preclude any appeal to anthropology, that is, to empirical knowledge of human nature, rather than to suggest that the reality of moral obligation can be deduced from the "mere concept" of a rational being. In fact, not only does Kant himself not attempt to deduce the moral law from this concept, but he also explicitly rejects the possibility of doing so. This is because Kant realized that for all that we can learn from its "mere concept," practical reason might involve nothing more than the capacity to determine the best possible means for the satisfaction of one's desires. As Kant puts it in a previously cited footnote from *Religion within the Limits of Reason Alone:*

For from the fact that a being has reason it by no means follows that this reason, by the mere representing of the fitness of its maxims to be laid down as universal laws, is thereby rendered capable of determining the will unconditionally, so as to be "practical" of itself; at least, not so far as we can see. The most rational mortal being in the world might still stand in need of certain incentives, originating in objects of desire, to determine his choice. He might, indeed, bestow the most rational reflection on all that concerns not only the greatest sum of these incentives in him but also the means of attaining the end thereby determined, without ever suspecting the possibility of such a thing as the absolutely imperative moral law which proclaims that it is itself an incentive and, indeed, the highest. (Rel 6: 26n; 21)

Since as we saw in the previous discussion of this passage in Chapter 8, Kant is here affirming the impossibility of deriving a capacity to be motivated by respect for the law from the mere concept of a rational being (the predisposition to rationality), it might be thought that this has no bearing on the question of whether the normative status of the moral law itself can be derived from a reflection on the nature of practical rationality. Such an inference, however, would be mistaken. Morality, as Kant construes it, requires not merely that one do one's duty but also that one act from duty. Consequently, if the possibility of the latter, which consists in the law or, more precisely, respect for it, serving as the sole and sufficient incentive, cannot be derived from the concept of a rational being, then neither can the bindingness of the law itself.

Nevertheless, the proper conclusion to be drawn from this is not that the argument sketched in the preceding is totally wrongheaded but merely that it is incomplete.[9] In particular, it ignores the fact that the real starting point of Kant's analysis is not the thin concept of a rational being, or even a rational agent *simpliciter,* but rather the thick concept of such an agent with a free will (in the transcendental sense). Accordingly, our next task is to see whether the argument encounters a better fate when it is buttressed with the strong, yet controversial premise of transcendental freedom.

III. Freedom and practical law: completing the argument

In order to understand the significance of the introduction of transcendental freedom, it is important to recall the contrast between mere practical freedom and transcendental freedom analyzed in Chapter 3. As was there suggested, the contrast is not to be understood, as it usually is, as between a compatibilist and an incompatibilist conception but rather as between two incompatibilist conceptions of freedom. The former roughly corresponds to the conception of freedom presupposed in the idea of rational agency, as presented in the *Critique of Pure Reason* and in *Groundwork* II, prior to the introduction of the principle of autonomy. As we saw, it involves a genuine, albeit limited, spontaneity or capacity for self-determination and therefore a capacity to act on the basis of imperatives, even though the incentives for obeying these imperatives might ultimately be traceable to our sensuous nature. By contrast, transcendental freedom, which is the conception of freedom required for genuine autonomy, involves, in Kant's terms, a complete "independence from everything empirical and hence from nature generally" (KprV 5: 97; 100).

Given this distinction, it follows that an agent would be free in the practical (but not in the transcendental) sense if that agent's choices were ultimately governed by some fundamental drive or natural impulse, for example, self-preservation or maximization of pleasure, which might be acted upon in any number of ways but could not be contravened. Such an agent would be practically free, even in an incompatibilist sense, because the drive or impulse serves to limit the agent's options rather than to necessitate causally a given choice. At the same time, however, the agent's choice would be ineluctably heteronomous, since it would be limited to the determination of the best means for the attainment of some end implanted by nature.

The situation with regard to transcendental freedom is quite different. According to this conception, the ground of the selection of a maxim can never be located in an impulse, instinct, or anything "natural"; rather, it must always be sought in a higher-order maxim and therefore in an act of freedom. Consequently, even if one posits a natural drive such as self-preservation, it remains the case that a transcendentally free agent is, *ex hypothesi,* capable of selecting maxims that run directly counter to its dictates. As we have seen, it is precisely this conception of freedom that underlies Kant's accounts of *Gesinnung* and radical evil as well as his insistence on the permanent possibility of a moral conversion of "change of heart."

Although this conception of freedom may be highly problematic in its own right, its implications for the problem of justification should be clear. First, without the assumption of such freedom, that is, assuming merely practical freedom, a maxim based on self-interest, happiness, or some such putatively ultimate, yet nonmoral end or motivational ground could be justified by an appeal to "human nature" or some given determinant of behavior. (The details are irrelevant to the argument.) With it, however, this familiar move is blocked. Put simply, if self-preservation, self-interest, or happiness is the principle of my behavior, if it dictates my maxims, it is I (not nature in me) that gives it this authority. At least this is the case under the presupposition that I am free in the transcendental sense.

Second (and this is an essential premise of the entire argument), since transcendental freedom is assumed to pertain to "rational" agents, the justification requirement is still in place. In fact, the presupposition of transcendental freedom not only blocks certain kinds of justification, it also extends this requirement to first principles or fundamental maxims. Since on the assumption of such freedom these maxims, like all others, are *ex hypothesi* freely adopted, it must be possible to offer reasons in support of their adoption. Moreover, since these principles or maxims are first or fundamental in the sense that they provide the ultimate grounds for the justification of lower-order maxims, they obviously cannot be justified by deducing them from some higher-order maxim.[10]

As indicated earlier, however, this does not mean that we are to regard fundamental maxims as adopted either in some mysterious pre- or nontemporal manner or by means of a self-conscious, deliberative process. It is rather that through reflection we find that we have been committed all along to such a maxim, understood as a fundamental orientation of the will toward moral requirements. Nevertheless, under the assumption of transcendental freedom, we are forced to acknowledge that this commitment may be imputed and, as such, is subject to the justification requirement. At the very least, we must acknowledge that our continued commitment to such a principle is a matter of "freedom" rather than "nature" and, as such, stands in need of rational justification.[11]

Given this conception of freedom, the issue becomes how such justification is possible. Although Kant never develops the point explicitly, it seems reasonable to maintain that implicit in his analysis is an argument to the effect that only conformity to an unconditional practical law could provide the required justification. This argument proceeds in two stages: The first contends that such conformity is a sufficient condition for the justification of these maxims; the second contends that it is also a necessary condition.

The first point seems to be relatively unproblematic. What stronger justification could there be for one's adoption of a maxim than its conformity to an unconditionally valid practical law? If a rule of action is "right" for all rational agents whatever their interests or desires, then clearly it is right for me. Again, if my reason for x-ing is that it is dictated by such a law (in Kant's deontic terms, that it is my duty), then I have all the justification I could conceivably need for x-ing. This is not to deny that there may be grave difficulties determining exactly what such a law requires in a given instance (what my duty is) and therefore that Kant's moral philosophy may run into severe difficulties in this regard. The present point is only that *if* a maxim can be shown to meet this requirement, then that maxim has been fully justified.

Obviously, then, the main difficulties concern the claim that conformity to such a law is also a necessary condition for justification. In dealing with this issue, it will be helpful to begin with the consideration of still another familiar, yet misguided criticism of Kant's moral theory. Couched in terms of the present discussion, the claim is that the requirement (at least as here construed) is too strong. If, so the argument goes, the only legitimate reason for adopting a maxim were its conformity to a practical law binding upon all rational agents, regardless of their interests or desires, then it would seem that no maxim to pursue one's interests or desires could ever be justified. But this is patently absurd. Thus, even if it is granted that conformity to a practical law is a sufficient condition for the justification of one's maxims, it is certainly not also a necessary condition. To claim otherwise is to commit oneself to the doctrine that only actions performed "for the sake of duty" are justifiable; and this is to conflate justifiability with moral worth.

Although there is undoubtedly a strand in Kant's moral philosophy that suggests this line of interpretation and therefore invites such criticism, it should be clear from the discussion of a good will, respect for the law, and virtue that it does not reflect his considered opinion. What this reading neglects is the centrality for Kant of the distinction between the permissible and the obligatory.[12] Not surprisingly, then, it also fails to recognize that the moral law is intended as a criterion of the former as well as of the latter.[13] For present purposes, however, the crucial point is simply that since no maxim could be regarded as justified if it were not *at least* shown to be permissible, our first goal will be attained if it can be shown that conformity to an unconditional practical law is a necessary condition of the permissibility of maxims.

Fortunately, this is not difficult to do. To begin with, permissibility, like other deontic notions, has both a specifically moral and a morally neutral sense. In the former case, it encompasses whatever is not contrary to duty and in the latter whatever is allowable within a given context or in light of some pregiven end (in accord with the "rules of the game").[14] But since we are concerned precisely with the conditions of the justification of the desire-

or interest-based maxims of transcendentally free rational agents, it is apparent that permissibility cannot be construed as a function of desires or interests, even the most fundamental ones. In other words, we are not looking for a rule or set of rules that determine what is permissible within the framework of some presupposed end. On the contrary, what must be determined is the rule or set of rules governing the pursuit of any end at all, including desire- or interest-based ends.

Finally, in view of the "transcendental" function of such a rule or set of rules (its function with respect to end-setting or maxim-selecting *überhaupt*), it is apparent that it must be both universal and "formal" in the specifically Kantian sense. In other words, it must not only apply to all transcendentally free rational agents, it must also apply to them regardless of what desires or interests they may happen to have. But such a rule or set of rules is precisely what Kant understands by an unconditional practical law. Consequently, it must either be denied that the maxims of transcendentally free agents can be justified at all (which amounts to a denial of rationality) or it must be acknowledged that conformity to such a law is the criterion governing the selection of the maxims and ends of such agents. This, then, is the Kantian argument for the "analytic" connection between transcendental freedom and an unconditional practical law.

IV. From practical law to the moral law

In order to complete the argument for the Reciprocity Thesis, however, it still remains to connect the vague notion of an unconditional practical law with the moral law as defined by Kant. Moreover, although Kant himself may have regarded such a move as relatively unproblematic, it certainly has not been taken in this way by many of his commentators. The basic difficulty is usually formulated in connection with the argument of the *Groundwork* rather than the *Critique of Practical Reason,* but it is presumably applicable to the latter text as well. In the language of Bruce Aune, it concerns the gap between the principle "Conform your actions to universal law" and the first formulation of the categorical imperative: "Act only on that maxim through which you can at the same time will that it should become a universal law." Aune allows that Kant establishes the former by showing that it is a requirement of rational willing; but he also contends that Kant either mistakenly treats the latter as equivalent to it or assumes, without argument, that it is readily derivable from it. That they cannot be regarded as equivalent is evidenced by the fact that the latter provides a decision procedure for the choice of maxims whereas the former does not.[15] Consequently, it becomes necessary to provide an argument showing how the latter follows directly from the former.

Aune attempts to provide such an argument, but he concludes that the project is a failure. According to his analysis, the key move turns on the implicit premise that "we conform to universal law when and only when we act on maxims that we 'can will' to be universal laws."[16] This premise would clearly yield the desired conclusion; but in spite of its initial plausibility, Aune contends that it does not withstand close scrutiny. Eschewing the details of his analysis, the root of the difficulty supposedly lies in the "notion of willing that a maxim shall be a law." As Aune sees it, this is because maxims lack the proper "logical form" to be laws. Consequently, it is not a maxim but, at best, the "generalization" of a maxim that is a candidate for being willed as a universal law. But this shift from talk about maxims *simpliciter* to talk about generalized maxims once again opens up a gap in the argument; for what must now be shown is that a maxim is consistent with a universal law "when and only when its *generalization* could be willed to be a universal law."[17] Aune concludes, however, that this cannot be shown, since there is no absurdity in the supposition that a maxim is consistent with universal law when its generalization is not.[18]

The difficulty to which Aune points is a real one, and it is related to the difficulty noted earlier regarding two distinct senses of universalizability. Thus, from the requirement to conform one's actions to universal law, it certainly follows that one should not adopt any maxim or rule of action that one would not also regard as valid (or reasonable) for any other rational agent in relevantly similar circumstances; but this is not equivalent to the requirement expressed in the categorical imperative. As before, this is shown by the fact that the rational egoist would be willing to grant the former but not the latter.

Moreover, in the *Groundwork* at least, Kant does seem to argue precisely in the way Aune indicates. For example, he states that in contrast to a hypothetical imperative the content of a categorical imperative (what it enjoins) can be derived immediately from the mere concept of such an imperative. This supposedly follows because

besides the law this imperative contains only the necessity that our maxim should conform to this law, while the law . . . contains no condition to limit it, there remains nothing over to which the maxim has to conform except the universality of a law as such; and it is this conformity alone that the imperative properly asserts to be necessary. (Gr 4: 420–1; 88)

Of itself, this shows merely that what the imperative requires is conformity to universal law as such; and as suggested in the preceding, this is something that even the rational egoist might accept. Just as Aune has noted, however, Kant proceeds immediately, without further argument, to derive the categorical imperative from this result. Clearly, then, there is a gap that needs to be filled, indeed, if it leaves room for rational egoism, perhaps even a more serious gap than Aune and other friendly critics realize.[19]

Since the analysis of the gap has focused on the derivation of the categorical imperative in the *Groundwork,* it is natural to look to the *Critique of Practical Reason,* particularly its version of the "Metaphysical Deduction" (§1–7) for a more helpful account. This deduction appears to be an argument to the nature of the categorical imperative from the analysis of the concept of a practical law. In other words, it seems to argue for the hypothetical: If

211

there is such a thing as a practical law, it must take the form of the categorical imperative, at least for imperfectly rational beings such as ourselves. Since the necessity of a practical law (for transcendentally free agents) has already been shown, this argument, if successful, would fill in the gap.

At first glance, however, this does not appear to be any more successful than the argument from the concept of a categorical imperative. In fact, the problems are similar to those already noted. For one thing, Kant speaks about maxims as if they could themselves be laws, thereby conflating the question of what an unconditional practical law might require of maxims (which is what we wish to learn) with the, strictly speaking, nonsensical question of what form our maxims must possess in order to themselves qualify as practical laws.[20] For another, he is guilty of a slide from one sense of "formality" to another, which parallels the previously noted slide between two senses of universality. Thus, after claiming, reasonably enough, that a universally and unconditionally valid practical law must be formal in the sense that it must abstract from any material (object) of the will (§2 and 4), he proceeds to argue (§5) that it must be formal in the quite different sense that it concerns merely the legislative form of maxims. Since by "legislative form" Kant means suitability as universal law, this slide turns out to be pivotal in the deduction of the categorical imperative.

Nevertheless, the situation is not as hopeless as it has so far appeared. What has been neglected is that the argument of the second *Critique* does not move straightforwardly from the concept of a practical law to the categorical imperative as the only conceivable candidate for such a law but rather from this concept *together with* the assumption of transcendental freedom. In other words, the derivation or metaphysical deduction of the categorical imperative in the *Critique of Practical Reason,* unlike that of the *Groundwork,* has transcendental freedom as an explicit premise.

The key step occurs at §5 and §6 (Problems I and II), where transcendental freedom is injected into the picture for the first time and where, in fact, Kant argues for the Reciprocity Thesis. As already noted, Kant there claims that "the legislative form, insofar as it is contained in the maxim, is the only thing which can constitute a determining ground of the [transcendentally free] will" (KprV 5: 29; 30). Since the move from legislative form to the categorical imperative is itself short and unproblematic (a maxim has legislative form just in case it can include itself as a "principle establishing universal law"), it seems clear that the gap can be filled if it can be shown that the requirement that one's maxims have legislative form is identical with or follows from the unconditional practical law to which the free will is subject.

This has, however, already been shown, at least implicitly. Moreover, in order to make this fully explicit, we need only to keep in mind that for a transcendentally free agent conformity to a practical law must provide the reason to adopt a maxim. In other words, one's maxim must not merely conform to such a law, it must also be adopted *because* it conforms or at least is taken to conform. Otherwise, this conformity would be purely contingent. The reasoning here parallels precisely that used in the case of moral worth (see Chapter 6). Thus, the mere fact that my maxim happens to conform to such a law does not of itself justify my adoption of it; the latter requires that this conformity be my reason for adopting it. Such conformity may be of itself a sufficient reason or, in the case of maxims based on inclination or an "empirical interest," an ineliminable component in a jointly sufficient reason. In either case, this is simply because nothing else could provide such a reason. As we have seen, an inclination or interest is never of itself a sufficient reason for a transcendentally free agent. It can become such only if a maxim based on it accords with the dictates of a practical law binding unconditionally on all transcendentally free rational agents.

But to say that conformity to universal law must be the reason for adopting a maxim is just to say that its mere legislative form must provide the reason or, in Kant's terms, the "determining ground" of the will; and this is precisely what the categorical imperative requires. By this line of reasoning, then, which turns crucially on the assumption of transcendental freedom, the apparently empty requirement to conform to universal law and, indeed, even the manifestly empty requirement to act only on maxims that are rationally justifiable, which presumably even the rational egoist could accept, becomes the contentful requirement to select only those maxims that one can also regard as suitable to be universal laws. In short, transcendental freedom is precisely the missing ingredient, which bridges the gap between the idea of conformity to practical law as such, or alternatively, the mere concept of a practical law and the moral law as Kant defines it.

Admittedly, the argument offered here for the Reciprocity Thesis hardly suffices to establish the Kantian version of morality. At most, it shows only that we cannot both affirm our freedom (construed in the transcendental sense) and reject the categorical imperative; and this is merely a first step in the Kantian justification of morality (albeit one that is common to both the *Groundwork* and the *Critique of Practical Reason*). Nevertheless, this result suffices to answer the familiar objection that Kant is engaged in a futile endeavor to derive substantive moral conclusions from morally neutral premises about the nature of rationality or rational agency. More specifically, it shows once again that Kant's actual starting point is the thick concept of a transcendentally free rational agent rather than the thin concept of a rational being or even a rational agent *simpliciter*.

Clearly, however, critics of Kant's moral theory would regard this as a Pyrrhic victory and most defenders as a mixed blessing at best. The problem is that by connecting Kantian morality so intimately to the presumably disreputable notion of transcendental freedom, it undermines any attempt to defend essential elements of the former without accepting the latter. Whether this inseparability is in fact as damaging to Kant's moral theory as it initially appears will be determined in the next two chapters, where we consider his attempts to move beyond the Reciprocity Thesis in the *Groundwork* and the *Critique of Practical Reason*.

213

12

The deduction in *Groundwork* III

The third part of the *Groundwork,* which is entitled "Passage from a Metaphysic of Morals to a Critique of Pure Practical Reason," is one of the most enigmatic of the Kantian texts. It is clear that its chief purpose is to ground or justify the "supreme principle of morality" articulated in the first two parts, and it would appear that Kant took this to require a deduction, presumably modeled on the transcendental deduction of the categories in the first *Critique.*[1] Nevertheless, although there is virtual unanimity that the attempt fails, there is little agreement concerning the actual structure of the argument that Kant advances. In fact, it is not clear whether the deduction is of the moral law, the categorical imperative, freedom, all three; or even whether it can be properly characterized as a "deduction" at all.[2]

In the present chapter I shall argue that *Groundwork* III does contain a deduction (albeit one that is seriously flawed) of the moral law and that the Reciprocity Thesis is its first premise or, better, underlying presupposition. The chapter is divided into four parts. The first analyzes the much-discussed "preparatory" argument, which is compressed into a single dense paragraph and which, as the caption indicates, is intended to show that "Freedom Must be Presupposed as a Property of the Will of all Rational Beings" (Gr 4: 447; 115). By focusing on the lacunae in this argument (lacunae that presumably would have been recognized by Kant), I explain why Kant fails to draw the inferences one might expect him to have drawn and that are frequently attributed to him by commentators.[3] The second part argues that these same lacunae explain why Kant raises the specter of a possible "hidden circle." The third part shows how the distinction between the "two standpoints" and the appeal to the intelligible world may be viewed as completing the deduction by filling in the lacunae and, therefore, removing the threat of a vicious circle. In addition, it discusses the sense in which there is a distinct deduction of the categorical imperative. The fourth part analyzes the reasons for the failure of the argument and suggests that Kant's own recognition of this failure might have led to the "great reversal" in the *Critique of Practical Reason.*

I. The preparatory argument

The argument in question is contained in the fourth paragraph in the text. In the first three paragraphs, Kant formulates the Reciprocity Thesis and remarks that in spite of the analytic connection between a free will and a will under moral laws, the principle of morality itself is synthetic. As such, Kant suggests, it requires some third term by means of which the subject and predicate terms are joined. He further suggests that the positive concept of freedom "directs" us to this third term. But instead of identifying this mysterious term, which, as we later learn, turns out to be the idea of an intelligible world, he insists that further preparation is required before we are in a position either to do this or, more important, to "make intelligible the deduction of the concept of freedom from pure practical reason and so the possibility of a categorical imperative" (Gr 4: 447; 115).

The ensuing paragraph, which supposedly supplies this needed preparation, begins by stating that the task is to show that freedom must be presupposed as a property of the will of *all* rational beings or, more precisely, of all rational beings with a will. The point here is simply that since the moral law is supposed to apply to us qua rational beings, and since (by the Reciprocity Thesis) it is supposed to be derived solely from the property of freedom, it is necessary to show that freedom must itself be presupposed as a universal property of rational beings with a will.

The importance of freedom to the Kantian project is already apparent from the Reciprocity Thesis. Given this thesis, the preferred strategy would clearly be to demonstrate the reality of freedom and from this infer the validity of the moral law. Indeed, as Dieter Henrich has shown, Kant was attracted to such a strategy for a considerable period of time and only abandoned it with the recognition of the impossibility of providing a theoretical proof of freedom.[4] With this no longer a viable option, the next best strategy would be to attempt to argue from the weaker thesis that freedom must necessarily be presupposed, and this is just what he seems to do. The argument, such as it is, consists of two steps:

1. "Now I assert that every being who cannot act except *under the idea of freedom* is by this alone – from a practical point of view – really free."
2. "And I maintain that to every rational being possessed of a will we must also lend the idea of freedom as the only one under which he can act." (Gr 4: 448; 115–16)

As Kant goes on to explain, the first step entails that all the laws "inseparably bound up with freedom" are valid for such a being, just as they would be if this freedom were established on theoretically valid grounds. In a footnote he further clarifies the point by stating that even if the question of freedom remains unsettled from a theoretical point of view, "the same laws as would bind a being who is really free are equally valid for a being who cannot act except under the idea of his own freedom" (Gr 4: 448n; 116). Accordingly, it is quite clear that the cash value of being free "from a practical point of view" is that one is subject to whatever laws one would be subject to if, *per impossibile,* it could be proven (theoretically) that one is free.

In support of the second step, Kant claims that a rational being with a will is one for whom reason is practical. He also advances his well-known argument to the effect that reason must regard itself as free in its cognitive activity (judgment), from which it supposedly follows that reason must likewise regard itself as free in its practical activity, that is, as will. As Kant succinctly puts it:

Reason must look upon itself as the author of its own principles independently of alien influences. Therefore as practical reason or as the will of a rational being, it must be regarded by itself as free; that is, the will of a rational being can be a will of his own [*ein eigener Wille sein*] only under the idea of freedom, and such a will must therefore – from a practical point of view – be attributed to all rational beings. (Gr 4: 448; 116)

Although Kant's premises are hardly immune from challenge, our immediate concern is not with their cogency but rather with the way in which he proceeds or, better, fails to proceed from them. Given these premises, together with the Reciprocity Thesis and the avowed goal of providing a justification or deduction of the moral law and the categorical imperative, one would expect him to continue the argument in roughly the following manner:

3. All laws "inseparably bound up with freedom" are valid for every being with reason and will.
4. But the Reciprocity Thesis establishes that the moral law is "inseparably bound up with freedom."
5. Therefore, the moral law is valid for every being with reason and will.
6. Since beings such as ourselves have reason and will, the moral law is valid for us.
7. Since we do not necessarily follow the dictates of the law (these dictates being "objectively necessary" but "subjectively contingent"), the law for us takes the form of a categorical imperative, that is, we are rationally constrained, although not causally necessitated, to obey it.

But instead of developing the argument in this natural manner, Kant shifts abruptly to a new topic: "The Interest Attached to the Ideas of Morality." Moreover, in addition to raising what would seem to be the wholly new problem of explaining the interest we take in morality and moral requirements, he makes it quite clear that he does not regard the argument sketched in the preceding as having established (even in a preliminary fashion) the validity of the moral law. On the contrary, he suggests that this argument has shown only that we must presuppose the idea of freedom if we are to regard a being as rational and as endowed with a will and that from the presupposition of this idea there "springs . . . consciousness of a law of action." Although this law is identified with the moral law, Kant remarks, in clear anticipation of the problem of the circle, that "it looks as if, in our idea of freedom, we have in fact merely taken the moral law for granted . . . and have been unable to give an independent proof of its reality and objective necessity" (Gr 4: 449; 117). Accordingly, the questions remain: "Why must the validity of our maxim as a universal law be a condition limiting our action?" and "On what do we base the worth we attach to this way of acting – a worth supposed to be so great that there cannot be any interest which is higher?" (Gr 4: 449; 117). Finally, lacking an answer to these questions, Kant concludes that we do not yet see *"how the moral law can be binding"* (Gr 4: 450; 118).

Even apart from the introduction of the problem of circularity, which is the topic of the next section, this portion of the text is deeply perplexing because of the presumably distinct considerations that Kant seems to run together with little in the way of clarification, namely, interest, validity, and bindingness.[5] Most surprising of all, however, is the fact that Kant proceeds as if the preliminary argument had done little or nothing toward establishing the validity of the moral law. Accordingly, it might be instructive to take a closer look at Kant's premises in order to see if there is something about them that may have deterred him from developing his argument in the natural manner suggested here. As we shall see, there is a problem with each of these premises that would give Kant himself, and not merely his critics, cause to refrain from drawing the desired conclusions.

The first premise, it will be recalled, states that from the point of view of practice the demonstration of the necessity of presupposing the idea of freedom is as good as the demonstration (on theoretical grounds) of the reality of freedom itself. Given the doctrine of the *Critique of Pure Reason* that neither the reality nor the possibility of freedom can be established on theoretical grounds, together with the connection between freedom and the moral law affirmed in the Reciprocity Thesis, it is easy to see why Kant would wish to affirm this. The problem, however, is that it is present in the text as a bald assertion without any supporting argument. (In fact, Kant explicitly presents both premises in this fashion.) It could, of course, be claimed that if one believes oneself to be free, one must also believe oneself to be subject to any laws (if there are such) to which one would be subject if one were in fact free. But to jump from this to the claim that one is really subject to those laws to which one believes oneself to be subject constitutes a colossal *petitio*.

The second premise seems close, in spirit at least, to Kant's precritical attempts to argue directly from the capacity for theoretical thinking to transcendental freedom discussed in Chapter 3. It is likewise quite close to the brief antifatalism argument, which Kant mounted in his "Review of Schulz's Theory of Ethics" (8: 14), published shortly before the *Groundwork*. Thus, one might assume that whatever its difficulties and limitations Kant remained attached to this basic line of argument.[6] Moreover, this is certainly true of the first part, in which Kant argues for the necessity of reason to regard itself as free in its epistemic capacity. In fact, this reflects the very line of argument discussed in Chapter 2 in connection with the analysis of epistemic spontaneity.

Nevertheless, it should be clear from our earlier analyses that Kant would have grounds to question the move from reason's freedom in its theoretical capacity to its analogous freedom in its practical capacity. The problem is not with the claim that reason must likewise regard itself as free in its practical capacity (this is just the argument for the necessity of appealing to the transcendental idea of freedom in its regulative capacity discussed in Chapter 2); it is rather with the underlying assumption that our reason has a practical capacity. As Henrich has pointed out, Kant's awareness of the limitations of this line of argument is reflected in the fact that the necessity of acting under (or presupposing) the idea of freedom is affirmed not of rational beings *überhaupt* but only of beings who possess both reason (or intelligence) and will. Since Kant here identifies practical reason with will (*Wille*), this means that the problem is that it has not yet been shown that rational beings such as ourselves possess a will.[7] This in turn invalidates the key sixth step and therefore the conclusion of the extended argument.

Such an agnosticism regarding will or, what amounts to the same thing, rational agency should not surprise us, since it is the very position we saw in Chapter 3 to underlie the account of freedom in the *Critique of Pure Reason*. Moreover, we need not limit ourselves to the passage presently under consideration to find evidence of it in the *Groundwork*. In fact, in the very beginning of the work, where Kant is concerned with criticizing the notion that the function of reason is to enable rational agents to achieve happiness (in contrast to a good will), he remarks that if that were nature's purpose, it could more readily be attained through instinct. Accordingly, he sketches a hypothetical scenario in which this "favoured creature" (one programmed for happiness) is also possessed of reason, but this reason serves "only for contemplating the happy disposition of his nature" and not for any practical purpose, that is, not as a guide for conduct (Gr 4: 395; 63). Similarly, near the end of the work, while commenting on the inexplicability of freedom and therefore the limits of practical philosophy, he writes: "It [freedom] holds only as a necessary presupposition of reason in a being who believes himself to be conscious of a will – that is, of a power distinct from mere appetition (a power, namely, of determining himself to act as intelligence and consequently to act in accordance with laws of reason independently of natural instincts)" (Gr 4: 459; 127). Although these passages raise issues that must be dealt with later, it should be already apparent that they show that Kant neither simply identified the class of rational beings with the class of rational agents nor assumed that one really has a will merely because one believes oneself to be conscious of having one.[8]

II. The hidden circle

Immediately after raising the problem of accounting for the possibility of taking an interest in morality and noting that it has not yet been shown how the moral law can be binding, Kant turns to the problem of the circle, which has proven so puzzling to generations of commentators. The nature of this circle is described in two passages. In the first, where Kant initially suggests that there seems to be no escape from it, the circle is said to consist in the fact that

in the order of efficient causes we take ourselves to be free so that we may conceive ourselves to be under moral laws in the order of ends; and we then proceed to think of ourselves as subject to moral laws on the ground that we have described our will as free. (Gr 4: 450; 118)

In the second, where Kant claims to have removed the suspicion of a "hidden circle" and therefore to have shown that the initial worry was unfounded, he locates the supposed difficulty in

our inference from freedom to autonomy and from autonomy to the moral law; that, in effect, we had perhaps assumed the idea of freedom only because of the moral law in order subsequently to infer the moral law in its turn from freedom; and that consequently we had been able to assign no ground at all for the moral law, but had merely assumed it by begging a principle which well-meaning souls will gladly concede us, but which we could never put forward as a demonstrable [*erweislichen*] proposition. (Gr 4: 453; 120–1)

The exegetical problem is that the circle Kant describes does not seem to pertain to his own preceding argument (what has here been termed the "preliminary argument"), at least not to the two premises Kant himself provides. As Paton, who both poses the problem and denies that Kant took the threat of a circle very seriously, puts it:

In plain fact the objection totally misrepresents his argument. He never argued from the categorical imperative to freedom, but at least professed, however mistakenly, to establish the presupposition of freedom by an insight into the nature of self-conscious reason quite independently of moral considerations. Perhaps when he came to the objection he was beginning to see dimly that the presupposition of freedom of the will did really rest on moral considerations; but it is surely unusual for a man to answer the sound argument which he has failed to put and to overlook the fact that this answer is irrelevant to the unsound argument which alone has been explicitly stated.[9]

Paton's suggestion reflects his view that Kant's real position, already in the *Groundwork,* is that there is no route to freedom from extramoral considerations and therefore no genuine deduction of morality from nonmoral premises. Thus, according to him, there is no major difference between the standpoints of the *Groundwork* and the second *Critique,* no "great reversal" after all.[10] Although we cannot deal with that issue until the next chapter, it should already be apparent that at least with respect to the account of the circle Paton's reading is implausible on the face of it. In fact, if we accept it, we must attribute to Kant either a total lack of insight into the structure of his own argument or the very patchwork mode of composition, which Paton himself took such pains to disparage as a possible reading of the first *Critique.*[11]

At the same time, however, Paton's account of the circle does point to a very real exegetical problem, one possible response to which is to maintain that the circle Kant describes is not, in fact, supposed to refer to his own position but to that of a view he is criticizing. Such a response has been mounted recently with considerable erudition and subtlety by Reinhard Brandt. According to Brandt, who emphasizes the importance of considering the problem of the circle in light of the overall structure of the *Groundwork* and particularly the function of the third part to provide a transition from a metaphysic of morals to a critique of pure practical reason, the circle belongs to the "metaphysics of morals (in the narrow sense)."[12] By the latter he means essentially the analytic procedure of the Wolffian school, by means of which Kant supposedly arrived at the following two propositions: (1) A free will is an autonomous will, that is, one subject to the categorical imperative and *vice versa,* and (2) a rational being is free in his own self-representation and can and must be taken by us as free and autonomous in a practical respect.[13] The circle arises, on this reading, when one endeavors to proceed from these analytic premises to the synthetic a priori conclusion regarding the necessitation of the will by the categorical imperative. Moreover, so construed, the circle can be avoided only by means of a critique of pure practical reason, which involves, of course, the distinction between the two standpoints and the appeal to the idea of an intelligible world. On this view, then, the circle plays an essential role in the transition from the metaphysic of morals to the critique of pure practical reason, which indicates that, *pace* Paton, Kant took it very seriously indeed.

In spite of its ingenuity and the light it sheds on the connections between the three sections of the *Groundwork* and between the argument of *Groundwork* III and other aspects of Kant's philosophy, Brandt's solution cannot be accepted as it stands. To begin with, the two propositions Brandt characterizes as pertaining to the "metaphysics of morals (in the narrow sense)" are not equivalent to those Kant affirms in this preliminary argument. The second corresponds roughly to the second of Kant's propositions; but the first corresponds to the Reciprocity Thesis, which is explicitly analytic but is presupposed by rather than a constitutive part of the preliminary argument. Moreover, neither the Reciprocity Thesis, the conception of autonomy, nor the necessity of presupposing the idea of freedom insofar as we take ourselves as rational agents can be regarded as elements that Kant simply takes over from elsewhere. On the contrary, as has been argued in previous chapters, all three are essential aspects of Kant's critical position.

In a larger sense, however, Brandt is certainly on the right track. The circle is to be found not in the argument Kant actually provides but in the natural extension (steps 3–7) he does not make. In that respect, then, it does not concern Kant's own explicit position. Moreover, by raising the threat of a circle at this point in the analysis, Kant is calling attention to the limitations of a merely analytic procedure, which, as such, is incapable of taking us beyond the Reciprocity Thesis and the necessity of presupposing the idea of freedom. Thus, the introduction of the threat of a circle, together with the discussion of the problems of moral interest and bindingness of which it is a part, may be taken as Kant's explanation of why the argument is not developed in the natural manner suggested and therefore of the need, in spite of the apparent availability of the extended argument, of embarking on the arduous path of a critique of pure practical reason.

In order to make this clear, we need only show how precisely the circle Kant describes arises when one endeavors to develop the argument on the basis of the unsupported premises, that is, without first removing the lacunae. Fortunately, this is easy to do. As already indicated, the most that Kant's explicit argument (steps 1 and 2) is able to show is that we must believe ourselves to be under the moral law insofar as we believe ourselves to be free (this much follows from the Reciprocity Thesis) and that we cannot regard ourselves as rational agents, that is, as rational beings with wills, without also regarding our wills as free. Together, they yield the hypothetical: If one regards oneself as a rational agent, then one must also regard oneself as free and therefore as standing under the moral law. But the extended argument sketched earlier maintains, in effect, the categorical claim that we stand under the moral law because we are rational agents. To argue in this way, however, without first providing any further support for the claim that we are rational agents may be aptly described as assuming "the idea of freedom only because of the moral law in order subsequently to infer the moral law in its turn from freedom" (Gr 4: 453; 120).

III. Completing the deduction

As already indicated, Kant's recipe for avoiding the circle and completing the deduction turns on the distinction between the two standpoints from which rational beings may regard themselves. From one of these they regard themselves as passive, causally conditioned members of the sensible world (*Sinnenwelt*) and from the other as free members of the intelligible world (*Verstandeswelt*). By adopting this distinction, which Kant here suggests has its basis in the ordinary human understanding, we are supposedly able to avoid the circle after all because "we now see that when we think of ourselves as free, we transfer ourselves into the intelligible world as members and recognize the autonomy of the will together with its consequence – morality" (Gr 4: 453; 121).

Presumably, the point here is that our membership in the intelligible world provides the needed nonmoral premise from which our freedom and (by means of the Reciprocity Thesis) our subjection to the moral law can be derived in a non-questioning-begging or circular manner. Moreover, if the previous analysis is correct, it would do so by remedying the deficiencies of the preliminary argument. In short, it must show that, qua members of the intelligible world, we are warranted in assuming that we really are rational agents and, as such, really subject to the moral law.

Even granting all of this, however, we still need sufficient (nonmoral) grounds for assigning to ourselves membership in the intelligible world in the first place. Otherwise, we would be once again trapped in the very circle that is supposedly being evaded by the appeal to the idea of the intelligible world. Accordingly, the deduction requires at least two further steps: (1) an argument that, without either appealing to the moral law or presupposing freedom, establishes our entitlement to regard ourselves as members of the intelligible world, if only from a "point of view" or "standpoint," and (2) an argument showing that, qua members of the intelligible world, we are justified in regarding ourselves as rational agents, that is, as rational beings with wills. Given this, the validity or bindingness of the moral law for us would follow by the Reciprocity Thesis.

The nonmoral evidence provided in support of our claim to membership in the intelligible world consists in our possession of reason, here construed as a theoretical capacity. After trying to show that even the ordinary, yet reflective human understanding (quite apart from an exposure to a critique of pure reason) is capable of arriving at the distinction between the two standpoints and of applying that distinction to the self, Kant writes:

> Now man actually finds in himself a power which distinguishes him from all other things – and even from himself so far as he is affected by objects. This power is *reason.* As pure spontaneity [*Selbstthätigkeit*] reason is elevated even above the *understanding* in the following respect. Understanding – although it too is spontaneous activity [*Selbstthätigkeit*] and is not, like sense, confined to representations which arise only when we are affected by things (and therefore are passive) – understanding cannot produce by its own activity any concepts other than those whose sole service is *to bring sensible representations under rules* and so to unite them in one consciousness. . . . Reason, on the other hand – in what are called "ideas" – shows a spontaneity so pure that it goes far beyond anything sensibility can offer: it manifests its highest function in distinguishing the sensible and intelligible worlds from one another and so of marking out limits for understanding itself. (Gr 4: 452; 120)

This passage is highly reminiscent of the one in the *Critique of Pure Reason* discussed in Chapter 2, where Kant claims that through mere apperception we are conscious of certain faculties (understanding and reason), "the action of which cannot be ascribed to the receptivity of sensibility" (A547/B575). There as well as here Kant distinguishes between the spontaneity of the understanding and reason and attributes a higher level to the latter. At the same time, it is also reminiscent of the claim in the preliminary argument to the effect that reason must regard itself as free in its theoretical capacity. Although Kant does not there distinguish between the spontaneity of reason and that of understanding, the basic point would seem to be the same: namely, that in the consciousness of our epistemic spontaneity we are directly aware of a capacity we cannot conceive as sensibly conditioned. Unfortunately, the latter resemblance serves only to exacerbate the problem of interpreting Kant's deduction; for if the present passage does not add anything of material significance to the one in the preliminary argument, it is difficult to see how it could help to remedy the deficiencies in that argument.

The sharp distinction between the spontaneity of understanding and that of reason is an important difference and should not be trivialized. It is in the end the capacity of reason to think the unconditioned that makes it the source of the moral law and that underlies the whole question of how pure reason can be practical. Nevertheless, this cannot be the main difference between the two passages; for Kant could very easily have included the contrast between the two levels of epistemic spontaneity in the preliminary argument without significantly changing things. Even buttressed in this manner, the preliminary argument would suffer from the same deficiencies and lead to the same circle.

If the salient difference between the two passages does not lie in the nature of the epistemic spontaneity to which they appeal, it must lie in the use that is made of this appeal. In the preliminary argument this appeal led directly to an analogous claim regarding reason in its practical capacity; and this raised the problem of whether we can be assured that reason has a practical capacity, that is, whether rational beings such as ourselves have wills (practical reason). Although Kant is still concerned with the problem of justifying the claim to rational agency (we have seen that this is necessary to complete the deduction), he does not now argue directly from epistemic to practical spontaneity. The move instead is from epistemic spontaneity (as manifested in reason rather than merely understanding) to membership in the intelligible world. Thus, immediately after the characterization of the spontaneity of reason, Kant remarks that it is because of this spontaneity that "a rational being must regard himself *qua intelligence* (and accordingly not on the side of his lower faculties) as belonging to the intelligible world, not to the sensible one" (Gr 4: 452; 120).

This move parallels that of the corresponding passage from the *Critique of Pure Reason,* where the consciousness of epistemic spontaneity is used as the basis for attributing an intelligible character to ourselves. Just as Kant there claims, in virtue of this consciousness, that each of us is to ourself not only a phenomenon with an empirical character but also a "merely intelligible object" (A547/B575), so he now claims, in virtue of the same consciousness, that each of us must regard ourself from two standpoints or, equivalently, as members of "two worlds."

Given this parallelism, it seems reasonable to assume that these claims are substantially equivalent or at least were construed as such by Kant. Consequently, the first of the two steps necessary to complete the deduction in the *Groundwork* consists in a reiteration of the claim that as cognitive beings we are conscious of capacities in virtue of which we cannot conceive ourselves merely as sensibly conditioned. Since this claim has already been analyzed at length in Chapter 2, there is no need to consider it any further here.

The second step involves the move from our membership in the intelligible world to the possession of a will, since this would supposedly legitimate the presupposition of freedom asserted in the preliminary argument. What Kant must do, then, according to this reconstruction, is to link membership in the intelligible world with the possession of a will. Moreover, this is precisely what we find him attempting. Thus, at one point Kant states explicitly that "a rational being counts himself, *qua* intelligence, as belonging to the intelligible world, and solely *qua* efficient cause belonging to the intelligible world does he give his causality the name of '*will*'" (Gr 4: 453; 121) and at another that "the concept of the intelligible world is thus only a *point of view* which reason finds itself constrained to adopt outside of appearances in *order to conceive itself as practical*" (Gr 4: 458; 126).

These passages indicate that Kant uses the concept of the intelligible world to link intelligence with the possession of a will, but they do not explain how this linkage is supposed to work. Moreover, the matter is far from clear, since the text of the *Groundwork* is virtually silent on the point, and it hardly seems obvious that one can deduce the possession of a will directly from membership in the intelligible world.

Nevertheless, we have the materials needed to develop this argument and therefore to fill in the gap in Kant's own account. The argument turns on a rational being's consciousness of possessing a will (practical reason). As already noted, in the *Critique of Pure Reason* Kant affirms the "fact" of such consciousness but intimates that it might possibly be illusory, that is, that our reason might not have causality. As was also noted, precisely the same possibility blocks the initial extension of the preliminary argument. If our consciousness of possessing a will were enough to certify our actual possession of one, then the argument could have continued without any appearance of a circle and without recourse to the intelligible world.

Assuming this to be Kant's problem, it is now clear how the appeal to the intelligible world must enter into the proposed solution. The essential point is that the connection of this consciousness with an activity that is "merely intelligible" and therefore located in the intelligible world serves to obviate any potential suspicions regarding its illusory character. It does so by undermining the assumption on which such suspicion could alone be based, namely, that our apparent practical rationality is really tropistic, the product of some hidden "mechanism of nature." Given transcendental idealism, the location of this activity in the intelligible world rules out the latter possibility and therefore any reductive, epiphenomenalistic treatment of the will because it exempts it, *ex hypothesi,* from this mechanism.

Although this line of argument will hardly appeal to someone not already committed to transcendental idealism and it may even seem somewhat speculative to attribute it to Kant, it is perfectly compatible with the underlying assumptions and problematic of the *Groundwork*. In fact, it can be taken as an illustration of how, as Kant suggests, the idea of the intelligible world is supposed to function as a middle term or "third thing" grounding the synthesis of conceptually distinct elements. Not only does it connect the possession of reason with subjection to the moral law, it also links the possession of reason with the possession of a will and ultimately with freedom. Moreover, in accomplishing these goals, it makes it possible to complete the deduction of the moral law (step 6 in the extended argument).

The deduction does not, however, stop at this point. In fact, Kant also speaks of a distinct deduction of the categorical imperative (step 7), and such a deduction appears to be contained in the three paragraphs headed by the caption "How is a Categorical Imperative Possible?" (Gr 4: 453–5; 121–3), which immediately follow the presentation of the argument outlined in the preceding. Moreover, some commentators take this not merely as an addendum but as the essential move in the argument because they regard the categorical imperative as the synthetic a priori proposition Kant is concerned with justifying.[14] Consequently, it is necessary to determine just how this additional deduction of the categorical imperative relates to that of the moral law.

Following Dieter Henrich, it seems reasonable to regard this deduction as a separate step in the argument, the intent of which is to account for the experience of the categorical imperative "as an imperative," that is, for the very feature of the ethical consciousness (the consciousness of duty) that has been the focal point of the *Groundwork* from the beginning.[15] As Henrich also points out, however, it presupposes the deduction of the moral law and, indeed, the distinction between the intelligible and the sensible worlds. Thus, appealing to this distinction, Kant notes that if one were solely a member (*Glied*) of the intelligible world, all of one's actions would be in perfect accord with the principle of autonomy; correlatively, if one were solely a part (*Stück*) of the sensible world, all one's action would accord with the law of nature governing desires and inclinations (Gr 4: 453; 121). With this as backdrop, the actual deduction proceeds as follows:

But the intelligible world contains the ground of the sensible world and therefore also of its laws; and so in respect of my will, for which (as belonging entirely to the intelligible world) it gives laws immediately, it must also be conceived as containing such a ground. Hence, in spite of regarding myself from one point of view as a being that belongs to the sensible world, I shall have to recognize that, *qua* intelligence, I am subject to the law of the intelligible world – that is, to the reason which contains this law in the Idea of freedom, and so to the autonomy of the will – and therefore I must look on the laws of the intelligible world as imperatives for me and on the actions which conform to this principle as duties. (Gr 4: 453–4; 121)

The nerve of this argument lies in the complex claim that since the intelligible world is (in general) the ground of the sensible world and its laws and since the will as member of the intelligible world is subject to its laws, it (the will) must also be conceived as a ground of the sensible world and its laws.[16] From this it supposedly follows that sensibly affected and therefore phenomenal beings such as ourselves who are likewise conscious of possessing a will experience the law stemming from this noumenal will as an unconditional command, that is, a categorical imperative addressed to them in their phenomenal nature. As Kant summarily puts it at the conclusion of this segment of his analysis: "The moral 'I ought' is thus an 'I will' for man as a member of the intelligible world; and it is conceived by him as an 'I ought' only insofar as he considers himself at the same time to be a member of the sensible world" (Gr 4: 455, 123).

As an analysis of obligation, this account is easy to criticize. Granting the general framework of transcendental idealism, which is obviously presupposed, the fundamental problem is that the putative addressee of the law, the phenomenal self, that is, the agent qua considered part of the sensible world, is *ex hypothesi,* incapable of recognizing any obligation, much less of acting in light of the "ought." This is because beings so considered are not merely sensibly affected (which is the point Kant wishes to emphasize in explicating the imperatival character of the law) but causally necessitated. As should be already clear from the account of agency in the *Critique of Pure Reason,* moral requirements (or more generally, practical principles) must not only be addressed to agents conscious of having an intelligible character (in the language of the *Groundwork* a will) but also be addressed to them in that character. Consequently, in order to explain the possibility of a categorical imperative for finite rational beings such as ourselves, it is necessary to show how the moral law addresses beings whose wills are sensibly affected but not necessitated. But such an argument cannot proceed, as Kant here seems to suggest, directly from general considerations about the phenomenal–noumenal relationship.[17]

With the benefit of hindsight, it seems clear that what Kant needs at this point but does not yet possess is precisely the *Wille–Willkür* distinction. Given this distinction, the point Kant here struggles to make in terms of the contrast between the intelligible and the sensible worlds can be formulated relatively straightforwardly, namely, the imperatival character of the law (and therefore its bindingness or necessitation) for finite rational beings such as ourselves is to be understood in light of the fact that the law as a product of pure *Wille* (or pure practical reason) confronts the sensibly affected (yet free) *Willkür* as an unconditional demand, one to which our needs as sensuous beings must be subordinated.[18]

Perhaps more to the point, however, Kant insists on the syntheticity of the moral law or principle of morality: "An absolutely good will is one whose maxim can always have as its content itself considered as a universal law" (Gr 4: 447; 115).[19] This means that a synthetic a priori proposition is first established with the deduction of the moral law (step 6), not with that of the categorical imperative (step 7). In underscoring the syntheticity of this principle, Kant remarks that it cannot be derived from the mere concept of an absolutely good will (which is presumably equivalent to that of a perfectly rational will[20]) but that such derivation is possible on the basis of the positive concept of freedom. This concept, we have seen, furnishes the "third term," which enables us to link the concept of an absolutely good will with the moral requirement. Since the *Groundwork* begins with the concept of a good will and attempts to derive the moral law from it, Kant's emphasis on the syntheticity of this proposition has seemed puzzling to many commentators, including Paton.[21] Nevertheless, both this and the assignment of a mediating role to the idea of freedom make perfect sense if we take Kant to be making the by now familiar point that one cannot derive the moral law from the concept of a rational agent, not even a perfectly rational one, unless (transcendental) freedom is also presupposed.

Finally, as Paton notes, once one has established the status of the moral law (which he terms the "principle of autonomy") as the principle on which rational agents would necessarily act if reason were fully in control, there is no further difficulty – or at least Kant would not find any – in claiming that it is also the principle on which rational agents *ought* to act should they be tempted to do otherwise.[22] Admittedly, Kant also refers to the categorical

226

imperative as a synthetic a priori proposition (Gr 4: 454; 122); but this does not entail that it requires a distinct deduction, since it follows directly from the moral law, which, as we have just seen, is itself a synthetic a priori proposition, indeed, the very proposition singled out by Kant as requiring a justification at the beginning of *Groundwork* III.

IV. The failure of the deduction

The concern in the first three parts of this chapter has been primarily exegetical. Accordingly, apart from the brief critique of the distinct deduction of the categorical imperative, relatively little has been said about the cogency of Kant's main line of argument. This should not be taken, however, as an endorsement of either the overall argument or its specific steps. On the contrary, the text contains a host of difficulties, most of which have been noted repeatedly in the literature, and the arguments here attributed to Kant on the basis of an analysis of the deficiencies of the preparatory argument are hardly immune from criticism.

Since a detailed critique of these arguments would require an extended discussion, I shall here focus only on two obvious difficulties that help us to understand why Kant significantly revised his procedure in the *Critique of Practical Reason*. Each of them involves a fatal ambiguity in a central notion. The first is in that of the intelligible world and the second in that of the will or practical reason. These are certainly not the only problems one can find; but they are the sort to which Kant himself would be sensitive and they are sufficient to undermine the deduction.

As we have just seen, the move from the possession of reason to membership in the intelligible world is the pivotal point in the deduction, since it provides both the needed nonmoral premise and the basis for removing global doubts about agency. Unfortunately, in making this key move Kant exploits an ambiguity in the notion of an "intelligible world." More precisely, Kant refers to both a *Verstandeswelt* and an *intelligibelen Welt* (both of which Paton renders as intelligible world) and he slides from the former to the latter without sufficient justification. The former is to be understood negatively as encompassing whatever is nonsensible or "merely intelligible," that is, whatever is thought to be exempt from the conditions of sensibility (the noumenon in the negative sense). The latter is to be understood positively as referring to a supersensible realm governed by moral laws, a "kingdom of ends" or, equivalently, "the totality of rational beings as things in themselves" (Gr 4: 458; 126). This is clearly noumenal in a positive sense.[23] The goal is to show that rational beings, including imperfectly rational beings such as ourselves, are members of such an *intelligibelen Welt* because this would entail that they really stand under the moral law. The problem is that the possession of reason, which is supposed to provide the *entrée* into this world, only gets us to the *Verstandeswelt*.[24]

The slide underlies the entire deduction, since it is the means by which Kant moves from the possession of reason (as a theoretical capacity) to subjection to the moral law. It is particularly evident, however, in a key passage in which Kant himself shows an awareness of the problem even while making the slide. Thus, he begins by admitting, quite appropriately, that the thought of the intelligible world (*Verstandeswelt*) is merely negative in the sense that it is "only a *point of view*." Unfortunately, having said this, he proceeds immediately to insist that with this thought or point of view comes "the idea of an order and a legislation different from that of the mechanism of nature appropriate to the world of sense" (Gr 4: 458; 126). In so doing, he begs the whole question at issue.

The ambiguity in the notion of will or practical reason mentioned in the preceding is closely related to the first problem and hardly requires a separate elaboration at this stage. The main point is simply that given the identification of will and practical reason the claim that rational beings possess a will can mean either merely that reason is practical or that pure reason is practical.[25] The former suffices to show that we are genuine rational agents rather than automata; but the latter is required to establish our autonomy. Alternatively, the former correlates with what has here been characterized as "mere practical" and the latter with genuine transcendental freedom. Once again, then, it is clear that Kant needs the latter and stronger claim but membership in the *Verstandeswelt* provides, at best, support for the weaker. Consequently, the attempt to establish the necessity of presupposing the kind of freedom that is both necessary and sufficient for morality (transcendental freedom) on the basis of a nonmoral premise about our rationality is doomed to failure even when buttressed by transcendental idealism.

Finally, assuming, as seems reasonable, that Kant himself may have been sensitive to these fatal defects in his deduction, we can readily understand why he saw fit to revise his procedure in the *Critique of Practical Reason*. More specifically, we can see why he would abandon the attempt to establish the practicality of pure reason on the basis of any nonmoral premise. Thus, instead of beginning with the concept of a rational agent and moving from this first to the presupposition of freedom and then, via the Reciprocity Thesis, to the moral law, Kant there moves directly from the consciousness of the moral law as the "fact of reason" to the practicality of pure reason and the reality of transcendental freedom.

Admittedly, as Paton and Henrich have noted, some of Kant's remarks near the end of *Groundwork* III appear to anticipate this shift. For example, in the closing section, "The Extreme Limit of Practical Philosophy," Kant underscores the limits of his deduction, pointing out the impossibility of explaining how pure reason can be practical (which would be equivalent to explaining how freedom is possible) and maintaining that the most that one can provide is a defense against those who would affirm the impossibility of freedom (Gr 4: 458–9; 127). Nevertheless, these disclaimers must themselves be viewed in light of the fact that Kant does provide what he takes to be a non-question-begging deduction of the moral law in *Groundwork* III.

As we have seen, this deduction must be judged a failure and quite probably was eventually recognized as such by Kant himself. Whether the new attempt to ground morality by means of the "fact of reason" meets with any greater success is the topic of the next chapter.

13

The fact of reason
and the deduction of freedom

Kant's appeal to the fact of reason in the *Critique of Practical Reason* has been greeted with even less enthusiasm than the ill-fated attempt at a deduction of the moral law in *Groundwork* III. The general consensus appears to be that even though this deduction failed, it was at least a step in the right direction. Consequently, by abandoning the effort to provide a deduction of the moral law and relying instead on a brute appeal to a putative fact of reason, which in turn is supposed to provide the basis for a deduction of freedom, Kant in effect reverted to a precritical dogmatism of practical reason. As Schopenhauer puts it, in commenting on the acceptance of this conception by Kant's followers:

Thus in the Kantian school practical reason with its categorical imperative appears more and more as a hyperphysical fact, as a delphic temple in the human soul. From its dark sanctuary oracular sentences infallibly proclaim, alas! not what *will*, but what *ought* to happen.[1]

In the present chapter I shall argue that far from being a reversion to a discredited standpoint, Kant's turn to the fact of reason marks a genuine advance, indeed, that given the basic principles of Kant's philosophy, it offers the best available strategy for authenticating the moral law and establishing the reality of transcendental freedom.[2] I shall also argue that given these principles, this strategy is reasonably successful on both counts, although it can hardly be expected to convince someone who rejects either the account of morality as based on a categorical imperative or transcendental idealism.

The chapter is divided into five parts. The first attempts to determine the nature of the "fact." It concludes that it is best construed as our common consciousness of the moral law as supremely authoritative. The second maintains that since the existence of this fact is not at issue, the key question is whether it may be regarded as the fact of *reason*. It then argues that this result follows if one assumes the correctness of Kant's account of morality and that this suffices to establish the rational credentials, although not the obligatory force, of the moral law. Appealing to the Reciprocity Thesis, it further suggests that the latter depends on the success of the deduction of freedom. The third part analyzes this deduction, arguing that it turns on the claim that the mere presence of an interest in morality suffices to establish the reality ("from a practical point of view") of transcendental freedom. The fourth considers the problem of the relationship between the fact of reason,

230

the deduction, and Kant's architectonic claims regarding the unity of theoretical and practical reason. Finally, the fifth part provides an assessment of
the deduction of freedom and of its place within Kant's overall theory of
freedom.

I. The nature of the fact

Before we are in a position to evaluate Kant's appeal to the fact of reason,
we must determine the nature of this fact or, as Kant terms it in his more
careful moments, "fact as it were" (*gleichsam als ein Faktum*). Moreover,
this is far from a trivial task, since Kant refers to it eight times in the *Critique
of Practical Reason* and it is by no means obvious that the various characterizations are equivalent. For convenience sake, I shall cite the relevant
passages:

[1] Now practical reason itself, without any collusion with the speculative, provides
reality to a supersensible object of the category of causality, i.e., to freedom. This
is a practical concept and as such is subject only to practical use; but what in the
speculative critique could only be thought is now confirmed by fact [*durch ein Faktum bestätigt*]. (KprV 5: 6; 6)
[2] The consciousness of this fundamental law may be called a fact of reason, since
one cannot ferret it out from antecedent data of reason, such as the consciousness of
freedom . . . and since it forces itself upon us as a synthetic *a priori* proposition based
on no pure or empirical intuition. . . . Still, in order to avoid misunderstanding in
regarding this law as given, one must note that it is not an empirical fact but the sole
fact of pure reason, which thereby proclaims itself as originating law (*sic volo, sic
jubeo*). (KprV 5: 31; 31)
[3] This Analytic proves that pure reason is practical, i.e., that of itself and independently of everything empirical it can determine the will. This it does through
a fact wherein pure reason shows itself actually [*in der That*] to be practical. This
fact is autonomy in the principle of morality by which reason determines the will to
action. . . . It shows at the same time this fact to be inextricably bound up with the
consciousness of freedom, and actually to be identical with it [*ja mit ihm einerlei
sei*]. (KprV 5: 42; 43)
[4] The moral law, although it gives us no such prospect [of speculative knowledge
of noumena through theoretical reason], does provide a fact absolutely inexplicable
from any data of the world of sense or from the whole compass of the theoretical use
of reason, and this fact points to a pure intelligible world . . . indeed, it defines it
positively and enables us to know something of it, namely, a law. (KprV 5: 43; 43)
[5] Moreover, the moral law is given, as an apodictically certain fact as it were of
pure reason [*gleichsam als ein Factum der reinen Vernunft*], of which we are *a priori*
conscious, even if it be granted that no example could be found in which it has been
followed exactly. (KprV 5: 47; 48)
[6] The objective reality of a pure will or of a pure practical reason (they being
the same) is given in the moral law *a priori* as it were by a fact [*gleichsam durch ein
Factum*], for one can so name a determination of the will which is ineluctable [*un-
vermeidlich*], even if it does not rest on empirical principles. (KprV 5: 55; 57)
[7] But that pure reason is of itself alone practical, without any admixture of any
kind of empirical grounds of determination – one had to show this from the com-

monest practical use of reason by producing evidence that the highest practical principle is a principle recognized by every natural human reason as the supreme law of its will, as a law completely *a priori* and independent of any sensuous data. It was necessary first to establish and justify it, by proof of the purity of its origin, in the judgment of common reason, before science could take it in hand to make use of it, so to speak, as a fact [*gleichsam als ein Factum*] which precedes all disputation about its possibility and all consequences which may be drawn from it. (KprV 5: 91; 94)

[8] Then it was only a question of whether this "can be" [thought of as free] could be changed into an "is"; it was a question of whether in an actual case and, as it were, by a fact [*gleichsam durch ein Factum*], one could prove that certain actions presupposed such an intellectual, sensuously unconditioned, causality, regardless of whether they are actual or only commanded, i.e., objectively and practically necessary. (KprV 5: 104; 108)

According to Beck, whose analysis is the mandatory starting point for any serious discussion of the fact of reason, these passages contain six distinct characterizations of the fact or fact as it were. These are (1) "consciousness of the moral law"; (2) "consciousness of freedom of the will"; (3) "the law"; (4) "autonomy in the principle of morality"; (5) "an inevitable determination of the will by the mere conception of the law"; and (6) "the actual case of an action presupposing unconditional causality."[3] Moreover, to complicate the picture further, Kant elsewhere identifies it with freedom, the practical law of freedom, and the categorical imperative.[4]

As Beck points out, these characterizations fall into roughly two classes. One (the objective class) identifies the fact with either the moral law or freedom (or their equivalents); the other (the subjective class) identifies it with the *consciousness* of the law (or its equivalents).[5] Leaving aside for the present the complexities introduced by the reference to freedom (these will be dealt with in the third section of this chapter), the problem raised by this classification is obvious. If the fact is construed subjectively as a mode of consciousness, its existence is readily granted but no inference to the validity of the law is warranted thereby. Conversely, if it is construed objectively and equated with the law itself, then the existence of this fact becomes the very point at issue and can hardly be appealed to in order to ground the reality of moral obligation.

In an effort to avoid this dilemma, Beck introduces a further distinction between a "fact for" and a "fact of" pure reason.[6] By the former is to be understood a pregiven, transcendentally real value that is somehow apprehended by pure reason, that is, by a direct nonsensuous insight or "intellectual intuition." Although Kant sometimes appears to construe the fact in this way and is frequently thought to have done so, such a reading stands in blatant contradiction with Kant's denial of a capacity for intellectual intuition.[7] Moreover, as Beck points out, if Kant is so interpreted, then his doctrine is subject to all the well-known difficulties of intuitionism.[8]

Beck also claims, however, that this result is avoided if we take Kant to be referring to the fact *of* pure reason, which he equates with the fact *that* pure reason is practical.[9] As the text indicates, the claim that pure reason is practical means that "of itself and independently of everything empirical it can determine the will" (KprV 5: 42; 43). Once again, this requires that pure reason provide both a rule or principle of action and a motive to act or refrain from acting in ways specified by this principle. Expressed in the terms of the *Lectures on Ethics,* it means that pure reason furnishes a *principium iudicationis bonitatis* and a *principium executionis bonitatis.*[10]

Beck's distinction between a fact for and the fact of pure reason is germane, and he is certainly correct to suggest that the fact of reason be construed in the latter sense. Nevertheless, we cannot simply identify it with the fact that pure reason is practical.[11] First, the major goal of the *Critique of Practical Reason* is precisely to show that pure reason is practical. Consequently, Kant could hardly appeal to it as a fact without begging the main question at issue. Second, the texts previously cited state that the fact of reason proves or shows that pure reason is practical, not that the latter is itself the fact. If the fact can do this, it must entail that pure reason is practical. But if Kant is to avoid begging the question at the most decisive point in the argument of the second *Critique,* there must be a genuine inference from the former to the latter.

Although the texts are far from unambiguous on this score, the bulk of the evidence suggests that the fact is best construed as the consciousness of standing under the moral law and the recognition of this law "by every natural human reason as the supreme law of its will" (7).[12] This cannot mean, however, that everyone is supposed to have a distinct and explicit awareness of the moral law as Kant defines it, that is, as a formal principle. It is rather that the consciousness attributed to "every natural human reason" is of particular moral constraints as they arise in the process of practical deliberation, with the law serving as the guiding rule (decision procedure) actually governing such deliberation.[13] Moreover, the latter is the law in its "typified" form, the rule of judgment: "Ask yourself whether, if the action which you propose should take place by a law of nature of which you yourself were a part, you could regard it as possible through your will." Kant claims explicitly that "everyone does, in fact [*in der That*] decide by this rule whether actions are morally good or bad" (KprV 5: 69; 72). And in anticipation of the doctrine of the "Typic," he states in the "deduction" itself that "the least attention to ourself shows that this idea really stands as a model [*gleichsam als Vorzeichnung zum Muster liegt*] for the determination of our will" (KprV 5: 43; 45).[14] By referring to this consciousness as a fact, Kant is emphasizing both its presumed universality (at least with regard to those capable of moral deliberation) and its status as a brute given, which cannot be derived from any higher principles or from a reflection on the nature of rational agency ("one cannot ferret it out from antecedent data of reason").

II. The fact as the fact of reason

If the fact in question is as just described, then the task is to show that this is the fact *of reason.* Although one certainly might quarrel with Kant's claim to have uncovered the universal form of moral deliberation, I shall assume that the process of such deliberation is universal and that it involves a consciousness of moral constraint. I shall further assume that his account of such deliberation, as involving something like an appeal to the moral law in its typified form, is sufficiently close to our intuitions as to be acceptable, at least for the sake of argument, even to the moral skeptic. In short, the skeptic's quarrel is not with the fact Kant describes but rather with the status he assigns to it. Consequently, it is this status that must be shown rather than simply assumed. Presumably, this would be accomplished if it could be shown both that this law as the operative rule of judgment is a product of pure (empirically unconditioned) practical reason and that the consciousness of its dictates is of itself sufficient to motivate or create an interest. If both of these could be shown, it would of course also be shown that pure reason is practical.

The proof strategy underlying Kant's appeal to the fact of reason is perhaps best indicated in a *Reflexion* in which the expression "fact of reason" does not appear but the idea is clearly present. In the first paragraph of this *Reflexion,* Kant characterizes the nature of the will (*Wille*), of an objective determining ground thereof, and the difference between moral obligation and pragmatic necessitation. In the second, which alone concerns us, he writes:

The distinction between empirically-conditioned and pure, yet still practical, reason is foundational for the critique of practical reason, which asks if there is such a thing as the latter. Its possibility cannot be comprehended *a priori,* because it concerns the relation of a real ground to its consequent. Something must therefore be given, which can stem only from it; and its possibility can be inferred from this reality. Moral laws are of this nature, and these must be proven in the manner in which we prove that the representations of space and time are *a priori,* with the difference being that the latter are intuitions and the former mere concepts of reason. Here the difference is only that, while, in the case of theoretical cognition, concepts have no significance and principles no use except with respect to objects of experience, in the practical realm they range much further: namely, to all rational beings in general and independently of all empirical determining grounds. Even if no object of experience corresponds to them, the mere character [*Denkungsart*] and disposition based on principles [*Gesinnung nach Principien*] is enough. (R 7201: 19; 275-6)[15]

According to this text, specific moral laws (rather than the moral law itself) are the given elements, the facts, as it were, from which the practicality of pure reason is to be inferred as the necessary condition of their possibility. Of particular interest, however, is the comparison of such laws with the representations of space and time. This is significant not simply because of Kant's insistence on the givenness of space and time[16] but also because of the suggestion that these laws are to be proven (their objective validity established) in the same manner as one proves the apriority of the representations of the latter. Since the apriority (universality and necessity) of the representations of space and time was accounted for in the Transcendental Aesthetic of the *Critique of Pure Reason* by showing that space and time are forms of human sensibility, the idea here is presumably that the objective validity of particular moral laws is to be established by showing that the principle in which they are grounded, the moral law, is a product of pure practical reason. If this were the case, then these laws would be applicable "to all rational beings in general . . . independently of all determining grounds." Finally, continuing the parallelism with the Transcendental Aesthetic, just as we cannot explain how or why space and time (rather than other possible forms) are the forms of human sensibility but can show that they must be regarded as such given the nature of our sensible intuition, so we cannot explain (comprehend a priori) how pure reason is practical but can show that it must be given our common consciousness of moral constraints.

Apart from the question of the cogency of the claim itself, the obvious problem with attributing such a proof strategy to the Kant of the second *Critique* is that it seems to come perilously close to construing the appeal to the fact of reason as a deduction after all, more specifically, a deduction from the nature of our moral experience or the "moral consciousness." In fact, the line of argument sketched in the preceding might seem to be precisely the sort that, according to Beck, one could reasonably expect from Kant at this point but that he explicitly repudiated with his denial of both the possibility and the necessity of providing a deduction of the moral law.[17]

The response to this objection is that the argument underlying the appeal to the fact of reason may indeed be a deduction of sorts but that it is not from moral experience (at least not in the sense assumed in the criticism). Moreover, it differs significantly enough from the deductions of both the first *Critique* and the *Groundwork* to justify Kant in his disclaimer of having provided a deduction.[18]

To begin with, a Kantian deduction from moral experience, modeled on that of the first *Critique*, would presumably move from this experience to the moral law as its necessary condition or ultimate presupposition. The law, according to such a deduction, would be justified as the only presupposition capable of accounting for the possibility of such experience. In the argument here attributed to Kant, however, the moral law is not so much a presupposition of experience as an ingredient given in it (in its typified form as the rule of judgment operative in our moral deliberation), with the inference being to the nature of this law as a product of pure practical reason. It is from this result, then, that its validity, and with it that of the particular moral judgments or "laws" based upon it, is established, much as the empirical reality (as well as transcendental ideality) of space and time is inferred from their status as forms of human sensibility. In this respect, then, the argument is, as *Reflexion* 7201 suggests, closer to that of the "Metaphysical Expositions" of space and time than it is to the deduction of the categories.

Although Kant does not refer to the parallel with the accounts of space and time in the second *Critique,* he does emphasize the difference between the justification of the moral law and the deduction of the categories. Thus, he notes that the procedure used in that deduction is not available in the case of the moral law, since the former was concerned with the conditions of the possibility of the knowledge of objects "given to reason from some other source" (sensibility), whereas the latter "concerns knowledge in so far as it can itself become the ground of the existence of objects" (KprV 5: 46; 47). Kant is typically cryptic here, but his main point seems to be that a deduction of the moral law from the conditions of the possibility of moral experience, comparable to the deduction of the categories, would have to show how this law can be the ground of the existence of objects (determinations of the will). And this, for Kant at least, is beyond our ken, since it amounts to explaining how pure reason could be practical. As he puts it, "Human insight is at an end as soon as we arrive at fundamental powers or faculties" (KprV 5: 46–7; 48).

In the last analysis, however, the real key to Kant's disclaimer of having provided a deduction of the moral law in the second *Critique* lies in the radical difference between the new proof strategy and the deduction in the *Groundwork*. This difference becomes apparent once one realizes that given the new proof strategy the desired goal has been already attained, implicitly at least, in and through the analysis of the nature of morality and its principle contained in the first two parts of the *Groundwork* and the first chapter of the Analytic of Pure Practical Reason in the second *Critique*. Thus, whereas in the *Groundwork* Kant takes seriously the possibility that morality might be nothing but a phantom of the brain, even after completing his analysis of its principle (the autonomy of the will), in the second *Critique* he appears (rightly or wrongly) to be burdened by no such concerns.

The justification for this dismissal of what was previously seen as a deep problem, that is, for the "great reversal," is simply that one could hardly accept the main points of Kant's analysis of morality and its supreme principle and deny that the fact in question (our consciousness of standing under the moral law) is the fact of reason in the sense indicated in the preceding. Similarly, one could hardly accept this result and deny the legitimacy of particular moral constraints (moral laws) insofar as they are seen to stem from the moral law. Moreover, this is precisely why the appeal to the fact of reason should be regarded as the procedure dictated by the overall logic of Kant's position rather than as a regression or lapse into some form of dogmatism of practical reason.

The point can be made clear by even a cursory consideration of what Kant's analysis of morality has supposedly shown. Certainly, its most basic result is that moral requirements are categorical in nature and, accordingly, that the principle operative in moral deliberation must be a categorical imperative. But this imperative addresses us in our capacity as rational agents and with a claim to universality and necessity that makes no concessions to our sensuous nature and no reference to empirical conditions. In its commands we find reason dictating on its own behalf and not in the interests of inclination. On the face of it, then, such a law could not be regarded as a

236

product of empirically conditioned practical reason; for in that case it would be reduced to a counsel of prudence.

The same conclusion is also reached by focusing on the moral law as the principle of autonomy. Here the key point is that for any heteronomously based moral theory the purely rational credentials of the moral law must be very much in doubt. In fact, any such theory must deny that the law has such credentials, since it presupposes some antecedent interest, some extrinsic reason to be moral. If, however, the law of which we are conscious is indeed one that the will legislates to itself, independently of any empirical interest, then that law must be a product of pure reason. At least that is the clear implication of Kant's conception of autonomy as analyzed in Chapter 5.

Furthermore, the analysis of morality as based on autonomy likewise suffices to resolve the motivational issue, the question of the *principium executionis*. If the moral law is self-legislated in the sense in which Kant maintains, then anyone who is conscious of being subject to it will also have a reason or incentive (*Triebfeder*) to obey it and therefore an interest in it. This is because in recognizing its validity one is taking it as the principle governing one's will (practical reason); and as such, one necessarily has an interest in it, indeed, an immediate and pure interest, since it is not dependent on any interests stemming from one's needs as a sensuous being. As Kant puts it in the *Groundwork*, "the law is not valid for us *because it interests us*" (that, he remarks, would be heteronomy); it is rather that "the law interests us because it is valid for us men in virtue of having sprung from our will as intelligence and so from our proper self" (Gr 4: 463–4; 128–9).

It is clear from this and other passages that, already in the *Groundwork,* Kant regarded it as a fact that we take an interest in the moral law or, more generally, moral requirements. At the same time, however, he also seems to have regarded it as something mysterious, which had to be accounted for by means of a deduction. Such a deduction could accomplish this goal if it could demonstrate that the will is autonomous. Unfortunately, as we have seen, this could not be shown, at least not on the basis of the available nonmoral premises.

The analysis of respect in the *Critique of Practical Reason* reflects a very different approach. Respect, as we saw in Chapter 6, is not simply the morally appropriate motive; it is also the feeling awakened in us by our consciousness of the moral law, the tribute we invariably, yet involuntarily, pay to it in virtue of our recognition of its supremely authoritative character as a rational norm. It was noted there that this analysis of respect presupposes the doctrine of the fact of reason, since it assumes the validity of the moral law and investigates the effects of the consciousness of this law on sensuously affected rational agents such as ourselves. It should now be clear, however, that this analysis also plays a crucial role in the presentation of the fact that is to be construed as the fact of reason.[19] It does this by showing that we do in fact take an interest in morality, an interest that must be regarded as pure and therefore shows pure reason to be practical. Thus, in the second *Critique,* the appeal to the fact that we take an interest in morality is part of the solution rather than, as in the *Groundwork,* part of the problem.

The conclusion to be drawn from all of this is that in a sense the analysis of morality is its deduction, which in turn helps us to understand why Kant denies that a deduction is necessary.[20] Nevertheless, as the account of respect makes clear, the justification of morality does not reduce entirely to its correct analysis. Even for the Kant of the second *Critique,* it remains one thing to show that morality rests on the principle of autonomy and quite another to show that the will is autonomous. Thus, an additional synthetic premise is still required. The significant difference is that this premise is now supposedly provided by something directly accessible, namely, our common consciousness of the moral law as supremely authoritative rather than by the problematic idea of our membership in the intelligible world. Given this consciousness together with its analysis, Kant now claims, in sharp contrast to the *Groundwork,* that morality is "firmly established of itself" and that it needs "no justifying grounds" (KprV 5: 47; 48–9).

The preceding account of Kant's strategy for the authentication of the moral law in the second *Critique* has tried to show that there is an argument at work rather than sheer assertion or appeal to intuition (intellectual or otherwise); that this argument marks a considerable improvement over that of *Groundwork* III; and that Kant has good, although hardly compelling, reasons for not characterizing it as a deduction. Clearly, however, since the argument attributed to Kant is tied so closely to his analysis of morality, it will have little appeal to those philosophers who have a significant disagreement with this analysis in the first place. For example, if with Philippa Foot one rejects the premise that morality must be based on a categorical imperative, then the appeal to the fact of reason is simply a "nonstarter."

Since the present work is not intended as a study of Kant's moral theory per se, it is impossible to explore here the possible Kantian response to external criticisms that challenge the very foundations of his analysis of morality. Nevertheless, there is an inner difficulty with Kant's position as here presented that cannot be ignored. The problem is simply that for all that has been learned so far, it seems quite possible both to accept the broad outlines of Kant's analysis of morality and to evade much of the force of his conclusion regarding the unconditioned nature of moral requirements. Thus, one might very well admit that these requirements stem from reason and even that their rational origin entails that we have a reason to obey them (what is usually referred to as Kant's "internalism") and yet deny that these requirements need be recognized as overriding.[21]

Why, after all, should the dictates of impartial and pure practical reason have the last word, even assuming that the moral law, as described by Kant, is that word? Otherwise expressed, might not all genuine duties be at bottom merely prima facie duties, that is, rationally grounded claims, which as such have legitimacy and provide a reason to act but which nonetheless may be set aside, at least occasionally, in favor of other "deeper" interests and values? As we have already seen, this view is rather like the story each of us supposedly tells ourself in virtue of our propensity to evil; but it is also quite close to the view advocated by critics of Kantian moral theory such as Bernard Williams. In any event, it is not at all clear that the appeal to the fact of reason suffices to remove this difficulty; and if not, then it has certainly not succeeded in grounding morality as Kant conceives it.[22]

In addition, there remains the problem of causal determinism. Freedom, after all, is supposed to be the *ratio essendi* of the moral law; so unless the will is free (in the transcendental sense), this law is not a law for it, that is, not a practical principle or determining ground. One might claim at this point that given the fact of reason the reality of freedom is established by appealing to the Reciprocity Thesis, and there is textual evidence to suggest that this was Kant's view. Thus, he maintains both that moral laws are necessary if the will is presupposed as free and "freedom is necessary because those laws are necessary, being practical postulates" (KprV 5: 46; 47). Such a move, however, would appear to beg the question and to raise once again the specter of circularity. Moreover, it ignores the possibility already noted that, of itself, the fact of reason might show something less than is claimed for it, in which case the deduction of freedom cannot proceed simply by appealing to the Reciprocity Thesis.

Although distinct, it is easy to see that these two problems are closely related and must be resolved by the same means, namely, by a deduction of freedom from the fact of reason that is not itself based on the Reciprocity Thesis. Given such a deduction, the second problem would be resolved directly, and it would be possible to use the Reciprocity Thesis in a non-question-begging manner to resolve the first. The latter is the case because, as we saw in Chapter 11, conformity to the moral law is a necessary (as well as sufficient) condition of the justification of the maxims of a transcendentally free agent; and this entails that such an agent could never be justified in allowing other (nonmoral) considerations or interests to override moral requirements. On both counts, then, it appears that the possibility of a deduction of transcendental freedom from the fact of reason is central to the grounding of morality as Kant conceives it.

III. The deduction of freedom: the basic argument

The deduction of freedom from the moral law, as certified through the fact of reason, turns essentially on the claim that "the moral law ... shows [freedom] to be not only possible but actual in beings which acknowledge the law as binding upon them" (KprV 5: 47; 49). Given the preceding analysis of the fact of reason, this claim must rest on the premise that the very consciousness of the moral law as binding produces an interest. Since for Kant "an interest is that in virtue of which reason becomes practical" (Gr

4: 461n; 128), and since the moral interest is pure, Kant takes the presence of such an interest as sufficient to show that pure reason is practical, which in turn is equivalent to showing the actuality of freedom.

But if this or something like it reflects Kant's reasoning at this point, then there is at least the appearance of a significant gap in the argument. The problem is that it does not seem to follow from the fact (assuming it is a fact) that we take an interest in the moral law that we also have the capacity to fulfil its requirements. Perhaps this interest is a weak one, so that it will always or for the most part be "overpowered" by other interests stemming from the needs (real or perceived) of our sensuous nature. In that case it would not follow that we possess the capacity to do what the law requires of us and therefore certainly not transcendental freedom, which, it will be recalled, involves an "independence from everything empirical and hence from nature generally" (KprV 5: 97; 100).

Actually, this line of objection points to two related, yet distinguishable problems that concern the positive and negative aspects of freedom respectively. As we have seen, freedom, positively understood, is equivalent to autonomy, that is, the capacity of the will to determine itself to act on the basis of self-imposed principles of rational willing (moral requirements), which in turn entails the capacity to act from respect for the law. Part of the problem described in the preceding is that this capacity or "property of the will" does not appear to be established by the mere presence of an interest in morality. Freedom, negatively understood, is just this previously noted independence from "everything empirical," which, given Kant's psychological determinism at the phenomenal level, amounts essentially to independence from "pathological necessitation." Even granting the analysis of the moral law as a product of pure practical reason, this independence cannot be established unless it can also be shown that it is possible for us to act on the basis of the law in spite of competing interests stemming from our sensuous nature. And this, clearly, cannot be shown merely by appealing to the fact that the former interest is present.

The first part of the problem, concerning freedom positively understood, can be dealt with fairly easily. To begin with, the "capacity" in question is merely for the appropriate motivation (respect for the law), not for the attainment of any particular end. In Kant's own terms, "The only concern here is with the determination of the will and with the determining ground of its maxims as a free will not with its results" (KprV 5: 45; 47). Moreover, it is not even a question of whether, in fact, one acts from respect for the law (recall Kant's agnosticism on this score) but merely whether one ever could be so motivated. That this is not a trivial issue is shown by the fact that psychological egoism and, indeed, for Kant all forms of heteronomy must deny the very possibility of such motivation.

Given Kant's account of interest, however, one cannot both affirm the existence of an interest in morality and deny the possibility of acting from respect for the law. As we saw in Chapter 5, interests, like maxims, are products of practical reason. Thus, one has an interest in something (as opposed to a mere inclination) only insofar as one spontaneously takes an interest, that is, makes it into a ground governing one's choice of maxims. But if one acknowledges the moral law as a ground in this sense, then one must also acknowledge an incentive or motive (an internal reason) to follow its dictates. Finally, one cannot acknowledge having a motive and deny the *possibility* of being motivated by it; although one can, of course, have a motive and refrain from acting on it.

Nevertheless, this is clearly not yet enough to establish our freedom, since as noted above, it does not of itself appear to rule out the possibility that our interest in morality and therefore our capacity for moral motivation might be eclipsed, totally or in great part, by interests and motives stemming from our needs as sensuous beings. In order to exclude this possibility, it is necessary to establish our negative freedom, that is, our independence from the "mechanism of nature" (broadly construed so as to include psychological causes). In short, unless it can be shown that freedom, so construed, likewise follows from (or is shown by) the fact of reason, there will be no real deduction of freedom and no grounding for judgments of imputation. Moreover, Kant himself is perfectly well aware of this; in fact, he insists that "without transcendental freedom, which is its proper meaning, and which alone is *a priori* practical, no moral law and no accountability to it are possible" (KprV 5: 97; 100).

Kant's solution to this problem rests largely on the claim that the requisite independence or negative freedom is shown in and through our positive freedom or autonomy. Given his initial appeal to the fact of reason, it is hard to see what other tactic is open to him at this point. Nevertheless, the claim does amount to something more than a bald assertion; for the argument seems to be that the capacity for moral motivation (autonomy) provides evidence of our membership in an intelligible world (*intelligibelen Welt*) from which our independence of the mechanism of nature may be inferred. Although this complete chain of reasoning is not unambiguously expressed in a single place in the text, the connection between freedom (positively construed as autonomy) and membership in an intelligible world is emphasized. Thus, at the very beginning of the deduction, after noting that the Analytic proves that pure reason is practical through a fact, which is characterized as "autonomy in the principle of morality" and is claimed to be identical with the consciousness of freedom of the will, Kant states:

By this freedom, the will of a rational being, which, as belonging to the sensible world, recognizes itself to be, like all other efficient causes, necessarily subject to the laws of causality, yet, at the same time, in practical matters [*im Praktischen*], in its other aspect as a being in itself, is conscious of its existence as determinable in an intelligible order of things. (KprV 5: 42; 43)[23]

The appeal to the notion of an intelligible world, or what amounts to the same thing, "an intelligible order of things," is reminiscent of the move made in *Groundwork* III. In reality, however, the line of reasoning is diametrically opposed. There, it will be recalled, it was our mere possession of a capacity to reason that was supposed to assure our membership in such a world (*Verstandeswelt*), which in turn assured our freedom in the sense of independence, from which our autonomy was then inferred. This accords with the procedure of *Groundwork* III, which begins with the negative definition of freedom and claims that the positive (autonomy) "springs" from it. Here, by contrast, it is our autonomy, as expressed in our interest in morality, that supposedly assures us of our supersensible or intelligible existence, from which our negative freedom is then inferred. If successful, this move would overcome one of the main difficulties of the deduction of *Groundwork* III, which was that such membership gets us, at best, to practical freedom, not to the autonomy necessary to establish the moral law.

The key to the connection between positive freedom and the intelligible world lies in the nature of the moral interest. As is clear already in the *Groundwork,* this is a pure interest, that is, one taken by reason independently of any antecedent empirically based interests (all of which reflect needs stemming from our nature as sensuous beings). It is also an interest in a merely intelligible or ideal order of things, specifically, a kingdom of ends or, equivalently, of rational beings under moral laws. In the second *Critique,* Kant characterizes this ideal order as a supersensible (*übersinnlichen*) nature and claims that we give objective, albeit merely practical, reality to such an order insofar as we take an interest in it (KprV 5: 44; 45).[24] But given Kant's account of rational agency, a will capable of determining itself by such a law must be independent of the mechanism of nature. Furthermore, with the consciousness of the law as binding comes the consciousness of this independence, an independence that is distinguished from the merely relative independence manifest in our ability to resist a given inclination for the sake of another.

Kant illustrates the latter point in a well-known passage in which he introduces a hypothetical subject who claims that his lust is irresistible when object and opportunity are at hand. Kant suggests that we ask such a person two questions. The first is whether he thinks that he would be able to control his lust if a gallows were erected at the appropriate location on which he would be hung immediately after performing the act. To this question, Kant suggests, the answer is obvious. The second question, addressed to the same subject, is whether he would be able to overcome his love of life (which presumably is stronger than his lust) if he were threatened with the same sudden death unless he made a false deposition against an honorable man. With respect to this question Kant remarks:

Whether he would or not he perhaps will not venture to say; but that it would be possible for him he would certainly admit without hesitation. He judges, therefore, that he can do something because he knows that he ought, and he recognized therein his freedom, which, without the moral law, would have remained unknown to him. (KprV 5: 30; 31)

Although this passage occurs prior to the "official" deduction of freedom in the text, it is crucial to the understanding of this deduction, since it clearly

242

illustrates the inseparability of the consciousness of the moral law and the consciousness of freedom (including negative freedom) as two aspects of the fact of reason. At the same time, it also shows why, in spite of their inseparability, Kant insists that it is the moral law that is established directly through the fact of reason and the reality of freedom that is "deduced" from it. The primacy of the moral law is conceptual, since it is precisely our consciousness of being subject to it (a consciousness we have even in violating its dictates) that makes us aware of our autonomy and, with it, our independence from the mechanism of nature.

This, in brief, is the deduction of freedom in the second *Critique*. In sharp contrast to that of the *Groundwork*, it moves from positive freedom, certified through the fact of reason, to negative freedom. It remains, of course, to evaluate this deduction and to determine its relationship to Kant's claims regarding freedom elsewhere, particularly in the first *Critique*. Before turning to these issues, however, it is necessary to consider a feature of the deduction that has so far been ignored but is emphasized by Kant, namely, its connection with the Third Antinomy of the first *Critique*.

IV. The deduction of freedom, the Third Antinomy, and the unity of theoretical and practical reason

In addition to affirming the connection between the moral law and freedom, Kant also includes in his deduction the claim that practical reason provides the solution to the problem posed by theoretical reason in the Third Antinomy, which, it will be recalled, is reason's need to think an unconditioned cause or ground for the series of conditioned causes. It is this claim to which Kant refers in the well-known and previously cited statement from the Preface to the second *Critique* that "the concept of freedom, in so far as its reality is proved by an apodictic law of practical reason, is the keystone of the whole architecture of the system of pure reason and even of speculative reason" (KprV 5: 4; 4). Since this claim is sometimes thought to be essential to both the authentication of the moral law through the fact of reason and the deduction of freedom, it requires examination at this point.

To begin with, we saw in Chapter 1 that the possibility of thinking this unconditioned is essential to reason in its speculative function and therefore arises quite independently of any moral concerns, indeed, independently of any concerns regarding rational agency. Kant underscores the speculative importance of this issue in the second *Critique* by characterizing the idea of absolute spontaneity (the unconditioned with respect to causality) as "not just a desideratum but, as far as its possibility was concerned, an analytical principle of pure speculation" (KprV 5: 48; 50). At the same time, however, he also reminds us that the first *Critique* was unable to establish the reality of an unconditioned causality but could merely defend it against the charge of inconceivability (because of its apparent conflict with the mechanism of nature) by creating a "vacant place" for it in an intelligible world.

243

The new claim is that pure practical reason fills this vacancy through the moral law, thereby resolving speculative reason's problem. In so doing, it also supposedly provides a "credential" for the law, which "is a sufficient substitute for any *a priori* justification" (KprV 5: 47–8; 49). The moral law earns this credential because as a "definite law of causality in an intelligible world (causality through freedom)," it both gives a positive definition to the intelligible causality, which is thought only negatively in the transcendental idea of freedom, and certifies its objective (although practical) reality. As a result, Kant notes, "Speculative reason does not herewith grow in insight but only in respect to the certitude of its problematic concept of freedom, to which objective, though only practical, reality is now indubitably given" (KprV 5: 49; 50).

This claim consists of two parts. The first is that the moral law gives a positive sense to the indeterminate notion of an intelligible causality and the second is that the fact of reason establishes the objective, yet practical reality of such causality. Since the second part amounts to the thesis of the deduction of freedom, nothing further need be said about it at this point, although we shall return to the distinctively Kantian notion of an objective, yet practical reality in the sequel. A word is in order regarding the first part of the claim, however, since it does introduce a fresh consideration.

The new element here is Kant's characterization of the moral law as a "law of causality in an intelligible world," or as he also terms it, a "law of causality through freedom" (KprV 5: 47; 49). This is puzzling on the face of it, since the moral law hardly corresponds to what one normally thinks of as a causal law, that is, one asserting a necessary connection between causes and effects. Nevertheless, it is possible to understand Kant's point if we keep in mind that the moral law supposedly describes the decision procedure or *modus operandi* of a hypothetical perfectly rational agent. Considered as such, it is both a causal law in a broad sense, since it depicts a *modus operandi,* and a "law of freedom" or of an intelligible world, since the activity falling under this law is independent of the mechanism of nature.[25] Moreover, this characterization of the moral law as a causal law is crucial for Kant because he also holds that freedom as a mode of causality can be thought determinately only if a law (*modus operandi*) of such causality can be given.[26] Since the moral law is just such a law, it provides positive content to the idea of an intelligible or noumenal causality, which reason requires in its theoretical function.[27]

As the text clearly indicates, Kant took this dual claim to support (if not establish) the unity of theoretical and practical reason. "The "credential" gained by the moral law is due to its ability to foster this end by providing something that theoretical reason requires but cannot attain on its own. Moreover, Kant's concern with this unity is readily understandable from a systematic standpoint, since it would seem to be a precondition of the unity of the first two *Critiques* and therefore of the critical philosophy as a whole.

The same concern is also evident from the texts. Thus, already in the *Groundwork,* in explaining why that work is to be distinguished from a

244

"Critique of Pure Practical Reason," Kant notes that such a critique, if it is to be complete, requires the demonstration of the unity of theoretical and practical reason in a single principle; and this is because "in the end there can only be one and the same reason, which must be differentiated solely in its application" (Gr 4: 391; 59). Similarly, in the *Critique of Practical Reason,* while arguing for the primacy of practical reason, he remarks: "But if pure reason of itself can be and really is practical, as the consciousness of the moral law shows it to be, it is only one and the same reason which judges *a priori* by principles, whether for theoretical or for practical purposes" (KprV 5: 121; 125).[28]

Even granting all this, however, the question of its relevance to the authentication of the moral law through the fact of reason and the deduction of freedom remains open. According to Beck, the claim that the moral law receives its "credential" through the concept of freedom, which, in his terms, itself has an "independent warrant" in virtue of its theoretical significance, is an essential feature of rather than an addendum to the overall deduction.[29] In fact, on his reading, the justification of the moral law itself would seem to stem largely from its capacity to provide the only "tenant" suitable to occupy the "vacant place" left by theoretical reason. As he puts it, "Only this independent warrant makes it possible for Kant to break out of the circle of using freedom to establish the moral law and the moral law to establish freedom."[30]

In spite of Kant's characterization of the credential for the moral law as a "sufficient substitute for any *a priori* justification" and the undeniable importance that he attached to the task of showing the unity of reason, it is difficult to accept the preceding account of his procedure in the deduction. First, there is no circle to avoid because Kant does not use freedom to establish the moral law. As we have seen, in the *Critique of Practical Reason* at least, Kant consistently maintains that the move is from the moral law to freedom. Second and most important, the alleged ability of the moral law to fulfil the need of theoretical reason already presupposes both its authentication as a fact of reason and the validity of the deduction of freedom from it. In other words, Kant is not arguing that the moral law is authenticated and freedom shown to be actual *because* these are somehow necessary to the unity of reason; the claim is rather that the unity of reason is illustrated or confirmed by the fact that the moral law, as self-authenticated, shows freedom to be actual (from a practical point of view).[31] Thus, we must return to this deduction in order to complete our examination of Kant's theory of freedom.

V. The deduction of freedom: a final consideration

Since the deduction, as previously characterized, rests ultimately on a claim regarding the consciousness or recognition of freedom, it appears open to the obvious retort that for all that has been said so far, this consciousness might be illusory. This is particularly true insofar as such freedom supposedly involves the complete independence from the mechanism of nature. Certainly, many philosophers have claimed as much. Moreover, it is still far from clear that Kant has anything to say to them beyond the appeal to transcendental idealism, which shows at most the conceivability of such independence and thus serves as a defense against the dogmatic denial of its possibility. In fact, we have seen repeatedly that in both the *Critique of Pure Reason* and the *Groundwork* Kant took seriously the epistemic possibility that our belief in our agency might be illusory. How, then, can Kant respond to this charge?

In dealing with this problem, it is necessary first of all to determine the nature of the consciousness of freedom, which, as we have seen, Kant at one point claims to be identical to the fact of reason, construed as "autonomy in the principle of morality" (KprV 5: 42; 42).[32] Clearly, this consciousness is not an experience; that is to say, Kant is not claiming that our independence of the mechanism of nature is somehow introspectively accessible. For Kant, any such "experience" not only could but necessarily would be illusory, since it would violate the conditions of the possibility of experience (KprV 5: 29; 29).[33] But neither is it the consciousness of an actual ability to act from duty when such action conflicts with one's strongest inclination, for example, the love of life. Such an ability would amount to virtue or autocracy; and as we have seen at length in the second part of this study, Kant emphasizes that the consciousness of being virtuous is always in danger of resting on self-deception. Moreover, the possession of this ability is explicitly put in doubt in Kant's illustration, since his hypothetical subject readily admits that he does not know how he would in fact behave if he were ever faced with the necessity of having to choose between betraying an innocent person or losing his own life.

This consciousness, then, is of a mere possibility rather than an actual capacity. What Kant's hypothetical subject admits "without hesitation" is simply that "it would be possible for him." This is not, however, merely the possibility, readily acknowledged by compatibilists, of acting in the morally required way "if one had chosen to"; it is rather the possibility of so choosing in spite of the presence and strength of the conflicting inclination.[34] In other words, it is the consciousness of freedom of choice or *Willkür*, not merely of freedom of action. It is this consciousness that, according to Kant, is present in everyone who recognizes the moral law as binding and therefore in "every natural human reason" because it is inseparable from the recognition of this law as binding. Moreover, together with this consciousness comes the recognition that the failure to live up to the moral requirement is itself something to be imputed, a matter of freedom, not nature, of the lack of autocracy, not of autonomy.[35] Thus, virtually the entire picture of moral agency analyzed in the second part of this study, including the accounts of *Gesinnung* and radical evil, may be seen as the presentation of the presuppositions and implications of this consciousness.

Given this analysis of the consciousness of freedom, we are now in a position to formulate the Kantian response to the objection that for all that has been shown so far, this consciousness might be illusory. Not surprisingly, it turns on the connection between this consciousness as already described and the fact of reason. The main point is simply that if it were illusory, then our autonomy or positive freedom and with it the whole conception of ourselves as moral agents would be also. But this has been shown to be actual by the fact of reason. Consequently, if the fact of reason is, indeed, the fact *of reason* then this consciousness cannot be regarded as illusory.

Admittedly, this argument still appears to derive rather strong conclusions from minimal premises; but this problem can be mitigated, to some extent at least, if we keep in mind Kant's own insistence that the claim concerning the reality of freedom holds only from a practical point of view (*in praktischer Absicht*) or in a practical context (*in praktischer Beziehung*).[36] This narrowing of the scope of the claim to the practical point of view leaves intact the purely epistemic possibility that this consciousness might be illusory, and that is precisely why it does not amount to a demonstration of freedom from a theoretical point of view. What is denied is merely the possibility of considering it as illusory from the practical point of view, that is, the point of view from which we regard ourselves as rational agents. This cannot be done because it would involve the denial of what the fact of reason has shown to be the very law of this agency.

Nevertheless, merely wrapping Kant's deduction in the banner of "the practical point of view" hardly suffices to resolve all of the problems, even the internal ones. In fact, if we recall the analogous claim made in connection with the analysis of the first *Critique* conception of agency, a fresh and potentially serious difficulty is suggested: namely, the possibility that this deduction may be redundant, the repetition in different terms, and with inflated claims made for it, of what has already been shown.

It was argued in Chapter 2 that already in the *Critique of Pure Reason* Kant assigns a necessary regulative role to the idea of freedom with respect to the conception of ourselves as rational agents. So construed, this idea is necessary from a practical point of view in the sense that it is a condition of the very possibility of taking a practical point of view. We have also seen that a similar line of thought is operative in the *Groundwork*, where Kant seems to equate being free from a practical point of view with the necessity of acting under the idea of freedom. How, then, one might very well ask at this point, does the present argument go beyond the earlier one, as it clearly must if it is to ground the authoritative status of the moral law?

The answer, in brief, is that it goes beyond it in two crucial respects, both of which are based on the fact of reason. First, it specifies the kind of freedom at issue as transcendental rather than practical freedom or, more precisely, rather than the "mere practical freedom" of the Canon. Since this issue has already been discussed at length, nothing further need be said about it here. Second and for present purposes most important, whereas the first *Critique* makes what is merely a conceptual claim concerning the necessity of the *idea* of freedom for our conception of ourselves as rational agents, in the deduction of the second *Critique* Kant purports to have established the *actuality* of freedom, albeit merely from a practical point of view. Moreover, in that respect it also goes beyond the *Groundwork,* which offers what amounts to a deduction of the idea of freedom.[37]

"Actuality" (*Wirklichkeit*), for Kant, always requires "givenness" in some sense as opposed to mere conceivability. According to the doctrine of the first *Critique,* in a theoretical context, it requires connection with some actual perception (A225/B272). Clearly, freedom is not actual in this sense, since it is not an item of possible experience. Kant's position is rather that freedom is actual, or better, actualized, in the interest that we take in the moral law. In other words, the claim is not simply that freedom must be presupposed as a condition of the conceivability of such an interest and of the possibility of obeying the dictates of the law (although this is certainly part of the story), it is also that our freedom – in the sense of autonomy and independence – is exhibited in our taking such an interest.

Once again, this claim rests on Kant's general account of interest together with the unique, pure character of the moral interest. Given this account, it follows that to take an interest in morality is not simply to find it interesting (or attractive), as if this were somehow how we happen to be constituted; it is rather to take or recognize the moral law as providing reasons for and restrictions on action. Moreover, since these reasons do not reflect (at least not directly) any of our needs as sensuous beings, this reveals to us our capacity to be motivated independently of these needs, which in turn shows us our independence from the mechanism of nature.

Finally, as revealed or manifested in an interest, freedom, like the moral law, is actual only from the practical point of view, since it is only from that point of view that one has interests.[38] Nevertheless, this is sufficient for practical purposes, that is, for any concerns we may have as rational agents, and even for the demonstration of the overriding nature of moral constraints. The latter is the case because, in showing our transcendental freedom to be actual, it also shows (by means of the Reciprocity Thesis) the unconditioned status of the moral law as the ultimate rational norm governing our conduct.

The deduction of freedom here attributed to Kant and defended against a possible line of objection obviously rests on a number of presuppositions. Foremost among these are transcendental idealism and the conception of morality as grounded in the categorical imperative and the autonomy of will. The former is necessary to defend the bare conceivability of freedom, as Kant construes it, and the latter to establish its practical reality. Both of these are, to say the least, controversial, although the latter certainly has many more contemporary adherents than the former. In spite of its controversial nature and the misunderstandings to which it is liable, I have simply assumed the truth, or at least the viability, of transcendental idealism in the present study, since I have attempted an extended analysis and defense of it elsewhere. Kant's conceptions of the categorical imperative and autonomy have certainly been discussed, and the former was even "deduced" from transcendental freedom in the analysis of the Reciprocity Thesis. Nevertheless, as already noted, the focus on the problem of freedom has precluded a detailed examination of Kant's moral theory per se, which gives a certain tentative character to the defense of the fact of reason (particularly since it was seen to presuppose the correctness of Kant's analysis of morality). And since the deduction of freedom is itself based on the authentication of the moral law through the fact of reason, the defense of it remains tentative as well. Thus, in the end, the most that can be said for this deduction, which is still more than most are willing to claim, is that it follows from Kant's premises and that together with the appeal to the fact of reason it constitutes Kant's definitive attempt to ground morality and freedom.

There is, however, a third fundamental presupposition of the deduction, which has been treated in detail in this study even though it has not figured prominently in the explicit argument of the last two chapters. This is the conception of rational agency, featuring the Incorporation Thesis, which clearly underlies the central notion of interest and, as we have seen, a good deal of Kant's moral psychology. What I wish to emphasize in closing is simply that this conception remains in place (as a necessary regulative idea) even if one rejects the claim that a unique and inexplicable interest in the moral law shows freedom to be actual from a practical point of view. Moreover, since this conception clearly involves an incompatibilist conception of freedom, we are left with the very real problem of reconciling the presupposition of freedom, so construed, with the causal determinism governing human actions, considered as natural occurrences.

For all its obscurity, verging at times on incoherence, Kant's theory of freedom is, in my judgment at least, the most profound and sustained attempt to deal with this problem in the history of Western philosophy. And this is what I have tried to show in the present study. Since compatibilism is so deeply embedded in the Anglo–American philosophical psyche, and since I have emphasized throughout Kant's incompatibilism or, better, his unique attempt to establish the compatibility of compatibilism and incompatibilism, this claim is bound to meet with a good deal of resistance. But if the interpretation and defense of Kant's theory of freedom presented here fails to convince critics of the profundity and overall coherence of Kant's position, I hope that it will at least convince would-be defenders of Kant of the folly of trying to gain a hearing for his views by depicting him as anticipating contemporary forms of compatibilism.

Notes

Introduction

1. Lewis White Beck, "Five Concepts of Freedom in Kant," *Philosophical Analysis and Reconstruction,* a Festschrift to Stephan Körner, 1987, pp. 35–51.
2. This problem is dealt with by Bernard Carnois, *The Coherence of Kant's Doctrine of Freedom.* Although he by and large makes a good case for the internal consistency of Kant's various accounts of freedom by treating them developmentally (an approach that will also be adopted here), he does, on crucial occasions, fall back on a "patchwork" reading in order to account for discrepancies in the text. The major limitation of Carnois's otherwise helpful book, however, is that it focuses almost exclusively on the problem of reconciling various Kantian texts with each other, so that he has relatively little to say regarding the cogency of Kant's doctrines themselves.
3. A particularly influential figure in this regard is August Wilhelm Rehberg, who in his review of the *Critique of Practical Reason* insisted that morality requires only a comparative conception of freedom. The review is reprinted in *Materialien zu Kants "Kritik der praktischen Vernunft,"* Rüdiger Bittner and Konrad Cramer, eds., pp. 179–96. For a detailed discussion of it and of Rehberg's influence on subsequent German critics of Kant's moral philosophy in general, and conception of freedom in particular, see E. G. Schulz, *Rehbergs Opposition gegen Kants Ethik.*
4. The gist of the standard line of criticism is expressed in a particularly sharp form by Jonathan Bennett, *Kant's Dialectic,* pp. 189–227, and "Kant's Theory of Freedom" (a commentary on Allen Wood's "Kant's Compatibilism"), in *Self and Nature in Kant's Philosophy,* Allen W. Wood, ed., pp. 102–12.
5. Two recent critics who attack Kant's appeal to the "fact of reason" are Gerold Prauss, *Kant über Freiheit als Autonomie,* esp. pp. 62–70, and Rüdiger Bittner, *Moralisches Gebot oder Autonomie,* esp. pp. 138–45.
6. I say primarily because there are passages where the terms "thing in itself" and "noumenon" do refer to entities that are ontologically distinct from the things that appear, but these are special cases. See Henry E. Allison, *Kant's Transcendental Idealism,* pp. 239–40, and for an extended discussion of the topic, Bernard Rousset, *La Doctrine kantienne de l'objectivité,* pp. 167ff.
7. See Karl Ameriks, "Recent Work on Kant's Theoretical Philosophy," *American Philosophical Quarterly* 19 (1982), pp. 1–11, esp. p. 5. I discuss this issue in Henry E. Allison, "Transcendental Idealism: The 'Two Aspect' View," *New Essays on Kant,* Bernard den Ouden and Marcia Moen, eds., pp. 155–78.
8. See Allison, *Kant's Transcendental Idealism,* especially pp. 10–13, 65, 86–7, 109, and "Transcendental Idealism: The 'Two Aspect' View," pp. 156–60.

Chapter 1

1. The major exception to this is Heinz Heimsoeth. See his "Zum kosmotheologischen Ursprung der kantischen Freiheitsantinomie," *Kant-Studien* 57 (1966), pp. 206–29.
2. I have dealt with many of these topics in more detail in Henry E. Allison, *Kant's Transcendental Idealism,* Chapter 3.
3. It should be noted that Kant argued in precisely that way in the Inaugural Dissertation with respect to the "laws of sensitive cognition." Thus, in his precritical version of the antinomical conflict his concern is to distinguish such "laws," which, if taken as objectively valid, yield "subreptive axioms," from intellectual concepts and principles, which do yield cognitions of things in themselves. See Diss 2: 410–19; 79–92.
4. See Sadik J. Al-Azm, *The Origins of Kant's Arguments in the Antinomies.*
5. See Proleg 4: 243; 90–95.
6. This is to be contrasted with the view that what supposedly (according to the thesis) requires a transcendentally free cause or unconditioned ground for its complete explanation is the series of appearances taken as a whole. This reading is argued for by Clark Zumbach, "A Note on the Thesis Argument of the Third Antinomy," *Ratio* 23(2), (1981), p. 119, on the grounds that, on the alternative interpretation, "the thesis argument is blatantly invalid." Zumbach's conclusion, however, rests on an interpretation of the thesis argument that is in essential agreement with that of Schopenhauer and Kemp Smith and that, we shall see, is mistaken.
7. See Heinz Röttges, "Kants Auflosung der Freiheitsantinomie," *Kant-Studien* 65 (1974), p. 37, and Birger Ortwein, *Kants problematische Freiheitslehre,* p. 24.
8. Kant's formulation here is confusing in that it suggests that the prior state must be the cause of the succeeding state, which is, of course, not the case. On this point see Allison, *Kant's Transcendental Idealism,* pp. 29–30.
9. Arthur Schopenhauer, *The World as Will and Representation,* Vol. 1, E. F. J. Payne, trans., pp. 497–8.
10. Norman Kemp Smith, *Commentary on the "Critique of Pure Reason,"* p. 493.
11. Jonathan Bennett, *Kant's Dialectic,* p. 185.
12. Ibid., p. 186.
13. See A. C. Ewing, *A Short Commentary on Kant's "Critique of Pure Reason,"* p. 218 (passage cited by Bennett, *Kant's Dialectic,* p. 184).
14. Bennett, *Kant's Dialectic,* p. 186.
15. See, e.g., Leibniz's Fifth Letter to Clarke, esp. secs. 1–20, *The Leibniz–Clarke Correspondence,* H. G. Alexander, ed. and trans., pp. 55–60.
16. Ibid., p. 95.
17. C. D. Broad, *Kant, An Introduction,* p. 271, is one of the few commentators who notes the contrast between law of nature and laws of nature. He also interprets each as I do but rejects the argument as resting merely on a verbal trick.
18. This fact and its potential significance for the argument was pointed out to me by Randy Wojtowicz.
19. See William Walsh, *Kant's Criticism of Metaphysics,* pp. 204–5, for a similar analysis.
20. For a development of this line of criticism, which can be traced back to Hegel, see Röttges, "Kants Auflosung," p. 36, and Ortwein, *Kants problematische Freiheitslehre,* pp. 24–6.

21. I discuss the nature of the connection between this principle and transcendental realism in more detail in Allison, *Kant's Transcendental Idealism,* pp. 52–6.
22. Schopenhauer, *The World as Will and Representation,* Vol. 1, p. 498.
23. P. F. Strawson, *The Bounds of Sense,* pp. 208–9.
24. See Röttges, "Kants Auflosung," p. 36, and Ortwein, *Kants problematische Freiheitslehre,* pp. 26–7.
25. Allison, *Kant's Transcendental Idealism,* p. 58.
26. See A471/B499, and for a discussion of the verificationist move in the antithesis position see Allison, *Kant's Transcendental Idealism,* pp. 46–7.
27. See Röttges, "Kants Auflosung," pp. 45–8, and Ortwein, *Kants problematische Freiheitslehre,* pp. 28–33.
28. Strawson, *The Bounds of Sense,* p. 209.
29. Cf. A523/B551.
30. Actually, what is self-contradictory is the concept of the sensible world as a whole existing in itself. For my analysis of this issue see Henry E. Allison, "Kant's Refutation of Realism," *Dialectica* 30 (1976), esp. pp. 239–46, and Allison, *Kant's Transcendental Idealism,* pp. 56–8.
31. See Allison, *Kant's Transcendental Idealism,* pp. 50–61.
32. Leibniz, *The Leibniz–Clarke Correspondence,* pp. 20, 30, 45–6, 97–8.
33. Ibid., p. 60.
34. Ibid., p. 59.
35. This point is emphasized by Al-Azm, *The Origins of Kant's Arguments in the Antinomies,* pp. 104–5.
36. Kant is explicitly criticized on this score by Wilfred Sellars, " . . . This I or He or It (the Thing) which Thinks . . . ," in *Essays in Philosophy and its History,* p. 77. According to Sellars, Kant's alleged antinomy arises from his conflation of the idea of a state of a system that is determined by a preceding state of the same system with the idea of a state that a system is determined to have by "foreign cases." As he cryptically puts it, *"The past is not something with respect to which we are passive."* Accordingly, what has here been called the "activity condition" can be met on compatibilist lines without any appeal to spontaneity or "contracausal freedom," simply by regarding genuine actions as those grounded in the antecedent state of the agent. Kant's reasons for rejecting such a solution will be considered in the next chapter and the plausibility of a compatibilist interpretation of Kant in Chapter 4.
37. Allen W. Wood, "Kant's Compatibilism," in *Self and Nature in Kant's Philosophy,* Allen W. Wood, ed., p. 74.

Chapter 2

1. Hermann Andreas Pistorius, "Rezension der *Kritik der praktischen Vernunft*" (1974), in *Materialien zu Kants "Kritik der praktischen Vernunft,"* Rüdiger Bittner and Konrad Cramer, ed., p. 175.
2. In his discussion of temperament in the *Anthropology* (7: 286–7; 150–3), Kant explicitly contrasts the psychological with the physiological point of view. He also suggests that anthropology assumes the former and that from this point of view the traditional classification of temperaments in terms of the composition of the blood (sanguine, melancholy, choleric, and phlegmatic) is to be taken merely as the expression of an analogy, useful for classification, but not as the assertion of an identity or even a causal dependence. Thus, although he does

acknowledge that temperaments may well have corporeal factors as "covertly contributing causes," he also insists that such factors play no role in the kind of explanation sought in anthropology or psychology.

3. This denial might seem to contradict Kant's affirmative claims about empirical psychology in the *Critique*. Thus, within the context of his introduction to the paralogisms, Kant characterizes it as "a kind of *physiology* of inner sense, capable perhaps of explaining the appearances of inner sense" (A347/B405), and again, in the Architectonic of Pure Reason, after denying that it belongs in metaphysics, he suggests that it will find its home in "a complete anthropology, the pendant to the empirical doctrine of nature" (A849/B877). In reality, however, there is no contradiction because in neither case is it assumed that the "science" is capable of providing anything more than a "natural description."

4. See Anthro 7: 161; 39 and R 1502 15: 802. For a brief but informative discussion of the procedure and scientific status of anthropology vis-à-vis both psychology and physiology see Mary J. Gregor, introduction to her translation of Kant's *Anthropology from a Pragmatic Point of View*, pp. xii–xv.

5. On this topic see Jürgen Henrichs, *Das Problem der Zeit in der praktischen Philosophie Kants*, pp. 38–42, and Bernard Carnois, *The Coherence of Kant's Doctrine of Freedom*, pp. 33–9.

6. See A546/B574, A551/B579, A556/B584.

7. See A541/B569, A546/B579, A553/B581, and R 5611 18: 253.

8. This is emphasized by Henrichs, *Das Problem der Zeit in der praktischen Philosophie Kants*, p. 39.

9. In the Preface to the *Anthropology* (7: 119; 3), Kant notes that in contrast to a physiological investigation of what "nature makes of man," he is there concerned with "what *man* as a free agent makes, or can and should make, of himself."

10. See Henry E. Allison, *Kant's Transcendental Idealism*, Chapter 10.

11. The best accounts in the literature of how these texts relate to the Second Analogy are by Gerd Buchdahl: *Metaphysics and the Philosophy of Science*, pp. 651–65; "The Conception of Lawlikeness in Kant's Philosophy of Science," in *Kant's Theory of Knowledge*, Lewis White Beck, ed., pp. 128–50; and "The Kantian 'Dynamic of Reason' with Special Reference to the Place of Causality in Kant's System," *Kant Studies Today*, Lewis White Beck, ed., pp. 187–208.

12. Admittedly, Kant himself is not very clear on this point, and there are many passages that suggest the contrary. See, in particular, A536/B569. This does not affect the present claim, however, which is concerned with what Kant is entitled to assume about the lawfulness of nature given his own arguments, not with what he in fact assumes.

13. For Kant's views on the scientific status of the chemistry of his day see, MAN 4: 470–1; 6–7.

14. See Terence Irwin, "Morality and Personality: Kant and Green," *Self and Nature in Kant's Philosophy*, Allen W. Wood, ed., esp. pp. 39–40, and Allen W. Wood, "Kant's Compatibilism," in *Self and Nature in Kant's Philosophy*, pp. 82–3.

15. Wood, op. cit., p. 83.

16. In Henry E. Allison, "Kant's Refutation of Materialism," *Monist* 72 (1989), pp. 190–208, I use this analysis to develop a Kantian critique of nonreductive forms of materialism.

17. On the latter point see Robert Pippin, "Kant on the Spontaneity of Mind," *Canadian Journal of Philosophy* 17 (1987), esp. pp. 459–63.

18. See also §24 and 25 of the B-Deduction, where Kant develops the contrast between apperception and inner sense. I discuss this contrast and the issues it raises in Allison, *Kant's Transcendental Idealism,* Chapters 12 and 13.

19. With regard to the latter point, the crucial text is *Reflexion* 5661, "Is It an Experience That We Think?" (18: 318–19). For a discussion of this text see Allison, *Kant's Transcendental Idealism,* pp. 274–8.

20. See A547/B575 and Gr 4: 452; 119.

21. See Ingeborg Heidemann, *Spontaneität und Zeitlichkeit,* pp. 226–7, and Allison, *Kant's Transcendental Idealism,* pp. 274–5.

22. We shall see in the second part of this study that elsewhere (e.g., in the *Groundwork*) Kant presents what I have called his model mainly in terms of the role of maxims in agency and only subsequently connects maxims with imperatives. This complicates but does not significantly change the picture.

23. In R 5611 18: 252, Kant speaks of "omissions of the understanding" (*Unterlassungen des Verstandes*) in a context in which understanding is clearly taken as equivalent to reason and in which such omissions are regarded as actions imputable to an agent. See also R 5619 18: 258 and R 6647 19: 124.

24. These are R 5611–20 18: 252–9. They are analyzed by Heinz Heimsoeth, "Freiheit und Charakter: Nach den Kant-Reflexionen Nr. 5611 bis 5620," *Tradition und Kritik,* pp. 123–44.

25. Kant's discussions of freedom in this lecture and in *Metaphysik Mrongovius* and *Moral Mrongovius* are analyzed by Karl Ameriks in an unpublished paper: "Kant on Spontaneity: Some New Data."

26. Much of what follows in the paragraph, although not the precise formulation, was suggested to me by my colleague, Robert Pippin.

27. There is a parallel passage in KprV 5: 99; 102.

28. That this is the regulative principle Kant has in mind is clear from the reference to the preceding paragraph. By referring to it in this manner, Kant is obviously attempting to link his account with his general strategy for the resolution of the antinomies, which involves finding a regulative function for the cosmological ideas. We shall see, however, that the recognition of a regulative function for the problematic notion of an intelligible character is crucial for the understanding of Kant's account of agency.

29. Kant expresses similar thoughts in R 5612 18: 253 and R 6812 19: 169. As we shall see in the second part of this study, this view is not to be confused with the familiar claim in the writings on moral philosophy, particularly the *Groundwork,* that we can never be certain of our own motivation.

30. Interestingly enough, in a series of *Reflexionen* dating from about the time of the *Critique,* Kant distinguishes sharply between causal explanation after the fact and predetermination, which would be required for prediction. Moreover, he maintains that the former, but not the latter, is compatible with freedom. Thus, at one point he writes, "We explain already performed [*begangene*] free actions according to laws of human nature, but we do not thereby know them as determined; otherwise we could not regard them as contingent and demand that they should and ought to have happened otherwise" (R 5612 18: 253). In another from the same series, he suggests that "acts of reason" can be explained after the fact according to "laws of sensibility" or "laws of appearance," but they cannot be "pre-determined" (*kan aber nicht vorher bestimt*) (R 5619 18: 257). See also R 5616 18: 255–6. These belong to the series of *Reflexionen* analyzed by Heimsoeth in "Freiheit und Charakter," pp. 123–44. Unfortunately, however, Heimsoeth does not really focus on this issue.

31. Irwin, "Morality and Personality: Kant and Green," p. 38.
32. For my analysis of the relationship between the concepts of the thing in itself, the noumenon, and the transcendental object see Allison, *Kant's Transcendental Idealism,* pp. 243–6.
33. In the *Critique of Pure Reason,* Kant defines "the practical" as "everything that is possible through freedom" (A800/B828). Similarly, in the *Groundwork,* he construes it to include both the morally and the technically practical. Starting with the *Critique of Judgment,* however, he distinguishes sharply between these two conceptions of the practical and connects only the former with freedom. See KU 5: 172–4; 10–12.
34. Similarly, in the *Critique of Practical Reason,* Kant refers to the concept of freedom as "the regulative principle of reason" and contends that "reason uses this concept only for a practical purpose." See KprV 5: 48–9; 50–1. As we shall see in later chapters, however, in the second *Critique* this use is exclusively morally practical.
35. Wood, "Kant's Compatibilism," p. 90.
36. Ibid., pp. 100–1.
37. Ibid., esp. pp. 99–101.
38. Ibid., p. 83.
39. Ibid., p. 82.
40. Ibid., p. 86. It is perhaps worth noting that unlike the interpretation offered here, Wood treats the claims that the empirical character is the effect and that it is the sensible schema of the intelligible character as nonproblematically equivalent.
41. Allen W. Wood, "The Emptiness of the Moral Will," *Monist* 73 (1989), p. 470.
42. Ibid.
43. Wood, "Kant's Compatibilism," p. 80.
44. At one point, however, Wood suggests that heteronomous actions are to be seen as the result of our failure to exercise our freedom, construed as the power to act autonomously, and as involving a submission to the motivation of natural impulses. See Wood, "Kant's Compatibilism," p. 79. Given Wood's reading, it would seem that this submission must itself be seen as "caused" by reason.
45. Ibid., pp. 96–7.
46. In fairness to Wood, it should be noted that he does not take Kant to be offering this theory as the correct account of agency but merely as a "device" used to disarm the dogmatic determinist by showing that freedom and determinism cannot be proven incompatible. See Wood, "Kant's Compatibilism," pp. 83–4, 99.
47. For Wood himself this does not appear to be a problem since he sees moral considerations, including the need to account for the possibility of autonomous agency given a hedonistic empirical psychology, as motivating the move to the adoption of an incompatibilist conception of freedom already in the first *Critique.* Thus, he does not seem to acknowledge any significant differences between Kant's accounts of freedom in the two works or, indeed, in the critical corpus as a whole. I have already indicated why I think it mistaken to attribute the first *Critique* theory of freedom, even in part, to a hedonistic psychology or to see it as motivated exclusively by moral considerations. In the next chapter I shall try to show that at the time of the first *Critique* Kant had not yet arrived at his conception of autonomy. Finally, it should be noted that a number of commentators have pointed to the differences between Kant's accounts of intelligible character in the *Critique of Pure Reason* and his later writings. On the latter point, see Josef Bohatec, *Die Religionsphilosophie Kants in der "Religion inner-*

halb der Grenzen der blossen Vernunft," pp. 306–9; Bernard Carnois, *The Coherence of Kant's Doctrine of Freedom,* pp. 34–9; Heidemann, *Spontaneität und Zeitlichkeit,* pp. 226ff; and Heinz Heimsoeth, *Transzendentale Dialectik,* pp. 349–61, 397–406.

48. The locution involving reason, pure practical reason, or the moral law as the "determining ground" of the will is more prevalent in the second *Critique,* where Kant is concerned with establishing the thesis that pure reason is practical, i.e., capable of itself of determining the will. In this context, he usually speaks of reason as the "ground" (*Grund*) of maxims, which certainly does not require being taken in a causal sense. Moreover, in one important passage in which he does use causal language, he immediately qualifies it. Thus, at the very end of the deduction he writes: "The significance which reason gives to it [the pure concept of causality] through the moral law is exclusively practical, since the idea of the law of a causality (of the will) has causality itself or is its determining ground" (KprV 5: 50; 51).

49. It should be noted that this reading has the advantage of reflecting Kant's considered view on the topic, which he articulated in the major writings of the 1790s in terms of the *Wille–Willkür* distinction. To anticipate a later discussion (Chapter 7), *Wille* (legislative will or practical reason) determines *Willkür* (executive will or the faculty of choice) in the noncausal sense that it is the source of the rule or principle governing its choice of maxims and, therefore, its specific actions. Even though Kant had not yet formulated this distinction, the preceding account of intelligible character suggests that this fundamental feature of his conception of agency, if not the doctrine of the autonomy of the will, is already at work in the first *Critique.*

Chapter 3

1. We shall see in the second part of this study that this negative–positive contrast does not correspond precisely to the well-known distinction between the negative and positive conceptions of freedom drawn in the *Groundwork.*

2. The list of scholars advancing such an interpretation includes Albert Schweitzer, *Die Religionsphilosophie Kants von der Kritik der reinen Vernunft bis zur Religion innerhalb der Grenzen der blossen Vernunft,* pp. 4–81; Victor Delbos, *La Philosophie pratique de Kant,* pp. 157–200; Martial Gueroult, "Canon de la raison pure et critique de la raison pratique," *Revue Internationale de Philosophie* 8 (1954), pp. 331–57; Norman Kemp Smith, *A Commentary to Kant's "Critique of Pure Reason,"* pp. 569–70; and Bernard Carnois, *The Coherence of Kant's Doctrine of Freedom,* p. 29.

3. See Lewis White Beck, *A Commentary on Kant's "Critique of Practical Reason,"* p. 190.

4. I defend this claim and advance an interpretation of Kant's first *Critique* theory of freedom based on it in Henry E. Allison, "Practical and Transcendental Freedom in the *Critique of Pure Reason," Kant-Studien* 73 (1982), pp. 271–90, and *Kant's Transcendental Idealism,* Chapter 15. Overall, however, the interpretation offered here differs from the earlier one in several respects, the most important of which is the present emphasis on the ambiguity in the conception of practical freedom.

5. For example, according to Bernard Carnois, "the ambiguity of practical freedom stems from the intermediate position it seems to occupy between nature, into

which it is in some manner inserted, and transcendental freedom, on which it is grounded" (*The Coherence of Kant's Doctrine of Freedom*, p. 29). This suggests that what is ambiguous is whether practical freedom is independent of the causality of nature, that is, whether it amounts to genuine freedom in an incompatibilist sense.

6. Yet see R 4338 17: 510, where Kant claims that "the freedom of our will from all outer necessitation is clear from experience."

7. Here I also differ with Carnois, *The Coherence of Kant's Doctrine of Freedom*, p. 29, where he suggests that the concept of practical freedom in the Canon, in contrast to the Dialect, is "completely" empirical.

8. In R 6007 18: 442, Kant states that it is not necessary to prove the reality of freedom, "for it lies as a psychological fact [*liegt als psychologische*] in the moral law." This suggests the later doctrine of the "fact of reason"; but the appearance of the term "psychological," which usually indicates something empirical for Kant, and the presumed date (Adickes, editor of the *Reflexionen*, suggests 1783–4) make it more likely that he is expressing the doctrine of the Canon. Even closer to the doctrine of the Canon is R 6859 19: 182. Kant there states that "in ethics we do not need any concept of freedom other than that our actions, according to experience, do not proceed on the basis of instinct [*am Faden des Instinkts*], but include reflection of the understanding." And later, in the same text, after discussing the practical use of the understanding, he states, "But how this use of the understanding becomes actual, whether it itself has its predetermined causes in the series of appearances is not a practical question." Admittedly, the language of this *Reflexion*, particularly the reference to instinct, strongly suggests a compatibilist reading. Nevertheless, it can be also interpreted in the same manner in which I interpret the analogous claims in the Canon.

9. See also ML₁ 28: 255.

10. See also R 4547 and R 4548 17: 589, which presumably stem from about the same time.

11. See also the whole set of *Reflexionen* from 4218–29 17: 462–7.

12. This passage is cited and discussed by Stephen Körner, "Kant's Conception of Freedom," *Proceedings of the British Academy* 53 (1967), p. 203. Other *Reflexionen* making a similar claim include 4220 17: 462–3, 4336 17: 509–10, 4723 17: 688, 5109 18: 90–2, 5441 18: 182–3.

13. It should be noted that Kant still wrestled with the same problem in KprV 5: 100–4; 103–7.

14. In R 6000 18: 420, Kant states that "practical freedom is the consciousness of absolute spontaneity [*Selbstthätigkeit*], freedom the capacity of the causality of pure reason." Correlatively, in R 6077 18: 443, he defines practical freedom as "the capacity to act from mere reason" and transcendental freedom as "absolute spontaneity." As in the lectures, the latter is distinguished from a *spontaneitas secundum quid;* but once again there is no indication that practical freedom is to be identified with *that* sort of spontaneity.

15. Karl Ameriks, "Kant's Deduction of Freedom and Morality," *Journal of the History of Philosophy* 19 (1981), pp. 55–6, and *Kant's Theory of Mind*, pp. 194–6.

16. Ameriks makes this latter point explicit in "Kant's Deduction," pp. 55–6, and *Kant's Theory of Mind*, pp. 193–4.

17. According to Adickes, the dating of this text is uncertain; but it presumably stems from some time in the 1770s subsequent to "Metaphysik L₁." Its signifi-

cance has been emphasized by Dieter Henrich, "Die Deduktion des Sitten-gesetzes," in *Denken im Schatten des Nihilismus,* Alexander Schwan, ed., pp. 64–70.

18. We shall see in the third part of this study that the same issue arises in *Ground-work* III, in the form of a distinction between a rational being *simpliciter* and a rational being with a will. We shall also see there that this distinction plays a crucial role in Kant's unsuccessful attempt to provide a deduction of the moral law.

19. Wilfred Sellars, ". . . This I or He or It (the Thing) Which Thinks . . . ," in *Essays in Philosophy and Its History,* pp. 80–1.

20. Such an interpretation is advocated by Walter Sims, "Did Kant Write the Canon before the Dialectic?" *De Philosophia* 2 (1981), pp. 14–31. Sims likewise traces this view back to the metaphysical lectures and uses it to refute the patchwork reading; but he does not note any ambiguity in Kant's conception of practical freedom in either the lectures or the Canon.

21. The incompatibilist nature of practical freedom, regarded as the causality of reason, is particularly clear in the *Prolegomena.* See 4: 346; 94.

22. Sellars, ". . . This I or He or It (the Thing) Which Thinks . . . ," pp. 81–2.

23. With respect to the question of the dating of these lectures, see Paul Menzer's "Anmerkungen" to *Eine Vorlesung über Ethik,* pp. 324–6, and his "Der Entwick-lungsgang der Kantischen Ethik in den Jahren 1760–1785," *Kant-Studien* 3 (1899), pp. 65–8. It should be noted, however, that nothing here hinges upon a precise dating. All that is necessary is that the position of the *Lectures* on the question of the relationship between morality and freedom be seen as in essential agreement with that of the *Critique of Pure Reason* and as differing in crucial respects from that of the *Groundwork* and the *Critique of Practical Reason.*

24. On the contrast between the two views of the postulates see Beck, *A Commentary,* pp. 266–7, 273; and Klaus Düsing, "Das Problem des höchsten Gutes in Kants praktischer Philosophie," *Kant-Studien* 62 (1971), esp. pp. 15–27. Apart from the *Critique,* this early view of the postulates and the moral psychology it involves is to be found as late as 1784–5, i.e., during the time of the composition of the *Groundwork.* Thus, in *Metaphysik Volkmann,* which dates from that period, Kant states, "The incentive for all actions is the desire for happiness; but this incentive is not satisfied by the knowledge of my moral obligations [*meiner Moral*]" and "All duties have no sufficient motive, if they do not at the same time bring with them rewards and punishments" (MV 28: 385–6). By contrast, in *Moral Mrongovius* II, which presumably stems from about the same period, Kant is recorded as distinguishing sharply between rewards as motivating grounds (*Bewegungsgrunde*) of morality and as confirmatory grounds (*Bestätig-ungsgründe*) of the correctness and truth of moral laws. His claim there is that morality requires the latter but not the former (MrM 29: 637).

25. See also *Critique of Pure Reason,* A589/B617, A634/B662, A811/B830.

26. See Allison, "The Concept of Freedom in Kant's 'Semi-Critical' Ethics," *Archiv für Geschichte der Philosophie* 68 (1986), pp. 96–115.

27. Menzer, "Der Entwicklungsgang," pp. 84ff. There is no need to conclude from this, however, as Menzer apparently did, that the *Lectures* antedate Kant's con-cern with transcendental freedom. On the contrary, there is ample evidence from the metaphysical lectures and the *Reflexionen* that Kant was concerned with this concept and the problems that it raises throughout the 1770s. A more likely explanation of its absence from the *Lectures on Ethics* is that here, as in the Canon, Kant regarded the question of the reality of transcendental freedom as

practically irrelevant. For a critique of Menzer on this issue see Josef Schmucker, *Die Ursprünge der Ethik Kants*, pp. 381ff.

28. On this issue see Schmucker, *Die Ursprünge der Ethik Kants*, esp. pp. 253–9, and Dieter Henrich, "Der Begriff der sittlichen Einsicht und Kants Lehre vom Faktum der Vernunft," p. 98, note 23.

29. Similar views are also expressed in R 3872 17: 319–20, R 4619 17: 611, R 5351 18: 159, R 5612 18: 253–4.

30. Kant seems to have been already aware of that problem in 1773. In a letter to Markus Herz stemming from near the end of that year, he writes: "The concept of morality must please in the highest degree, must have moving power; and though it is indeed intellectual, it must also have direct relation to the basic incentives of the will" (10: 145; 78).

31. This conception of a *habitus* and its role in the formation of character is also prominent in the *Reflexionen*. See, e.g., R 5611 18: 252, R 5612 18: 253–4, R 6763 19: 153–4, R 6859 19: 182–3, R 7097 19: 248.

32. Henrich, "Der Begriff der sittlichen Einsicht," pp. 100–1. According to Henrich, this is merely one of two proof strategies found in the Kantian *Nachlass*. The other involves a direct proof from the concept of freedom. We shall return to these issues in the third part of this study.

33. Ibid., pp. 101–2, and Henrich, "Das Prinzip der kantischen Ethik," p. 36.

34. The tension between these two lines of thought is particularly evident in R 6858 19: 181. The quasi-eudaemonistic point of view is found, however, in numerous *Reflexionen*, the most important of which is R 7202 19: 276–82. For a discussion of the latter with respect to the question of the moral incentive see Beck, *A Commentary*, p. 215.

Chapter 4

1. This critique is formulated in Lewis White Beck, *A Commentary on Kant's "Critique of Practical Reason,"* pp. 191–4, and "Five Concepts of Freedom in Kant," *Philosophical Analysis and Reconstruction*, a Festschrift to Stephan Körner, 1987, pp. 35–51.

2. The others are empirical and moral freedom, spontaneity, and postulated freedom. See Beck, "Five Concepts of Freedom in Kant." The most controversial item on this list is the third; and Beck himself admits that the title is not entirely suitable. It is clear from his account, however, that what he has in mind here is the nonspecifically moral conception of freedom that is a condition of imputability. By distinguishing this (and, indeed, moral freedom) from the transcendental variety, Beck raises issues that will be dealt with in the second part of this study.

3. Beck, "Five Concepts of Freedom in Kant," p. 42.

4. Ibid., pp. 42–3. The citation from Kant is from KprV 5: 99; 102.

5. Lewis White Beck, *The Actor and the Spectator*, esp. pp. 123–5.

6. See KprV 5: 99–100; 102–3.

7. Beck, "Five Concepts of Freedom," p. 47.

8. Ibid., pp. 43–9, and Beck, *Commentary* pp. 192–4.

9. See, e.g., G. W. Leibniz, *Theodicy, Essays on the Goodness of God, the Freedom of Man and the Origin of Evil*, par. 288, where Leibniz remarks that intelligence, spontaneity, and contingency, with the latter defined negatively as the exclusion of logical or metaphysical necessity, are the defining characteristics of freedom.

10. See *Critique of Pure Reason*, A538/B566.

11. The main critique of compatibilism on this score in the recent literature is Peter van Inwagen, *An Essay on Free Will,* esp. pp. 55–105.
12. See, e.g., KprV 5: 98; 102, where Kant implicitly equates being in possession of one's freedom with being in one's senses (*bei Sinnen*); and KU 6: 272n; 132, where, in distinguishing affects (*Affecten*) from passions (*Leidenschaften*), he remarks that the latter are "inclinations that make it difficult or impossible to determine our power of choice [*Willkür*] through principles." Since practical freedom essentially involves the capacity to act on principles, this means that passions can limit or even undermine such freedom. The same thought is also expressed in Anthro 7: 251; 119.
13. The same considerations apply to similar moves by Stephen Körner, "Kant's Conception of Freedom," *Proceedings of the British Academy* 53 (1967), pp. 193–217, and John Silber, "The Ethical Significance of Kant's Religion," in the introduction to the English translation of *Religion Within the Limits of Reason Alone,* esp. pp. xcvii–viii.
14. For an analysis of this issue, including a survey of the recent literature on the topic, see Werner S. Pluhar, translator's introduction to his translation of the *Critique of Judgment,* pp. lxxxvi–cix.
15. Among the foremost proponents of this strategy are Wilfred Sellars, " . . . This I or He or It (the Thing) Which Thinks . . . ," and "Metaphysics and the Concept of a Person," in *Essays in Philosophy and its History,* pp. 63–90 and 214–41; and Patricia Kitcher, "Kant on Self-Identity," *Philosophical Review* 91 (1982), pp. 41–72, "Kant's Paralogisms," *Philosophical Review* 91 (1982), pp. 515–47, and "Kant's Real Self," in *Self and Nature in Kant's Philosophy,* Allen Wood, ed., pp. 113–47. I criticize this strategy and attempt to show the inability of even nonreductive, causal models of mind to capture the spontaneity of the understanding as Kant conceives it in "Kant's Refutation of Materialism," in *Monist* 72 (1989), pp. 190–208. I believe that similar considerations apply, *mutatis mutandis,* in the present context.
16. Donald Davidson, "Mental Events," in *Essays on Action and Events,* p. 207. See also pp. 209 and 225.
17. Meerbote's interpretation is contained in Ralf Meerbote, "Wille and Willkür in Kant's Theory of Action," in *Interpreting Kant,* S. Gram Moltke, ed., 1982, pp. 69–89; "Kant on the 'Nondeterminate Character of Human Actions,'" in *Kant on Causality, Freedom, and Objectivity,* William A. Harper and Ralf Meerbote, eds., pp. 138–63; and "Kant on Freedom and the Rational and Morally Good Will," a commentary on an essay by Terence Irwin, in *Self and Nature in Kant's Philosophy,* Allen W. Wood, ed., pp. 57–72.
18. Meerbote, "Kant on the Nondeterminate Character of Human Actions," p. 140.
19. Ibid., p. 141.
20. See Meerbote, "Wille and Willkür in Kant's Theory of Action," p. 71.
21. Meerbote, "Kant on the Nondeterminate Character of Human Actions," p. 145.
22. Meerbote, "Kant on Freedom and the Rational and Morally Good Will," p. 63.
23. Ibid.
24. Ibid., p. 149.
25. Ibid., p. 150.
26. See Daniel C. Dennett, "Mechanism and Responsibility," in *Essays on Freedom of Action,* Ted Honderich, ed., pp. 159–84, and, more recently, *Elbow Room.*
27. Thomas Nagel, *The View from Nowhere,* p. 119. At the beginning of the paragraph in which this passage occurs, Nagel refers to Kant's "unintelligible idea of the noumenal self which is outside time and causality," which he sees as an

expression of "the literally unintelligible ambition of intervening in the world from outside."
28. Ibid., p. 127.
29. Ibid., pp. 120–3, 137.

Chapter 5

1. In the present instance, I have translated the key phrase *"nach der Vorstellung der Gesetze"* as "in accordance with the conception of laws," which is closer to the common reading than Paton's *"in accordance with his idea* of laws."
2. A very helpful survey and analysis of these interpretations has been provided by Pierre Laberge, "La Volonte, la representation des lois et la fin," *Grundlegung zur Metaphysik der Sitten. Ein kooperativer Kommentar,* Otfried Höffe, ed., 1989. He shows that the claim in question has been taken to mean that rational agents act according to the conception of moral laws, laws of nature, both kinds of laws, that is, objective principles of one kind or another, as well as according to maxims. His own view is that the text is interpretable in each of these ways, so that, in effect, every interpretation is correct in what it affirms and wrong in what it denies.
3. See, e.g., Paton, *The Categorical Imperative: A Study in Kant's Moral Philosophy,* pp. 80–1; John Silber, "The Copernican Revolution in Ethics: The Good Reexamined," *Kant-Studien* 51 (1959), p. 86; Stephen Körner, *Kant,* p. 134; and Rüdiger Bittner, "Maximen," *Akten des 4. Internationalen Kant-Kongresses, Mainz, 6–10 April 1974,* G. Funke and J. Kopper, eds., pp. 485–98. These references are cited by Konrad Cramer, "Hypothetische Imperative?" in *Rehabilitierung der praktischen Philosophie,* p. 168n. Cramer himself defends the view that Kant has laws of nature in mind here. Following Bittner, however, I think it more appropriate to claim that rational agents act in light of their knowledge of laws of nature but not according to such laws. Similarly, I shall argue that rational agents act in light of but not according to objective practical principles, which leaves maxims as the principles according to which rational agents actually act.
4. See, e.g., Ethik 52; 43.
5. Lewis White Beck, *A Commentary on Kant's "Critique of Practical Reason,"* p. 81. Beck notes that, logically, "maxim" and "principle" have the same meaning and law is only a species of them.
6. A similar point is made by Aune with respect to the relationship between maxims and laws. See Bruce Aune, *Kant's Theory of Morals,* pp. 24–5.
7. This reading of the phrase is suggested by Beck, *Commentary,* p. 81. He speaks of a "general setting of the will."
8. I am again following Beck, *Commentary,* p. 81. He notes the puzzle generated by the juxtaposition of *Bestimmung* and *Bedingung* and points out in a note that one commentator (Bruno Käubler, *Der Begriff der Triebfeder in Kants Ethik,* p. 41) has suggested that the latter is a misprint for the former. Although Beck rejects this suggestion, he does assume the rough equivalence of these two terms and explains Kant's use of the second on the basis of his logical terminology (the point being that the middle term in a practical syllogism is termed the condition).
9. Beck, *Commentary,* pp. 81–2.
10. Kant himself characterizes maxims based on a subjective condition as *"blosse Maximen,"* KprV 5: 26; 25. For a discussion of these locutions, see also Paton, *The Categorical Imperative,* pp. 59–61.

11. See KprV 5: 26–7, 36, 74, 76; 25–6, 37, 76, 78.
12. This is emphasized by Bittner in "Maximen."
13. For this account of the relationship between pure and empirical concepts see Robert Paul Wolff, *Kant's Theory of Mental Activity,* pp. 24–5, and Henry E. Allison, *Kant's Transcendental Idealism,* p. 117.
14. See, e.g., Gr 4: 427; 94, where Kant assigns to empirical psychology the explanation of how maxims arise from inclinations and desires "with the cooperation of reason." The significance of this passage is noted by Gerold Prauss, *Kant über Freiheit als Autonomie,* p. 153.
15. See KprV 5: 19–20; 17–18.
16. See Gr 4: 413n; 81n and 460n; 128n.
17. I take this to be the point of Kant's claim that "an interest is that in virtue of which reason becomes practical – that is, becomes a cause determining the will" (Gr 4: 460n; 128n).
18. Rüdiger Bittner, *Moralisches Gebot oder Autonomie,* pp. 155–6, construes the generality of what he terms a "subjective law" in this sense, although he regards maxims as merely a subclass of such laws.
19. It is worth noting that in the other two examples intended to illustrate the function of the categorical imperative in evaluating maxims, Kant fails to specify any principle that could reasonably be construed as a maxim. Thus, in the case of the man who refuses to develop his talents, the "maxim" in question is described merely as one of "neglecting my natural gifts," which hardly specifies a course of action; whereas in the case of the person who rejects the duty of beneficence, Kant does not even attempt to stipulate a maxim but merely an attitude (*Gesinnung*). See Gr 4: 423; 90.
20. This point is emphasized by Andreas Wildt, *Autonomie und Anerkennung,* p. 56n. Rather than making it implicit, however, he insists that it must be explicit. Thus, for him all maxims have the form: "Immer wenn ich durch die Handlung H das Result R herbeifuhren kann, so will ich H tun."
21. See Otfried Höffe, "Kants kategorischer Imperativ als Kriterium des Sittlichen," in *Ethik und Politik,* Otfried Höffe, ed., esp. pp. 87–96, and Bittner, "Maximen." A similar view was already advocated, although not really developed, by Beck, who states (*Commentary,* p. 78) that a maxim "must contain or express a lasting policy or settled disposition of the will, not a capricious resolve or a variable rule of thumb."
22. This seems particularly clear in the account of Bittner, "Maximen."
23. Onora O'Neill, "Kant after Virtue," *Inquiry* 26 (1983), p. 394. See also Onora O'Neill, "Universal Laws and Ends in Themselves," *Monist* 73 (1989), p. 344.
24. O'Neill, "Kant after Virtue," p. 394.
25. Basically, O'Neill argues that since the particular rules or intentions under which agents act, which presumably cannot be equated with the *Vorsätze* of the Höffe–Bittner interpretation, are not maxims, the question of whether or not they are universalizable without contradiction is morally irrelevant. Correlatively, since maxims, as the locus of moral evaluation are underlying intentions rather than the specific intentions expressed in particular acts, it follows, on her view, that Kant's moral theory is not so much concerned with the rightness or wrongness of particular actions or action types as it is "with the underlying moral quality of a person's life or aspects of his life" (O'Neill, "Kant after Virtue," p. 395). In fact, in the same essay (p. 397) she goes so far as to deny that Kant's moral philosophy is a rule-based theory at all and argues instead that it is virtue based.

It should be noted, however, that this is a polemical piece in which O'Neill is concerned with countering the wholesale attack on Kant's moral theory launched by Alasdair MacIntyre in *After Virtue*.

26. O'Neill, "Kant after Virtue," pp. 393–4.
27. This point is also noted by Robert B. Louden, "Kant's Virtue Ethics," *Philosophy* 61 (1986), p. 481.
28. Onora O'Neill, *Acting on Principle*, pp. 34–42.
29. Louden, "Kant's Virtue Ethics," pp. 480–1.
30. The idea that maxims are arranged hierarchically is also advanced by Beck, *Commentary*, p. 118; Paton, *The Categorical Imperative*, pp. 136–7; and more recently Christine Korsgaard, "Kant's Analysis of Obligation: The Argument of Foundations I," *Monist* 73 (1989), p. 324.
31. The problem, at least with respect to the maxim–*Vorsatz* distinction, seems to have been grasped by Bittner. See "Maximen," p. 488.
32. The distinction between instances in which the relatively specific rule is the morally relevant factor and those in which it is the underlying intention would seem to correspond, at least roughly, to Kant's distinction between perfect and imperfect duties. But since this distinction itself is far from unproblematic, I do not wish to insist on that here.
33. This dual concern of Kantian morality is emphasized, and I think quite correctly, by Louden in response to O'Neill's strong virtue reading of Kant. See Louden, "Kant's Virtue Ethics," esp. pp. 484–5.
34. See Thomas Hill, "Kant's Argument for the Rationality of Moral Conduct," *Pacific Philosophical Quarterly* 66 (1985), pp. 8–15.
35. Hill, "Kant's Argument for the Rationality of Moral Conduct," pp. 7–8, provides a good sketch of this line of interpretation and of the difficulties which it involves. He also identifies Robert Paul Wolff, *The Autonomy of Reason*, as its main proponent. Like many interpreters, he correctly points out that it is incompatible with Kant's later views but fails to note that it conflicts with his earlier views as well.
36. This view has a large number of advocates, but it is perhaps best known to English language students of Kant through the interpretation of John Silber, "The Ethical Significance of Kant's Religion." By far the most detailed and sophisticated statement of this position, however, is by Prauss, *Kant über Freiheit als Autonomie*.
37. Bittner, *Moralisches Gebot oder Autonomie*, p. 151. Although, as will become clear in the next section of this chapter and in later chapters, I have profound differences with Bittner regarding his criticisms of the overall Kantian project of justifying the moral law, I am in agreement with many aspects of his analysis of Kant's conception of agency, particularly with respect to his claim that rational agents can act only according to self-given laws.
38. Bernard Carnois, *The Coherence of Kant's Doctrine of Freedom*, p. 45. I believe that Carnois is also correct in suggesting that Kant himself viewed the introduction of autonomy as analogous to the Copernican revolution in his theoretical philosophy.
39. See KprV 5: 33–4; 33–4.
40. Hill, "Kant's Argument for the Rationality of Moral Conduct," pp. 13–14. The following analysis is largely based on Hill's.
41. Kant makes this fully explicit in KprV 5: 29; 28.
42. For my account of the contrast between transcendental idealism and transcendental realism, see Allison, *Kant's Transcendental Idealism*, Chapter 2.

43. This heading is supplied by Paton in his translation to the argument on 443–4. See H. J. Paton, trans., *Groundwork to the Metaphysic of Morals,* p. 111.

44. One of the best known criticisms of this type is offered by Philippa Foot, "Morality as a System of Hypothetical Imperatives," in *Virtues and Vices,* pp. 157–73.

45. Kant's own uncertainty in this regard is perhaps best evidenced by the differences in the classificatory schemata offered in the *Groundwork* and the *Critique of Practical Reason.* In the former, the basic division is between those based on empirical principles, which stem from the "principle of happiness," and those based on rational principles, which stem from the "principle of perfection" (Gr 4: 441–3; 108–11). In the latter, the basic division is between subjective and objective material principles (KprV 5: 40; 40–1). In addition, there are earlier attempts at classification, which antedate the autonomy–heteronomy contrast, in *Reflexionen* 6631 and 6637 (19: 118–19 and 121–2) and the *Lectures on Ethics* (Ethik 14–17; 12–15). For a discussion of this issue see Beck, *Commentary,* pp. 103–8.

46. This problem pertains particularly to Kant's "indirect proof" of transcendental idealism by means of the refutation of its alleged contradictory opposite, transcendental realism. For my analysis of this issue see Allison, *Kant's Transcendental Idealism,* pp. 50–61.

47. T. H. Green, *Collected Works,* Vol. 2, p. 119, cited by Terence Irwin, "Morality and Personality: Kant and Green," in *Self and Nature in Kant's Philosophy,* Allen W. Wood, ed., p. 43.

48. Andrews Reath, "Hedonism, Heteronomy and Kant's Principle of Happiness," *Pacific Philosophical Quarterly* 70 (1989), esp. pp. 46–50. Much of the following analysis is indebted to Reath's important paper.

49. See Gr 4: 413n; 81. Other important discussions of inclination, which include references to their aetiology are Rel 6: 29n; 24; MS 6: 211; 8–9, and Anthro 7: 251; 119. We shall return to Kant's account of inclination in the next chapter.

50. Reath, "Hedonism, Heteronomy and Kant's Principle of Happiness," esp. pp. 50–9.

51. Hutcheson's theory, with which Kant was quite familiar, might seem to be the most obvious counterexample to the claim that all heteronomous theories are based on the principle of happiness or self-love. Thus, it is frequently thought that Kant seriously misrepresents this theory when, in the *Critique of Practical Reason,* he claims that for it, as for all forms of heteronomy, "everything is reduced to the desire for one's own happiness" (KprV 5: 38; 40). On the interpretation offered here, however, Kant need not deny the nonegoistic nature of Hutcheson's conception of natural sympathy, understood as an "instinct" or "disinterested affection," which leads us, independently of any consideration of our own interests, to be concerned with the good of others (Francis Hutcheson, "An Inquiry concerning the Original of Our Ideas of Virtue or Moral Good," Introduction, section ii, in *British Moralists,* Vol. 1, p. 72). In fact, the Kantian critique of this and similar moral sense theories has nothing to do with the issue of hedonism or even eudaemonism as it is usually construed. It concerns rather the assumption that the presence of a feeling can serve as the ground of an obligation. Put simply, Kant's view is that the fact, assuming it is a fact, that I am so constituted as to take pleasure in virtuous action or the well-being of others cannot ground a categorical imperative. It cannot do so because such an imperative, by its very nature, dictates the (moral) necessity or impossibility of a course of action independently of how an individual or, indeed, a species happens to

be constituted. For a further discussion of this point see Beck, *Commentary,* pp. 101–2.

52. See §5, Problem I (5: 28–29; 28). Although Kant there claims that what is required is freedom "in the strictest, i.e., transcendental, sense," rather than autonomy, this really amounts to the same thing, since as we have seen, to attribute the property of autonomy to the will is to regard it as free in the transcendental sense.

53. That it is properly only a principle in the first sense is argued most forcefully by T. C. Williams, *The Concept of the Categorical Imperative,* especially Chapter 3, "The 'Supreme Principle of Morality.'"

Chapter 6

1. For a discussion of the thesis itself and of many of the standard criticisms, see Karl Ameriks, "Kant on the Good Will," in *Grundlegung zur Metaphysik der Sitten: Ein kooperativer Kommentar,* Otfried Höffe, ed., pp. 45–65.

2. This does not, of course, mean that it is the sole intrinsic good. Thus, happiness is clearly an intrinsic good (its goodness does not consist in its suitability as a means for the attainment of some other good); yet Kant maintains that it is not an unqualified good, since "a good will seems to constitute the indispensable condition of our even being worthy of happiness" (Gr 4: 493; 61). For discussions of this point see Bruce Aune, *Kant's Theory of Morals,* p. 6; Christine Korsgaard, "Two Distinctions in Goodness," *Philosophical Review* 92 (1983), p. 178; and Ameriks, "Kant on the Good Will," p. 46.

3. For example, H. J. Paton, *The Categorical Imperative,* p. 46, states that "a good will *under human conditions* is one which acts for the sake of duty." Ameriks terms this the "'particular intention' view," and he criticizes it on the grounds that it is incapable of offering a non-question-begging account of why such a will could be regarded as an unconditioned good. See Ameriks, "Kant on the Good Will," pp. 46–51.

4. In his discussion of conscience in the *Doctrine of Virtue,* Kant does admit that one can err in one's "objective judgment as to whether something is a duty or not." Similarly, in the *Anthropology* he admits the possibility that the principles adopted by a person of character (*Denkungsart*) "might occasionally be mistaken and imperfect." See MS 6: 401; 61 and Anthro 7: 292; 157. In the *Groundwork* this possibility seems to be precluded.

5. See Gerold Prauss, *Kant über Freiheit als Autonomie,* p. 249.

6. This version is taken from Paton, *The Categorical Imperative,* p. 48.

7. Ibid., pp. 48–9; Lewis White Beck, *A Commentary on Kant's "Critique of Practical Reason,"* p. 120n. See also KprV 5: 92–3; 95–6.

8. See Barbara Herman, "On the Value of Acting from the Motive of Duty," *Philosophical Review* 90 (July 1981), pp. 378–9.

9. See, e.g., KprV 5: 118; 122.

10. The importance of this distinction is emphasized by Hans Reiner, *Duty and Inclination,* esp. pp. 25–7, and Prauss, *Kant über Freiheit als Autonomie,* esp. pp. 70–83.

11. See Herman, "On the Value of the Motive of Acting from Duty," pp. 365–6.

12. See Gr 4: 422n; 89 and MS 6: 390–1; 50–51. For a discussion of some of the problems raised by this distinction see Mary Gregor, *Laws of Freedom,* pp. 95–112.

13. See, e.g., Rel 6: 4n; 3, where Kant notes that even an intended altruistic act

"must, first of all, itself be weighed according to the moral law before it is directed to the happiness of others." The point is also emphasized by Herman, "On the Value of Acting from the Motive of Duty," p. 365.

14. See note 9.

15. In fact, this is how Kant's requirement is generally understood in the recent literature. See, e.g., Paul Benson, "Moral Worth," *Philosophical Studies* 51 (1987), pp. 365–82.

16. Richard G. Henson, "What Kant Might Have Said: Moral Worth and the Over-determination of Dutiful Action," *Philosophical Review* 88 (1979), pp. 39–54, esp. pp. 42–4.

17. Ibid., p. 48.

18. Ibid., pp. 44–5.

19. Herman, "On the Value of Acting from the Motive of Duty," pp. 367–70.

20. Ibid., p. 369.

21. Herman has communicated to me in correspondence that she did not intend to suggest that counterfactual considerations are *never* relevant in the determination of moral worth and it is quite true that she never states it explicitly. Nevertheless, I continue to believe that it is a consequence, albeit unintended, of the account that she does give.

22. This weakness of Herman's account has not escaped notice in the literature. Perhaps the most pointed response is by Benson, "Moral Worth," esp. pp. 370–3. Contrary to Herman, Benson insists (and I think correctly) that examining nonactual circumstances is crucial in determining moral worth because it is crucial in determining whether an action is nonaccidentally right in a given set of circumstances. See also Tom Sorrell, "Kant's Good Will," *Kant-Studien* 78 (1987), p. 93.

23. Herman, "On the Value of Acting from the Motive of Duty," p. 371.

24. See Gr 4: 393, 399; 61, 67 and Rel 6: 71; 65. For discussions of this point in the secondary literature see Warren G. Harbison, "The Good Will," *Kant-Studien* 71 (1980), pp. 47–59, and Ameriks, "Kant on the Good Will." Kant's conception of *Gesinnung* will be analyzed in the next chapter.

25. In *Moral Mrongovius* II (29: 611), Kant defines virtue as the "enduring maxim to make one's will accord with the moral law," but this can, more properly, be taken as referring to a good will. Strictly speaking, a good will is one that adopts such a maxim, i.e., one that strives with all of its power to make the law the ultimate determinant of its conduct, whereas "virtue" refers to the strength or capacity (*Fertigkeit*) of the will to achieve that goal. Kant's doctrine, of course, is that for finite rational beings such as ourselves, success is at best partial. These issues will be discussed in detail in Chapter 9.

26. The Kantian rejection of moral luck has been the topic of considerable discussion and criticism in the recent literature. See, e.g., Bernard Williams, "Moral Luck," in *Moral Luck,* pp. 22–39; Thomas Nagel, "Moral Luck," in *Mortal Questions,* pp. 24–38; and Martha Nussbaum, *The Fragility of Goodness.* Issues raised by this critique will be dealt with in subsequent chapters. Our present concern is merely with the interpretation of the Kantian conception of moral worth.

27. The contrary view is affirmed by Henson, "What Kant Might Have Said," p. 44. For a retort see Herman, "On the Value of Acting from the Motive of Duty," pp. 370–1.

28. Herman, "On the Value of Acting from the Motive of Duty," pp. 372–6.

29. Marcia Baron, "The Alleged Moral Repugnance of Acting from Duty," *Journal*

of Philosophy 81 (4) (1984), p. 207. Since Baron does not present her analysis as an interpretation of Kant, I shall not deal with it here.

30. Benson, "Moral Worth," pp. 379–80.
31. Ibid.
32. Benson, "Moral Worth," pp. 378–9.
33. We shall see in Chapter 9 that the picture is complicated, although not radically altered, by the introduction in *The Doctrine of Virtue* of the conception of imperfect duties as obligations to adopt certain maxims rather than to perform (or refrain from performing) certain actions.
34. It should be noted that I am here differing from Paton in translating *Achtung* as respect rather than as reverence.
35. The implications of the claim that pure reason is, or can be, practical, as well as its basis, will be explored at length in Part 3 of this study.
36. The expression is used by Andrews Reath in the title of his paper, "Kant's Theory of Moral Sensibility: Respect for the Moral Law and the Influence of Inclination," *Kant-Studien* 80 (1989), pp. 284–302. Kant himself points to the analogy with the Aesthetic (KprV 5: 90; 92). For a discussion of the point, see Beck, *Commentary*, pp. 211–12.
37. This is in essential agreement with the way in which the chapter is read by Beck. See *Commentary*, p. 212.
38. See Gr 4: 445; 112–13.
39. This is to say that, for purposes of exposition, I am following the analytic method of the *Groundwork* rather than the synthetic method of the *Critique of Practical Reason*, even when dealing with material from the latter work and Kant's later writings.
40. See Beck, *Commentary*, p. 216.
41. Following Kant's usual usage, I am here equating a divine with a holy will. We shall see in Chapter 8, however, that this raises certain difficulties.
42. See, e.g., KprV 5: 79; 81–2, where Kant explicitly links the concepts of inclination, interest, and maxims and notes that they are all only applicable to finite beings.
43. This is noted by Beck, *Commentary*, p. 221–2. It also accords with the account in the *Groundwork*, where Kant equates respect with the "consciousness of the *subordination* of my will to a law without the mediation of external influences of my senses" (Gr 4: 401n; 69).
44. For Kant's account of moral fanaticism, see KprV 5: 83–7; 85–9. Some of the issues raised by this account will be discussed in Chapter 8.
45. I am here following the extremely helpful account of Reath in "Kant's Theory of Moral Sensibility: Respect for the Moral Law and the Influence of Inclination," p. 287. Reath terms this recognition of supreme authoritativeness the "'intellectual' aspect of respect."
46. At this point I differ somewhat from Reath's account in "Kant's Theory of Moral Sensibility," esp. pp. 292–4. Appealing mainly to a passage in the *Doctrine of Virtue* in which Kant describes self-conceit as "lack of modesty in one's claims to respect from others" (MS 6: 131) and to Rawls's distinction between general and first-person egoism, he takes it to be an inclination to make one's own desires the source of value (or laws) for others and to be perceived as superior to others. There is no doubt that what Reath describes is an important manifestation of self-conceit. But this attitude toward others and the aspect of vanity seem to be a consequence rather than the essence of self-conceit. The crucial point, at least

with respect to the *Critique of Practical Reason,* is that one assumes that acting on the basis of one's desires is a matter of right, whatever the consequences to others. This, in turn, entails that others are regarded merely as means, which violates the categorical imperative.

47. This point is emphasized by Reath, "Kant's Theory of Moral Sensibility," esp. p. 294.

48. One is reminded here of Kant's assignment to the concept of a noumenon in the *Critique of Pure Reason* the function of curbing "the pretensions of sensibility" to be coextensive with the real (A255/B311).

49. See also KprV 5: 75, 79, 80; 77, 81, 82.

50. Thus, Kant insists that "respect applies to persons only, never to things." KprV 5: 76; 79.

51. Reath, "Kant's Theory of Moral Sensibility," p. 296.

52. My major difference with Reath concerns his views regarding the justification of maxims. We agree that the Incorporation Thesis (or, as he terms it, the "principle of election") entails that when an agent adopts a maxim there is an implicit assumption that this is in some sense rationally justified. Apparently, however, he takes this to mean that Kant is committed to the view that we always adopt maxims we think could serve as universal laws and thus that a reference to the standpoint of others is built into our justificatory procedure, even in nonmoral contexts. As he puts it, "The presumption is that someone who understands your maxim can at some level accept your way of acting." Given this view, which he presents as an aspect of the fact of reason (construed in Rawlsian fashion as the "consciousness of the moral law in everyday life"), he is forced to contend that this intersubjective universality standard is recognized even by the champion of self-love. (See Reath, "Kant's Theory of Moral Sensibility," pp. 296–7.) On my view, the agent operating on the principle of self-conceit denies the legitimacy of the perspective of others and, therefore, rejects the assumption that his choice of maxims must pass the universalizability test encoded in the categorical imperative. These issues will be discussed in Part 3.

53. Dieter Henrich, "Das Problem der Grundlegung der Ethik bei Kant und im spekulativen Idealismus," in *Sein und Ethos,* Paulus Engelhardt, ed., pp. 372–5. This critique is endorsed by Andreas Wildt, *Autonomie und Anerkennung: Hegels Moralitätskritik im Lichte seiner Fichte-Rezeption,* pp. 92–3.

Chapter 7

1. See Lewis White Beck, *A Commentary on Kant's Critique of Practical Reason,* p. 200.

2. For a thorough discussion of the translation problems see Ralf Meerbote, "*Wille* and *Willkür* in Kant's Theory of Action," *Interpreting Kant,* Moltke S. Gram, ed., pp. 69–84.

3. The first is exemplified by Beck in his translation of the *Critique of Practical Reason* and Mary Gregor in her translation of *The Doctrine of Virtue;* the second is exemplified by T. M. Greene and H. H. Hudson in their translation of *Religion within the Limits of Reason Alone.*

4. See Meerbote, "*Wille* and *Willkür* in Kant's Theory of Action," pp. 71–2.

5. Yet elsewhere (23: 248) Kant speaks of maxims of *Willkür.*

6. In the *Critique of Practical Reason,* however, Kant confuses matters considerably by referring to the autonomy of *Wille* and heteronomy of *Willkür.* See KprV 5: 33, 36; 33, 37–8.

7. Beck, *Commentary,* pp. 199–200.
8. John Silber, in his lengthy review of Beck's *Commentary,* notes the untenability of Beck's attribution of freedom in the sense of autonomy to *Wille;* but he then proceeds to commit the opposite mistake of attributing autonomy to *Willkür.* See John Silber, "The Highest Good in Kant's Ethics," *Ethics* 73 (1963), p. 181.
9. Carl Leonhard Reinhold, "Eröterungen des Begriffs von der Freiheit des Willens," in *Materialien zu Kants "Kritik der praktischen Vernunft,"* Rüdiger Bittner and Konrad Cramer, eds., pp. 252–74.
10. Carl Leonhard Reinhold, "Einige Bemerkungen über die in der Einleitung zu den 'Metaphysischen Anfangsgründen der Rechtslehre' vonn. I. Kant aufgestellten Begriffe von der Freiheit des Willens," in *Materialien zu Kants "Kritik der praktischen Vernunft,"* Rüdiger Bittner and Konrad Cramer, eds., pp. 310–24.
11. Ibid., p. 112.
12. For the discussion and critique of Reinhold on this issue see Gerold Prauss, *Kant über Freiheit als Autonomie,* pp. 85–9.
13. Ibid., pp. 99–100. Prauss argues that in addition to allowing for the possibility of genuinely free actions that are not motivated by respect for the law, this also leaves room for a transcendental deduction of the moral law.
14. Reinhold, "Einige Bemerkungen," pp. 313–14.
15. In "Metaphysik L_2" (28: 589), Kant states that animals can have a *Willkür* but not a *Wille,* since they cannot form a representation of a thing that they desire, much less formulate a reason (*Zweck*) why they want or do not want something.
16. Although he refers to the critique of Sidgwick rather than to that of Reinhold or Prauss, a similar analysis of this text and its relevance to the general problem of the possibility of free and yet nonmoral action for Kant is provided by Nelson Potter, Jr., "Does Kant Have Two Concepts of Freedom?" in *Akten des 4. Internationalen Kant-Kongresses,* G. Funke and J. Kopper, eds., 590–6.
17. For an account of *Gesinnung* and its connection with *Willkür* see John Silber, "The Ethical Significance of Kant's Religion," pp. cxiv–cxxvii.
18. This claim is made by Daniel O'Connor, "Good and Evil Disposition," *Kant-Studien* 76 (1985), p. 291.
19. This aspect of Kant's conception is emphasized by Silber, "The Ethical Significance of Kant's Religion," pp. cxv–cxviii.
20. This reduction is presented in its sharpest form by Ralph Walker, *Kant. The Arguments of the Philosophers,* p. 149. An attempt to avoid this consequence while accepting the interpretation of Kant's position from which it presumably stems is offered by Allen W. Wood, "Kant's Compatibilism," in *Self and Nature in Kant's Philosophy,* Allen W. Wood, ed., pp. 91–3. Wood's attempt is, in turn, criticized by Jonathan Bennett, "Commentary: Kant's Theory of Freedom," also in *Self and Nature,* Allen W. Wood, ed., pp. 103–5.
21. The suggestion of this as a *possible* reading of Kant on this point is made by Ralph Walker, "*Achtung* in the *Grundlegung,*" in *Grundlegung zur Metaphysik der Sitten: Ein kooperativer Kommentar,* Otfried Höffe, ed., 1989. Walker, of course, goes on to argue that, on this reading, Kant's theory makes no sense. By contrast, the importance of distinguishing sharply between Kant's theory and the theory implicit in the Platonic myth is emphasized by Bernard Carnois, *The Coherence of Kant's Doctrine of Freedom,* pp. 100–1. It is not clear to me, however, that his alternative metaphysical reading, which emphasizes that the choice is nontemporal rather than "pretemporal," makes the position attributed to Kant any more coherent.

22. Cf. Arthur Schopenhauer, *The World as Will and Representation*, Vol. 1, pp. 286–307; *Essay on the Freedom of the Will*, pp. 26–64; and *On the Basis of Morality*, pp. 109–15.
23. For a contrary view on this point, see Wood, "Kant's Compatibilism," pp. 97–101.
24. O'Connor, "Good and Evil Disposition," p. 293, suggests that the Kantian text is ambiguous between these two conceptions.
25. See Anthro 7: 285; 151.
26. See Carnois, *The Coherence of Kant's Doctrine of Freedom*, p. 34.
27. It should be noted, however, that it is not necessarily incompatible with the conception of "mere" practical freedom discussed in Chapter 3.
28. See Anthro 7: 292; 157. In *Religion within the Limits of Reason Alone*, Kant denies that we are responsible for the existence of our inclinations. See Rel 6: 35; 30.
29. On this point see Yirmahu Yovel, *Kant and the Philosophy of History*, p. 53. For the contrary reading see O'Connor, "Good and Evil Disposition," pp. 294–5.
30. For Kant's views on the social contract as an idea of reason see, especially, *On the Old Saw: That May be Right in Theory but It Won't Work in Practice* (8: 297).
31. It will be recalled that, already in "Metaphysik L_1," Kant spoke of freedom as not operative in early childhood and madness. See Chapter 3, note 10. Presumably, the point now is that the same conditions would rule out the attribution of a *Gesinnung*.
32. The notion of an original acquisition also plays a crucial role in the *Rechtslehre*, where it provides the cornerstone of Kant's justification of private property. See 6: 260–70. Although this account is itself relevant to the issue currently before us, since it indicates that the concept of an original acquisition is treated by Kant as a product of juridically practical reason rather than as the designation of a historical occurrence, pursuing the details of this account would take us too far afield. For an illuminating discussion of the role of the notion in the *Rechtslehre* see Mary Gregor, "Kant's Theory of Property," *Review of Metaphysics* 41 (1988), pp. 157–87.
33. See the Inaugural Dissertation, §15 (Diss 2: 406; 73–4), and *On a Discovery*, 8: 221–2. I also discuss this notion in *The Kant–Eberhard Controversy*, pp. 82–83.
34. In the Introduction to the *Metaphysic of Morals*, Kant defines a person as "a subject whose actions can be *imputed* to him" and moral (in distinction from psychological) personality as "the freedom of a rational being under moral laws" (MS 6: 223; 22).

Chapter 8

1. In a letter to G. Koerner, dated February 22, 1793, Schiller described Kant's essay as "scandalous," and in a letter to Herder, dated June 7, 1793, Goethe wrote: "Kant required a long lifetime to purify his philosophical mantle of many impurities and prejudices. And now he has wantonly tainted it with the shameful stain of radical evil, in order that Christians too might be attracted to kiss its hem." Both references are taken from Emil Fackenheim, "Kant and Radical Evil," *University of Toronto Quarterly* 23 (1954), p. 340.
2. A recent criticism in this vein is by Stephen Engstrom, "Conditioned Auton-

omy," *Philosophy and Phenomenological Research* 48 (1988), pp. 435–53. In addition to rejecting Kant's rigorism and his "purism," i.e., Kant's view of the moral requirement, Engstrom attempts a positive reconstruction of Kant's thought on the basis of the notion of a "conditioned autonomy," understood as a person's capacity, under certain circumstances, to act from duty or respect for the law.

3. See MS 6: 421–47; 84–114.

4. See John Silber, "The Ethical Significance of Kant's Religion," in *Religion within the Limits of Reason Alone,* T. M. Greene and H. H. Hudson, trans., p. cxxix.

5. See Allen Wood, *Kant's Moral Religion,* pp. 210–15. A similar analysis is also suggested by Fackenheim, "Kant and Radical Evil," pp. 347–8.

6. See Fackenheim, "Kant and Radical Evil," p. 349.

7. See also Gr 4: 424; 91–2.

8. The basic idea here seems to be that the formulation and clear presentation of the categorical imperative as the supreme principle of morality, which is the main concern of the *Groundwork,* is a means for resolving this dialectic by making evident the unconditioned status of this imperative.

9. A critique of Kant's conception of a propensity to evil along the lines suggested here is offered by Daniel O'Connor, "Good and Evil Disposition," *Kant-Studien* 76 (1985), pp. 296–7. According to O'Connor, Kant's argument for a universal propensity to evil turns partly on a misguided analogy with a medical notion and partly on an illicit generalization.

10. Kant himself treats the innateness of this propensity as a postulate although he terms it a *Satz* (proposition) rather than a *Postulat.* In their translation, however, Greene and Hudson render *Satz* as "postulate." See Rel 6: 50–1; 46.

11. It is interpreted in this way by Philip L. Quinn, "In Adam's Fall, We Sinned All," *Philosophical Topics* 16 (1988), p. 111.

12. See O'Connor, "Good and Evil Disposition," pp. 297–8.

13. On the question of Kant's intentions here, see Wood, *Kant's Moral Religion,* pp. 224–5.

14. See also KprV 5: 82, 84; 84, 86.

15. Although it does not mention the propensity to evil, one of the most helpful texts in this regard is the introduction to *The Doctrine of Virtue.* See MS 6: 379–81, 394; 37–40, 55.

16. As we shall see in the next chapter, there is a somewhat different conception of vice at work in *The Doctrine of Virtue.*

17. Lest one assume that this insistence is merely a feature of the *Groundwork* and the *Critique of Practical Reason,* it should be noted that Kant makes precisely the same claim in *Religion within the Limits of Reason Alone,* indeed, in connection with the account of radical evil. See Rel 6: 30–1; 27–8.

18. Some of these difficulties are noted by Engstrom, "Conditioned Autonomy," pp. 441–2.

19. Strong support for such an assumption is provided by Kant's account of lying in *The Doctrine of Virtue.* (See MS 6: 429–31; 92–6.) In contrast to his earlier treatment of lying in the *Lectures on Ethics,* Kant here characterizes it as a violation of a perfect duty to oneself. Moreover, not only does he distinguish between an outer and an inner lie and claim that the latter is worse, he also explicitly connects the inner lie with an insincerity (*Unlauterkeit*) that "man perpetrates upon himself" and that "seems to be rooted in human nature itself." Although the expression is not used, it seems reasonably clear that what Kant has in mind here is precisely radical evil. The claim is that this corrupting evil,

manifested in the lie to oneself or self-deception, prepares the ground for the deceitful treatment of others and for immorality in general.

20. Alexander Broadie and Elizabeth M. Pybus, "Kant and Weakness of Will," *Kant-Studien* 73 (1982), pp. 406–12, argue that self-deception plays a significant role in Kant's account of weakness of will, which they tend to equate with an account of the possibility of immoral action. They do not refer, however, to the text currently under consideration or, indeed, to *Religion within the Limits of Reason Alone* at all.

21. Although he does not refer explicitly to radical evil, Kant expresses his agreement with this line of thought, together with an account of self-deception, in the section entitled "On Permissible Moral Semblance" (*Von dem erlaubten moralischen Schein*) in the *Anthropology* (Anthro 7: 151–3; 30–2).

22. See also *Moral Mrongovius* II, 29: 608. In the latter text Kant also refers (605) to "a naturally good will" (*einen natürlichen guten Willen*). This is clearly equivalent to a holy will, however, since it needs no imperative and pertains only to God.

Chapter 9

1. As Kant indicates, the reason ethics contains duties we cannot be compelled by others to fulfill is that no one can compel someone else to make something their end. Hence the only compulsion possible here is self-compulsion. See MS 6: 381; 39. Kant also holds, of course, that there can be no duty without some sort of compulsion or constraint.

2. See also MS 6: 380, 383–4; 405, 407–8; 38, 42–3, 67–8, 69–72, and *Moral Mrongovius* II, 29: 603–4.

3. These texts include *Religion within the Limits of Reason Alone*, 6: 24n; 19 (which we shall discuss in the next chapter in connection with the analysis of Kant's response to Schiller); *The Doctrine of Virtue*, 6: 409, 484–5; 72, 159–160; *Anthropology*, 7: 235–6; 103–4; and *Moral Mrongovius* II, 29: 617, 639.

4. Karl Americks, "Kant on the Good Will," in *Grundlegung zur Metaphysik der Sitten: Ein kooperativer Kommentar*, Otfried Höffe, ed., p. 40.

5. See also MS 6: 394; 55–6.

6. See also *Vorarbeiten*, 23: 396, 398; *Moral Mrongovius* II, 29: 626; and *On the Progress of Metaphysics*, 20: 295.

7. I am here differing with Mary Gregor, who in her translation of *The Doctrine of Virtue* takes the pronoun *diese* to refer to habit rather than aptitude (*Fertigkeit*). Both are grammatically possible, but the former seems better to capture Kant's point.

8. See also MS 6: 407, 479; 69–70, 152–3 and Anthro 7: 153, 32.

9. In the recent literature, this aspect of Kant's thought has been most fully explored by Onora O'Neill. See particularly her "Kant after Virtue," *Inquiry* 26 (1983), p. 396, where she states that "Kant offers primarily an ethic of virtue rather than an ethic of rules."

10. See also MS 6: 387, 394, 402, 405; 47, 55–6, 63–4, 67–8.

11. Recent authors who emphasize the increased complexity of the moral psychology of Kant's later writings include Gerold Prauss, *Kant über Freiheit als Autonomie*, esp. pp. 248–59, who focuses on the significance of love, and Karl Americks, "The Hegelian Critique of Kantian Morality," in *New Essays on Kant,* Bernard den Ouden and Marcia Moen, eds., esp. pp. 192–5, who calls attention also to the role of religious hope and who appeals to this complexity as a part of a

response to the Hegelian critique. The latter issue will be taken up in the next chapter.

12. The reader should be apprised of the fact that I am glossing over a number of very controversial issues and complexities in Kant's moral theory with which it is impossible to deal adequately here. One such issue is whether imperfect duties can ever require particular actions. For an interesting argument that they can, see Paul Eisenberg, "From the Forbidden to the Supererogatory: The Basic Ethical Categories in Kant's *Tugendlehre*," *American Philosophical Quarterly* 4 (1966), esp. pp. 9–10. Another, perhaps the major, issue concerns the interpretation of the nature and extent of the leeway granted by duties of wide obligation. At the heart of the problem is the apparent conflict between the characterization in the *Groundwork* of a perfect duty as "one which allows no exception in the interests of inclination" (Gr 4: 421n; 88), which implies that imperfect duties do allow for such an exception, and the account in *The Doctrine of Virtue* where Kant claims that "a wide duty is not to be taken as permission to make exceptions to the maxim of actions, but only as a permission to limit one maxim of duty by another" (MS 6: 390; 49). The difference between these two texts amounts to the difference between a rigoristic and a nonrigoristic view of imperfect duty. The former does not allow any exceptions "in the interests of inclination," whereas the latter does. In my analysis I am assuming the nonrigoristic reading, which tends to underscore the problem of temptation. For discussions of this issue that, on balance, support the nonrigoristic reading see Mary Gregor, *Laws of Freedom*, pp 104–12, and Thomas Hill, "Kant on Imperfect Duty and Supererogation," *Kant-Studien* 62 (1971), esp. pp. 56–65.

13. I am indebted to Eckart Förster for reminding me of this connection in a conversation.

14. See also KprV 5: 267;126.

15. Kant's treatment of Aristotle is criticized on these grounds by Peter Louden, "Kant's Virtue Ethics," *Philosophy* 61 (1986), p. 481.

16. For a different interpretation of the relationship between these two treatments of weakness see Stephen Engstrom, "Conditioned Autonomy," *Philosophy and Phenomenological Research* 48 (1988), p. 451.

17. Kant identifies the former with virtue's "empirical" and the latter with its "intelligible" character (*virtus phaenomon* and *virtus noumenon*).

18. An insightful discussion of the problem, which he takes as a significant weakness in Kant's moral theory, is provided by Ameriks, "The Hegelian Critique of Kantian Morality," p. 201.

19. See also *Moral Mrongovius* II, 29: 604–5.

20. For a discussion of the issues and some of the critical literature, see Lewis White Beck, *A Commentary on Kant's "Critique of Practical Reason,"* pp. 270–1, and Allen W. Wood, *Kant's Moral Religion*, pp. 116–24.

21. This difficulty is noted by Beck, *Commentary* p. 268.

22. G. W. F. Hegel, *Phenomenology of Spirit*, A. V. Miller, trans., pp. 374–83.

23. Wood, *Kant's Moral Religion*, pp. 119–20. My entire account of this problem is greatly indebted to Wood's lucid analysis.

24. This analysis can be compared to Wood's *Kant's Moral Religion*, p. 121. Focusing on the dialectical problem raised by the antinomy of practical reason (the attainability of the Highest Good), Wood claims that the postulate of immortality solves only part of the problem by allowing for the possibility of an endless progress. It does not solve the whole problem because, as he puts it, "it does not tell us how this endless progress (or the disposition corresponding to it)

fulfills the condition of the Highest Good." Here, by contrast, the focus is not on the attainability of the Highest Good but rather on the justification of the requirement to pursue an unrealizable goal. From this point of view, Kant gives not a partial answer but no answer at all.

25. See also "The End of All Things" 8: 334.
26. See Wood, *Kant's Moral Religion,* pp. 236–48.
27. Ibid., p. 236.
28. For an interesting discussion of Kant's views on the vicarious satisfaction, see Philip L. Quinn, "Christian Atonement and Kantian Justification," *Faith and Philosophy* 3 (1986), pp. 440–62.
29. The point is made more explicitly here in connection with the preliminary discussion of the obligation to cultivate morality.
30. See Rel 6: 38; 33 and MS 6: 392–3; 53–4.
31. A defense of Kant along these grounds is also offered by Paul Dietrichson, "What Does Kant Mean by 'Acting from Duty?'" in *Kant: A Collection of Critical Essays,* Robert Paul Wolff, ed., pp. 315–30. In his defense of Kant, however, Dietrichson seems to slide (as does Kant) from talking about the duty to act from duty alone to the duty of appraising the worth of our actions. See particularly pp. 321–2.
32. On this matter see Kant's discussions of conscience, lying, and above all, what he terms "the first *command* of all duties to oneself," namely, "*know* (scrutinize, fathom) *yourself.*" *The Doctrine of Virtue,* 6: 400–1, 429–31, 441; 61–3, 93–7, 108.
33. See Barbara Herman, "On the Value of Acting from the Motive of Duty," *Philosophical Review* 90 (1981), pp. 370–1. A very different defense of Kant on this point is attempted by John Beversluis, "Kant on Moral Striving," *Kant-Studien* 65 (1974), pp. 67–77. Beversluis argues that we can know whether we are trying as hard as we can because behavioral criteria are available. As an example, he cites someone striving to master the performance of a piece of music. The obvious problem with this, however, is that it is not at all like striving to act from duty alone. Moreover, there are no behavioral criteria available for the latter.
34. For a helpful discussion of this problem, see Gregor, *Laws of Freedom,* pp. 113–27. It is perhaps worth noting that in spite of heroic efforts Gregor ends up admitting that "ethical duties of omission remain something of an anomaly, participating in certain characteristics of both juridical duties and duties of virtue, yet inclining, apparently, toward duties of virtue" (p. 126).
35. For a very different analysis, see Gregor, *Laws of Freedom.* pp. 170–6.
36. W. D. Ross, *The Right and the Good,* p. 5.
37. This criticism is raised by Paul Eisenberg in his unpublished dissertation, "Duties to Oneself: Leading Arguments Concerning Them from Kant to the Present Day and a Defense of Them," Harvard University, 1966, p. 111.
38. See MS 6: 386–7, 391–3, 444–7; 45–7, 51–5, 111–14.

Chapter 10

1. Friedrich Schiller, *Über Anmut und Würde, Schillers Werke,* Bd. 11, pp. 238–96.
2. Ibid., p. 270.
3. Among recent commentators, Hans Reiner, *Duty and Inclination,* pp.41–9, and Dieter Henrich, "Das Prinzip der kantischen Ethik," *Philosophische Rundschau*

2 (1954–5), pp. 29–34, agree that there is a serious disagreement between Kant and Schiller but differ as to its nature and significance. According to Reiner, who thinks that Schiller got the best of the dispute, the main point of contention is the impossibility, for Kant, of the ethical cultivation of the inclinations emphasized by Schiller. According to Henrich, Kant not only allows for but insists upon such cultivation, and the issue is how it is to be interpreted. As Henrich notes, a positive relationship between sensibility and moral reason is the essential feature of Schiller's position, which means that a well-developed sensibility is constitutive (in a motivational sense) of good moral character or virtue. For Kant, however, for whom the relationship to the law is always mediated by respect, it is merely a mark of a virtuous character, not an ingredient in moral motivation. The latter view, which I take to be the correct one, is also advocated by Andreas Wildt, *Autonomie und Anerkennung: Hegels Moralitätskritik im Lichte seiner Fichte-Rezeption*, p. 157. In a somewhat different vein, Gerold Prauss, *Kant über Freiheit als Autonomie*, pp. 240–77, provides an interesting, albeit highly speculative, analysis of the Kant–Schiller dispute. According to Prauss, Kant had already shown the untenability of Schiller's key conception of an inclination to duty in the *Critique of Practical Reason*, but he failed to mount the kind of response to Schiller that was necessary to bring out the real basis and strength of his own position, namely, his radical conception of spontaneity. If he had done so, Prauss suggests, Kant would have recognized a third possible source of motivation besides duty and inclination, namely, love. This in turn would have led to the dissolution of the analytic connection between autonomy (construed as spontaneity) and moral autonomy.

4. Schiller *Über Anmut und Würde, Schillers Werke*, Bd. 11, p. 271.
5. Ibid., p. 274.
6. Ibid.
7. Ibid., pp. 275–6, for the characterization of the "beautiful soul."
8. See Rel 6: 23–4n; 18–19 and *Vorarbeiten*, 23: 98–101.
9. Prauss, *Kant über Freiheit als Autonomie*, pp. 247–8.
10. This point is noted by Wildt, *Autonomie und Anerkennung*. p. 157. In his discussion of the "social virtues" in *The Doctrine of Virtue*, however, Kant does echo Schiller in claiming that "the graces will accompany virtue; it is even a duty to bring this about" (MS 6: 473; 146).
11. See KprV 5: 84; 86–7. I here differ with Prauss, who argues that Kant's treatment of action based on love (*aus liebe*) and related notions is ambiguous, sometimes equating it with action *aus Neigung* and sometimes with action *aus Pflicht*, whereas he should have recognized it as a distinct third category. See Prauss *Kant über Freiheit als Autonomie*, esp. pp. 250ff. On the view advocated here, Kant is referring to the moral requirement to pursue an unobtainable ideal, not introducing a distinct type of motivation.
12. See KprV 5: 82; 84–5.
13. Kant characterizes fantastic virtue as "a micrology which, were it admitted into the doctrine of virtue, would turn the sovereignty of virtue into a tyranny" (MS 6: 409; 72 and MrM 23: 641). It refers to the attitude for which there is nothing morally indifferent. This should not, however, be taken to mean that the moral law is always functioning as a background condition determining what is permissible (since this is a mark of genuine virtue or good willing for Kant); it is rather that every decision (e.g., whether to eat meat or fish) is viewed as morally momentous, an occasion for fulfilling a duty. For a discussion of fantastic virtue

and its relevance to the issue of the rigoristic versus the nonrigoristic construals of the latitude permitted by imperfect duty see Mary Gregor, *Laws of Freedom,* pp. 74–5, 107.

14. See, e.g., G. W. F Hegel, *The Philosophy of Right,* §135 R, English translation, p. 90, and *Phenomenology of Spirit,* English translation, pp. 260–2.

15. Among the best defenses of the Kantian position against this type of criticism in the recent literature are Onora O'Neill, *Acting on Principle: An Essay on Kantian Ethics,* particularly Chapter 5, and Christine Korsgaard, "Kant's Formula of Universal Law," *Pacific Philosophical Quarterly* 66 (1985), pp. 24–37.

16. See Karl Ameriks, "The Hegelian Critique of Kantian Morality," in *New Essays on Kant,* Bernard den Ouden and Marcia Moen, eds., pp. 198–9.

17. Wildt, *Autonomie und Anerkennung,* esp. pp. 84–95, and Allen W. Wood, "The Emptiness of the Moral Will," *Monist* 72 (1989), pp. 454–5.

18. G. W. F. Hegel, *Hegels theologische Jugendschriften,* Herman Nohl, ed., p. 267. For a discussion of this Hegelian critique, see Hegel, *On Christianity: Early Theological Writings,* English translation by T. M. Knox, p. 213; Ameriks, "The Hegelian Critique of Kantian Morality," pp. 196–8.

19. Hegel, *Hegels theologische Jugendschriften,* p. 266, and *On Christianity,* p. 211. The passage is cited by Wood, "The Emptiness of the Moral Will," p. 457.

20. Hegel, *Phenomenology of Spirit,* English translation, p. 386.

21. See Wood, "The Emptiness of the Moral Will," p. 462.

22. Ibid., p. 463.

23. Ibid., p. 464.

24. Ibid., p. 466.

25. Ibid., p. 467.

26. Ibid., p. 466.

27. Ibid., pp. 473–4.

28. It is interesting to note in this regard that at one time Wood himself emphasized Kant's distinction between end and motive in order to respond to an essentially Hegelian objection by T. H. Greene. See Allen W. Wood, *Kant's Moral Religion,* pp. 49–53.

29. Wood, "The Emptiness of the Moral Will," p. 470.

30. Ibid., p. 471.

31. Interestingly enough, appealing mainly to Hegel's account of will in the published text of the *Philosophy of Right* and to materials from the *Vorlesungen über Rechtsphilosophie,* Wood attributes an explicitly noncausal theory of free agency to Hegel, which in many ways appears similar to the Kantian Incorporation Thesis. Thus, at one point he suggests that "Hegel denies that the will stands in any causal relation to its motives or to other circumstances which determine it." Wood, "The Emptiness of the Moral Will," p. 471.

32. See KprV 5: 34; 34–5. In arguing against the view that the principle of happiness is qualified to serve as the foundation of a necessary and universal rule, Kant writes: "Thus the happiness of others may be the object [*Object*] of the will of a rational being, but if it were the determining ground [*Bestimmungsgrund*] of the maxim, not only would one have to presuppose that we find in the welfare of others a natural satisfaction but also one would have to find a want such as that which is occasioned in some men by a sympathetic disposition." This text is also cited by Adrian Piper, "Moral Theory and Moral Alienation," *Journal of Philosophy* 84 (1987), pp. 111–12. Piper, however, takes Kant to be distinguishing between intention and "motive" in the sense of psychological cause. Thus, she, like Wood, attributes a causal theory of motivation to Kant.

276

33. For this distinction see Gr 4: 427; 95 and Lewis White Beck, *Commentary,* pp. 90–1, note 2.
34. Wood, "The Emptiness of the Moral Will," p. 472.
35. Ibid., p. 473.
36. This objection was raised by Robert Pippin in an unpublished commentary on an earlier version of Wood's paper. As far as I can judge, it still applies.
37. In his latest work, *Ethics and the Limits of Philosophy,* Bernard Williams expresses (p. 104) his appreciation of Hegel's critique of "abstract" Kantian morality and even for the Hegelian formulation (although not the solution) of the moral problem. This problem, in Williams's gloss on Hegel, is "how a concretely experienced form of life can be extended, rather than . . . how a universal program is to be applied." He also suggests that conceptions of self-consciousness are still very relevant to the latter problem. The similarities between the Kant criticisms of Williams and other contemporary philosophers in the "analytic" tradition and those of Schiller and Hegel is emphasized by Ameriks, "The Hegelian Critique of Kantian Morality," esp. pp. 183–5, 197–8.
38. This critique of Kantian moral psychology is contained in essays such as Bernard Williams, "Morality and the Emotions," in *Problems of the Self,* pp. 207–29, and "Persons, Character and Morality," "Moral Luck," "Utilitarianism and Moral Self-indulgence," and "Internal and External Reasons," in *Moral Luck.* In *Ethics and the Limits of Philosophy,* Chapter 4, he also explicitly criticizes the Kantian attempt to ground morality in practical reason.
39. This aspect of Williams's critique and its similarity to Hegel's is noted by Wildt, *Autonomie und Anerkennung,* pp 169–70.
40. See, e.g., Williams, "Persons, Character and Morality," in *Moral Luck,* p. 13.
41. This suggests that Williams's critique, like Hegel's, has both an ontological or conceptual and normative dimension to it. Although he does not mention Hegel, this point is noted by Kenneth Rogerson, "Williams and Kant on Integrity," *Dialogue* 22 (1983), pp. 461–78.
42. See Williams, *Ethics and the Limits of Philosophy,* pp. 64–5.
43. Ibid., p. 65. In the context of a comparison of Kant and Aristotle, a similar critique of Kant's conception of agency is advanced by Jonathan Lear, *Aristotle: the Desire to Understand,* esp. pp. 149–51, 186–91.
44. Williams, *Ethics and the Limits of Philosophy,* p. 67.
45. Ibid., p. 69.
46. Williams, "Persons, Character and Morality," in *Moral Luck,* p. 18.
47. Critics who take roughly this line, sometimes in combination with a critique based on the notion of alienation from oneself, include Michael Stocker, "The Schizophrenia of Modern Ethical Theories," *Journal of Philosophy* 73 (1976), pp. 453–66; Lawrence Blum, *Friendship, Altruism and Morality;* Susan Wolf, "Moral Saints," *Journal of Philosophy* 79 (1982), pp, 419–38; Michael Slote, *Goods and Virtues* and with specific reference to Kant, Lawrence Hinman, "On the Purity of our Moral Motives: A Critique of Kant's Account of the Emotions and Acting for the Sake of Duty," *Monist* 66 (1983), pp. 251–66. Important responses to this line of criticism include Barbara Herman, "Integrity and Impartiality," *Monist* 66 (1983), pp. 233–49; Marcia Baron, "The Alleged Moral Repugnance of Acting from Duty," *Journal of Philosophy* 81 (1984), pp. 197–220; Adrian Piper, "Moral Theory and Moral Alienation"; and Kenneth Rogerson, "Williams and Kant on Integrity."
48. The first two are clearly expressed by Herman, "Integrity and Impartiality," the first and third by Rogerson, "Williams and Kant on Integrity," the fourth by

Piper, "Moral Theory and Moral Alienation," and the fifth by Baron, "The Alleged Moral Repugnance of Acting from Duty."

49. Herman, "Integrity and Impartiality," p. 246. My entire analysis of this issue is greatly indebted to hers.

50. The contrast between a "colloquial" and a genuinely moral sense of acting from duty is clearly drawn by Baron in "The Alleged Moral Repugnance of Acting from Duty," esp. pp. 199–200.

Chapter 11

1. Kant distinguishes between the moral law or supreme practical principle and the categorical imperative, with the former being a law of holiness descriptive of the actions of a perfectly rational being and the latter the law as it presents itself to sensuously affected beings such as ourselves. See, e.g., Gr 4: 428; 96 and KprV 5: 82; 84–5. At the same time, however, he is notorious for not keeping strictly to this distinction and for treating them as virtually equivalent. For a discussion of this issue see Lewis White Beck, *Commentary*, pp. 72–3, 211–12. For the purposes of this chapter they will be treated as equivalent, since the difference is not directly relevant to the main issue. In the next chapter, however, we shall consider the question of whether the *Groundwork* contains a deduction of the categorical imperative distinct from that of the moral law.

2. Karl Ameriks, *Kant's Theory of Mind*, p. 226.

3. This point is noted by Dieter Henrich, "Die Deduktion des Sittengesetzes," in *Denken im Schatten des Nihilismus*, Alexander Schwan, ed., pp. 89–90.

4. See also Gr 4: 447; 115.

5. It should be noted that practical freedom as Kant here defines it differs significantly from the conception of practical freedom discussed in Chapter 3, which will itself be appealed to later in this chapter in order to underscore its difference from transcendental freedom. Practical freedom, construed as "the will's independence of everything except the moral law," involves transcendental freedom in the sense that the latter is the negative pole of the former.

6. Marcus Singer, *Generalization in Ethics*, p. 57.

7. I am obviously ignoring the whole problem of specifying "relevantly similar circumstances," which is a critical issue in its own right. I think, however, that I am here in agreement with the analysis provided by Singer, *Generalization in Ethics*, pp. 17–33.

8. Concise versions of this criticism are given by Allen W. Wood, "Kant on the Rationality of Morals," *Proceedings of the Ottawa Congress on Kant in the Anglo–American and Continental Traditions Held October 10–14, 1974*, P. Laberge, F. Duchesneau, and B. C. Morrisey, eds., pp. 94–109, and by Gilbert Harman, *The Nature of Morality*, pp. 76–7. In Harman's case, however, there is absolutely no attempt to connect the criticism to the Kantian texts.

9. One of the few recent commentators to grasp this point is Thomas Hill, "The Hypothetical Imperative," *Philosophical Review* 82 (1973), pp. 429–50. In discussing the syntheticity of the principle that Kant attempts to justify in *Groundwork* III, Hill correctly notes that subjection to the moral law cannot be derived analytically from the concept of a rational person but that the freedom of the person plays an essential role in the argument. In fact, Hill states clearly that Kant's argument rests on two poles: (1) the claim that any person that is negatively free is also positively free (which is supposed to be a matter of conceptual analysis) and (2) the claim that every rational being is also negatively free (which

is not a matter of conceptual analysis). More recently, he has argued for a similar view in more detail in "Kant's Argument for the Rationality of Moral Conduct," *Pacific Philosophical Quarterly* 66 (1985), pp. 3–23. Some of my differences with Hill regarding the interpretation of *Groundwork* III will emerge later in the present and in the subsequent chapter.

10. Lewis White Beck, "The Fact of Reason: An Essay on Justification in Ethics," *Studies in the Philosophy of Kant*, pp. 200–14, provides the best discussion, from a Kantian point of view, of the problems involved in the justification of fundamental practical principles.

11. There are obvious affinities between this line of argument and those that appeal to the is–ought distinction and the "naturalistic fallacy." For an important discussion of the relevance of such arguments to Kant's own position see Karl-Heinz Ilting, "Der naturalistische Fehlschluss bei Kant," in *Rehabilitierung der praktischen Philosophie*, Vol. 1, Manfred Riedel, ed., pp. 79–97.

12. See, e.g., Gr 4: 439; 107 and MS 6: 222; 20–1.

13. This was emphasized in Chapter 6. For further discussion of the issue see H. J. Paton, *The Categorical Imperative*, pp. 141–2, and Beck, *Commentary*, p. 122.

14. Kant himself suggests such a distinction in KprV 5: 11n; 11.

15. Bruce Aune, *Kant's Theory of Morals*, pp. 29–30. A similar objection is noted, although not developed, by Thomas Hill, "Kant's Argument for the Rationality of Moral Conduct," *Pacific Philosophical Quarterly* 66 (1985), p. 19.

16. Aune, *Kant's Theory of Morals*, p. 87.

17. Ibid., p. 88.

18. Ibid., p. 89.

19. This includes Thomas Hill, who, as noted, shares Aune's reservations regarding Kant's derivation of the categorical imperative but who still wishes to defend the argument of *Groundwork* III (including the Reciprocity Thesis) on the grounds that it establishes the necessity of desire-independent norms of practical reason, if not the categorical imperative as Kant defines it. See Hill, "Kant's Argument for the Rationality of Moral Conduct," p. 20.

20. This conflation seems to run through Kant's analysis, but it becomes explicit in §4 (Theorem III), KprV 5: 27; 26.

Chapter 12

1. Kant himself characterizes the argument as a deduction in three places: GR 4: 447, 454, 463; 115, 122, 128. The suggestion that this deduction should be regarded as "transcendental" has been challenged by Reinhard Brandt, "Der Zirkel im dritten Abschnitt von Kants Grundlegung zur Metaphysik der Sitten," in *Kant Analysen-Probleme-Kritik*, Hariolf Oberer and Gerhard Seel, eds., p. 183 and note 14. Brandt notes that Kant himself does not characterize the deduction as transcendental and that in the first *Critique* he is careful to distinguish transcendental from practical philosophy. Even granting this, however, the fact remains that Kant is attempting to provide a justification for a synthetic a priori proposition, that is, to answer a *quid juris*, and this supposedly always requires a transcendental deduction. See *Critique of Pure Reason*, A84–7/B116–20.

2. The richest and most authoritative account of the difficulties in interpreting the text of *Groundwork* III is provided by Dieter Henrich, "Die Deduktion des Sittengesetzes," in *Denken im Schatten des Nihilismus*, Alexander Schwan, ed., pp. 55–112. According to Henrich, these difficulties stem from Kant's lack of

clarity concerning his own intentions and argumentative strategy. Although Kant, on Henrich's reading, describes his project as that of providing a deduction of the supreme principle of morality comparable to that of the categories, what he actually delivers is something much weaker and, in all essentials, in accord with the view of the *Critique of Practical Reason* that one cannot provide a justification of morality based on nonmoral premises. In fact, in the summary of his overall argument, Henrich contends (pp. 108–10) that the difficulties in the text can be traced to Kant's failure to draw (at least explicitly) seven distinctions. These are (1) between a proof and a deduction; (2) between a strong form of the deduction, such as is provided of the categories in the first *Critique,* and a weak form, such as is alone appropriate in the present context; (3) between different forms of a weak deduction; (4) between the consciousness of having a will, the consciousness of freedom, and the consciousness of the law; (5) between a deduction of the idea (or consciousness) of freedom and a deduction of the moral law (on his reading, the *Groundwork* provides only the former, from which the validity of the law is supposed to follow without further argument); (6) the deduction (or justification) of the law from that of the categorical imperative; and (7) the establishment of the validity of moral principles from their importance (construed as their supremacy and overridingness). Although I disagree with Henrich on a number of fundamental points, including his central claim that the *Groundwork* does not contain a serious attempt to provide a deduction (from nonmoral premises) of the moral law and/or the categorical imperative, my discussion is greatly indebted to his analysis. An additional helpful, albeit brief and schematic, account of the ambiguities in Kant's deduction is provided by Manfred Moritz, "Die Probleme der Deduktion des kategorischen Imperativs (ein Vorbericht)," in *Proceedings of the Third International Kant Congress,* Lewis White Beck, ed., pp. 424–33.

3. This is done explicitly by Michael H. McCarthy, "The Objection of Circularity in *Groundwork* III," *Kant-Studien* 76 (1985), p. 34. McCarthy only stops short of finding a complete argument embedded here because of his assumption that the final and crucial step is to demonstrate the necessitation of the will for imperfectly rational beings such as ourselves.

4. Dieter Henrich, "Der Begriff der sittlichen Einsicht und Kants Lehre vom Faktum der Vernunft," in *Kant: Zur Deutung seiner Theorie von Erkennen und Handeln,* G. Prauss, ed., pp. 107–10.

5. For an excellent analysis of this section and of the problems it raises, particularly that of the circle, see Pierre Laberge, "L'Espèce de cercle dont, à ce qu'il semble, il n'y pas moyens de sortir," *Dialogue* 21 (1982), pp. 745–53. I believe that my own account differs from his more in emphasis than in substance.

6. This is the view of Karl Ameriks, who notes these connections. See his *Kant's Theory of Mind,* pp. 213–14.

7. See Henrich, "Die Deduktion des Sittengesetzes," esp. pp. 91–100. A similar point is noted by Ameriks, *Kant's Theory of Mind,* pp. 203–4, and by Laberge, "L'espèce de Cercle Dont, à ce Qu'il Semble, Il N'y Pas Moyens de Sortir," pp. 746–7.

8. On this point see also KprV 5: 32, 36; 32, 37.

9. H. J. Paton, *The Categorical Imperative, A Study in Kant's Moral Philosophy,* p. 225.

10. Ibid., pp. 255–6.

11. See Brandt, "Der Zirkel im dritten Abschnitt von Kants Grundlegung zur Metaphysik der Sitten," p. 170.

12. Ibid., p. 186.
13. Ibid., pp. 184–5.
14. This view is argued by Brandt and McCarthy, both of whom claim that the main thrust of the argument of *Groundwork* III, indeed, the synthetic a priori proposition in need of justification, concerns the necessitation of the will of an imperfectly rational being by the categorical imperative. For Brandt's analysis, see "Der Zirkel im dritten Abschnitt von Kants Grundlegung zur Metaphysik der Sitten," pp. 169–91; for McCarthy's see Michael H. McCarthy, "Kant's Application of the Analytic/Synthetic Distinction to Imperatives," *Dialogue* 18 (1979), pp. 373–91; "Kant's Rejection of the Argument of *Groundwork* III," *Kant-Studien* 73 (1982), pp. 169–90; and "The Objection of Circularity in *Groundwork* III."
15. Henrich, "Die Deduktion des Sittengesetzes," p. 95.
16. See Paton, *The Categorical Imperative,* pp. 251–2.
17. This is noted by Henrich, "Die Deduktion des Sittengesetzes," p. 97. Strangely enough, however, it is neglected by McCarthy, who takes the point of the deduction of the categorical imperative to be to show that "Every sensible rational being – as it presents itself to empirical intuition – is subject to, and hence motivated to act in accordance with, the principle of autonomy." See McCarthy, "The Objection of Circularity," p. 37. The problem, of course, is that qua presented to itself in empirical intuition, the rational being is a causally conditioned object in the phenomenal world and therefore incapable of being motivated to act in accordance with the principle of autonomy.
18. Although he does not refer explicitly to the *Wille–Willkür* distinction, the basic point is made by Henrich ("Die Deduktion des Sittengesetzes," p. 97) when he remarks that a further development of the conception of the rational will is necessary if the Kantian account is to become at all plausible.
19. I am here following Beck, *Commentary,* p. 122, in identifying this principle with the moral law.
20. Paton, *The Categorical Imperative,* p. 201.
21. Ibid., pp. 201–2.
22. Ibid., p. 247.
23. The contrast between the negative and positive senses of noumenon is drawn in the *Critique of Pure Reason* (B 307). The former refers to "a thing so far as it is *not an object of our sensible intuition*" and the latter to the problematic *"object of a nonsensible intuition."* I discuss this contrast and related issues in Henry E. Allison, *Kant's Transcendental Idealism,* pp. 242–6.
24. This problem is noted by Henrich, "Die Deduktion des Sittengesetzes," pp. 72–3.
25. Henrich notes this same ambiguity but suggests that it is merely apparent and that Kant finally comes down unambiguously for the second sense of will (Henrich, "Die Deduktion des Sittengesetzes," p. 67). I agree with Henrich that the second sense is the one that Kant is interested in, but I contend that the first sense is the only one that the argument is capable of establishing.

Chapter 13

1. Arthur Schopenhauer, *On the Basis of Morality,* E. F. P. Payne, trans., p. 79. A similar sentiment is expressed by Hegel, who remarks: "Chill duty is the final undigested lump left within the stomach, the revelation given to reason" (*Lectures on the History of Philosophy,* E. S. Haldane and Frances H. Simpson, Vol.

NOTES TO PP. 230–233

3, trans., p. 461). Both passages are cited by Dieter Henrich, "Der Begriff der sittlichen Einsicht und Kants Lehre vom Faktum der Vernunft," in *Kant: Zur Deutung seiner Theorie von Erkennen und Handeln,* G. Prauss, ed., pp. 93–4. Recently this general line of criticism has been forcefully expressed by Gerold Prauss, *Kant über Freiheit als Autonomie,* esp. pp. 66–70, and Rüdiger Bittner, *Moralisches Gebot oder Autonomie,* esp. pp. 138–45.

2. An important account of the development of Kant's thinking on this issue is provided by Dieter Henrich, who shows that Kant only turned to the fact of reason after having exhausted all available strategies for deriving morality or, more precisely, the bindingness of the moral law, from nonmoral premises. For Henrich, then, this turn, which as noted in the last chapter he sees to be already at work in the *Groundwork,* is likewise the true culmination of Kant's moral philosophy rather than a lapse into a dogmatism of practical reason. See Henrich, "Der Begriff der sittlichen Einsicht und Kants Lehre vom Faktum der Vernunft," esp. pp. 107–10. But in spite of his rich and nuanced account of the development of Kant's thought and of the historical–philosophical significance of the turn to the fact of reason, his actual discussion of this fact and its grounding is neither particularly illuminating nor very sympathetic. For example, in "Das Problem der Grundlegung der Ethik bei Kant und in Spekulativen Idealismus," in *Sein und Ethos,* Paulus Englehardt, ed., esp. pp 370–7, Henrich presents what amounts to an essentially Hegelian critique of the fact of reason and of the conception of respect, which he regards as inseparable from it. I have discussed his critique of respect in Chapter 6.

3. Lewis White Beck, *Commentary,* p. 166. For Beck's full discussions see *Commentary,* pp. 166–75, and "The Fact of Reason: An Essay on Justification in Ethics," in *Studies in the Philosophy of Kant,* pp. 200–14. Although I disagree with many aspects of his analysis, including his characterization of the fact of reason, I follow him closely in the setting up of the problem.

4. Beck, *Commentary,* p. 166, note 10.

5. Ibid., pp. 166–7. Beck also notes that Kant cannot speak of the consciousness of freedom as a fact because he denies that we can have an immediate consciousness thereof.

6. Ibid., p. 168, and "The Fact of Reason," pp. 210–11.

7. For example, Jürgen Heinrichs, *Das Problem der Zeit in der praktischen Philosophie Kants,* p. 45, calls it a "quasi-Anschauung."

8. For an account of these difficulties and their relevance to Kant see Beck, "The Fact of Reason," pp. 202–4.

9. Beck, *Commentary,* p. 169. A somewhat similar interpretation is advanced by Bernard Rousset, *La Doctrine Kantienne de L'objectivité,* p. 257.

10. This terminology is used by Henrich to describe the two aspects of the practicality of pure reason in "Das Problem der Grundlegung der Ethik bei Kant und in Spekulativen Idealismus," p. 356.

11. Here and at many other points in this chapter I differ from my earlier treatment of this topic in Henry E. Allison, "Justification and Freedom in the *Critique of Practical Reason,*" in *Kant's Transcendental Deductions,* Eckart Förster, ed., pp. 114–30. Although she did not discuss this point, many of the changes between the present and my earlier account of the fact of reason are the result of an effort to rethink my position in light of the criticisms of that earlier account made by Barbara Herman in "Justification and Objectivity: Comments on Rawls and Allison," *Kant's Transcendental Deductions,* Eckard Förster, ed., pp. 131–6.

12. Three of the eight passages cited (2, 3, and 5) include a reference to conscious-ness in the characterization of the fact; whereas three others (1, 4, and 8) do not really characterize it at all but merely state what it confirms, provides, or proves. Passage 6 suggests that it is a determination of the will. Although 7 does not refer to the consciousness of the law, the common recognition of the law's su-premely authoritative status, which it does emphasize, is certainly part of the content of consciousness.

13. In emphasizing that the "fact" must be construed as the consciousness of specific moral constraints rather than of the formal principle of morality, I am following the lead of T. C. Williams, *The Concept of the Categorical Imperative,* pp. 103–11. He does not refer, however, to the "Typic" or "Law of Nature Formula" in this context.

14. For an analysis of the doctrine of the "Typic," see Beck, *Commentary,* pp. 154–62.

15. The significance of this *Reflexion* for the interpretation of the fact of reason is noted by Beck, *Commentary,* p. 166n.

16. I discuss the "givenness" of space in Henry E. Allison, *Kant's Transcendental Idealism,* pp. 94–8.

17. See Beck, *Commentary,* pp. 171–2. Beck's analysis is referred to approvingly at this point by John Rawls, "Themes in Kant's Moral Philosophy," *Kant's Tran-scendental Deductions,* Eckard Förster, ed., p. 105 and note 15.

18. It is certainly a deduction in the sense that it is concerned with a *quid juris,* i.e., with the legitimation of a synthetic a priori proposition. For an account of the distinction between deduction and proof in Kant and of the various senses in which he construes the former, see Henrich, "Die Deduktion des Sittengesetzes," pp. 76–84.

19. The relationship between the fact of reason and respect is emphasized by Hen-rich, who notes that these are the two pivotal concepts of the *Critique of Practical Reason.* See Henrich, "Der Begriff der sittlichen Einsicht und Kants Lehre vom Faktum der Vernunft," pp. 112–13.

20. In this respect, Kant's position is similar to his treatment of the sublime in the third *Critique.* Thus, in denying that in contrast to the beautiful in nature, it requires a deduction, he also insists that the analysis of the sublime is its de-duction in the sense that this analysis is sufficient to justify the claim of such judgments to universally necessary validity. See KU 5: 280; 142–3.

21. An extremely helpful and lucid account of Kant's internalism is provided by Christine Korsgaard, "Skepticism about Practical Reason," *Journal of Philosophy* 83 (1986), pp. 8–11.

22. I take it that the problem raised here is equivalent to what Henrich regards as that of the importance of moral rules, which he distinguishes from that of their validity. See Henrich, "Die Deduktion des Sittengesetzes," pp. 104–7.

23. See also KprV 5: 43, 46, 94; 44, 47, 97.

24. See also KprV 5: 49, 93–100; 51, 96–104.

25. Unfortunately, I did not adequately grasp this point in Henry E. Allison, "Mo-rality and Freedom: Kant's Reciprocity Thesis," *Philosophical Review* 95 (1986), p. 398. Following Paton and W. D. Ross, I there accused Kant of a gross equiv-ocation in his formulation of the Reciprocity Thesis at the beginning of *Ground-work* III (Gr 4: 446–7; 114–15), since he there seemed to jump from the notion of a causal law, understood as a law connecting causes and effects, to a "law of freedom." I now wish to withdraw that accusation.

26. Kant describes freedom as one of two conceivable kinds of causality in the *Cri-*

tique of Pure Reason (A532/B560). The other is, of course, causality according to nature. As we saw in Chapter 2, by insisting that every cause must have a character, he is making the point that a definite causal law (understood as a *modus operandi*) is necessary in order to conceive of a causal activity. What we now learn is that the moral law is the law governing rational agency in its intelligible character. In the case of imperfectly rational agents such as ourselves, however, the moral law is a *modus obligandi* rather than *operandi*.

27. It is clearly the pure or unschematized concept of causality that is at issue here. In fact, in sharp contrast to his "official" position in the first *Critique* that the categories, apart from their schemata, "are merely functions of the understanding for concepts and represent no object" (A147/B187), Kant now emphasizes that precisely because these concepts have their seat in the pure understanding, they are available, for all practical purpose, for the thought of noumena. See, in particular, KprV 5: 53–7; 55–8.

28. Yet at one point, in commenting on the symmetry between the Analytics of the two *Critiques*, Kant writes: "Whoever has been able to convince himself of the truth of the propositions of the Analytic will get a certain enjoyment out of such comparisons, for they correctly occasion the expectation of bringing some day into one view the unity of the entire pure rational faculty (both theoretical and practical) and of being able to derive everything from one principle. The latter is an unavoidable need of human reason, as it finds complete satisfaction only in a perfectly systematic unity of its cognitions" (KprV 5: 90–1; 94). As Beck notes (*Commentary*, p. 47), this passage suggests that Kant thinks that he does not yet have a satisfactory proof of the unity of reason, even though one of the fundamental concerns of the second *Critique* is to demonstrate this unity.

29. As Karl Ameriks notes in *Kant's Theory of Mind*, p. 290, Beck insists that there is a strict deduction of morality, as well as of freedom, in the second *Critique*.

30. Beck, *Commentary*, p. 174. Recently, a somewhat similar interpretation has been advanced by Rawls, "Themes in Kant's Moral Philosophy," p. 108. Relying heavily on Henrich's account of Kant's unsuccessful efforts in the 1770s to provide a deduction of the moral law, particularly from the nature of theoretical reason, Rawls argues that by the time of the second *Critique* Kant had arrived at a "coherentist" account of the authentication of practical reason, which he sees as the key to the doctrine of the fact of reason. Thus, on Rawls's view, "pure practical reason is authenticated finally by assuming primacy over speculative reason and by cohering into, and what is more, by *completing* the constitution of reason as one unified body of principles: this makes reason self-authenticating as a whole." For Rawls, this "coherentist" account of justification goes together with what he terms a "constructivist conception of practical reason," which itself is supposed to provide support for the doctrine of autonomy. For a brief but helpful discussion of Rawls's views on justification, see Herman, "Justification and Objectivity," pp. 136–7.

31. A criticism of Beck's interpretation along somewhat similar lines is presented by Ameriks, *Kant's Theory of Mind*, pp. 220–1. Ameriks also points out that there is nothing in the idea of transcendental freedom that requires it to be understood in terms of the kind of intelligible causality thought in the moral law. In fact, although I do not wish to belabor the point, one could go beyond Ameriks and note that this kind of intelligible causality makes a rather unsuitable "tenant" for the vacant space left by the Thesis of the Third Antinomy.

32. See also KprV 5: 29; 29.

33. In this connection it should also be recalled that as was noted in Chapter 3, Kant

explicitly denied the possibility of proving the negative (independence from pathological necessitation) empirically, since the possibility of unconscious stimuli always remains open. See MM 29: 896–7.

34. A standard compatibilist strategy for reconciling causal determinism with the capacity to do otherwise, which is supposedly needed for the ascription of moral responsibility, is to interpret the latter to mean that one could have done otherwise if one had chosen to. For a contemporary discussion of this issue from a broadly Kantian perspective see Roderick M. Chisholm, "Human Freedom and the Self," in *Free Will,* Gary Watson, ed., pp. 24–35.

35. The contrast between autonomy and autocracy, which is implicit in Kant's illustration, also provides the key to understanding why, in the Dialectic of the second *Critique,* Kant treats freedom, together with God and immortality, as a postulate of practical reason after claiming to have provided a deduction of it in the analytic. The solution lies in the fact that Kant is using freedom in two distinct senses in the two portions of the *Critique.* The freedom that receives its deduction in the Analytic is autonomy (including, as its negative side, independence). The freedom that is postulated in the Dialectic is autocracy. Freedom in the latter sense is not a condition of imputation, since as we have seen, those of us who are lacking it are still responsible for our actions, indeed, for this very lack. It is, however, a condition of the attainment of virtue, and since virtue is a component of the Highest Good, it is a condition of the realization of this good. That is why it must be postulated, that is, assumed to be possible of attainment. Consequently, freedom in the first sense is an object of (practical) knowledge, whereas freedom in the second sense is an article of (practical) faith. On this point see Beck, *Commentary,* pp. 207–8, and Bernard Carnois, *The Coherence of Kant's Doctrine of Freedom,* pp. 116–21.

36. These and similar locutions occur repeatedly in the KprV. See, particularly, 5: 42–57; 43–59.

37. This is noted by Henrich, "Die Deduktion des Sittengesetzes," esp. pp. 84–91.

38. Kant holds that "every interest is ultimately practical, even that of speculative reason being only conditional and reaching perfection only in practical use" (KprV 5: 121; 126).

Bibliography

Al-Azm, Sadik J. *The Origins of Kant's Arguments in the Antinomies.* Oxford: Oxford University Press, 1972.

Allison, Henry, E. "The Concept of Freedom in Kant's 'Semi-Critical' Ethics." *Archiv für Geschichte der Philosophie* 68 (1986), pp. 96–115.

"Empirical and Intelligible Character in the *Critique of Pure Reason,*" in *Kant's Practical Philosophy Reconsidered,* Proceedings of the 7th Jerusalem Philosophical Encounter, Yirmahu Yovel, ed. Dordrecht: Kluwer, 1989, pp. 1–21.

"The Hidden Circle in *Groundwork* III," in *Proceedings: Sixth International Kant Congress,* G. Funke and Th. M. Seebohm, ed. Washington, DC: The Center for Advanced Research in Phenomenology and the University Press of America, 1989, pp. 147–58.

"Justification and Freedom in the *Critique of Practical Reason,*" in *Kant's Transcendental Deductions: The Three "Critiques" and the "Opus Postumum"* Eckart Förster, ed. Stanford, CA: Stanford University Press, 1989, pp. 114–30.

"Kant's Preparatory Argument in *Groundwork* III," in *Grundlegung zur Metaphysik der Sitten: Ein kooperativer Kommentar,* Otfried Höffe, ed. Frankfurt am Main: Vittorio Klostermann, 1989, pp. 314–24.

"Kant's Refutation of Materialism." *Monist* 72 (1989), pp. 190–208.

"Kant's Refutation of Realism." *Dialectica* 30 (1976), pp. 223–53.

Kant's Transcendental Idealism. New Haven and London: Yale University Press, 1983.

"Morality and Freedom: Kant's Reciprocity Thesis." *Philosophical Review* 95 (1986), pp. 393–425.

"Practical and Transcendental Freedom in the *Critique of Pure Reason.*" *Kant-Studien* 73 (1982), pp. 271–90.

"Transcendental Idealism: The 'Two Aspect' View," in *New Essays on Kant,* Bernard den Ouden and Marcia Moen, eds. New York and Bern: Peter Lang, 1987, pp. 155–78.

Ameriks, Karl. "The Hegelian Critique of Kantian Morality," in *New Essays on Kant,* Bernard den Ouden and Marcia Moen, eds. New York and Bern: Peter Lang, 1987, pp. 179–212.

"Kant on the Good Will," in *Grundlegung zur Metaphysik der Sitten: Ein kooperativer Kommentar,* Otfried Höffe, ed. Frankfurt am Main: Vittorio Klostermann, 1989, pp. 45–65.

"Kant on Spontaneity: Some New Data," unpublished.

"Kant's Deduction of Freedom and Morality." *Journal of the History of Philosophy* 19 (1981), pp. 53-79.

Kant's Theory of Mind. Oxford: Clarendon Press, 1982.

"Recent Work on Kant's Theoretical Philosophy." *American Philosophical Quarterly* 19 (1982), pp. 1–24.

BIBLIOGRAPHY

Aune, Bruce. *Kant's Theory of Morals*. Princeton, NJ: Princeton University Press, 1979.

Austin, J. L. "Three Ways of Spilling Ink." *Philosophical Review* 75 (1966), pp. 427–40.

Baron, Marcia. "The Alleged Moral Repugnance of Acting from Duty." *Journal of Philosophy* 81 (1984), pp. 197–220.

Beck, Lewis White. *The Actor and the Spectator*. New Haven, CT: Yale University Press, 1975.

A Commentary on Kant's "Critique of Practical Reason." Chicago: University of Chicago Press, 1960.

"Five Concepts of Freedom in Kant," in *Philosophical Analysis and Reconstruction*, a Festschrift to Stephan Körner, J. T. J. Srzednick, ed. Dordrecht: Martinus Nijhoff, 1987, pp. 35–51.

Studies in the Philosophy of Kant, Indianapolis, IN: Bobbs-Merrill, 1965.

(ed.). *Kant Studies Today*. La Salle, IL: Open Court, 1969.

(ed.). *Kant's Theory of Knowledge*. Dordrecht: Reidel, 1974.

(ed.). *Proceedings of the Third International Kant Congress*. Dordrecht: Reidel, 1972.

Bennett, Jonathan. *Kant's Dialectic*. Cambridge: Cambridge University Press, 1974.

"Kant's Theory of Freedom" (a commentary on Allen Wood's "Kant's Compatibilism"), in *Self and Nature in Kant's Philosophy*, Allen W. Wood, ed. Ithaca and London: Cornell University Press, 1984, pp. 102–12.

Benson, Paul. "Moral Worth." *Philosophical Studies* 51 (1987), pp. 365–82.

Beversluis, John. "Kant on Moral Striving." *Kant-Studien* 65 (1974), pp. 67–77.

Bittner, Rüdiger. "Maximen," in *Akten des Kongresses,* G. Funke and J. Kopper, eds. Berlin: de Gruyter, 1974, pp. 485–98.

Moralisches Gebot oder Autonomie, Freiburg/München: Verlag Karl Alper, 1983.

(ed.), with Konrad Cramer. *Materialen zu Kants "Kritik der praktischen Vernunft."* Frankfurt am Main: Suhrkamp Verlag, 1975.

Blum, Lawrence, *Friendship, Altruism and Morality,* London: Routledge & Kegan Paul, 1980.

Bohatec, Josef. *Die Religionsphilosophie Kants in der "Religion innerhalb der Grenzen der blossen Vernunft" Mit besonderer Berücksichtung ihrer theologisch-dogmatischen Quellen.* Hildesheim: Georg Olms, 1966.

Brandt, Reinhard. "Der Zirkel im dritten Abschnitt von Kants Grundlegung zur Metaphysik der Sitten," in *Kant Analysen-Probleme-Kritik,* Hariolf Oberer and Gerhard Seel, eds. Würtburg: Königshausen & Neumann, 1988, pp. 169–91.

Broad, C. D. *Kant, An Introduction*. Cambridge: Cambridge University Press, 1978.

Broadie, Alexander, and Pybus, Elizabeth M. "Kant and Weakness of Will." *Kant-Studien* 73 (1982), pp. 406–12.

Buchdahl, Gerd. "The Conception of Lawlikeness in Kant's Philosophy of Science," in *Kant's Theory of Knowledge,* Lewis White Beck, ed. Dordrecht: Reidel, 1974, pp. 128–50.

"The Kantian 'Dynamic of Reason' with Special Reference to the Place of Causality in Kant's System," in *Kant Studies Today,* Lewis White Beck, ed. La Salle, IL: Open Court, 1969, pp. 187–208.

Metaphysics and the Philosophy of Science. Cambridge, MA: MIT Press, 1969.

Carnois, Bernard, *The Coherence of Kant's Doctrine of Freedom,* English translation by David Booth. Chicago and London: University of Chicago Press, 1987.

Chisholm, Roderick M. "Human Freedom and the Self," in *Free Will,* Oxford Readings in Philosophy, Gary Watson, ed. New York: Oxford University Press, 1982, pp. 24–35.

Cramer, Konrad. "Hypothetische Imperative?" in *Rehabilitierung der praktischen Philosophie,* Vol. 1, Manfred Reidel, ed. Freiburg: Rombach 1972, pp. 159–212.

Davidson, Donald. "Mental Events," in *Essays on Actions and Events.* Oxford: Clarendon, 1980, pp. 207–27.

Delbos, Victor. *La Philosophie pratique de Kant,* 3rd ed. Paris: Presses Universitaires de France, 1969.

Dennett, Daniel C. *Elbow Room: The Varieties of Free Will Worth Wanting,* Cambridge MA: MIT Press, 1984.

"Mechanism and Responsibility," in *Essays on Freedom of Action,* Ted Honderich, ed. London: Routledge & Kegan Paul, 1973, pp. 159–84.

den Ouden, Bernard, and Moen, Marcia (eds.). *New Essays on Kant.* New York and Bern: Peter Lang, 1987.

Dietrichson, Paul. "What Does Kant Mean by 'Acting from Duty?' " in *Kant: A Collection of Critical Essays,* Robert Paul Wolff, ed. Garden City, NY: Doubleday, 1967, pp. 315–30.

Duncan, A. R. C. *Practical Reason and Morality.* London: Thomas Nelson and Sons, 1957.

Düsing, Klaus. "Das Problem des höchsten Gutes in Kants praktischer Philosophie." *Kant-Studien* 62 (1971), pp. 5–42.

Eisenberg, Paul. "Duties to Oneself: Leading Arguments Concerning Them from Kant to the Present Day and a Defense of Them." Ph.D. dissertation, Harvard University, 1966.

"From the Forbidden to the Supererogatory: The Basic Ethical Categories in Kant's Tugendlehre." *American Philosophical Quarterly* 4 (1966), pp. 1–15.

Engstrom, Stephen. "Conditioned Autonomy." *Philosophy and Phenomenological Research* 48 (1988), pp. 435–53.

Ewing, A. C. *A Short Commentary on Kant's "Critique of Pure Reason,"* 2nd ed. London: Methuen, 1950.

Fackenheim, Emil. "Kant and Radical Evil." *University of Toronto Quarterly* 23 (1954), pp. 339–53.

Foot, Philippa, "Morality as a System of Hypothetical Imperatives," in *Virtues and Vices.* Berkeley and Los Angeles: University of California Press, 1981, pp. 157–73.

Förster, Eckart (ed.). *Kant's Transcendental Deductions: The Three "Critiques" and the "Opus Postumum."* Stanford, CA: Stanford University Press, 1989.

Funke, G., and Kopper, J. (eds.). *Akten des 4. Internationalen Kant-Kongresses, Mainz, 6–10 April 1974.* Berlin: de Gruyter, 1974.

Gregor, Mary. "Kant's Theory of Property." *Review of Metaphysics* 41 (1988), pp. 157–87.

Laws of Freedom, Oxford: Basil Blackwell, 1963.

Gueroult, Martial. "Canon de la raison pure et critique de la raison pratique." *Revue Internationale de Philosophie* 8 (1954), pp. 331–57.

Harbison, Warren G. "The Good Will." *Kant-Studien* 71 (1980), pp. 47–59.

Harman, Gilbert. *The Nature of Morality.* New York: Oxford University Press, 1977.

Hegel, G. W. F. *Hegels theologische Jugendschriften,* Herman Nohl, ed. Tübingen: J. C. B. Mohr, 1907.

Lectures on the History of Philosophy, Vol. 3, English translation by E. S. Haldane and Frances H. Simpson. London: Routledge & Kegan Paul, 1963.

BIBLIOGRAPHY

On Christianity: Early Theological Writings, English translation by T. M. Knox. New York: Harper, 1961.

Phenomenology of Spirit, English translation by A. V. Miller. Oxford: Oxford University Press, 1979.

Philosophy of Right, English translation by T. M. Knox. Oxford: Oxford University Press, 1942.

Heidemann, Ingeborg. *Spontaneität und Zeitlichkeit.* Köln: Kölner Universitäts-Verlag, 1958.

Heimsoeth, Heinz. "Freiheit und Charakter Nach den Kant-Reflexionen Nr. 5611 bis 5620," in *Tradition und Kritik,* Festschrift für Rudolf Zocher zum 80, Geburtstag, Wilhelm Arnold and Hermann Zeltner, eds. Stuttgart: Friedrich Frommann, 1967, pp. 123–44.

"Persönlichkeitbewusstsein und Ding an sich in der kantischen Philosophie," in *Studien zur Philosophie Immanuel Kants: metaphysische Ursprüng und ontologische Grundlagen.* Köln: Kölner Universitäts-Verlag, 1956, pp. 227–57.

Transzendentale Dialectik, Ein Kommentar zu Kants Kritik der reinen Vernunft, 4 vols. Berlin: Walter de Gruyter, 1967.

"Zum kosmotheologischen Ursprung der kantischen Freiheitsantinomie." *Kant-Studien* 57 (1966), pp. 206–29.

Henrich, Dieter, "Das Prinzip der kantischen Ethik." *Philosophische Rundschau* 2 (1954–5), pp. 29–34.

"Das Problem der Grundlegung der Ethik bei Kant und in spekulativen Idealismus," in *Sein und Ethos,* Paulus Engelhardt, ed. Mainz: Matthias-Grünewald Verlag, 1963, pp. 351–85.

"Der Begriff der sittlichen Einsicht und Kants Lehre vom Faktum der Vernunft," in *Kant: Zur Deutung seiner Theorie von Erkennen und Handeln,* G. Prauss, ed. Köln: Kiepenheuer & Witsch, 1973, pp. 77–115.

"Die Deduktion des Sittengesetzes," in *Denken im Schatten des Nihilismus,* Alexander Schwan, ed. Darmstadt: Wissentschaftliche Buchgesellschaft, 1975, pp. 55–112.

Identität und Objektivität, Eine Untersuchung über Kants transzendental Deduktion. Heidelberg: Carl Winter Universitäts-Verlag, 1976.

Henrichs, Jürgen. *Das Problem der Zeit in der praktischen Philosophie Kants.* Bonn: Bouvier, 1968.

Henson, Richard G. "What Kant Might Have Said: Moral Worth and the Overdetermination of Dutiful Action." *Philosophical Review* 88 (1979), pp. 39–54.

Herman, Barbara. "Integrity and Impartiality." *Monist* 66 (1983), pp. 233–49.

"Justification and Objectivity: Comments on Rawls and Allison," in *Kant's Transcendental Deductions: The Three "Critiques" and the "Opus Postumum,"* Eckart Förster, ed. Stanford, CA: Stanford University Press, 1989, pp. 131–6.

"On the Value of Acting from the Motive of Duty." *Philosophical Review* 90 (1981), pp. 359–82.

Hill, Thomas. "The Hypothetical Imperative." *Philosophical Review* 82 (1973), pp. 429–50.

"Kant on Imperfect Duty and Supererogation." *Kant-Studien* 62 (1971), pp. 55–76.

"Kant's Argument for the Rationality of Moral Conduct." *Pacific Philosophical Quarterly* 66 (1985), pp. 3–23.

Hinman, Lawrence. "On the Purity of our Moral Motives: A Critique of Kant's Account of the Emotions and Acting for the Sake of Duty." *Monist* 66 (1983), pp. 251–66.

BIBLIOGRAPHY

Höffe, Otfried. "Kants kategorischer Imperativ als Kriterium des Sittlichen," in *Ethik und Politik,* Otfried Höffe, ed. Frankfurt: Suhrkamp, 1979, pp. 84–119.

(ed.) *Grundlegung zur Metaphysik der Sitten: Ein kooperativer Kommentar.* Frankfurt am Main: Vittorio Klostermann, 1989.

Hutcheson, Francis. *"An Inquiry Concerning the Original of Our Ideas of Virtue or Moral Good,"* in *British Moralists,* Vol. 1, L. A. Selby-Bigge, ed. Indianapolis and New York: Bobbs-Merrill, 1964, pp. 69–175.

Ilting, Karl-Heinz. "Der naturalistische Fehlschluss bei Kant," in *Rehabilitierung der praktischen Philosophie* Vol. 1, Manfred Riedel, ed. Freiburg: Rombach, 1972, pp. 79–97.

Irwin, Terence. "Morality and Personality: Kant and Green," in *Self and Nature in Kant's Philosophy,* Allen W. Wood, ed. Ithaca and London: Cornell University Press, 1984, pp. 31–56.

Käubler, Bruno. "Der Begriff der Triebfeder in Kants Ethik." Ph.D. dissertation, Leipzig, 1917.

Kemp Smith, Norman. *A Commentary to Kant's "Critique of Pure Reason,"* 2nd ed., revised and enlarged. New York: Humanities, 1962.

Kitcher, Patricia, "Kant on Self-Identity." *Philosophical Review* 91 (1982), pp. 41–72.

"Kant's Paralogisms", *Philosophical Review* 91 (1982), pp. 515–47.

"Kant's Real Self," in *Self and Nature in Kant's Philosophy,* Allen W. Wood, ed. Ithaca and London: Cornell University Press, 1984. pp. 113–47.

Körner, Stephen. *Kant.* Harmondsworth, Middlesex: Penguin Books, 1955.

"Kant's Conception of Freedom." *Proceedings of the British Academy* 53 (1967), pp. 193–217.

Korsgaard, Christine. "Kant's Analysis of Obligation: the Argument of Foundations I." *Monist* 73 (1989), pp. 311–40.

"Kant's Formula of Universal Law." *Pacific Philosophical Quarterly* 66 (1985), pp. 24–37.

"Skepticism about Practical Reason." *Journal of Philosophy* 83 (1986), pp. 5–25.

"Two Distinctions in Goodness." *Philosophical Review* 92 (1983), pp. 169–95.

Laberge, Pierre. "L'Espèce de cercle dont, à ce qu'il semble, il n'y pas moyens de sortir," *Dialogue* 21 (1982), pp. 745–53.

"La Volonte, la representation des lois et la fin," in *Grundlegung zur Metaphysik der Sitten. Ein kooperativer Kommentar,* Otfried Höffe, ed. Frankfurt am Main: Vittorio Klostermann, 1989, pp. 83–96.

Lear, Jonathan. *Aristotle: the Desire to Understand.* Cambridge: Cambridge University Press, 1988.

Leibniz, G. W. *The Leibniz–Clarke Correspondence,* Alexander, H. G., ed. and trans. Manchester: Manchester University Press, 1956.

Theodicy, Essays on the Goodness of God, the Freedom of Man and the Origin of Evil, English translation by E. M. Huggard. London: Routledge & Kegan Paul, 1951.

Louden, Robert B. "Kant's Virtue Ethics." *Philosophy* 61 (1986), pp. 473–89.

McCarthy, Michael H. "Kant's Application of the Analytic/Synthetic Distinction to Imperatives." *Dialogue* 18 (1979), pp. 373–91.

"Kant's rejection of the Argument of *Groundwork* III." *Kant-Studien* 73 (1982), pp. 169–90.

"The Objection of Circularity in *Groundwork* III." *Kant-Studien* 76 (1985), pp. 28–42.

290

BIBLIOGRAPHY

Mac Intyre, Alasdair. *After Virtue,* 2nd ed. Notre Dame, IN: University of Notre Dame Press, 1984.

Martin, Gottfried. *Kant's Metaphysics and Theory of Science,* English translation by P. G. Lucas. Manchester: Manchester University Press, 1955.

Meerbote, Ralf. "Kant on Freedom and the Rational and Morally Good Will," a commentary on an essay by Terence Irwin, in *Self and Nature in Kant's Philosophy,* Allen W. Wood, ed. Ithaca and London: Cornell University Press, 1984, pp. 57–72

"Kant on the 'Nondeterminate Character of Human Actions,' " in *Kant on Causality, Freedom, and Objectivity,* William A. Harper and Ralf Meerbote, eds. Minneapolis: University of Minnesota Press, 1984, pp. 138–63.

"Wille and Willkür in Kant's Theory of Action," in *Interpreting Kant,* Moltke S. Gram, ed., Iowa City: University of Iowa Press, 1982, pp. 69–89.

Menzer, Paul. "Anmerkungen" to *Eine Vorlesung über Ethik.* Berlin: Rolf Heise, pp. 322–8.

"Der Entwicklungsgang der Kantischen Ethik in den Jahren 1760–1785." *Kant-Studien,* 3 (1899), pp. 41–104.

Moritz, Manfred. "Die Probleme der Deduktion des kategorischen Imperativs (ein Vorbericht)," in *Proceedings of the Third International Kant Congress,* Lewis White Beck, ed. Dordrecht: Reidel, 1972. pp. 424–33.

Nagel, Thomas. *Mortal Questions.* Cambridge: Cambridge University Press, 1979. *The View from Nowhere.* Oxford: Oxford University Press, 1986.

Nussbaum, Martha. *The Fragility of Goodness.* Cambridge: Cambridge University Press, 1986.

O'Connor, Daniel. "Good and Evil Disposition." *Kant-Studien* 76 (1985), pp. 288–302.

O'Neill (formerly Nell), Onora. *Acting on Principle: An Essay on Kantian Ethics.* New York and London: Columbia University Press, 1975.

"Kant after Virtue." *Inquiry* 26 (1983), pp. 387–405.

"Universal Laws and Ends in Themselves." *Monist* 73 (1989), pp. 341–61.

Ortwein, Birger. *Kants problematische Freiheitslehre.* Bonn: Bouvier, 1983.

Paton, H. J. *The Categorical Imperative, A Study in Kant's Moral Philosophy,* 3rd ed. London: Hutchinson & Co., 1958.

Piper, Adrian. "Moral Theory and Moral Alienation." *Journal of Philosophy* 84 (1987), pp. 102–18.

Pippin, Robert. "Kant on the Spontaneity of Mind." *Canadian Journal of Philosophy* 17 (1987), pp. 449–75.

Pistorius, Hermann Andreas. "Rezension der *Kritik der praktischen Vernunft"* (1794), in *Materialien zu Kants "Kritik der praktischen Vernunft,"* Rüdiger Bittner and Konrad Cramer, eds. Frankfurt am Main: Suhrkamp Verlag, 1975, pp. 161–78.

Pluhar, Werner S. "Translator's Introduction." *Critique of Judgment.* Indianapolis: Hackett Publishing Co., 1987, pp. xxiii–cix.

Potter, Nelson Jr. "Does Kant have Two Concepts of Freedom?" in *Akten des 4. Internationalen Kant-Kongresses,* G. Funke and J. Kopper, eds. Berlin: de Gruyter, 1974, pp. 590–6.

Prauss, Gerold. *Kant über Freiheit als Autonomie.* Frankfurt am Main: Vittorio Klostermann, 1983.

Quinn, Philip L. "Christian Atonement and Kantian Justification." *Faith and Philosophy* 3 (1986), pp. 440–62.

BIBLIOGRAPHY

"In Adam's Fall, We Sinned All." *Philosophical Topics* 16 (1988), pp. 89–118.

Rawls, John. "Themes in Kant's Moral Philosophy," in *Kant's Transcendental Deductions*, Eckart Förster, ed. Stanford, CA: Stanford University Press, 1989, pp. 81–113.

Reath, Andrews. "Hedonism, Heteronomy and Kant's Principle of Happiness." *Pacific Philosophical Quarterly* 70 (1989), pp. 42–72.

"Kant's Theory of Moral Sensibility: Respect for the Moral Law and the Influence of Inclination." *Kant-Studien* 80 (1989), pp. 284–302.

Rehberg, August Wilhelm. "Rezension der *Kritik der praktischen Vernunft*" (1788), in *Materialen zu Kants "Kritik der praktischen Vernunft,"* Rüdiger Bittner and Konrad Cramer, eds. Frankfurt am Main: Suhrkamp Verlag, 1975, pp. 179–96.

Reidel, Manfred (ed.). *Rehabilitierung der praktischen Philosophie,* Vol. 1. Freiburg: Rombach, 1972.

Reiner, Hans. *Duty and Inclination: The Fundamentals of Morality Discussed and Redefined with Special Regard to Kant and Schiller,* English translation by Mark Santos. The Hague: Martinus Nijhoff, 1983.

Reinhold, Carl Leonhard. "Einige Bemerkungen über die in der Einleitung zu den 'Metaphysischen Anfangsgründen der Rechtslehre' von. I. Kant aufgestellten Begriffe von der Freiheit des Willens," in *Materialen zu Kants "Kritik der praktischen Vernunft,"* Rüdiger Bittner and Konrad Cramer, eds. Frankfurt am Main: Suhrkamp Verlag, 1975, pp. 310–24.

"Eröterungen des Begriffs von der Freiheit des Willens," in *Materialien zu Kants "Kritik der praktischen Vernunft,"* Rüdiger Bittner and Konrad Cramer, eds. Frankfurt am Main: Suhrkamp Verlag, 1975, pp. 252–74.

Rogerson, Kenneth. "Williams and Kant on Integrity." *Dialogue* 22 (1983), pp. 461–78.

Ross, W. D. *Kant's Ethical Theory.* Oxford: Clarendon Press, 1954.

The Right and the Good. Oxford: Clarendon Press, 1930.

Röttges, Heinz. "Kants Auflosung der Freiheitsantinomie." *Kant-Studien* 65 (1974) pp. 33–49.

Rousset, Bernard. *La Doctrine kantienne de l'objectivité.* Paris: Librairie Philosophique J. Vrin, 1967.

Schiller, Fredrich. *Über Anmut und Würde, Schillers Werke.* Stuttgart: J. G. Cotta-'schen Buchhandlung, 1867, Bd. 11, pp. 238–96.

Schmucker, Josef. *Die Ursprünge der Ethik Kants,* Monographien zur philosophischen Forschung, Band XXII. Meisenheim am Glan: Verlag Anton Hain Kg, 1961.

Schopenhauer, Arthur. *Essay on the Freedom of the Will,* English translation by Konstantin Kolenda. Bobbs-Merrill Co., 1960.

On the Basis of Morality, English translation by E. F. P. Payne. Indianapolis: Bobbs-Merrill Co., 1965.

The World as Will and Representation, English translation by E. F. P. Payne. Indian Hills, Colorado: Falcon's Wing, 1958.

Schulz, Eberhard Günter. *Rehbergs Opposition gegen Kants Ethik.* Köln: Böhlau Verlag, 1975.

Schweitzer, Albert. *Die Religionsphilosophie Kants von der Kritik der reinen Vernunft bis zur Religion innerhalb der Grenzen der blossen Vernunft.* Freiburg: J. C. D. Mohr, 1899.

Sellars, Wilfred. *Essays in Philosophy and Its History.* Dordrecht/Boston: D. Reidel, 1974.

292

BIBLIOGRAPHY

Silber, John. "The Copernican Revolution in Ethics: The Good Reexamined." *Kant-Studien* 51 (1959), pp. 85–101.

"The Ethical Significance of Kant's Religion," in the introduction to the English translation of *Religion within the Limits of Reason Alone,* T. M. Grene and H. H. Hudson, trans. New York: Harper & Row, 1960, pp. lxxix–cxxxvii.

"The Highest Good in Kant's Ethics." *Ethics* 73 (1963), pp. 179–97.

Sims, Walter. "Did Kant Write the Canon Before the Dialectic?" *De Philosophia* 2 (1981), pp. 14–31.

Singer, Marcus. *Generalization in Ethics.* New York: Alfred A. Knopf, 1961.

Slote, Michael. *Goods and Virtues.* New York: Oxford University Press, 1983.

Sorrell, Tom. "Kant's Good Will," *Kant-Studien* 78 (1987), pp. 87–101.

Stocker, Michael. "The Schizophrenia of Modern Ethical Theories." *Journal of Philosophy* 73 (1976), pp. 453–66.

Strawson, P. F. *The Bounds of Sense, an Essay on Kant's Critique of Pure Reason.* London: Metheun, 1966.

van Inwagen, Peter. *An Essay on Free Will.* Oxford: Clarendon, 1983.

Walker, Ralph. "*Achtung* in the *Grundlegung,*" in *Grundlegung zur Metaphysik der Sitten: Ein kooperativer Kommentar,* Otfried Höffe, ed. Frankfurt am Main: Vittorio Klostermann, 1989, pp. 97–116.

Kant. The Arguments of the Philosophers. London: Routledge & Kegan Paul, 1978.

Walsh, W. H. *Kant's Criticism of Metaphysics.* Edinburgh: Edinburgh University Press, 1975.

Wildt, Andreas. *Autonomie und Anerkennung: Hegels Moralitätskritik im Lichte seiner Fichte-Rezeption.* Stuttgart: Klett-Cotta, 1982.

Williams, Bernard. *Ethics and the Limits of Philosophy.* Cambridge MA: Harvard University Press, 1985.

Moral Luck. Cambridge: Cambridge University Press, 1981.

Problems of the Self. Cambridge: Cambridge University Press, 1973.

Williams, T. C., *The Concept of the Categorical Imperative.* Oxford: Clarendon, 1968.

Wolf, Susan. "Moral Saints." *Journal of Philosophy* 79 (1982), pp. 419–38.

Wolff, Robert Paul. *The Autonomy of Reason, A Commentary on Kant's Groundwork of the Metaphysic of Morals.* New York: Harper & Row, 1973.

Kant's Theory of Mental Activity. Cambridge, MA: Harvard University Press, 1963.

(ed.). *Kant: A Collection of Critical Essays.* Garden City, NY: Doubleday, 1967.

Wood, Allen W. "The Emptiness of the Moral Will." *Monist* 73 (1989), pp. 454–83.

"Kant on the Rationality of Morals," in *Proceedings of the Ottawa Congress on Kant in the Anglo–American and Continental Traditions Held October 10–14, 1974,* P. Laberge, F. Duchesneau, and B. C. Morrisey, eds. Ottawa: University of Ottawa Press, 1976, pp. 94–109.

"Kant's Compatibilism," in *Self and Nature in Kant's Philosophy,* Allen W. Wood, ed. Ithaca and London: Cornell University Press, 1984, pp. 73–101.

Kant's Moral Religion. Ithaca and London: Cornell University Press, 1970.

(ed.). *Self and Nature in Kant's Philosophy.* Ithaca and London: Cornell University Press, 1984.

Yovel, Yirmahu. *Kant and the Philosophy of History.* Princeton: Princeton University Press, 1968.

Zumbach, Clark, "A Note on the Thesis Argument of the Third Antinomy." *Ratio* 23 (1981), pp. 114–23.

Index

act, intelligible and empirical, 5, 82, 139, 153–4
actuality, 248
agency, *see* rational agency
alienation, 193, 194
Ameriks, Karl, 62, 163, 201, 265, 272–3, 284
anomalous monism, 71, 76, 77–81
anthropology, 31, 32, 33, 43, 46, 154, 206, 253
Anthropology from a Practical Point of View, 34, 252, 253, 265
antinomy of judgment, *see Critique of Judgment*
Antinomy of Pure Reason, 11, 252
 antinomial conflict in, 12–13, 18–19, 22, 251
 distinction between mathematical and dynamical, 14, 22, 23–5
 Third Antinomy, 14–27, 54, 243; *see also Critique of Judgment*; antithesis of, 14, 19–22, 23–4, 27; and Beck's reconstruction of Kant's theory, 73, 75–6; resolution of, 12, 15, 22–25, 76, 243, 254; thesis of, 14–19, 21, 22, 23–4, 27, 251; verificationism in, 20, 22, 27
appearances, 33, 46
 and things in themselves, 3–4, 12, 14, 19, 250
apperception, 36–7, 40, 78–9, 90, 222, 254
arbitrium, *see* will
Aristotle, 137, 191
 concept of *hexis*, 139, 141, 143
 conception of virtue, 168
Aune, Bruce, 210–11, 261, 279
autocracy, 164, 246, 285
autonomy, 247, 263
 and analytic connection to practical reason, 134, 220, 228
 and autocracy, 164, 246, 285
 and categorical imperative, 94–5, 99–101, 105–6, 225
 and heteronomy, 95, 96–105, 237, 240, 264
 and incompatibilism, 95, 255

 and independence of empirical inclination, 97–9, 231, 237, 240–2, 248
 and membership in the intelligible world, 241–2
 and moral law, 2, 95, 98, 219, 221, 226, 237, 240
 and practical freedom, 96–9, 140
 as practical spontaneity, 96, 134–5
 principle of, 99–106
 as property of will, 94–9, 104–6, 202, 240, 265
 and transcendental freedom, 207
 see also Critique of Practical Reason; *Groundwork*; *Wille–Willkür*

Baron, Marcia, 119, 278
Beck, Lewis White
 and *The Actor and the Spectator*, 72
 on disparity between Dialectic and Canon, 57–8, 64
 on fact of reason, 232–3, 235, 245, 279, 282, 284
 and five concepts of freedom in Kant, 1, 71, 259
 on incentive, 121
 interpretation of freedom in *Critique of Pure Reason*, 71–6
 on maxims, 87–8, 261, 262, 263
 and reasons–causes distinction, 72, 75
 on *Wille–Willkür* distinction, 131, 132
Bennett, Jonathan, 16–17, 250, 269
Benson, Paul, 119–20, 266
Beversluis, John, 274
Bittner, Rudiger, 91, 92, 96, 261, 262, 263
Brandt, Reinhard, 219–20, 279, 281
Broad, C. D., 251
Broadie, Alexander, 272
Buchdahl, Gerd, 253

Canon
 discussion of freedom in, 35–6, 54–9, 63–4, 66, 257
 and "patchwork theory," 54, 56–8
Carnois, Bernard, 250, 256, 257, 263, 269

295

practical, 233, 234–6
practical and theoretical (two standpoints), 192, 194–5
and spontaneity, 38–9
and transcendental apperception, 36, 78–9
Denkungsart (mode of thought), 47, 137, 140, 165, 170, 234
Dennett, Dan, 81
descriptions of events, 43–4, 77–8
desire, 35, 108, 168, 194, 195, 210
faculty of, 127, 130
see also inclination
determinism
causal, 2, 28, 33, 41, 43, 44, 239, 249
psychological, 31, 34, 189, 240
diabolical will, 150, 158, 160, 168
Dialectic, 35, 38, 39, 45–6, 63, 65
contrast with Canon discussion of freedom, 54–9, 63
and "patchwork theory," 54, 56–8
Dietrichson, Paul, 274
divine grace, *see* virtue
divine will, 17, 121–2, 267
Doctrine of Virtue, The, 108, 119, 149, 181, 265
holiness in, 171, 175–9
nature of virtue in, 162–71
dogmatism, 13, 230
of practical reason, 3, 236
duty
of beneficence, 112, 119, 162, 166–7
distinction between action from and in accordance with, 103, 108, 112–13, 156, 190–1, 207
and inclination, 108–9, 114, 117, 156, 159, 163–5, 182–4, 190–1
juridical, 162–3, 274
of justice, 112
as motivation, 118–19, 164–7, 186–8, 193, 225, 238, 258
as necessary for moral worth, 6, 85, 107, 167, 186
perfect and imperfect, 112–13, 166–7, 175–8, 263, 267, 273
and predisposition to good, 164
and propensity to evil, 156
to pursue holiness, 162, 171, 172, 175–9
as respect for law, 119
of virtue (ethical duty), 112, 162–3, 165, 169, 175, 177, 274
see also moral worth; motivation; virtue

egoism, 206, 211, 213, 240
Eisenberg, Paul, 273
empiricism, 13, 22
"End of all Things, The," 166

Engstrom, Stephen, 270–1, 273
Epictetus, 60
Epicurus, 13
epistemic condition, 4, 44, 52
eudaemonism, 69–70, 180, 259
evil, *See* propensity to evil *(Hang)*; radical evil
Ewing, A. C., 16–17
explanation, 14, 16–17, 72
causal, 17–19, 30, 42, 74
mechanistic and teleological, in *Critique of Judgment*, 33, 73, 76, 77
teleological, 33, 34, 77

fact of reason, 3, 121, 123, 229, 239, 282
and consciousness of freedom, 231–2, 243, 246–7
as consciousness of moral law, 67, 195, 224, 230, 232–9, 242–3, 246, 257, 283
construed subjectively and objectively, 232–3
and deduction, 235–9, 241–5, 249
and fact for reason, 232–3
nature of, 230–4
and transcendental freedom, 230, 239
see also Beck, Lewis White; categorical imperative; *Critique of Practical Reason*; deduction, freedom; moral law
fatalism, 50
Foot Philippa, 238, 264
Forster, Eckart, 273
free will *(arbitrium liberum)*, 66–7, 95, 220
and animal will *(arbitrium brutum)*, 55, 59–60, 68, 122, 132, 135
freedom
acting under idea of, 215–16, 218, 247
in Canon, 35–6, 54–9, 63–4, 66, 247, 257
causality of, 14–15, 25–7, 49, 202, 231, 232, 243–5, 283–4
comparative concept of, 34, 57, 61, 250
consciousness of, 231–2, 243, 246–7
deduction of, 3, 201, 214, 219, 221–4, 230, 239–48, 249; through fact of reason, 3, 224, 230, 232, 239–43, 245
in Dialectic, 39, 54–9, 63, 65
idea of, 25–7, 45–6, 57–8, 145, 215–18, 219, 220, 225, 226, 244
illusion of, 19, 20, 63, 80, 224, 246–7
as independence of empirical necessitation, 1, 133, 240–8 *passim*, 257
positive and negative aspects of, 55, 133, 240, 242, 243, 256, 285
postulation and deduction of, 285
from practical point of view, 1, 3, 201, 215–17, 230, 244, 247–8
psychological concept of, 25, 33, 34, 54

freedom *(cont.)*
  reality (actuality) of, 1, 217, 230, 239–40,
    244, 246–8
  and Reciprocity Thesis, 214–17, 219–21
  regulative function of, 26, 45–6, 145, 247,
    255
  See also autonomy; Beck, Lewis White;
    compatibilism; *Critique of Judgment*;
    Critique of Pure Reason; fact of reason;
    incompatibilism; Meerbote, Ralf; prac-
    tical freedom; transcendental freedom
Fried, Charles, 193
friend of man example, *see* moral worth
functionalism, 76

Garve, Christian, 11
Gesinnung, 136–45, 169, 208, 234, 246
  choice of, 137–9, 141–4, 270
  as fundamental maxim, 94, 140–3, 148,
    153–4, 165
  as ground of adoption of maxims, 136–8
  and intelligible character, 138, 140, 144–5
  as moral propensity, 153, 156, 173
  as presupposing moral law, 142–5
  as regulative notion, 140
  and timeless choice, 50–2, 138–9, 140–1,
    143–4, 153–4, 269
  and *Wille–Willkür* distinction, 142
  see also character, intelligible; good will
God
  as *causa sui*, 61, 62
  and Highest Good, 171–2
  idea of, 45–6
  and moral progress, 173, 174, 175
  postulate of, 67, 69–70, 171
  and timeless agency, 138
Goethe, Johann Wolfgang von, 146, 270
good, 265
  Highest, 67, 171–3, 178, 273–4
  see also predisposition *(Anlang)* to good
good will
  and character *(Gesinnung)*, 116, 136
  in *Groundwork*, 107–8, 136, 161, 226
  and lack of virtue, 108, 159–60
  and moral worth, 107–8, 116, 120, 136,
    187, 190, 209, 226, 266
  as motivated by duty, 107, 120, 161, 183
  perfect and imperfect, 156, 161
  and radical evil, 159–61
  see also moral worth
Green, T. H., 35, 102
Gregor, Mary J., 253, 273, 276
Groundwork, 41, 66–7, 218, 246
  autonomy in, 85, 94–6, 134–5, 220, 236,
    237, 242
  critique of heteronomy in, 99–102, 104–6

conception of good will, 107–8, 136, 161,
  226
deduction in, 2–3, 201, 219, 223–30, 237,
  241–2, 243, 279–80
definitions of "maxim", in, 86–8, 94
moral worth in, 108–13, 163, 166
radical evil in, 151–2, 161
rational agency in, 85–94
Reciprocity Thesis in, 202–3, 210–13,
  214–17, 220–1
respect in, 120, 123, 125

happiness, 66, 124, 163, 218, 264, 265, 276
  desire for, 67, 151, 155
  and heteronomy, 101, 102, 103
  and virtue, 70, 171–2
hedonism, 35, 102–3, 255
Hegel, G. W. F., 79, 173, 251, 276, 281
  critique of Kant's moral theory, 2, 180,
    184–92, 277
Heimsoeth, Heinz, 16, 251, 254
Henrich, Dieter, 69, 127
  on deduction, 215, 218, 225, 228, 259,
    279–80, 281, 283
  on fact of reason, 282, 283
  on Schiller's critique, 274–5
Henson, Richard, 113–14, 116–18, 126, 164
Herman, Barbara, 108, 111, 114–16, 118–20,
  197, 266, 282
heteronomous action, 6, 39, 50, 136, 255
heteronomy, 33, 96–7, 207
  Kant's critique of, 99–106, 237, 240, 264
  and self-love, 102, 103
  see also autonomy; imperatives, categor-
    ical and hypothetical; inclination
Hill, Thomas, 97–8, 263, 273, 278–9
Höffe, Otfried, 91, 92
holiness as moral ideal, 147, 162–3, 164,
  170, 171–9, 183
  see also duty; maxims, virtue
holy will, 49, 50, 156, 161, 184, 267, 272
  as free of incentive, 176–7
"honest shopkeeper" example, *see* moral
  worth
human nature, 148, 154, 159, 166, 176, 206
Hume, David, 4, 28, 29, 137, 191, 196
  compatibilism of, 5, 27, 34, 39
Hutcheson, Francis, 103, 264

idea
  cosmological, 11, 13, 254
  of transcendental freedom, *see* freedom,
    idea of
Ilting, Karl-Heinz, 279
immortality, Kant's postulate of, 67, 171–3,
  273–4

INDEX

Wood, Allen (*cont.*)
  causal determinist theory of action, 49–50,
    188–90, 255
  critique of Kantian account of moral moti-
    vation, 185–90, 192, 276
  on holiness, 173, 174–5, 273–4

  on malignant will, 150
  on psychological hedonism, 35
  on timeless agency, 47–51

Zumbach, Clark, 251

304